Y0-BCW-415

the language of graphic design

ROCKPORT

Quarto is the authority on a wide range of topics.

Quarto educates, entertains and enriches the lives of our readers—enthusiasts and lovers of hands-on living.

www.QuartoKnows.com

© 2011 Rockport Publishers, Inc.
Paperback edition published 2012

First published in the United States of America
by Rockport Publishers, a member of Quayside Publishing Group
100 Cummings Center
Suite 406-L
Beverly, Massachusetts
01915-6101
Telephone: (978) 282-9590
Fax: (978) 283-2742
www.QuartoKnows.com
Visit our blogs at www.QuartoKnows.com

Library of Congress Cataloging-in-Publication Data
Poulin, Richard.
 The language of graphic design : an illustrated handbook for
understanding fundamental design principles / Richard Poulin.
     p. cm.
Includes bibliographical references and index.
ISBN-13: 978-1-59253-676-4
ISBN-10: 1-59253-676-X
1. Graphic arts. 2. Design. I. Title.
NC997.P63 2011
741.6--dc22

                                          2010049318
                                          CIP

ISBN: 978-1-59253-825-6

Digital edition published in 2011
eISBN-13: 978-1-61058-0359

Design: Poulin + Morris Inc.

Printed in USA

Richard Poulin

the language of graphic design

An Illustrated Handbook for Understanding Fundamental Design Principles

ROCKPORT PUBLISHERS

BEVERLY MASSACHUSETTS

contents

lan·guage \ˈlaŋ-gwij, -wij\ *n*
1 a: the words, their pronunciation, and the methods of combining them used and understood by a community
2 b: form or manner of verbal expression; *specif:* style

Anyone trying to communicate in a new language has to first gain a complete understanding of its fundamentals; the ABCs of that language—definitions, functions, and usage. *The Language of Graphic Design* provides graphic design students and practitioners with an in-depth understanding of the fundamental elements and principles of their language—graphic design—what they are, why they are important, and how to use them effectively.

Similar books on the market today limit their focus and content to a student audience, using their work only to demonstrate a premise. This book goes beyond the student experience. It includes work by some of the most successful and renowned practitioners from around the world and how they have applied these fundamental principles to their work. By examining both student and professional work, this comprehensive handbook is a more meaningful, memorable, and inspiring reference tool for novice design students as well as young designers starting their careers.

The foundation of any successful graphic designer relies upon an understanding of the fundamentals of graphic design. Throughout a designer's education and career, these basic tenets are constantly referred to for inspiration and provide the basis for designing meaningful, memorable, and communicative work.

To understand visual communications, a graphic designer has to first understand by "seeing." To develop this discipline or visual sense is similar to learning a new language with its own unique alphabet, lexicon (vocabulary), and syntax (sentence structure). This book provides clear and concise information that will enhance visual literacy, while using dynamic, memorable, visual references to inform, inspire, and reinforce a sense of "seeing."

> **"It's not what you look at that matters, it's what you see."**
> HENRY DAVID THOREAU (1817–1862), *American, Author, Naturalist, Poet*

The Language of Graphic Design is organized in twenty-six chapters with each chapter defining a fundamental element (basic building blocks of the graphic designer's vocabulary) and principle of graphic design. Please note that the inclusion of twenty-six elements and principles should not be interpreted as a definitive number—they are solely a reference to the standard alphabet; the building blocks for Western language.

Each chapter includes a narrative and visual sidebar referencing a historical graphic design benchmark to further illustrate each element or principle being explored, while continuing with an in-depth, illustrated overview of what it is, why it is important, and how to use it effectively.

Additionally, dictionary definitions begin each chapter to illustrate one of my convictions as a teacher. I have always reinforced to my students the value of the written word. Furthermore, I have stressed that words should never be taken for granted. Graphic designers are visual interpreters; however, we can't be effective communicators without first having a deep and continued appreciation and respect for narrative form. To further this point, I insist that my students always refer to a dictionary to remind themselves of the meaning of words (familiar or not). I believe this strengthens their understanding of what they ultimately need to interpret visually. With this book, I hope to achieve the same with you—the reader.

Visual communications, like written and verbal communications, involve analysis, planning, organizing, and, ultimately, problem solving. When you write or speak, you intuitively choose which words to use and how to use them together to effectively communicate your message. In visual communications, the same end result can be achieved; however, the graphic designer needs to be as intuitive.

"The challenge is for the graphic designer to turn data into information and information into messages of meaning."
KATHERINE McCOY (B. 1945). *American, Educator, Graphic Designer*

8

9

The principles of graphic design are the framework for using elements in the most appropriate and effective manner to create meaningful and understandable visual communications. Elements are the "what" of a graphic designer's visual language, and principles are the "how." When carefully considered and utilized together, they allow graphic designers to "speak" in an accessible, universal, visual language. We never think of writing a sentence as an unusual or extraordinary act. We are taught at an early age about the principles and elements of written and verbal communications. Unfortunately, the same cannot be said for visual communications. However, as we were taught the basics of spelling, grammar, and syntax, we can also be taught the same fundamentals of visual communications.

> **"Creativity . . . involves the power to originate, to break away from the existing ways of looking at things, to move freely in the realm of the imagination, to create and recreate worlds fully in 'one's mind—while supervising all this with a critical inner eye."**
>
> OLIVER SACKS (B. 1933), *British, Author, Educator, Neurologist*

The elements and principles of graphic design such as point, line, shape, light, color, balance, contrast, and proportion are a graphic designer's vocabulary for giving voice and, ultimately, meaning to any visual communication. Without a reliance on these fundamentals, visual communications will be ineffective, non-communicative, and will not "speak" to any audience.

"The hardest thing to see is what is in front of your eyes."
GOETHE (1749-1832), German, Author

My goal for this design reference book is that the reader will be able to refer back to the contents of it on a regular basis for essential information, inspiration, and guidance. Design students, as well as practitioners, are in dire need of a comprehensive reference book that provides them with essential information and inspirational resources on the basic tenets of visual communications and graphic design fundamentals.

Hopefully, *The Language of Graphic Design* will become one of the few primary resources and references that will be referred to time and time again.

point \ˈpȯint\ *n*

4 a: a geometric element that has zero dimensions and a location determinable by an ordered set of coordinates

point

1

12

13

"An idea is a point of departure and no more. As soon as you elaborate it, it becomes transformed by thought."

PABLO PICASSO (1881–1973), *Spanish, Painter, Sculptor*

A point is the fundamental building block of all visual communication elements and principles. It is also the simplest and purest of all geometric elements in a graphic designer's vocabulary and used as an essential element in geometry, physics, vector graphics, and other related fields.

Paris Diderot Université's logotype is literally based on an "X marks the spot" graphic representation or, in this case, the intersection of two visual elements or lines creating a singular point. Additionally, the dots of the lowercase *i*'s in the words *Paris* and *Diderot* are shared to create a visual focal point and integration between the two words, providing a much stronger and cohesive unity to the overall message.

CATHERINE ZASK
Paris, France

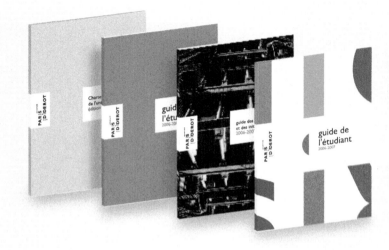

Definitions

A point has many definitions. It is often considered within the framework of Euclidean geometry, where it is one of the fundamental objects. Euclid (325–625 BC), creator of modern geometry, originally defined the point vaguely, as "that which has no part."

It is an abstract phenomenon indicating a precise location; however, it cannot be seen or felt. It is a location or place without area. In typography, a point is a period. It is a dot character such as a full stop, decimal point, or radix point. It is also the smallest (continued on page 16)

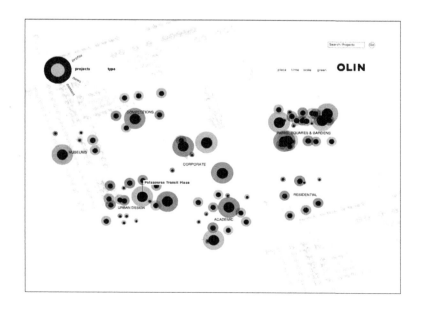

The website for Olin, a landscape architecture, urban design, and planning firm, relies solely upon varied size points, or dots, as the primary navigational tools for accessing specific information, such as profile, project types, and news on the firm. It also visually symbolizes the macrocosm and microcosm of the organization through the fluid, kinetic movements of the site's interface, further conveying Olin as an organic, living entity.

PENTAGRAM
New York, New York, USA

AEG Lamp Poster
PETER BEHRENS
Munich, Germany

PETER BEHRENS (1868–1940) was a true visionary and the first Renaissance designer of the modern age, moving with ease from one discipline to another—painting, architecture, product design, furniture design, and graphic design. His creative interests were boundless. Behrens was the first to pursue a seamless integration of visual communications and architecture and was an inspiration to the founders of the modernist movement.

As a young man, he worked as a fine artist, illustrator, and bookbinder in his native Hamburg. In 1899, Behrens became the second member of the recently created Darmstadt Artists' Colony, where he designed and built his own house as well as everything inside it—from furniture and textiles to paintings and pottery. While at Darmstadt, he realized that he was more interested in simplified geometric forms than the more organic and curvilinear forms of the current Jugendstil (New Art) or art nouveau. In the early 1900s, he became one of the leaders of architectural reform in Germany and one of the first architects of factories and office buildings utilizing a modernist materials palette of brick, steel, and glass.

As a teacher, his ideas and teachings on design for industry, as well as everyday objects and products, influenced a group of students that would ultimately alter the direction of twentieth-century architecture and design worldwide, including Ludwig Mies van der Rohe, Le Corbusier, Adolf Meyer, and Walter Gropius, founder of the Bauhaus school in Dessau, Germany.

In 1907, Allegemein Elektricitäts-Gesellschaft (AEG), Germany's largest electrical utility and industrial producer, hired Behrens as their new artistic consultant. It was at AEG that he created a unified brand for every aspect of the company's visual environment—office buildings, factories, and visual communication materials.

A primary example of Behrens's design philosophy at AEG was a promotional poster he designed advertising AEG's newest product in 1910—a technologically advanced lamp or lightbulb. The design of the poster is clearly based on fundamental modernist design elements and principles. Its orthogonal graphic composition is organized with an articulated grid and comprises basic geometric shapes—a continuous frame or square, a circle, and an equilateral triangle. The triangle provides a focal location for the lightbulb and a simplified, abstract dot pattern represents brilliance and illumination. The pattern and lines framing and dividing the composition of the poster, as well as the outline of the circle and triangle, are all composed of a series of dots or points, which symbolize and communicate light.

In defining his approach, Behrens stated, "Design is not about decorating functional forms—it is about creating forms that accord with the character of the object and that show new technologies to advantage."

His visionary approach not only influenced the entire AEG corporate culture, it became the first seminal example of corporate identity and branding that would inevitably become a primary force within the design professions in the later part of the twentieth century.

Peter Behrens and the AEG Brand

This book cover for *The Verificationist* uses a diminuitive-scaled, universal symbol of man as a visual metaphor that supports the book's title and main character—a middle-aged psychotherapist in the midst of a midlife crisis. The head of the symbol—a point represented in a larger scale—is divorced and distant from its body, creating an immediate and jarring focal point to an otherwise restrained graphic cover composition.

JOHN GALL
New York, New York, USA

unit of measurement, being a subdivision of the larger pica—one point is equal to 0.0148 inches, 1/72 of an inch, whereby twelve points equals one pica. It also describes the weight or thickness of paper stock.

Visual Characteristics

In visual communications, a point takes the form of a visible mark or dot. It can stand alone, identified solely by its own presence, or become an integrated element of a larger collective whole. A point can be realized in many ways and take on many graphic forms. A series of points can create a line. A mass of points can create shape, form, texture, tone, and pattern. While it is a visible mark, it has no mass. It is a design element that has a location in space but has no extension. It is defined by its position in space with a pair of *x*- and *y*-coordinates.

Every shape or mass with a recognizable center is also a point, no matter what its size. A point simultaneously radiates inward and outward. An infinite set of points is also a line. Any two points can be connected by a straight line. A plane or shape with a center is a closed form and can also be described as a point. Even when its size is increased, it still retains its essential identity as a point.

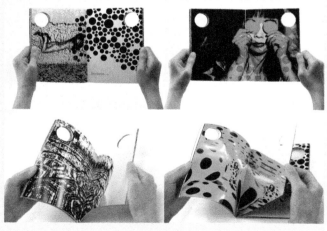

Point—or dot—is shown in a variety of different forms, scales, and configurations throughout this monograph brochure on the work of Japanese avant-garde artist Yayoi Kusama. Dot matrix letterforms, die-cut circles, varying-scale dot patterns, dot-patterned images, and linear dotted frames juxtaposed with black and white, as well as saturated, intense color fields, all add to the visual celebration of this artist's work.

SANG LEE JIN, Student
TRACY BOYCHUK, Instructor
School of Visual Arts
New York, New York, USA

This assignment requires sophomore students to consider fundamental design elements—in this case, point—found in their environment and in everyday objects. With photography they explore their surroundings and document examples of point found in surprising and intriguing situations. The final images are cropped to a 3 X 3-inch (7.6 X 7.6 cm) square and then composed in a 3 X 3 nine-square composition, further communicating the student's examination of interrelationships in form, color, texture, scale, and contrast between the various images. This visual exercise helps design students increase their understanding of fundamental design elements, increase their awareness of the natural and built environment, become more comfortable with a camera and with composing compelling and communicative photographic images, crop images to create interesting and dynamic compositions, identify visual relationships between seemingly disparate images, and become familiar with image software such as Camera Raw, Adobe Photoshop, and Adobe Bridge.

NEIL AGUINALDO, Student
ANNABELLE GOULD, Instructor
University of Washington
Seattle, Washington, USA

Conventional offset printing is also solely based on a point, since it is the single common denominator for creating color, tone, value, gradients, and halftones. A spatial point describes a specific object within a given space that consists of volume, area, length, or any other higher dimensional form. It is an object with zero dimensions.

While it can be defined in many ways and take on a variety of visual realities, when used in a meaningful scale and in an appropriate context, a point can communicate a multitude of visual meanings.

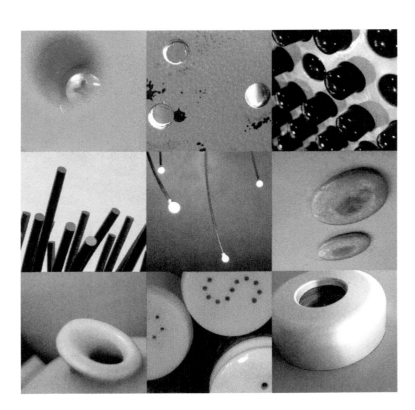

A free-form mass of minuscule, graphic points is the primary visual element on this identity program for the Museum of the African Diaspora (MoAD), a first-voice museum that explores and celebrates the history, culture, and contributions of the people of the African Diaspora around the world. These graphic points, in this context, communicate the brand and mission of the institution and can be found in the building's architecture, exhibition design, graphic identity, collateral materials, and environmental graphics. Here, the museum's acronym and logotype comprise thousands of points, further reinforcing that the MoAD is about the individual and their own unique experiences.

SUSSMAN/PREJZA & COMPANY
Los Angeles, California, USA

This simple, iconic eclipse logotype represents summer as well as the elements of risk and mystery found in the diverse work of the performing artists appearing at this independent theater and arts festival in Toronto, Ontario. An organizational grid of different suns based on a common graphic point and juxtaposed on an intense, neon-yellow background further reinforces this message, as well as creates an eye-catching and memorable visual for the festival.

MONNET DESIGN
Toronto, Ontario, Canada

This information-based poster titled *The Shape of Globalization: World Auto Industry* and designed for the U.S. Department of Energy documents the designer's analysis of the global auto manufacturing industry and its impact on sales and use throughout the world. The poster is composed of a series of points—dots and circles of varying scale, used as primary identification elements for specific auto types, manufacturers, brands, and subsidiaries. Adjacent and overlapping circles communicate statistical data relating to the collaborative partnerships between two or more automakers. Color is used as a codification for the six primary countries that produce automobiles and trucks worldwide.

CHRISTINA VAN VLECK
Lexington, Massachusetts, USA

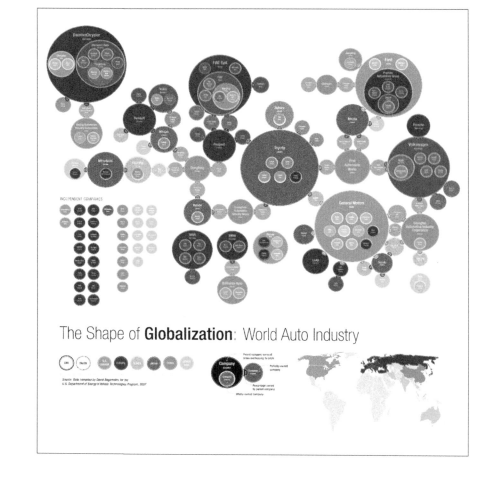

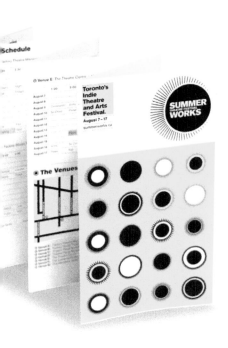

This visual identity system for Huasen Architecture Company's touring exhibition titled *Seeds of the Cities* relies solely on perforated letterforms derived from a series of LED indicator displays found throughout the traveling exhibition. These dot-based characters and symbols are either printed or literally punched through various paper stocks for the project logotype, promotional posters, exhibition catalog, invitations, and shopping bags. In some situations, the dot-based characters are composed as a visual continuum, similar to a typical LED zipper display, where the information is literally traveling from one surface to another.

SENSE TEAM
Shenzhen, China

The visual branding program for AOL reflects the fluid, flexible, and ever-changing content of the digital media world. The program's only stable, rigid, and consistent element is its logotype—a bold sans serif acronym followed by a period or point. The counter of the lowercase *o* in AOL, as well as the period at the end of the acronym, reinforces this logotype's singular clarity and focus. Its asymmetrical placement and juxtaposition to various photographic and graphic images, such as a set of black balloons, the extended wing of a hawk, or an expressive texture of colorful brushstrokes, further enhance its unique and unconventional visual characteristics.

WOLFF OLINS
New York, New York, USA

line \\'līn\\ *n*
1: the path traced by a moving point
2: a thin, continuous mark, as that made by a pen, pencil, or brush applied to a surface

2

line

"The geometric line is an invisible thing. It is the track
made by the moving point . ... Here, the leap out of the static
into the dynamic occurs."
WASSILY KANDINSKY (1866-1944), *Russian, Painter*

One of the most basic and
pervasive visual elements
of a graphic designer's
visual vocabulary is a line.

A line's functions are limitless. It can join, organize, divide, direct,
construct, and move other graphic objects. A line can be read as
a positive mark or a negative gap. Lines can be actual or implied.

This brand design standards guide for Point Loma Nazarene University, a liberal arts teaching university in San Diego, California, uses a singular, free-flowing line (made of string) as a youthful, energetic, authentic, and fun information element for the reader. It literally is "a common thread" to follow for the reader and functions as a visual information cue and guide throughout the various sections of this user reference guide.

MIRIELLO GRAFICO
San Diego, California, USA

They can be realized as edges or boundaries to objects as well as contours to shapes and forms. A line can lead the reader's eye as well as provide movement and energy to any composition. When used properly, a line can improve readability, immediacy, and the ultimate meaning of any visual message.

Historical References

We are taught "a line is the shortest distance between two points." While this fact is true, we have never been taught to appreciate the other inherent characteristics and qualities of a line. Since man felt the need to visually (continued on page 24)

Kinetic, fluid lines used in this logotype and environmental graphics program play multiple roles. First, they convey Signature Theatre Company's brand and mission to provide a venue for an evolving series of diverse voices and visions in the theater. The logotype's linear composition is constructed of layered, handwritten signatures of the company's history of playwrights-in-residence. They also create a cloud of signatures that serves a myriad of uses such as a frame, backdrop, and even as a container to hold photographs or artwork. The relationship between the logotype's linear elements and the vibrant color palette used in various applications creates a dynamic and memorable identity.

C+G PARTNERS LLC
New York, New York, USA

Zurich Tonhalle Concert Poster
JOSEF MÜLLER-BROCKMANN
Zurich, Switzerland

JOSEF MÜLLER-BROCKMANN (1914–1996), designer, writer, artist, and educator, was one of the pioneers of functional, objective graphic design and the Swiss International Typographic Style. His poster series for the Zurich Tonhalle is a seminal example of this modernist, constructivist style and set the standard for the use of pure geometry, mathematical systems, and the grid in visual communications.

During the 1950s, he explored various theories of nonrepresentational abstraction, visual metaphor, subjective graphic interpretation, and constructive graphic design based on the sole use of elements of pure geometry without illustration, nuance, or embellishment.

Each poster in the Tonhalle series uses geometric elements such as circles, squares, arcs, and lines as visual metaphor and is visually orchestrated with rhythm, scale, and repetition. Müller-Brockmann said that these posters were "designed in which the proportions of the formal elements and their immediate spaces are almost always related to certain numerical progressions logically followed out."

For example, the Zurich Tonhalle poster he designed for a concert featuring the work of Igor Stravinsky, Alan Berg, and Wolfgang Fortner was based on a series of photographic studies he had been working on earlier. One study was composed of intersecting lines of varied thickness and lengths, where the dimensions of each line were determined in relationship to each adjacent line. These spatial relationships were also used in defining the spaces between each line. The overall composition is angled by 45 degrees so that each line appears to move diagonally in two directions across the poster.

This approach supported Müller-Brockmann's interpretive view that visual form is comparable to nonrepresentational structures and mathematical systems found in all musical composition. Here, the structural and compositional framework of lines expresses the true nature of the composer's music. At the time, it was said that Müller-Brockmann was a musician composing without an instrument.

All of his work can be analyzed in a similar manner. A precise mathematical plan, logically constructed, is always employed. Every element has a reason for its size, placement, and position.

In reviewing the poster series, Paul Rand said, "They reveal an artist at work, as well as one who fathoms the world of communication, the particular audience for a particular function. These posters are comfortable in the worlds of art and music. They do not try to imitate musical notation, but they evoke the very sounds of music by visual equivalents."

Müller-Brockmann's integration of typography and pure geometry illustrates a timeless relationship between image and music—vocabulary and message.

Josef Müller-Brockmann and the Zurich Tonhalle Posters

The exhibition Brno Echo: Ornament and Crime from Adolf Loos to Now is a lively dialogue between historical and contemporary design on "modern ornament." Adolf Loos's 1908 manifesto "Ornament and Crime" serves as the conceptual foundation for this exhibition, which looks at the recurrence of lines and patterns that constitute a fundamental grammar of modern ornament, connecting everything from the Wiener Werkstätte through pop art to current variants of retro-futurism. Here, geometric striping and concentric forms are a type of ornamentation that is acceptably modern. This, in turn, leads the viewer through an archaeology of concentric striping that links early modernism with other stylistic visual languages throughout the last century. The exhibition's graphic identity is based on the *B* designed for the original Brno Biennial identity, and these posters utilize this line-composed letterform to create "BRNO ECHO."

PENTAGRAM
New York, New York, USA

This promotional poster for Design UK, one component of a comprehensive public awareness and branding program for the British Embassy in Tokyo, is based on an abstract Union Jack created from red and white illuminated neon tubes attached to a blue background. The resulting linear construction, symbolically British with futuristic Japanese overtones, was used to brand the entire event and appeared on a diverse set of collateral print materials and websites.

FORM
London, United Kingdom

communicate his day-to-day experiences by making marks on cave walls, he has unconsciously relied upon line. This fact is evident in cave paintings in southern France, burial messages in Egyptian hieroglyphics, inscriptions on Roman tribunal arches, and medieval crests adorning castle walls. Line has always been a fundamental element of our visual communications palette.

In reexamining these historical references, we can further identify the many functions that man has given to line.

Character and Meaning

A line is composed of a number of points located next to one another in one direction; the number of points can be infinite or there can be two endpoints—a beginning point and an endpoint—or a vector. Its path defines the quality and character of the resulting line. It can be straight, meander, or curve across itself or it can follow the precise arc of a circle segment. The end result gives specific character and meaning to each line.

A line is elemental in visual communications. It is also a fundamental element of visual geometry. Without it, the circle, square, and triangle would not exist, nor could we visually represent them. As an elemental geometric form, a line always has length, but never breadth. When this proportional relationship occurs, a line inevitably becomes a plane or surface.

The primary function of a line in visual communications is to connect or separate other elements in a composition. A line's inherent nature is directional. When it is articulated as a smooth gesture, the eye follows it in an easy and unconscious manner; when it is rough or irregular, it impedes movement, thereby slowing the eye's connection with it. Lines create boundaries and ultimately define shape and form. They are inherently dynamic gestures as opposed to points that are always static. Lines communicate movement because they move in two directions.

Man created line as the simplest means to visually communicate. We see lines as boundaries in objects and are initially taught to draw lines as a way to convey or communicate naïve shapes and forms.

Tone and Message

A line communicates division, organization, emphasis, sequence, and hierarchy. These inherent functions can change in tone and

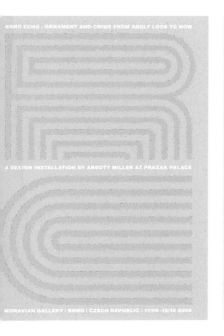

Stories from the Field

The United Nations
Documentary Film Festival

This logotype and promotional poster use a series of dramatic calligraphic lines rendered in bold, kinetic brushstrokes to represent the Asian influences of this documentary film festival's program offerings to the general public.

TAKASHI KUSUI, Student
JI LEE, Instructor
School of Visual Arts
New York, New York, USA

This logotype for the restaurant Txikito Cocina Vasca, featuring cuisine from the Basque region of Spain, is based on curvilinear wrought-iron signs found throughout the region and was reproduced in gold leaf on its entrance doors.

LOUISE FILI LTD.
New York, New York, USA

The Prix Émile Hermès competition focuses on young European designers and rewards them for their creative and innovative contributions to the functionality of designed objects. The awards program is named in honor of Émile Hermès, a creative visionary and pioneer who recognized the value of form and function in design as well as the relationship between craftsmanship and the end product. The logotype for the prize captures the spirit of function, craft, and innovation through the use of line, letterform, and metaphor.

CATHERINE ZASK
Paris, France

PRIX
ÉMILE
HERMÈS

LE SENS DE L'OBJET

message through the tool used to articulate a line. Lines are expressive. They can be long, short, thick, thin, smooth, or irregular and can convey a wide range of emotions. A straight line is mechanical and cold; a curvilinear line is natural and approachable; a thin line is soft and restrained; a bold line communicates strength and power. If a line is drawn with a brush, it conveys a more fluid and undisciplined message as opposed to a line created with a mechanical pen that conveys precision and a disciplined message.

Another aspect of line quality is determined by the tool that makes it; for example, the sketched quality of a charcoal pencil line, the precision of a line drawn with a digital pen tool, or the organic quality of a line brushed with ink. Again, history confirms this to be true. From the naïve nature of a line drawn by a hand's finger or a branch from a tree to a metal scribe or a calligraphic pen nib, the communicative nature of the line has evolved over time at the same pace as man's reliance on different tools and technologies.

Graphic Forms

The orientation and position of a line can also further influence a visual message. A horizontal line is calm, quiet, and serene; a

This exercise requires sophomore graphic design students to consider fundamental design principles—in this case, line found in the environment. With photography, they explore their surroundings and document examples of line found in surprising and intriguing situations. The final images are cropped and composed in a unique and compelling manner, further communicating the students' exploration of line, color, form, and contrasts between images. This exercise helps students increase their understanding of fundamental design principles; increase their awareness of the natural and built environment; become more comfortable with a camera and with composing compelling and communicative photographic images; crop images to create interesting, dynamic compositions; find visual relationships between seemingly disparate images; and become familiar with image software such as Camera Raw, Adobe Photoshop, and Adobe Bridge.

AMBER JOEHNK, Student
ANNABELLE GOULD, Instructor
University of Washington
Seattle, Washington, USA

The identity and collateral material for a fund-raising event, Safe Horizon, was based on work contributed by a number of artists who created their own interpretations of the word *safety*. The majority of art was based on line, as well as form, texture, and pattern created by line. The art was displayed and auctioned at the event.

ROGERS ECKERSLEY
DESIGN
New York, New York, USA

vertical line communicates strength, height, and aspiration. Vertical lines appear more active and communicate a more powerful and immediate message than a series of horizontal lines. Diagonal lines are much more suggestive, energetic, and dynamic.

While we have always been told to "color within the lines," we should consider that lines can be realized in a variety of different graphic forms. They can be straight, curvilinear, thin, thick, solid, and dotted. Multiple lines, whether parallel or juxtaposed at right angles, create texture, movement, tension, pattern, tone, value, perspective, and structure.

This poster is from an exercise, "Visual Storytelling and Narrative Form," and requires a student to read, analyze, and visually interpret the narrative themes of the Pulitzer Prize–winning play *Angels in America*. Each student conceptualizes and photographs imagery that visually communicates his or her point of view. Here a loose, frayed thread on the verge of breaking is a metaphor for the main characters of the play undergoing extreme challenges in their lives. The purity of the image, as well as the supporting typography, allows the line to be emotional, provocative, and highly communicative.

MIKIHIRO KOBAYASHI,
Student
RICHARD POULIN, Instructor
School of Visual Arts
New York, New York, USA

A Gay Fantasia on National Themes
Part One: Millennium Approaches

TONY KUSHNER

Center Theatre Group/Mark Taper Forum
213.628.2772
www.centertheatregroup.org

Angels In America

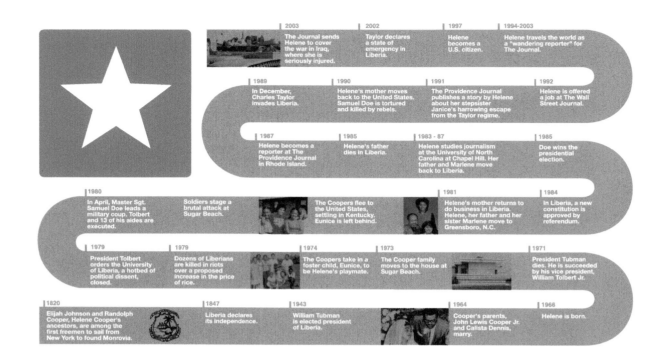

This dramatic three-dimensional, textural wall mural for PMP Limited Melbourne is composed of horizontal lines dimensionalized in an abstract manner symbolizing the activities of this media production and magazine distribution company. Spectrum-colored up-lighting and an exaggerated bas-relief of each horizontal band further create a spatial and ascending focal point to this two-story, double-height office reception space.

EMERYSTUDIO
Victoria, Australia

The graphical articulation of a line also impacts its presence, subtle or obvious, on any given surface. Shaded lines recede as they change from thick to thin, creating a subtle illusion of space. The thicker the line, the more it comes forward or advances.

Another way to think of line is as an edge. When it is given this function, it allows the eye to perceive an object from its background. We also immediately understand line as edge when a horizontal line distinguishes land from sea or land from sky. A linear edge can also exist along the side of any straight or curved shape or as the result of shapes sharing the same edge.

A line can also be implied, meaning it occurs as the result of an alignment of shapes, edges, or even points. Implying the existence of a line in that way can be very engaging for the viewer. Implying lines also activates the compositional space.

This information graphic for the *New York Times Book Review's The House at Sugar Beach: In Search of a Lost African Childhood*, by Helene Cooper, visually highlights specific developments and dates found throughout her emotional memoir. The graphic is composed of a serpentine bold stripe chronologically identifying key dates in her country's development as well as her own life, finally arriving at a symbolic star or home. The graphic composition is based on the Liberian flag and shows the circuitous route that the reader will travel when reading her book.

JULIA HOFFMANN
New York, New York, USA

This information graphic, titled "The Bilbao Effect" from *Metropolis* magazine, contains a list of cultural institutional buildings conceived since 1991—the year that the Guggenheim in Bilbao, Spain, opened. Line weights and line lengths vary based on the specifics of each building project, which is further identified at the end of each line graphic: commission, completion date, location, architect, and time span of project. The lines are organized in a curvilinear manner, evoking the forms and massing of the Bilbao building, and further create a unified and cohesive message. Each individual line is coded with specific building project information: new museum/institution (green), new building (pink), expansion or addition (blue), canceled (red), and in progress (orange).

PURE + APPLIED
New York, New York, USA

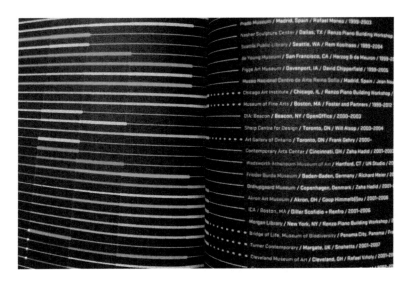

The Quality of a Line

Lines have a variety of functions in visual communications. They can serve as the contour of an object or human figure or exist purely to serve themselves as elements used to separate information, lead the eye in a particular direction, or imply alignment. Lines can also become textures or patterns. The quality of a line can communicate the nature of what is being described; for example, delicate, precise, angular, architectural, chemical, anatomical, fluid, or awkward.

One of the most prevalent uses of line is in print material, such as newspapers, magazines, publications, and websites. Here, lines are used to organize information, separate and emphasize content, and direct the eye to specific areas of interest. In all of these situations, line is used primarily to improve readability, allow easy access to information, and reinforce the immediacy of any visual message.

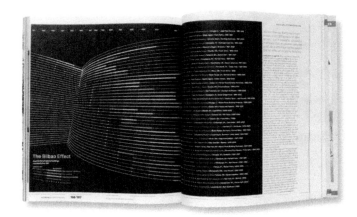

shape \'shāp\ *n*
1: spatial form or contour,
or the characteristic surface
configuration of a thing; an outline
or a contour; see *form*

"The object of art is to give life a shape."
JEAN ANOUILH (1910-1987), *French, Dramatist*

From ancient glyphs to contemporary symbols, shape is one of the fundamental elements of a graphic designer's vocabulary. Generally, *shape* is defined by boundary and mass. It refers to a contour or an outline of a form. A plane or shape is a point or dot that has become too large to

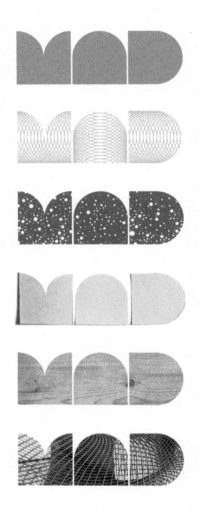

retain its pure identity due to its weight or mass, even if it still has a flat appearance. When this transformation occurs, a dot becomes a shape.

A shape is a graphic, two-dimensional plane that appears to be flat and is defined by an enclosing, contour line, as well as by color, value, texture, or typography. It is the external outline of a plane that results from a line that starts at one point and continues back to its beginning, creating an enclosed space or shape. It is composed of width and height but never depth. It is a line with breadth. Shapes are used to define layouts, create patterns, and compose countless elements in a composition.

Basic Characteristics

Examples of basic shapes are the circle, square, and triangle. All other complex shapes, such as an oval, rectangle, trapezoid, pentagon, hexagon, and octagon, are derived from these three elemental shapes. A shape can be solid or outline, opaque or transparent, smooth or textured.

Basically, shapes are either geometric, organic, or random. Their overall configura-

(continued on page 34)

The playful and unconventional shapes for the Museum of Arts and Design (MAD) identity program are reminiscent of forms evident in the building's original interior architecture and represent the museum's unique home, expanded collections, and diverse program offerings. A broad and visually diverse set of colors, textures, materials, forms, and images allows the museum's acronym to constantly evolve and change from application to application, furthering the eclectic nature and public message of this institution's mission.

PENTAGRAM
New York, New York, USA

The Sold Appetite Poster
VLADIMIR AND GEORGII STENBERG
(STENBERG BROTHERS)
Moscow, Russia

VLADIMIR STENBERG (1899–1982) and GEORGII STENBERG (1900–1933), also known as the Stenberg brothers, were Soviet artists and designers who came to renown following the Russian Revolution of 1917.

After an initial interest in engineering, the Stenbergs attended the Stoganov School of Applied Art (later renamed the State Free Art Workshops) in Moscow from 1917 to 1922, where they designed the decorations and posters for the first May Day celebration of 1918. In 1919, the Stenbergs along with a group of comrades founded the OBMOKhU (the Society of Young Artists) and participated in its first group exhibition in May of 1919. During the 1920s and '30s, they were well established and members of the avant-garde community, collaborating with other artists, architects, and writers such as Alexandr Rodchenko, Varvara Stepnova, and Kasimir Malevich.

They worked in a wide range of media, initially as sculptors and then as theater designers, architects, and draftsmen, designing everything from clothing and furniture to costumes and stage sets. However, their greatest achievement was in graphic design, particularly with the design of mass-produced posters used to advertise a new and powerful form of universal communication—film.

In the early 1900s, the commercial film poster provided artists and designers, such as the Stenbergs, with new and uncharted approaches for communicating a diverse range of visual themes. Up to this point in time, film posters usually relied upon a narrow point of view for communicating their story—either a single scene from the film or an image of the featured star of the film—to gain the public's attention.

The Stenbergs were at their prime during this revolutionary period of politics, propaganda, and artistic experimentation in Russia. They started to experiment with collage, photomontage, and assemblage, as well as portions of photographic images and preprinted paper created by others. They realized a new approach and methodology for creating imagery and compositions that were no longer connected to conventional realism.

While the visual characteristics of their posters included perspective, texture, scale, contrast, and movement as well as an innovative use of color, pattern, and typography, shape was a primary compositional element used in all of their work. Whether its scale is exaggerated, its graphic form distorted, or its visual composition jarring, the Stenbergs used shape to create identity and visual immediacy, as well as to reinforce a poster's story. Their posters were groundbreaking, abstract studies of line, plane, and shape composed in space and reflected a kinship to Suprematist painting, Russian Constructivism, and the work of El Lissitzky, Vladimir Mayakovsky, and Wassily Kandinsky.

The majority of their posters, radical even by contemporary standards, were produced within a nine-year period from 1924 to 1933, the year of Georgii's untimely death at age 33. Vladimir continued to design film posters and organized the decorations of Moscow's Red Square for the May Day celebration of 1947.

Film Poster

The Stenberg Brothers and the Russian Avant-Garde

The soft inviting shape of this four-sided wine label for Terrazzo Prosecco provides an appropriate frame and background for its delicate, linear border, as well as for its symmetrical typography and fluid script lettering of the wine name.

LOUISE FILI LTD.
New York, New York, USA

tion can determine their inherent message and meaning. For example, a soft, curvilinear shape may appear warm and welcoming, whereas a sharp, angular shape may appear cold and threatening.

Straight lines and angular corners create rectilinear, geometric shapes. Curvilinear lines create amorphous, organic shapes. Circles, squares, triangles, and rectangles are geometric shapes that are crisp and mathematically precise with straight lines and consistent, curved profiles. A natural or organic shape can either be irregular or regular.

The pairing of these two pure geometric shapes provides a strong visual counterpoint for this identity for the University of Kentucky's Arts in HealthCare program. The dynamic juxtaposition of the shapes fully depends upon the visual clarity of the square representing the institution, combined with the imperfect dots of the concentric circles symbolizing the human connection of the visual and performing artists represented in this program.

POULIN + MORRIS INC.
New York, New York, USA

Three thick, sturdy, and bold custom letterforms are composed as one shape to further communicate the strength and power of New York City's branding and identity program. Used alone or collectively as a visual texture and pattern, this unique mark is designed as one continuous shape, organized in a variety of compositional configurations. Due to the shape of this logotype, it is still immediately understood as three separate and distinct letterforms with an unmistakable visual characteristic that is immediate, durable, impactful, and strong.

WOLFF OLINS
New York, New York, USA

A bold, six-sided, vertically proportioned shape functions as a distinctive frame and containment element for the name and logotype of Darden Studio, a type foundry housed in a historic building in downtown Brooklyn. Framed on a black field and outlined with a thin, white hairline, this shape communicates a strong sense of craft in the studio's aesthetic, is rooted in centuries of type founding, and is reminiscent of historical board and flag signs found in the area.

MUCCA DESIGN
New York, New York, USA

This poster series for the Cleveland International Film Festival relies upon unusual, random, free-form shapes representing the festival's attendees. Overscale, bold, black shapes set against vibrant color backgrounds strengthen the overall identity of these memorable and eye-catching profiles and are further married with smaller dynamic shapes containing typographic information and visual textures for added nuance and character.

TWIST CREATIVE INC.
Cleveland, Ohio, USA

The stylized, machinelike, curved shape of this *M* represents Mac Industries, a precision machining and fabrication company, and the image is further conveyed with a corner of the *M* separated and set apart from the body of the letter functioning as a dotted *i*. This dynamic void creates a visual intersection within the stylized shape of the letterform, reinforcing

a level of detail and precision in the firm's identity and secondary descriptive line.

INFINITE SCALE DESIGN
Salt Lake City, Utah, USA

Categories of Shape

There are three categories of shape, each with their own unique visual characteristics and criteria:

Geometric

The most familiar shapes are geometric in character—circles, squares, rectangles, and triangles. They are based on mathematical formulas relating to point, line, and plane. Their contours are always regularized, angular, or hard edged. We are most familiar with geometric shapes because they are the first shapes we tend to encounter when we are small children.

Organic

Shapes that are created or derived from nature and living organisms are organic. These shapes are used more freely than geometric shapes are usually irregular and soft.

Random

Shapes created from invention and imagination are random and have no sense of order, semblance, or relationship to geometric or organic shapes.

The amorphous, free-form shape of a stylized window, projected back in space and framed with soft corners, symbolizes a youthful appeal for this Seattle-based boutique urban realtor named Funky Lofts.

URBAN INFLUENCE
DESIGN STUDIO
Seattle, Washington, USA

These letterforms are unconventional not only in their shape, but also in their subtle variations in profile, proportion, counter, and stroke thickness. Reinforced with nonalignment to a common baseline and a pronounced dot over the letter *i*, the active and lyrical typographic statement is unique and memorable. Color is also used as an alternating, pulsating visual element to further unify the varying shapes and meaning of the logotype.

WINK
Minneapolis, Minnesota, USA

The visual strength, immediacy, and simplicity of a pure geometric-shaped letterform is the central focal point and singular message of this lecture-series poster. A large-scale, sans serif, white *C* centered within the vertical composition of this poster and contrasted against a dramatic black background further reinforces the purity and beauty of this geometric shape, as well as the design philosophy and career of the designer, Ivan Chermayeff.

PISCATELLO DESIGN CENTER
New York, New York, USA

The fluid profile of the black letter *T* and star ligature combined with the purity of the starlike, circular seal for this identity and stationery program creates a strong visual integrity and counterpoint between an organic shape and a geometric-based shape that become one and the same with the firm name of Thomas & Star.

MARKATOS MOORE
San Francisco, California, USA

This promotional poster was part of a series that was developed by Scholastic, Target, and AIGA to help educators introduce design to their K-8 curriculums. The pro-bono project invited designers to "respond" to an art piece by creating a poster that celebrates its themes or formal elements. The dual nature of Picasso's painted terra-cotta piece titled

Vase-Bird inspired the random, half animal, half object, and hybrid shapes evident in this poster. These playful, whimsical letterforms are further strengthened by an intense two-color palette, a strong figure-ground relationship, and an unusual overall texture that is engaging to the viewer.

ALFALFA STUDIO LLC
New York, New York, USA

Shape versus Form

The terms *shape* and *form* are commonly used interchangeably; however, they have two separate and distinct meanings. A shape has a two-dimensional character, whereas a form is perceived to have a three-dimensional character. Other terms commonly used for form are *mass* and *volume*.

A form, mass, or volume is a three-dimensional shape because it has height, width, and depth.

In compositional terms, a shape functions as a figurative element in or on a ground, surrounding background, or space. It is a positive element within a negative space. This is a fundamental principle of figure-ground and an integral characteristic of balance in a visual composition.

The traditional, cruciform shape of this symmetrical, ornamental medallion is derived from unique architectural features of the Old Police Headquarters building, a renovated, historic, mixed-use real estate development in downtown San Diego.

URBAN INFLUENCE
DESIGN STUDIO
Seattle, Washington, USA

form \ˈfȯrm\ *n*
1 a: the shape and structure
of something as distinguished from
its material, or the shape
and structure of an object

4

"Art is nothing without form."
GUSTAVE FLAUBERT (1821-1880), *French, Novelist, Playwright*

Basic forms are derived from basic shapes—a square becomes a cube, a circle becomes a sphere, a triangle becomes a pyramid. The terms *shape* and *form* are often confused with one another as if they meant the same thing. In chapter 3, criteria and characteristics that define shape were

The **CNN** Grill was a "wired hub of political activity" for journalists, political operatives, and celebrities during the national political conventions. Bold, illuminated geometric forms and typography, coupled with patriotic colors, created a strong and memorable identity for this temporary gathering venue.

COLLINS
New York, New York, USA

explained. Form is achieved by integrating depth or volume to the equation of shape. It is a three-dimensional element of design that encloses volume. It has height, width, and depth. For example, a two-dimensional triangle is defined as a shape; however, a three-dimensional pyramid is defined as a form. Cubes, spheres, ellipses, pyramids, cones, and cylinders are all examples of geometric forms.

Form is always composed of multiple surfaces and edges. It is a volume or empty space created by other fundamental design elements—points, lines, and shapes. (continued on page 44)

The paper slit of this magazine cover for *Camera Work* creates a three-dimensional, concave surface on a two-dimensional plane that is furthered strengthened by the asymmetrical placement of typography on the cover.

MENDE DESIGN
San Francisco, California, USA

The pop art, cartoonlike visual character of this dialog box creates a dynamic and playful three-dimensional form for the containment of "Pop Justice," a logotype for one of England's most popular blogs. Vibrant, analogous colors and bold letterforms, sans their counters, further create visual impact without overpowering the logotype's spatial depth and volume.

FORM
London, United Kingdom

1983

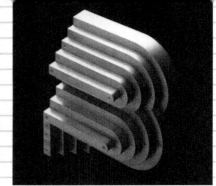

Aluminum Alphabet Series
TAKENOBU IGARASHI
Tokyo, Japan

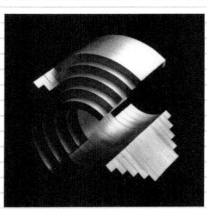

TAKENOBU IGARASHI (b. 1944) is a sculptor and designer who has continually explored the fusion of two-dimensional and three-dimensional form. His work is based on a language of basic elements—point, the purest element of design; line, which delineates locations and boundaries between planes; shape, realized flat or dimensional; texture, visual or tactile; and grid, whose horizontal and vertical axes provide order and logic to a composition.

While the majority of his work for the last thirty years has been in graphic identity, environmental graphics, and product design, his exploration and experimentation with letterform and isometric grids has brought him international attention and recognition. In the early 1980s, his two-dimensional, isometric alphabets, first conceived as a series of poster calendars for the Museum of Modern Art in New York City, quickly evolved into three-dimensional alphabetic structures that Igarashi called architectural alphabets.

The *Aluminum Alphabet Series*, the first to involve typographic sculptures, comprises twenty-six three-dimensional, aluminum letterforms. Each sculptural form consists of a series of aluminum plates of varying thickness joined together by flat-head aluminum fasteners. Here, Igarashi uses letterform to explore the potential of three-dimensional form. He says, "One of the charms of the Roman letter is its simple form. The wonderful thing is that it is created with the minimum number of elements; the standard structure is based on the circle, square, and triangle, which are the fundamentals of formation."

Letterforms are basically symbols or signs written on paper in a flat, two-dimensional world. Design of letterforms can be varied by extending their two-dimensional characteristics into a three-dimensional world. Letterforms can also be considered as simple graphic compositions of basic geometric elements—circles, squares, and triangles—and within these compositions are hidden possibilities for developing a greater set of shapes and forms.

Igarashi's approach for this series was to conceive letterforms as solid volumes divided into positive and negative spaces. A three-dimensional composition is realized when the form of the letter is extended in both its positive and negative directions; in other words, by generating spatial tensions in both directions. He states, "This is one example of my attempt to find a geometric solution between meaning and aesthetic form. Based on a 5-millimeter [1/4 inch] three-dimensional grid system, the twenty-six letters of the alphabet from A to Z were created by adding and subtracting on the x-, y-, and z-axes."

The *Aluminum Alphabet Series* is a unique, groundbreaking result of taking a conceptual, spatial, and mathematical view of letterforms and revealing some of the many possibilities of shape and form. It is the ultimate study in letterform, material, detailing, visual interpretation, and three-dimensional form.

Takenobu Igarashi and the Aluminum Alphabet Series

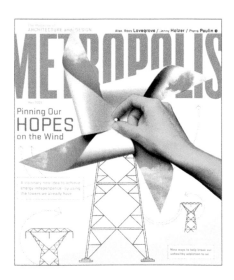

In this cover for *Metropolis* magazine, the juxtaposition of three-dimensional forms—a pinwheel and a person's hand—on a two-dimensional representation of the same form creates a visually dynamic, engaging, and memorable cover.

COLLINS
New York, New York, USA

Types of Forms

Forms can be real or illusory. Real, three-dimensional form contains actual volume or physical weight while illusory, two-dimensional form is perceptual. Real forms are three-dimensional such as objects, sculpture, architecture, and packaging. Illusory forms are illusions of three-dimensional shapes in two-dimensional spaces and can be realized three-dimensionally by using several graphic conventions to achieve illusory results.

Projections

Representing several surfaces or planes of a two-dimensional form all at once is one way to visually represent a three-dimensional form without it receding in space or in scale. The most common types of projections are as follows:

Isometric

An isometric projection is the easiest of projection methods where three visible surfaces of a form have equal emphasis. All axes are simultaneously rotated away from the picture plane and kept at the same angle of projection (30 degrees from the picture plane), all lines are equally foreshortened, and the angles between lines are always 120 degrees.

These three marks represent the breadth and spirit of the Smithsonian's Cooper-Hewitt National Design Week, an annual education initiative on design, by implying a three-dimensional volume or environment that contains iconic forms of furniture, lighting, and related functional objects. The figure-ground relationships evident in each of these marks further reinforce a dynamic, visual interplay between two-dimensional and three-dimensional forms.

WINK
Minneapolis, Minnesota, USA

Types of Projections

Isometric

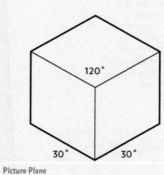

120°

30°　　30°

Picture Plane

Plan Oblique (30°–60°)

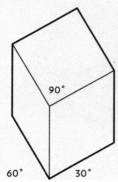

90°

60°　　30°

Plan Oblique (45°–45°)

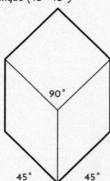

90°

45°　　45°

Types of Perspective

One-Point

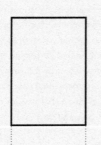

Picture Plane

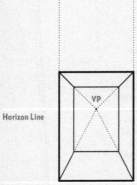

VP

Horizon Line

Picture Plane

Two-Point

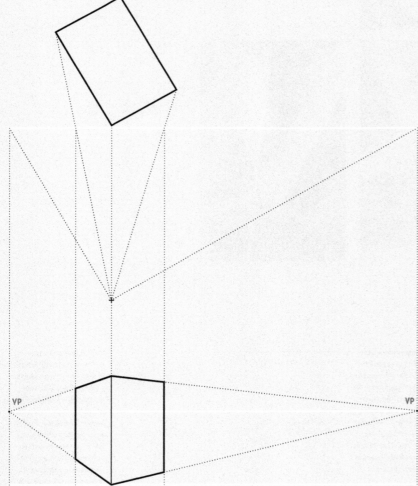

VP　　　　　　　　　　　　　　　　VP

VP = Vanishing Point

This paper promotion for Neenah Paper uses a single ink color and laser die-cut shapes on a duplex cover to reveal custom display letterforms spelling out "1/2 the job." The layered cover provides depth, volume, and shadow to this typographic treatment, further strengthening these unique forms and ultimately the identity of the promotional message.

AND PARTNERS
New York, New York, USA

Axonometric (or Plan Oblique)
An axonometric, or plan oblique, projection is a parallel projection of a form viewed from a skewed direction to reveal more than one of its sides in the same picture plane.

In isometric and axonometric projections, all vertical lines remain vertical and all parallel lines remain parallel.

Spatial Depth

Three-dimensional space and depth can also be achieved when one surface of a form is overlapped and partially obscured by another form. One- and two-point perspective drawings exemplify creation of a form's spatial depth with two-dimensional shapes overlapping on a two-dimensional picture plane. (See diagrams on page 45.)

Tone and Shading

Form can also be visually indicated through tone, shade, and texture. The surfaces of a form curving or facing away from a directed light source appear darker than surfaces facing a directed light source. This effect suggests the rounding of a two-dimensional shape into a three-dimensional form.

This assignment requires the student to explore the visual relationships between typographic form and architectural form. This student based their photographic exploration and analysis on the angles and geometry found in Daniel Liebskind's Denver Art Museum and in the typeface, Futura.

CASSANDRA BARBOE,
Student
HENRIETTA CONDAK,
Instructor
School of Visual Arts
New York, New York, USA

This promotional poster series for the McGill School of Architecture uses form as a primary vehicle for communicating an emblematic element in architecture. Each lecturer's name is printed on a colored strip of paper and folded to evoke an architectural form. These paper strips were photographed together to announce the series and individually to announce each lecture. Each three-dimensional, photographic composition is unique, adding a strong visual dynamic to the series. An organizational grid for narrative, informational text is used consistently on all posters and is a contrasting juxtaposition to each free-form, three-dimensional photographic composition.

ATELIER PASTILLE ROSE
Montreal, Quebec, Canada

The primary visual element of this promotional poster celebrating the second anniversary of Casa da Musica, Portugal's world-renowned concert hall, relies upon its unique and unconventional symbol—a stylized, trapezoidal form derived from the building's architecture. This form is fragmented by facet and color, further implying a three-dimensional appearance as well as communicating the diversity of music performances scheduled during the anniversary season.

SAGMEISTER INC.
New York, New York, USA

Michael Rotondi
RoTo Architects Inc
Los Angeles
20.10.08
David J. Azrieli Lecture in Architecture

Lecture starts at 6pm
Moyse Hall, Arts Building
853 Sherbrooke Street West
Reception to follow in the Exhibition Room
of the School of Architecture

La conférence commence à 18h
Moyse Hall, Pavillon des Arts
853, rue Sherbrooke Ouest
Une reception est offerte après la conférence
à la salle d'exposition de l'École d'architecture

light \\'līt\\ *n*
1 a: something that makes vision possible

5

"Light is the ultimate messenger of the universe."
ANONYMOUS

Light is a constant source of kinetic energy, ever changing on the infinite continuum of day into night. It is also an essential design element in visual communication because it fundamentally allows us to "see" and visually experience our world as we know it. In visual communications, light

This dramatic book cover relies solely upon extreme contrast, subtle color, and intense light to bring a strong focal point to the eye in the photographic portrait of Martin Heidegger and his seminal book entitled *Introduction to Philosophy*.

CASA REX
São Paulo, Brazil

In each of these covers, X-ray photographic images of flowers accentuate the texture, linear structure, beauty, and illuminated brilliance of each cropped image, as well as the pure human emotions of each opera libretto. Pure, bright, saturated colors paired with asymmetrical placement of symmetrically composed labels containing serif type and decorative bordered line elements also reinforce the visual and narrative themes of each composition.

TAKAKO SAEGUSA, Student
MICHAEL IAN KAYE,
Instructor
School of Visual Arts
New York, New York, USA

is either used as a sensation of light, a source of light or illumination, a representation of it, or an awareness of it, on design elements in a graphic composition.

Technically, light is defined as an electromagnetic radiation of wavelengths that are visible to the human eye. It also refers to other wavelengths that are not detectable by the eye such as ultraviolet (UV) and infrared.

Historical References
In the fifth century, the Greeks recognized a direct link between the human eye and (continued on page 52)

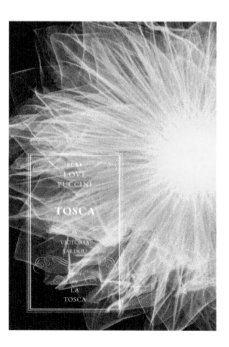

bauhaus zeitschrift (*Bauhaus* magazine) Cover
HERBERT BAYER
Berlin, Germany

HERBERT BAYER (1900–1985), was a pioneering designer, typographer, architect, painter, photographer, and educator.

After completing his military service, he was an architect's apprentice working on commissions including interiors, furniture, and packaging.

In 1921, Bayer enrolled as a student at the Bauhaus in Weimar, where he studied under Wassily Kandinsky and later under Lazlo Moholy-Nagy. Following the closing of the Bauhaus, arrangements were made to transfer the school to Dessau, and in 1925 Bayer and five other former students including Marcel Breuer, Joost Schmidt, and Josef Albers were appointed teachers.

As an educator, he transformed the Bauhaus by eliminating the use of lithography and woodcuts and introducing movable type and mechanical presses to the Dessau workshops. The use of serif, black letter, and capital letterform ended; the use of sans serif, lowercase letterforms began. Typographic form was now asymmetric, simple, and direct.

During his years at Dessau, Bayer had been strongly influenced by Moholy-Nagy's enthusiasm for photography as a contemporary means of visual communication and started to experiment with various photographic techniques including collage, photomontage, and light.

Bayer's most original use of light (and shadow) was with his photomontage for the 1928 cover of the *bauhaus zeitschrift*. In this memorable composition, he uses light in a dramatic and striking manner. Additionally, Bayer makes use of a cube, ball, and cone (solidifications of Kandinsky's iconic square, circle, and triangle) along with sharpened pencil and transparent triangle juxtaposed over the surface of the magazine's cover. This image, classically simple and evocative, was one of the most widely produced examples of Bayer's graphic design. It not only identified the publication in a provocative manner, but it fully communicated the essence and philosophy of the Bauhaus and its avant-garde educational programs.

Bayer left the Bauhaus in 1928 and relocated to Berlin. In 1938, like many artists and designers in Germany at the time, he fled the Nazis and immigrated to the United States, where he became a self-appointed spokesperson for the Bauhaus movement.

Herbert Bayer and *bauhaus zeitschrift*

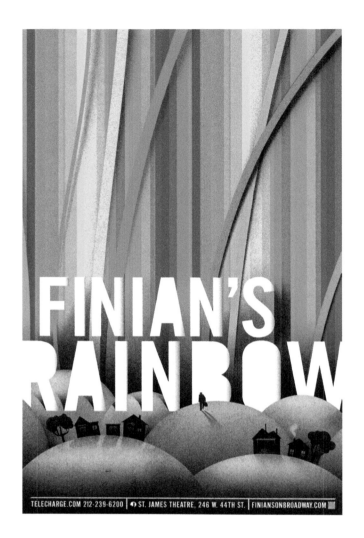

Both informational-based posters reveal and illuminate the beauty hidden within complex data. Each poster diagrammatically charts twenty-four hours of light and dark for each day of the year and is scientifically accurate and visually engaging.

ACCEPT & PROCEED
London, United Kingdom

how we see objects. Earlier thinking was that there was a visual "fire" or glow emanating from the human eye that allowed us to see. In the fourth century BC, Aristotle rejected this premise by concluding "if vision were produced by means of a fire emitted by the eye, like the light emitted by a lantern, why then are we not able to see in the dark?"

In the history of fine arts, the visual representation of light has inspired generations of artists and designers. One needs to consider only the paintings of Leonardo da Vinci, Rembrandt, Claude Monet, and Georges Seurat to understand how these visionaries captured and used light subtly, effectively, and meaningfully. In contemporary work, the photography of Ansel Adams and Robert Mapplethorpe provides the same insightful lessons and insights.

Properties and Characteristics

A graphic designer can determine how light ultimately influences and affects two-dimensional design elements in any composition. For example, light can be illusory by overlapping a shape or form with color, shade, tone, and texture, creating a sense of transparency or opacity. This graphic effect creates the appearance that light is coming through each

Light is represented in this theatrical production poster for *Finian's Rainbow* by a full spectrum of saturated color—cut paper with just a few strips within this pure graphic pattern breaking away from their strong, rigid vertical axis to create the start of a rainbow. Cut-out letterforms and landscape forms appear three-dimensional and in bas-relief due to light and shadow projected onto each of these compositional elements, further reinforcing light, depth, volume, and three-dimensional space.

SPOTCO
New York, New York, USA

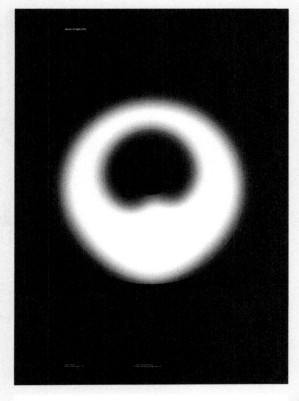

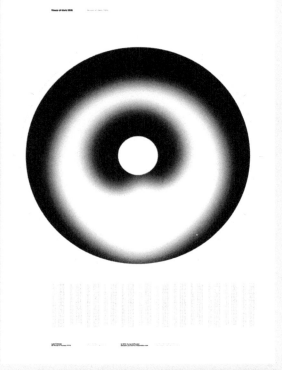

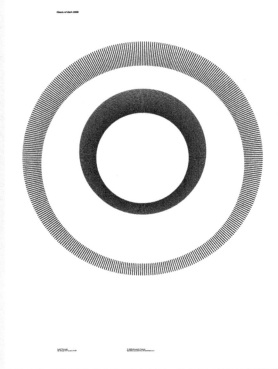

This assignment requires the student to explore the visual relationships between typographic and architectural form. This student based her photographic exploration and analysis on the monolithic proportions and use of light and transparency found in Pierre Chareau's modernist masterpiece building, La Maison de Verre, and the typeface, Futura Condensed.

MEAGHAN TIRONDOLA,
Student
HENRIETTA CONDAK,
Instructor
School of Visual Arts
New York, New York, USA

of these elements, or it can be completely impermeable and prevent light from appearing through another shape or form.

Light can also create the illusion of a third dimension on a two-dimensional surface through the use of shadow. This can be achieved by carefully determining where a light source is located above, below, behind, or beside compositional elements.

Light also assists with another design principle—contrast, allowing our eyes to perceive a broad range of colors and tones from light to dark. In addition to creating the illusion of three-dimensionality, light is critical for creating the illusion of depth on

In this promotional poster for a lecture given by the toy designer Jarvis Rockwell, light is projected through childlike, translucent, primary-colored plastic letters, creating colored shadows that are projected onto the poster's white background. The effect is iconic, playful, and immediately identified with a child's point of view.

ROGERS ECKERSLEY
DESIGN
New York, New York, USA

a two-dimensional plane. And it is also an essential element in any three-dimensional space where there is a need to emphasize objects and forms, such as in a retail display or museum exhibition.

Light is also a critical and essential element, property, and dimension of color, defined as a reflection and how we perceive the brightness of any color within the spectrum of colors. The amount of light in a color has a direct connection to its amplitude, strength, and visual impact. Other visual effects, such as shadow and contrast, are also visually perceived as varied light levels on a scale from light to dark.

This logotype for an independent boutique hair salon, is based on a clear-cut, powerful idea that relies upon the Miller & Green initials and the essential hairdressers' tool—a pair of scissors. The vibrant color combination of a bright lime green and dark brown reflects the salon's elegant yet vivacious character and was implemented across various applications including business stationery, promotional materials, and environmental graphics.

LANDOR
Paris, France

THE NEW GROUP

THE STARRY MESSENGER

WRITTEN & DIRECTED BY
**KENNETH
LONERGAN**

Matthew Broderick
Stephanie Cannon
Kieran Culkin
Merwin Goldsmith
Catalina Sandino Moreno
Grant Shaud
J. Smith-Cameron
Missy Yager

SETS DEREK McLANE COSTUMES MATTIE ULLRICH LIGHTS JASON LYONS SOUND SHANE RETTIG PROJECTIONS AUSTIN SWITSER
ASSISTANT DIRECTOR MARIE MASTERS PRODUCTION SUPERVISOR PETER R. FEUCHTWANGER / PRF PRODUCTIONS
PRODUCTION STAGE MANAGER VALERIE A. PETERSON CASTING JUDY HENDERSON, CSA
PUBLIC RELATIONS BRIDGET KLAPINSKI / THE KARPEL GROUP GENERAL MANAGER ELISABETH BAYER
EXECUTIVE DIRECTOR GEOFF RICH ARTISTIC DIRECTOR SCOTT ELLIOTT MANAGING DIRECTOR, DEVELOPMENT OLIVER DOW

STARTS OCTOBER 24, 2009
THEATRE ROW 410 WEST 42ND STREET 212.279.4200 www.TheNewGroup.org

Simple, dramatic black-and-white photography and a bold figure–ground give this theatrical poster a strong yet subtle visual metaphor for the theme of the play *The Starry Messenger*. The texture of a starlit sky set against the stark white, background further reinforces the character-driven reference in the play's title.

ROGERS ECKERSLEY
DESIGN
New York, New York, USA

The element of light is directly connected to other visual characteristics such as brilliance, chiaroscuro, fluorescence, gradient, luminosity, pearlescence, reflection, refraction, value, shade, tint, and tone.

Light provides graphic designers with the essential means to understand other visual elements, principles, and techniques such as color, shape, form, movement, texture, perspective, shading, motion, visual acuity, and depth perception. It is a critical element of visual communications for obvious reasons. Without it, the phenomena of visual perception and understanding would not exist.

The fundamental element of light can be conveyed through shadow and depth, as shown in this book cover. Light is directed upward from the bottom of the image, lengthening projected shadows vertically above each red element as well as giving them a more pronounced, three-dimensional appearance. The twenty unique and subtly distinct red dotlike elements represent the twenty love poems written by the Chilean poet Pablo Neruda. This visually distinctive cover is further strengthened by the symmetrical placement of these elements in contrast with an asymmetrical placement of the cover's typography.

KATYA MEZHIBOVSKAYA
New York, New York, USA

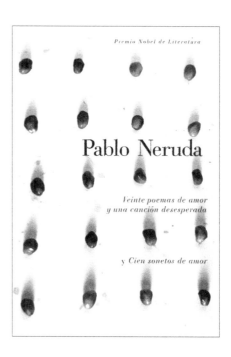

Premio Nobel de Literatura

Pablo Neruda

*Veinte poemas de amor
y una canción desesperada*

y Cien sonetos de amor

The use of a subtle color palette with the varied scaled decorative patterns for this branding and identity program for a San Francisco-based home furnishings company creates light, transparency, and depth on a two dimensional surface.

VOLUME
San Francisco, California, USA

A highly reflective material, contrasted with an over-scaled, large matte black dot, reinforces the message and meaning of this promotional poster for a light festival in Porec, Croatia. The poster's base material allows any light to be either absorbed or reflected, depending on where it is displayed.

STUDIO SONDA
Porec, Croatia

col·or \ˈkə-lər\ *n*

1 a: a phenomenon of light (as red, brown, pink, or gray) or visual perception that enables one to differentiate otherwise identical objects

color

6

"Color is the place where our brain and the universe meet."
PAUL KLEE (1879-1940), *Swiss, Author, Educator, Painter*

Color is one of the most powerful and communicative elements in a graphic designer's language. It affects all of us by providing visual energy and variety in what we see and experience on a daily basis. Color is used to attract attention, group disparate elements, reinforce meaning, and enhance

visual compositions. It can also immediately convey an attitude or an emotion, provoke a response, create emphasis and variety, communicate a specific message, and further strengthen an established hierarchy.

Color increases visual interest and can reinforce the meaning and organization of elements in any visual composition. As a primary visual element, color enhances the emotional and psychological nuances of any visual message. It assists in creating the mood you desire. For example, light colors produce pleasant responses whereas darker colors produce quieter effects.

(continued on page 62)

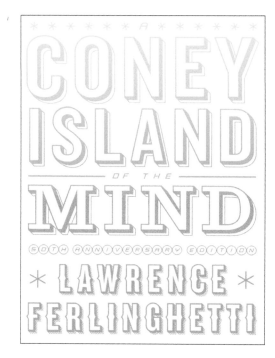

Vibrant, tertiary color combinations create a strong visual dynamic in these covers for Mohawk Papers' Via notebooks. Repeating horizontal patterns set in a variety of typographic treatments for "Via" further strengthens the diversity and broad applications of the paper line, as well as create a campaign that is fresh, bold, and vibrant.

ADAMSMORIOKA INC.
Beverly Hills, California, USA

A full-color gradient, from yellow to blue, is used on this book cover, *Coney Island of the Mind*, communicating the playful and festival-like spirit of the title and theme of the book. An intense color palette, as well as an eclectic set of typographic letter-forms, further expresses the central celebratory mood and emotional content of the book's poetry.

RODRIGO CORRAL DESIGN
New York, New York, USA

1984 Los Angeles Summer Olympics
SUSSMAN/PREJZA & COMPANY
Los Angeles, California, USA

Since 1980, DEBORAH SUSSMAN (b. 1931) and her firm, Sussman/Prejza & Company, have advanced the field of environmental graphic design, creating urban sign programs for numerous cities in California as well as environmental graphics for Disney, Hasbro, and Apple Computer.

In the 1960s, Sussman worked with two pioneers of twentieth-century American design, Charles and Ray Eames, whose creative imprint revolutionized the look of postwar America. It was during this mentoring period that she became rooted in an Eamesian joy of color, pattern, cultural influences, and ethnic design.

Her environmental graphics program for the 1984 Summer Olympics literally changed the way we experience color in an urban environment. This comprehensive program guided an enormous international audience through a series of complex venues, while visually celebrating the games and the surrounding city on a grand scale and in a festival-like manner. Sussman's system of temporary structures, scaffolding, striped columns, large-scale graphics, and bright colors were inventive, functional, and extremely accessible.

The Olympic colors were unexpected, exciting, and distinct from the everyday visual fabric of an urban city. Magenta was the base color on which the color palette was built. Sports pictograms were white on magenta; freeway signs were magenta with aqua; the interaction of magenta against yellow, vermilion, and aqua was the most important interrelationship of the palette. The colors also had strong ties to locale—magenta and yellow are of the Pacific Rim, Mexico, and the Far East. Aqua is Mediterranean and a strong counterpoint to the warmer Pacific colors.

Colors were generally used in combinations of three or more, and the palette was divided to produce enormous visual variety. Each venue had its own palette that related to the character of its specific sport and to the ambient color and lighting of its surroundings. For example, gymnastics was represented by vermilion, yellow, and green; swimming by aqua and white. The colors worked very effectively in southern California light, appearing brilliant and vibrant at different times of the day.

Color made the 1984 Los Angeles Olympics a truly visual event. It transformed one of the largest cities in the world into an intimate, cohesive experience, as well as the manner in which visual communications would be approached for all future Olympics.

In considering color in her work, Sussman says, "My work with color is informed by content. It has roots in contextual sources and is inspired by geography, cultural history, user's needs, architecture, urban characteristics, and available materials. I work intuitively when selecting the actual palettes, often relating them to musical iconography. Ray Eames and Alexander (Sandro) Girard were my mentors. Wassily Kandinsky said, 'In general, color is a medium that has a direct impact on the soul.' This has been my experience and remains my belief."

Deborah Sussman and the 1984 Summer Olympics

This promotional shopping bag series for Cass Art Stores in London celebrates color in art through typographic compositions that feature traditional oil colors and communicate their provenance throughout art history. Scarlet lake, phthalo turquoise, quinacridone magenta, and viridian are just a few colors that are used on these eye-catching moving billboards.

PENTAGRAM
London, United Kingdom

Colors also inherently contain subjective meanings that communicate immediately without words or images. For example, red is associated with fire, blood, and sex; blue is associated with ice, sea, and sky.

Numerous classification systems have been developed to identify and categorize color for a variety of visual applications. These include systems and theories developed by Sir Isaac Newton (1701), Johann Wolfgang von Goethe (1810), Albert Munsell (1915), Johannes Itten (1961), and Josef Albers (1975).

Fundamental Properties
There are three fundamental visual properties of color:

Hue
Color in its purest form, or hue, is the identification given to each color such as yellow, red, or blue. This identification is the result of how we "see" light being reflected from an object at a specific frequency. Of these three fundamental properties, hue is the most absolute—we may "see" a color as yellow, red, or blue, but it is identifiable only when it is adjacent to another color with which it can be compared. A color with no visible hue, such as gray, is a neutral color.

Value
The lightness or darkness of a color is identified as its value. This property is also referred to as a color's luminance, brightness, or tone. It is fully dependent on a color's hue and intensity. Adding white to a color creates a lighter value, or tint; adding black creates a darker value, or shade of a color.

Value can be used to exaggerate the meaning of any visual message. When elements have changing color value, a viewer's eye is guided in, around, and through a visual composition. The degrees of contrast and relative amounts of value also provide movement to the composition. Because distant objects appear lighter in nature, value can also create the illusion of space and depth.

Saturation (also chroma)
Intensity or saturation is the brightness or dullness of a color, or its level of saturation. It is the measure of a color's purity, brightness, or grayness. A saturated color is vibrant and intense, as opposed to a desaturated color that is restrained and somber. Saturation is

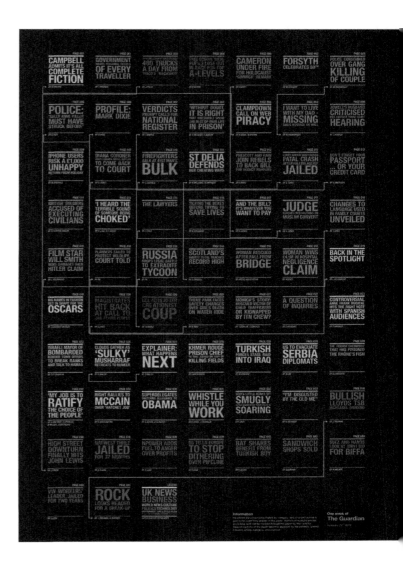

the amount of gray in a color. As it increases, the amount of gray decreases. Brightness is the amount of white in a color. As it increases, the amount of white increases. A color with little or no saturation contains a large amount of white.

Saturated colors attract the viewer's attention. Use desaturated colors when function and efficiency are the priority. Desaturated, light colors are seen as friendly; desaturated, dark colors are seen as formal; saturated colors are seen as exciting and dynamic. Exercise caution when combining saturated colors, as they can visually interfere with one another and increase eye fatigue.

Emblem, an international group of branding specialists, relies solely upon bright, vibrant colors on their website for reinforcing the visual immediacy of their identity, as well as the site's navigational tools.

BLANK MOSSERI
New York, New York, USA

Color is used as a primary organizational and wayfinding tool in this information-based poster titled *One Week of the Guardian*. Based on the periodic table of elements, information is organized by category of interest and popularity. Relying upon a color key at the bottom of the poster, the viewer can interact with content in an easy and accessible manner by immediately identifying a specific topic with a limited number of colors—in this case, ten different color variables for categories such as News, Business, Culture, and Media.

DESIGNING THE NEWS
London, United Kingdom

A sophisticated color palette of vibrant and muted colors in a range of values and saturations is the primary element in the rebranding of Sprint's new retail experience. These diverse colors, combined with product- and user-based imagery, create a visual system that is clean and contemporary for the brand, as well as appealing to a younger audience.

MIRIELLO GRAFICO
San Diego, California, USA

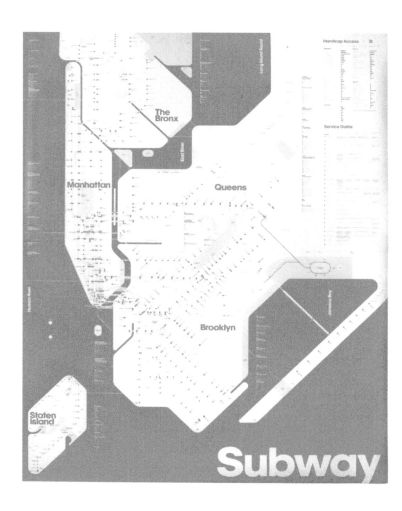

This rethinking of the iconographic New York City subway map in fluorescent red strips away the familiar color-coding of the circa-1970s version while still maintaining a level of hierarchy and functionality. The fluorescent red color becomes an unpredictable variable, as legibility changes completely under different lighting conditions.

The neon effect is intense and uncomfortable in some lighting conditions, while washed out and unreadable in other environments. Color is the primary element used in the extreme simplification of this visually complex information diagram.

TRIBORO DESIGN SOLUTIONS
Brooklyn, New York, USA

This standards manual is part of a student's senior thesis project for the rebranding and repositioning of Microsoft Corporation. In the overall program, as well as throughout the manual itself, color is used as a symbolic, functional communication device. For example, a palette of three secondary colors—orange, green, and purple—is used for the containment border of the MS logotype, reinforcing the diversity of the company's products and services. A subdued, muted color palette is used to organize, emphasize, and allow information to be clear and accessible without competing with the primary tricolors of the new logotype and symbol.

JOHN CLARK, Student
RICHARD POULIN, Instructor
School of Visual Arts
New York, New York, USA

Organizational Categories

Primary Colors
Yellow, red, and blue are primary colors. They are pure in composition and cannot be created from other colors. All other colors are created by combining primary colors.

Secondary Colors
Colors identified as secondary are created by combining two primary colors. Yellow and red create orange; red and blue create purple; and yellow and blue create green.

Tertiary Colors
Colors identified as tertiary are created by combining one primary color with one secondary color—red-orange, red-purple, purple-blue, blue-green, and yellow-green.

Complementary Colors
Colors, such as red and green, blue and orange, and yellow and purple, are complementary and are opposite one another on a color wheel. When mixed together, they desaturate or neutralize each other. However, when they are placed next to each other they increase in intensity.

Monochromatic Colors
Colors created with varying values of a single color are identified as monochromatic. This is achieved by adding white or black to a color. Monochromatic color schemes are perceived as homogenous and unified.

Analogous Colors
Colors created from adjacent colors on a color wheel and have minimal chromatic differences are identified as analogous colors. Analogous color schemes are also perceived as unified, but are more varied than monochromatic color schemes.

Triadic Colors
Colors created from colors equidistant from one another or located at the corners of an equilateral triangle juxtaposed on a color wheel are identified as triadic colors. Triadic color schemes are perceived as strong, dynamic, and vibrant.

Quadratic Colors
Colors created from colors located in the four corners of a square or rectangle juxtaposed on a color wheel are identified as quadratic colors.

In this poster, overlapping lines of intense colors are layered on a solid, black background, creating brighter hues, as well as an optical third dimension to the overall composition.

RYOTA IIZUKA, Student
SIMON JOHNSTON, Instructor
Art Center College of Design
Pasadena, California, USA

A subtle palette of rich, warm colors is evident throughout this admissions viewbook for Middlebury, a liberal arts school in Vermont. Each chapter begins with a typographically bold narrative followed by a series of diagrams, illustrations, and iconic duotone and four-color photographic imagery that gives the reader an understanding of the diversity and varied experiences of the multicultural student body at the school.

PHILOGRAPHICA
Brookline, Massachusetts, USA

Comparative Relationships

All color relationships are relative. Colors can be identified as darker or lighter only when they are compared to other colors. Yellow is perceived as light; violet as dark. Yellow, for example, appears darker than white and has the lightest value of any color. A deep blue or violet appears bright against black and has the darkest value of any color (black being the absence of any reflected light).

Each color also has different levels of saturation. For example, red, blue, and yellow have different levels of intensity from bright to dull. Blue is not as bright as red or yellow; therefore, its intensity is not as high a level of brightness as found in the other two colors.

When complementary colors are juxtaposed with one another, each color appears brighter than the other. When analogous colors are juxtaposed, they tend to blend visually and therefore may be more difficult to distinguish from one another.

Color schemes, or color harmonies, have been developed to assist designers in choosing colors that work well together. The color wheel, a visual representation of the primary, secondary, and tertiary colors, forms the basis for color schemes.

Color Wheels

Color theorists have developed many different methods and systems for organizing and describing fundamental and comparative color relationships. In the late seventeenth century, Sir Isaac Newton (1643–1727) discovered that a prism separates light into a spectrum of seven colors—red, orange, yellow, green, blue, indigo, and violet. He also noticed that the colors at one end of the visible spectrum appear very similar to the colors at the other end of the spectrum. He then drew these two ends of the visible spectrum together, creating the first color wheel. This rudimentary model is very similar to color wheels used today to codify and organize all color relationships.

The structure of color is represented in a color wheel, which is organized in twelve units: three primary colors, three secondary colors, and six tertiary colors. A color wheel is a visual reference tool that illustrates comparative relationships between colors. Color wheels are two-dimensional diagrams of fundamental color relationships and only reference hues—the identification of colors, such as yellow, red, and blue. (see diagrams on page 68, 69)

By using a color wheel as a visual reference, designers can create meaningful relationships such as harmony or tension among color combinations.

A graduated color wheel contains a progressive series of values, or tints and shades, for each color. This visual reference also illustrates that a color's highest saturation point is not the same for each hue. For example, yellow is at its highest intensity toward the lighter end of the value scale, while blue is more intense at the darker end of the value scale. (See diagrams on page 183.)

A graduated color wheel is an effective reference tool for determining combinations of colors that are similar in value or saturation or determining contrast relationships.

Light and Temperature

Color is a property of light and can only be perceived when light is emitted or reflected by an object.

Additive color is created from a light source emitted from a video screen, computer monitor, or theatrical lighting. Additive primary colors are red, green, and blue with all other additive colors derived from them. *(continued on page 70)*

Vibrant and intense colors, are used in this magazine cover, *Latina*, to convey the spirit and culture of the Latin experience in Mexico. This message is further strengthened with the rich and varied color palette in the circular textile of the cover image as well as its juxtaposition with the intense yellow background color of the cover.

RODRIGO CORRAL DESIGN
New York, New York, USA

Color Wheels and Organizational Categories

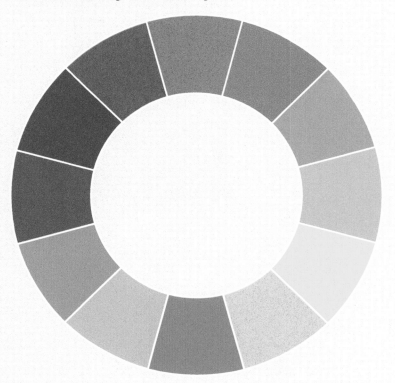

This color wheel illustrates the fundamental relationships among colors. The eight smaller color wheels shown here illustrate basic color relationships that can be applied to an infinite number of color palette combinations.

Primary Colors

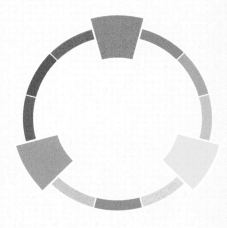

Secondary Colors

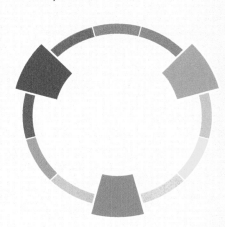

Tertiary Colors

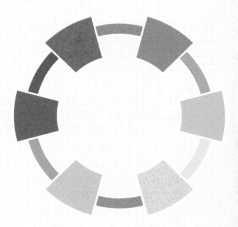

Complementary Colors

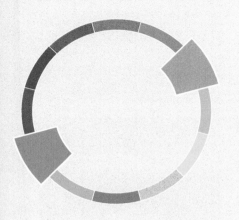

Triadic Colors

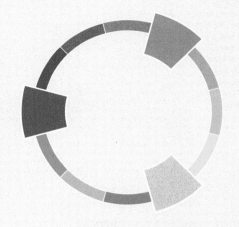

Monochromatic Colors

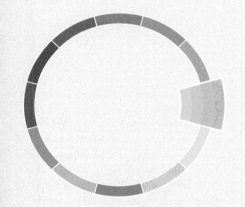

Quadratic Colors

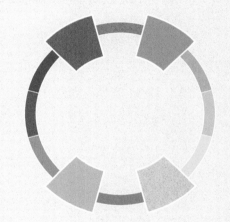

Analogous Colors

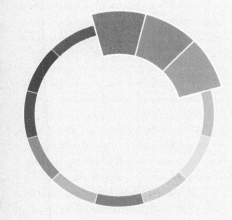

In this well-defined study of analogous colors used in an environmental graphics program for Cincinnati's Civic Center, color is also used as a metaphor for the Ohio River. It enhances the sense of movement in the river with analogous, saturated blues. These cool colors, although at times appearing alone as calming and meditative, in this context convey energy and a kinetic movement throughout the interior public spaces of the center. The main concourse, two city blocks long, and potentially a vacuous and impersonal public space, becomes transformed as a colored canvas on which the river unfolds in wall, ceiling, and floor treatments.

SUSSMAN/PREJZA
& COMPANY
Culver City, California, USA

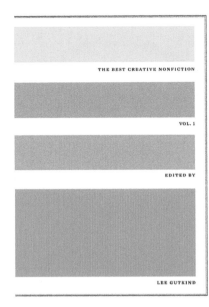

Combining two additive primary colors creates additive secondary colors such as magenta from red and blue, cyan from blue and green, and yellow from red and green. Combining all three additive primary colors creates white, such as when spotlights of red, green, and blue are focused on the same area or subject to create a white spotlight. The absence of all additive primary colors—in other words, no light—creates black. RGB (red, green, and black) is an additive color system used for designing on screen.

Subtractive color is created from light reflected off a colored or pigmented surface. Subtractive primary colors are red, yellow, and blue. Combining two subtractive primary colors creates subtractive secondary colors: orange from red and yellow, green from yellow and blue, and purple from blue and red. Combining all three subtractive primary colors creates black. The absence of all subtractive primary colors—in other words, no pigment—results in white. CMYK (cyan, magenta, yellow, and black) is a subtractive color system used in offset printing.

Temperature of a color is also another subjective quality and relates to our visual experience. Colors considered "warm," such as red, orange, and yellow, remind us of heat

Value and saturation are both critical color considerations in the success of this cover, *The Best Creative Nonfiction*, Volume 1, for a collection of nonfiction writing. Four distinct colors, three warm and one cool, attract the reader's attention by communicating a bold visual for the nonfiction theme of this book, as well as frame the restrained, small-scale serif typography.

RODRIGO CORRAL DESIGN
New York, New York, USA

bideaŵee™

bideaŵee™

and communicate a feeling of warmth. Cool colors such as blue and green remind us of water and nature and communicate a feeling of coolness. Warm colors are brighter and more energetic; cool colors are calmer and more relaxed.

In addition to typography, color is one of the most valuable and influential elements in a graphic designer's vocabulary. It is a profoundly useful tool and has the power to communicate a wide range of emotions, codify diverse information, and establish an immediate connection with the viewer.

The bold, simple use of one bright, intense color—magenta—in this brand identity program for Bideawee, a New York City-based animal adoption center, conveys a message of friendliness, accessibility, and warmth without being literal. Vibrancy and visibility are further strengthened with a warm black background set against the intense value of the prominent magenta color. Lowercase, sans serif letterforms and simple line pictograms further convey a friendly and accessible message. The color also functions as a visual indicator to correctly pronounce this unusual name.

CARBONE SMOLAN AGENCY
New York, New York, USA

tex·ture \ˈteks-chər\ *n*
3 b: the visual or tactile surface characteristics and appearance of something

texture

7

"One touch of nature makes the whole world kin."
WILLIAM SHAKESPEARE (1564-1616), *English, Author, Playwright, Poet*

Texture is defined as the look and feel of any surface. It is the surface quality of an object, be it smooth, rough, soft, or hard, and essentially a visual effect that adds richness and dimension to any visual composition. It can be seen and experienced by human touch or interpreted tactilely

A diverse set of compositional elements, such as large and small-scale typography, borders, frames, diagrams, and colors are used in this page spread to further enhance the textural qualities of the page and ultimately the reader's experience.

160OVER90
New York, New York, USA

by visual means. Textures can be described as flat, shiny, glossy, glittery, velvety, wet, feathery, gooey, furry, sandy, leathery, furry, cracked, prickly, abrasive, puffy, bumpy, corrugated, rusty, slimy, and so on.

Texture, along with other elements in a composition, can communicate a variety of different emotions and messages. Rough textures are visually active and kinetic, while smooth textures are passive and calm.

Primary Characteristics

Texture has characteristics similar to color. Like color, texture cannot function inde-

pendently without being integrated to other design elements such as line and form. It is used primarily to enhance other elements relying on shape and space to exist.

In visual communications, texture is the surface character of an object. It can be either two-dimensional or three-dimensional and distinguished by visual and physical properties such as rough or smooth and shiny or dull. A tactile texture such as sandpaper can be actually felt by touch; however, visual texture can only be suggested, interpreted, and understood by the human eye.
(continued on page 77)

(continued on page 77)

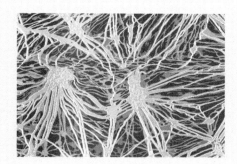

This capabilities showroom for W. L. Gore—maker of fluoropolymer Gore-tex products, presents the company's technical superiority in making ingredient products for a wide range of industries—from medical, to military, to leisure. Large-scale photographic images of material textures are used as emblematic and engaging visual backdrops for the presentation of complex data and scientific information in a compelling and accessible manner for a wide audience.

CARBONE SMOLAN
AGENCY
New York, New York, USA

1959

Goodbye, Columbus and 5 Short Stories Book Cover
PAUL RAND
New York, New York, USA

PAUL RAND (1914–1996) was a designer, author, and educator who shaped and influenced the course of twentieth-century graphic design. For forty years, he also devoted himself to teaching graphic design at Cooper Union, Pratt Institute, and Yale University. Through his work, writings, and teaching, he has educated and inspired generations of graphic designers worldwide.

Rand was educated at Pratt Institute, Parsons School of Design, and the Art Students League under George Grosz. In 1937, at the age of twenty-three, he became art director of both *Esquire* and *Apparel Arts* magazines, for which he created a series of now classic covers.

In 1941, he left the publishing world to become an art director for the William H. Weintraub Advertising Agency, where he created a series of innovative campaigns for Coronet Brandy, Dubonnet Aperitif, El Producto Cigars, and Orbach's.

With his early work for American publishers such as Meridian, Knopf, and Vintage, Rand proved that modernism did not have to be serious, cold, and clinical. Rand gave modernism "heart and soul." His whimsical approach, as well as his use of unconventional methods and familiar elements to communicate a variety of different emotions and messages, proved to be a new and groundbreaking interpretation of the European modernist movement in American graphic design.

His 1959 cover for Philip Roth's *Goodbye, Columbus* is a pivotal prototype for the use of familiar, humanistic, textural elements—irregular, cut-out shapes, the designer's own handwriting, and the powerful use of a graphic "kiss." The slightly parted lips, rendered in a bright, red lipstick on a stark, white field, are another example of visual texture that reinforced a real sense of physicality. This provocative image immediately and memorably communicates the sexually obsessive theme of the author's text, as well as the hands-on approach of the designer's process. Here, the textured image is a visual metaphor not only for the book's theme but also for the designer's creative, interactive response.

Rand continued to explore a broad range of possibilities with texture and abstraction in his publishing work—pure color fields, organic and ragged cut-out shapes, splatters of ink and paint, as well as the use of his distinctive handwriting. He approached book covers as if they were small canvases or sculptures where the artist or, in this case, the graphic designer, could express his individuality, intuition, and most importantly, creativity.

In American book publishing during the 1950s and 1960s, Rand influenced numerous graphic designers such as Alvin Lustig, Leo Lionni, Ivan Chermayeff, Tom Geismar, and Paul Bacon, who continued to pursue their beliefs that design in book publishing was an act of creative expression and invention.

Rand's "play" instinct transformed the written word through book-cover designs with wit, humor, and a timelessness unmatched in the history of graphic design.

Paul Rand
and Goodbye, Columbus

SOULPEPPER THEATRE 10TH ANNIVERSARY SEASON **AUG 23 — SEPT 20**

08 RING ROUND THE MOON

JEAN ANOUILH ADAPTED BY CHRISTOPHER FRY

416.866.8666
soulpepper.ca

SOULPEPPER THEATRE 10TH ANNIVERSARY SEASON **MAY 13 — JUN**

08 'NIGHT, MOTHER

MARSHA NORMAN

416.866.8666
soulpepper.ca

MUCH ADO ABOUT NOTHING
WILLIAM SHAKESPEARE

TWELFTH NIGHT
WILLIAM SHAKESPEARE

THE PLAY AND PLAIN ENGLISH

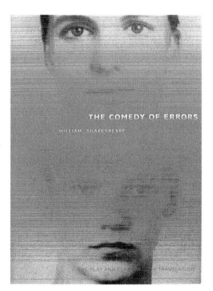

THE COMEDY OF ERRORS
WILLIAM SHAKESPEARE

ULPEPPER THEATRE **10TH ANNIVERSARY SEASON** FEB 27 — APR 19

08 AS YOU LIKE IT
WILLIAM SHAKESPEARE

416.866.8666
soulpepper.ca

The character-based figurative illustrations in this series of posters for Soulpepper Theatre's 2008 season of plays have a visual textural quality that captures and strengthens each of the play's diverse themes while still communicating the essence of each of the main characters. In this context, texture is used as a common visual element, represented as line, pattern, tone, modeled color, and varied scale typography in each composition.

EDEL RODRIGUEZ
Mt. Tabor, New Jersey, USA

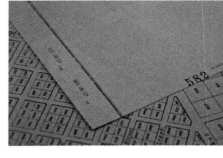

Types of Texture

There are three types or classifications of texture in visual communications:

Physical or Literal

Tactile texture, also defined as physical or literal texture, is an actual tactile variation on an object's surface. For example, wood, grain, sand, fur, glass, leather, canvas, and metal are all physical textures. This type of texture differentiates itself from visual texture by having a physical quality that can only be felt by human touch. One of the most obvious ways to evoke a response to texture is by using physical or literal textures—materials that already have noticeable and familiar textures. The specific use of this type of physical or literal texture in a visual communication can provide further emphasis, rhythm, movement, tension, pattern, and contrast, ultimately having a direct effect on its message and meaning.

Light is also important when considering physical or literal texture in a composition since it can influence how a surface is viewed and understood. Intense light on a smooth surface can obscure the immediacy and readability of an image, while the same effect can create a strong, visible contrast on a textured surface like wood or canvas.

The book covers for these three plays, Shakespeare's *Much Ado about Nothing*, *As You Like It*, and *The Comedy of Errors*, use a subtle and consistent visual metaphor to support each play's character-driven themes of identity. The primary visual element of each book cover uses a linear texture as a symbolic theatrical scrim or veil that partially hides or reveals photographic portraits or the identities of the each of the play's main character(s).

TAKASHI KUSUI, Student
JI LEE, Instructor
School of Visual Arts
New York, New York, USA

Inspired by the ancient Roman taverns it was named for, Aventine's identity and branding program has a strong textural appearance derived from the inline letterforms paired with smaller serif and sans serif typography. These contrasting typographic forms are further enhanced with line drawings, frames, and maps, as well as debossing and letterpress, which further enhances the textural identity, richness, and warmth of this program.

MARKATOS MOORE
San Francisco, California, USA

Kanuhura, a luxury resort located on a remote atoll in the Maldives, celebrates its authentic and remote locale with a wide range of textured brand elements—a hand-woven *K* monogram based on a repeating line pattern device; a custom typeface made of palm leaves; and a color palette evocative of white sand contrasted by aqua sea, sunsets, and local spices. This textural theme continues with hand-stitched "recycled" leather holders for information, wood stationery, and driftwood signs made in the island's craft workshops.

PENTAGRAM
London, United Kingdom

Visual

The illusion of a physical texture on an object's surface is identified as visual texture. These illusory effects can be achieved through the use of design elements such as point, line, shape, form, light, tone, contrast, and pattern.

Every material and structure has its own inherent texture and needs to be taken into account when creating a composition. Materials such as canvas and watercolor paper are considerably rougher than bristol board or laser paper and may not be the most suitable for creating a flat, smooth surface.

Implied

An implied texture is a visual texture that has no basis in everyday reality. It is most often utilized in works of abstraction.

Creating Texture

Textures can be created through a variety of design elements and techniques such as repetition, typography, collage, assemblage, impasto, rubbings, transfers, moirés, erasures, and computer-generated effects.

Visual textures can be created by reproducing the color, tone, and pattern of actual textures; darks and lights can be used to suggest the grooves and irregular surface of the bark of a tree or the three-dimensionality of an irregular stone surface.

Lines of typographic text, painted surfaces, applications of dry media such as pencil or charcoal, or actual surfaces photographed or digitally scanned replicate actual texture but function as visual texture.

Texture provides any graphic design element with visual surface and feel. This can be achieved with line, shape, or even photographic images of specific surfaces.

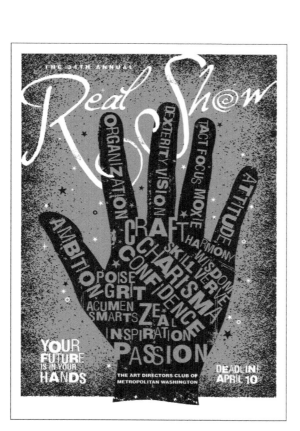

This poster, titled the *Real Show* for the Art Directors Club of Metropolitan Washington, DC, combines different sizes and weights of sans serif typography with fluid, scriptlike hand lettering to enhance the visual texture of the poster's promotional message. Additionally, the textured border of the composition, as well as the extreme color contrasts between black and red and red and white, further enhances the textural characteristics of the poster's two-dimensional surface.

FUSZION
Alexandria, Virginia, USA

Continuous typographic line treatments are used as visual backdrops for the branding and identity of this Charles Shaw wine label series. These textural background treatments describe the taste, flavor, and character of each wine—Valdiguié, Shiraz, and Merlot—and are further enhanced by their subtle monochromatic color palettes, which provide maxi-

mum contrast for identifying the wine name, year, vintage, and vineyard.

ANDREW LIM, Student
MICHAEL IAN KAYE, Instructor
School of Visual Arts
New York, New York, USA

The Everything Italian postcard series for Fox River Paper is composed of a set of eight themed postcards—all letterpressed to celebrate the textural surface qualities and properties of a new line of paper to add to its popular ESSE collection. All postcards use a diverse sampling of typography, patterns, and line drawings, all unified with the same color palette.

MIRIELLO GRAFICO
San Diego, California, USA

This dual front-and-back book jacket for *Miss Lonelyhearts* and *The Day of the Locust* uses texture as the primary element to communicate the essence of both novels—*Miss Lonelyhearts* with a repetitive pattern of hearts organized in a series of free-form, horizontal lines and with *The Day of the Locust* treated in the same manner but as filmstrips. Both communicate the essence of each narrative, create a thematic connection with the reader, and ultimately convey a cohesive and unified message.

RODRIGO CORRAL DESIGN
New York, New York, USA

Built-up media, such as oil or acrylic paint, can produce rough textures from brushstrokes or palette knives. Type can also be used to create a visual texture that ultimately has more importance in a composition than the legibility of the letters themselves. In traditional printing with letterpress or metal type, each letterform or number to be printed consists of a raised image—an actual texture—on a flat background.

Texture gives a "tonal" quality to the surface of any design element such as a line, shape, or form, enhancing its visual presence as well as the viewer's emotional response. In this case, textural characteristics and qualities can be defined as descriptive adjectives in visual communications. Appropriate and meaningful texture can give the simplest visual element resonance and a spark of life. Effective use of texture can communicate a variety of emotions and messages.

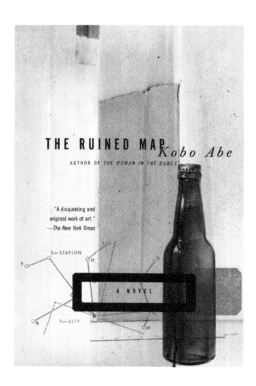

In this book cover for Kobo Abe's *The Ruined Map*, the visual characteristics of collage, assemblage, and photomontage of paper, board, object, line, image, and typography are used in various sizes and styles to enrich the overall textural power of the composition. Light and shadow, as well as a diverse range of tones coupled with a monochromatic color palette, add to the surface character and visual power of this active and kinetic book cover.

JOHN GALL
New York, New York, USA

Freehand line drawings, collage, and hand lettering add enhanced visual impact, strength, and texture to this poster series for the National Theatre School of Canada. The sole structured element evident in each composition is the framed typographic information at the top of each poster identifying the times, dates, and locations for each production.

LAURENT PINABEL
Montreal, Quebec, Canada

OCTOBER
21-25
2008

::: HYDRO-QUÉBEC STUDIO MONUMENT-NATIONAL

PUBLIC PERFORMANCE
OF THE 2009 GRADUATING CLASS

ent-nts.ca

National Theatre School
of Canada

THE IMPORTANCE
OF BEING
EARNEST

by OSCAR
WILDE

directed by
BRENDAN
HEALY

DECEMBER
9-13

::: LUDGER-DUVERNAY THEATRE MONUMENT-NATIONAL

PUBLIC PERFORMANCE
OF THE 2009 GRADUATING CLASS

ent-nts.ca

National Theatre School
of Canada

By Arthur MILLER
Directed by
Sarah Stanley

All
my Sons

10–14
MARS
2009

::: STUDIO HYDRO-QUÉBEC MONUMENT-NATIONAL

EXERCICE PUBLIC
DE LA PROMOTION 2009

ent-nts.ca

École nationale de théâtre
du Canada

LE BRAS
CANADIEN
ET autres
VANITÉS

de Jean-Philippe Lehoux
MISE EN SCÈNE Gill Champagne

APRIL 28
> MAY 02
2009

::: HYDRO-QUÉBEC STUDIO MONUMENT-NATIONAL

PUBLIC PERFORMANCE
OF THE 2009 GRADUATING CLASS

ent-nts.ca

National Theatre School
of Canada

NEW WORDS
FESTIVAL
CAUTIONARY TALES FOR KIDS
AND GROWN-UPS...

THE BATTERY
BY MEGAN COLES
DIRECTED BY PHILIP MCKEE
APRIL 28, 29, 30 & MAY 2 . 7 PM
MAY 1 . 5 PM

TICK
BY MATTHEW MACKENZIE
DIRECTED BY VAHID RAHBANI
APRIL 28, 29 & 30 . 8:30 PM
MAY 1 . 6 PM & MAY 2 . 2 PM

scale \\'skāl\ *n*
5 b: a distinctive relative size, extent, or degree

"If you don't scale the mountain, you can't view the plain."
CHINESE PROVERB

The visual principle of scale is defined as a relative, progressive classification of proportion or a degree of size, amount, importance, and rank in a composition. Proportion and scale are related design principles in visual communications. Proportion refers to the size relationships of design

The primary communication element of this branding and identity program for Evolutiva, a firm specializing in leadership coaching, is a typographic poster composed of narrative content in varying scales and sizes that reflects the firm's values and explains key concepts of the firm's metaphor-based training programs. Words and statements are cropped, flipped, and fragmented in a variety of different configurations to further engage and provoke the viewer. Staff business cards were also cut from this same poster to emphasize both the element of surprise and the strategic thinking that highlights different leadership concepts.

BLOK DESIGN
Mexico City, Mexico

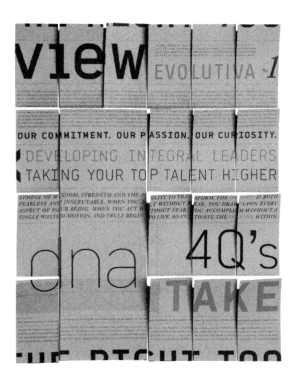

The inaugural issue of the McGill School of Architecture alumni newsletter uses extreme typographic scale as an eye-catching, attention-getting device. Small-scale, narrative-based typography is printed on newsprint in a single color—blue (evoking architectural blueprints)—with a vibrant, fluorescent orange overprint highlighting important information on select pages. To emphasize the school's many alumni, the names of all living alumni (approximately 3,000 names) were listed on the front cover with "I was here" overprinted in orange. The visual impact of this oversized typographic message juxtaposed with the diminuitive columnar text of the newsletter creates a bold, engaging invitation for the reader, as well as making it extremely personal for the reader to engage with and ultimately explore.

ATELIER PASTILLE ROSE
Montreal, Quebec, Canada

elements relative to the space they occupy in an overall composition. Scale refers to the size comparisons of the design elements in a composition, or a size relationship when comparing one design element to another.

On a day-to-day basis, we all make scale comparisons relating to size, distance, and weight.

These types of visual comparisons are usually based on known and familiar experiences that constantly provide us with a visual reference or orientation. For example, a skyscraper or snow-capped mountain on the horizon may be difficult to judge in terms of size. However, when we juxtapose either of these with a familiar scale reference such as a person, car, or even a book, it is easier for us to immediately quantify and understand.

Types of Scale
The visual principle of scale can be categorized as either objective or subjective.

Objective
This type of scale is the literal, or objective, definition of scale and is the actual dimensions of a physical object or a literal correla-
(continued on page 86)

Normandie Poster
ADOLPHE JEAN-MARIE MOURON (A. M. CASSANDRE)
Paris, France

NORMANDIE
Cⁱᵉ Gⁱᵉ **TRANSATLANTIQUE**
LE HAVRE — SOUTHAMPTON — NEW-YORK

ADOLPHE JEAN-MARIE MOURON, also known as A. M. Cassandre (1901–1968), was one of the most influential poster designers of the twentieth century. Born in Khrakov, Ukraine, in 1901, Cassandre spent most of his life in Paris following his family's emigration to France during the Russian Revolution of 1917. As a young man, he studied drawing and painting at the Ecole des Beaux-Arts and at the Academie Julian.

Cassandre was a man of many talents and, like most creative individuals, he experimented throughout his life and career with a wide variety of techniques and styles. From 1922 to 1940, he devoted himself to the art of the poster. In the latter part of his life, he returned to his first love, painting, as well as teaching graphic design at the Ecole des Arts Decoratifs and then at the Ecole d'Art Graphique.

In 1936 his work was exhibited at the Museum of Modern Art in New York City, which led to numerous cover commissions from *Harper's Bazaar*.

At the age of 24, he furthered his growing reputation with works such as *Bucheron (Woodcutter)*, a poster created for a French cabinetmaker that won first prize at the 1925 Exposition Internationale des Arts Decoratifs et Industriels Modernes. Additionally, his innovative approach for the Dubonnet wine company was among the first posters and advertisements designed to be seen and read by passengers in moving vehicles.

His love of fine art, combined with his typographic sensitivity and natural ability to combine these two distinct disciplines into coherent and visually dynamic design solutions, enabled Cassandre to become one of the earliest and most successful commercial artists and poster designers in the world. Inspired by surrealism and cubism, his posters are memorable for their innovative graphic solutions and their frequent references to twentieth-century avant-garde painters such as Max Ernst and Pablo Picasso.

Normandie, an iconic poster that afforded him international fame and recognition, is a primary example of how Cassandre used scale as a dynamic compositional element in all of his work.

The poster's frontal view is completely symmetrical with an extreme upward angle that emphasizes the ship's monumental scale and art deco lines. It is composed in a manner that draws our eyes irresistibly upward to the sky. The immense scale of the ship's prow is further emphasized by the French flag at the prow's apex as well as a group of tiny gulls and sea foam close to the horizon line where ship meets sea. This reductive, erect composition towers over the monolithic text NORMANDIE that also functions as a stable, typographic pedestal for the image of the ship.

The majority of Cassandre's posters were based on a true sense of proportion and scale, which governed their overall structure, rhythm, and final composition. His primary objective was always to make the object the center of a poster's attention. Through exaggerated scale, he was able to celebrate the geometry of form as well as use this fundamental principle as a memorable, storytelling device.

A. M. Cassandre and the Art of the Modern Poster

Large-scale letterforms and numbers such as **W** for whole wheat, **2** for 2% fat content, **L** for large eggs, and **4** for four sticks of butter are primary communication elements in Archer Farms food packaging. This unorthodox typographic treatment creates an impactful and informative visual hierarchy of scale that clearly identifies product, type, and amounts for the shopper.

WERNER DESIGN WERKS
St. Paul, Minnesota, USA

tion between an actual object and its graphic representation. An example of objective or literal scale is a "scale" drawing of a chair that is realized on a sheet of 8 1/2 X 11-inch (21.6 X 28 cm) paper; however, the actual chair in "real" scale is of a size to accommodate the human figure.

This type of scale is also used in maps, architectural plans, and models. It is a scale ratio defined numerically as two quantities separated by a colon (:). For example, a scale noted as 1:50 is one unit of measurement, such as inches or meters, and represents fifty of the same units at full size.

Subjective

This type of scale refers to a person's impression of an actual object. For example, a car or a house may be described as having an immense or intimate scale due to how it relates to our physical selves, as well as our knowledge and familiarity with cars and houses. Subjective scale is relative only to our own personal experiences and is, therefore, subjective in nature.

Effective Use of Scale

Scale can be used as an effective design principle to create variety, emphasis, and

This identity and packaging for a new product line of disposable and biodegradable wooden cutlery made by Aspenware, named **WUN** (wooden utensils naturally), elevates the product above the "natural food" niche. Sans serif typography in large-scale caps contrasted with small-scale numbers and lowercase identifiers on the front of the packaging further reflects the restraint and eco-conscious nature of the brand.

BLOK DESIGN
Mexico City, Mexico

One Degree, an employee-based awareness program at News Corporation, was developed from a simple premise: If everyone were to change their behavior by just one degree, it would change the planet's future. The logotype for this program relies upon scale as a primary compositional principle that is evident in all applications throughout the program.

LANDOR
Paris, France

visual hierarchy in any visual communication. A proper use of scale contributes to the stability, visual comfort, and memorable aspects of any composition, while an incorrect scale will create discomfort, dysfunction, and a cramped awareness in a composition.

An element within a composition can appear larger or smaller depending on the size, placement, color, texture, and visual weight of the elements around it. Additionally, contrast in size can create visual emphasis, hierarchy, depth, movement, and tension within any composition.

When compositional elements are all the same size and equal in visual scale, the composition will appear flat and one-dimensional. It will lack contrast, tension, rhythm, and movement. It's as if we were listening to a musical composition and heard only one, continuous, monotonous note—always the same, never fluctuating in tone or resonance. All of the previous design elements referenced, when used in an effective, appropriate, and meaningful manner, can create a sense of depth and movement in any visual composition. Scale is also an essential design element and critical consideration in achieving this end result.

Scale can be used to direct a viewer's attention through a singular design element, such as an image or typography, as well as a composition of multiple visual elements.

A graphic designer also needs to consider scale in practical and functional ways. Professional work today requires graphic designers to consider a variety of different media and vehicles for conveying their work. From the traditional realms of printed matter, to the small-scale requirements of the digital world of websites and electronic interfaces, and the large-scale requirements of environmental graphics and exhibitions, scale is an important and constant consideration.

Context

The visual principle of scale is also fully dependent on context. In visual communications, familiar comparisons are less intuitive; therefore, the graphic designer relies upon scale to communicate those comparisons in an immediate and understandable way.

We all have experienced the jarring visual phenomenon of first printing out a sheet of paper with work we have been designing on screen, and to our surprise, something is amiss. We have methodically

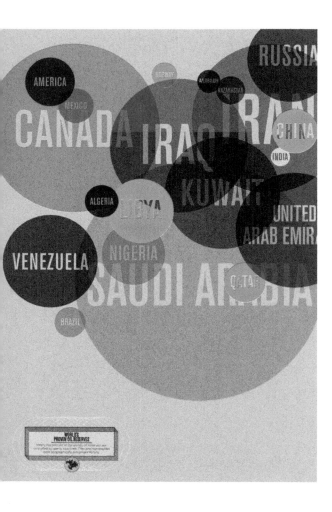

This information-based poster, titled *World's Proven Oil Reserves*, uses various scales and sizes of transparent color circles to create a visually dynamic composition that communicates which major countries around the world have the largest oil reserves. Overlapping circles also create distinct color combinations that further convey another layer of information on the relationship of oil dependency from one country to another. The poster's asymmetrical composition expands beyond its edges, which further reinforces the extreme scale changes from one country to another.

BRYAN FAREVAAG, Student
GENEVIEVE WILLIAMS, Instructor
School of Visual Arts
New York, New York, USA

evaluated and resolved a visual composition in one scale (on screen) and now expect the same spatial and visual relationships to be achieved and maintained at a completely different scale when they are printed out on an 8 1/2 X 11-inch (21.6 X 28 cm) sheet of paper. This consistently happens often among most designers today.

We automatically make comparisons every time we receive sensory information. Objects are "too hot" or "safe to touch" because we immediately compare them to our previous experiences. Additionally, as human beings we tend to make size comparisons based on our own relationships to human scale. For example, our perception of scale in the adult world is completely different from our perception as small children.

Optical Effects and Scale

Scale is a fundamental design principle that also helps the viewer perceive spatial illusion, such as the size of objects and their relative scale in a composition. Small elements recede, larger ones come forward. Compositional elements that are closer to us appear larger than objects of the same size that are located farther away.

Restraint in typographic scale and an effective use of a monochromatic color palette provides a unique visual identity for this brand of hair care products—Frizz. The unusual shape and small scale of the packaging further reinforce the distinct qualities of this product line.

WOLFF OLINS
New York, New York, USA

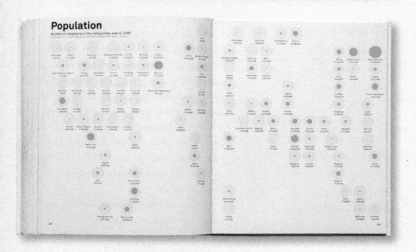

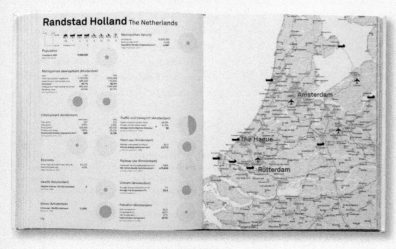

A system of varied-scale orange dots is used as a primary
communication device in
this atlas and accompanies
the reader through the
analysis and comparison
of 101 capital cities around
the world. These functional
dots, sized according to
comparative data on each
city, communicate specific
statistical information and
data such as population,
area, and crime. A strict page
grid develops into a type of
three-dimensional chart, as
successive pages of circles are
stacked, allowing a quick flip
through the book to reveal
changes in pollution, density,
public transport, and other
statistics.

JOOST GROOTENS
Amsterdam, The Netherlands

The following compositonal treatments
can be used to achieve optical and spatial
illusions in a visual composition:

Overlapping and Position
An optical device that can automatically
interpret scale and depth, as well as evoke
either realistic or unusual spatial effects,
is overlapping. A compositional element
partially hidden by another appears to be
located behind it in space and therefore
will appear smaller in scale. Each element
obscuring part of another helps the viewer
make spatial sense of the composition.

In addition to overlapping, the position
of elements relative to the overall picture
plane helps the viewer organize them in a
composition. The area at the bottom of the
picture plane is often seen as foreground—
the portion of a visual composition that is
closest to the viewer. The area at the center
of the picture plane is often interpreted as
middle ground—the portion of a visual composition of varying depth that is at midpoint
distance to the viewer. The upper area of a
visual composition is often seen as background (with the exception of landscapes in
which the sky seems to project forward from

In the third edition of this annual, ongoing project, the designer investigates ways to analyze, capture, depict, and ultimately encapsulate a year of personal activity graphically. Bar charts, area charts, maps, and pie charts illustrate the textures and experiences of a complex and diverse life in New York City over a period of 365 days. In this context, scale plays a critical role in helping the reader engage with a variety of dense and detailed statistical data and narrative information in an accessible and intuitive manner.

NICHOLAS FELTON
New York, New York, USA

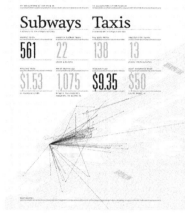

the background over the head of the viewer). In Western culture, we tend to interpret the lower portion of a composition as closer than the upper portion because representational paintings in art history have been composed in this manner.

Atmospheric Perspective
In addition to overlapping and position in a composition, graphic designers can rely on atmospheric perspective to further indicate scale and spatial depth. This effect can be used when there is need for a specific element or area to appear more distant than the other elements in the composition. This can be achieved by using softer edges, less value or contrast, and less detail in these elements so that they appear farther back in the compositional space.

When compositional elements are extremely close to the viewer, they may be seen in reverse atmospheric perspective: The closest elements are blurred or brought out of focus, with the sharpest edges and strongest value contrast in the elements that are a bit farther away.

No matter what size a designer's work will be when finally realized, it must have its own true sense of scale.

Scale is used as an effective communication tool in the permanent exhibition areas of the California Academy of Sciences. Here, scale provides an immediate visual hierarchy to exhibition content, whether it is object or artifact, large photographic imagery, or small narrative and interpretive information-based panels allowing the visitor to get an immediate overview of the exhibition's themes or an in-depth presentation of detailed information on a specific exhibition theme.

VOLUME INC.
San Francisco, California, USA

This promotional poster announcing exhibitions, performances, workshops, and lectures at the Pump House Gallery in London uses extreme scale changes in typography and imagery to further capture the viewer's attention as well create a visually dynamic and memorable composition.

FRASER MUGGERIDGE
London, United Kingdom

move·ment \ˈmüv-mənt\ *n*
5 a: the suggestion or illusion of motion in a painting, sculpture, or design

movement

"Everything in the universe has rhythm. Everything dances."
MAYA ANGELOU (B. 1928), American, Actor, Author, Civil Rights Activist, Poet

Movement is defined as the act or process of moving or a change of place, position, or effort. It can be actual or implied. In a painting or photograph, for instance, movement refers to a representation or suggestion of motion. In sculpture, movement refers to implied motion, with the exception

This symbol for the Darien Library is derived from the simple movement seen when flipping the pages of a book, and in this identity interpreted through a progression of transparent, overlapping color tints. The symbol also refers to an ocean wave or the wing of a bird, all suggesting movement and ascent.

C+G PARTNERS LLC
New York, New York, USA

of mobiles and kinetic sculptures that have actual motion, such as found in the work of Alexander Calder.

In visual communications, movement apparent in a drawing, painting, photograph, book cover, or even magazine spread forces our eyes to move constantly and attend to one or more elements within the composition. Our eye may be brought to the center of the composition because there is a bright color there and then to another location that contains typography functioning as a headline in a bold typeface. Here, the responsibility of the graphic designer is to direct the viewer's attention through a specific sequence of visual experiences, as opposed to letting the eye randomly go from one element to another in a composition.

The primary function of movement in visual communications is to guide the eye of the viewer through and around any visual message. In a three-dimensional composition or space, a graphic designer needs to consider not only movement realized with light and color, but also with the physical movement of the viewer through, in, and around the total environment.

(continued on page 96)

This assignment requires sophomore students to consider fundamental design principles—in this case, movement—found in their environment and in everyday objects. With photography, they explore their surroundings and document examples of "movement" found in surprising and intriguing situations. The final images are cropped to a 3 X 3-inch (7.6 X 7.6 cm) square and then composed in a 3 X 3 nine-square composition further communicating the student's examination of interrelationships in form, color, texture, scale, tension, contrast, and pattern between the various photographic images. This visual exercise helps students increase their understanding of fundamental design elements; increase their awareness of the natural and built environment; become more comfortable with a camera and with composing compelling and communicative photographic images; crop photographic images to create interesting, dynamic and impactful compositions; find visual relationships between seemingly disparate images; and become familiar with digital image software such as Adobe Photoshop, Adobe Bridge and Camera Raw.

JONATHAN SIKOV
CASTELLANO, Student
ANNABELLE GOULD,
Instructor
*University of Washington
Seattle, Washington, USA*

1948

Gran Premio dell'Autodromo di Monza (Monza Grand Prix) Poster
MAX HUBER
Milan, Italy

MAX HUBER (1919–1992) was one of the most significant graphic designers of the twentieth century and an influential figure in the history of modern graphic design.

He studied at the Kunstgewerbeschule in Zurich and worked as an art director before moving to Milan in 1940, where he became art director of Studio Boggeri. Huber was also a member of the distinguished association of Swiss modernists called the Allianz—a group whose members included Hans Arp, Max Bill, Le Corbusier, Paul Klee, Leo Leuppi, and Richard Paul Lohse.

In his early career, Huber was greatly influenced by the teachings of modernist masters such as Max Bill and Lazlo Moholy-Nagy and therefore among the first designers in Italy to apply avant-garde principles and aesthetics to commercial graphic design such as posters, jazz record album covers, and book covers. Some of Huber's most memorable achievements were on a completely different scale and remain in the minds of generations of Italians, such as his identity programs for the department store chain La Rinascente, the supermarket chain Esselingsa, and for media giant RAI.

One celebrated example of this modernist approach is Huber's memorable posters for the Monza races. Starting in 1928, Huber designed promotional posters and flyers for the Monza car races in Italy, mainly for the Grand Prix and the Lottery Race. This poster series illustrates how he brought the visual element of movement to two-dimensional compositions.

Huber's 1948 poster for the motor races at Monza incorporated illusions of visual perspective that reinforced a great sense of movement and speed—letterforms are disappearing in the distance and are in counterpoint to the arrows moving forward. Additionally, varied typographic sizes and vibrant transparent colors laid over one another provide exaggerated depth, rhythm, and movement to the poster's overall composition. For example, the red and blue arrows give direction to the street. The type identifying the event, *Gran premio dell' Autodromo*, rushes across the field of the poster with visual speed as if it transformed itself into one of the cars racing at that very moment.

This innovative poster illustrates Ettore Sottsass's dictum of 1947: "One can state that the people of Greece would never have existed without the sea, and that the sea is their great story. I believe our great story, by contrast, is speed (velocita)."

It is also important to note here that the dramatic and distorted visual effects Huber created with typography were highly readable and impactful without the assistance of contemporary methods of photocomposition, digital composition, and computerized image manipulation software.

Huber relied upon the basic tenets of perspective to convey distance, depth, and motion in a unique and memorable way. This poster is a classic visual representation that is simultaneously suggestive and powerful on the theme of movement.

The Monza posters and flyers embody a joyfulness conveyed by combining vibrant colors, balanced lines, and oblique angles, all lending rhythm and spatial harmony to the composition. It is a choreographed composition of visually moving dynamics.

Max Huber and the Monza Grand Prix

Elements and Techniques

Movement in any visual composition is realized and fully dependent upon combining the basic elements of visual communications, such as line, shape, form, and texture to produce the look and feel of motion. These design variables can create a collective sense of movement that causes the viewer's eye to move through an overall composition or focus specifically on an isolated group of elements within a composition.

Visual techniques, such as repetition and rhythm, can also enhance the characteristics of movement in a two-dimensional or (three-dimensional) composition. In many

The primary project section of this website for Diller Scofidio + Refro, an architectural design firm, as well as its interface navigation from section to section, provides a series of extremely kinetic movements that immediately engage and hold the viewer's interest. With each inquiry, a new and dynamic composition is achieved through one-point perspective and the dimensionalization of flat photographic images into three-dimensional planes located in space. Additionally, as the cursor moves off the common one-point perspective left or right of that common point, so does the composition. It is fluid, organic, and immediate.

PENTAGRAM
New York, New York, USA

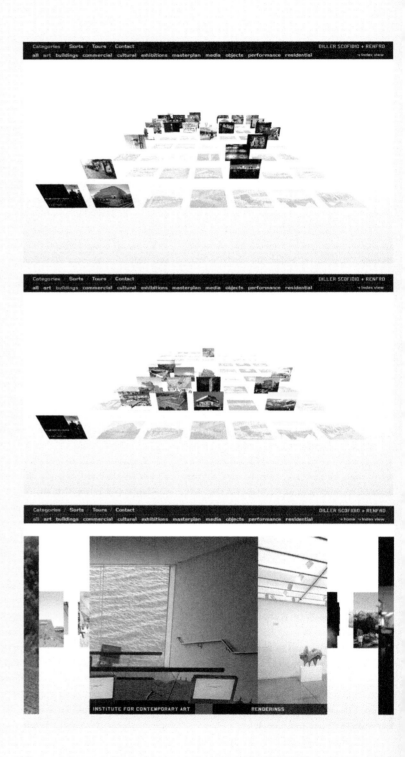

CATHERINE ZASK
Paris, France

ways, these two techniques can be thought
of as visual "music" since they relate directly
to creating the "tempo" of any composition.

With the repetition of line, shape, form,
and color, a visual sequence can also guide
the eye of the viewer along a specific visual
path or defined sequence of events. A repetitive visual sequence in a composition can
be regular, irregular, gradual, or exaggerated
in its visual character.

Rhythm

Rhythm is most often thought of in terms
of sound and music, defined as alternating
occurrences of sound and silence. In visual

The visual principle of
movement is apparent in
the streamlined figurative
element of this symbol for
Seagull, a manufacturer of
custom courier bags.

ELEMENT
Columbus, Ohio, USA

The branding and identity program for Media Trust, an organization that works in partnership with the media industries throughout the United Kingdom in building effective communications for charities and nonprofit organizations, uses movement as a fundamental visual element in all levels of its branding system. The company's brand architecture relies upon a one-color, contemporary logotype for the parent brand, a series of subbrand logotypes defined for all of its service organizations, and a "box fan" symbol that adds visual interest to related print collateral material.

FORM
London, United Kingdom

CHRISTOPHER ISHERWOOD

THE BERLIN STORIES

INTRODUCTION BY ARMISTEAD MAUPIN

This provocative book cover for Christopher Isherwood's *The Berlin Stories* symbolizes the dual presence of two paths or points of view in the book, comprising two short novellas—*Goodbye to Berlin* and *Mr. Norris Changes Trains*. Movement is articulated in dynamic and meaningful ways in this composition; from the cropping of the figure at the top of the cover, to the shadows projected in opposing directions, to the typography angled and aligned with the direction of the man walking.

MOTHER DESIGN
New York, New York, USA

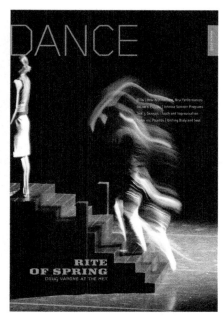

communications, it can be described in the same way. Sound and silence are replaced with form and space—active and passive, primary and secondary. Creating rhythm with visual elements in a composition is similar to the role of choreography in dance. With visual form, choreography is the implied movement of compositional elements perceived by the eye of the viewer.

Rhythm can also be acheived with the repetition or alternation of compositional elements, often with defined intervals organized between them. It can create a sense of movement, as well as establish pattern and texture in any composition.

Types of visual rhythm are often defined with the following characteristics:

Regular
A regular visual rhythm occurs when the graphic intervals between the compositional elements, and often the actual elements themselves, are similar in size, length, weight, or visual character.

Flowing
A flowing visual rhythm can convey a sense of movement and is often perceived as a more organic and natural graphic form in its visual character.

With the redesign of *Dance* magazine, this student effectively redefined movement with unusual croppings of photographs to further celebrate the art of dance, as well as active and inactive zones for related information necessary for an effective magazine cover. Here the use of perimeter or edge, typographic variation on graphic form, texture, and composi-tion, and scale collectively contribute to the strong dynamic movements of each of the cover compositions.

LAURA GRALNICK, Student
RICHARD POULIN, Instructor
School of Visual Arts
New York, New York, USA

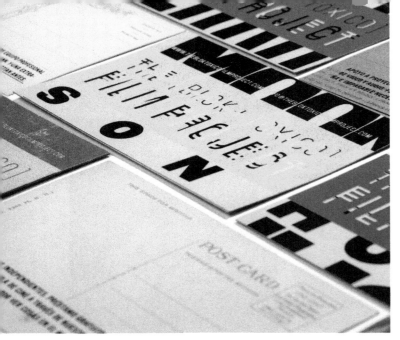

Progressive

A progressive rhythm is created with a sequence of compositional elements through a defined progression of steps.

Rhythm gives character to movement in a composition. Visual rhythms can be evenly paced and static or irregular and full of exaggerated gestures.

Other Considerations

Movement and rhythm are critical to the compositional aspects of any singular work of graphic design, as well as the construction and organization of multiple images, pages, and frames, such as books, magazines, motion graphics, and websites. In these examples, movement and rhythm enhance variation and change in content while providing a variety of scales, tonal values, and textural variations while maintaining a visual and structural cohesiveness.

In many ways, both movement and rhythm are transparent in visual communications. They exist only in an implied sense through the arrangement and organization of elements of varying size, shape, form, color, texture, and contrast in a composition.

"Film Project" was created by Blok Design and Toxico to support independent filmmakers and videographers who face challenges in developing and completing their films. To avoid wasting limited resources, postcards, mailers, and stationery were created by recycling overruns from their own existing projects, along with old postcards and jackets from discarded vinyl LPs; the project's logotype was silk-screened as a layered overprint to this previously printed material. With these cost-savings methods, a kinetically dynamic visual program was developed that clearly expresses the essence of film, pacing, rhythm, and movement, as well as smart use of limited resources and creative risk.

BLOK DESIGN
Mexico City, Mexico

A series of highly kinetic
photographic images by Bill
Beckley is used in a variety
of scales, color palettes,
pairings, and croppings
throughout this monograph
brochure to further celebrate
the visual qualities and nuances of movement found in
this photographer's work.

KATYA MEZHIBOVSKAYA
New York, New York, USA

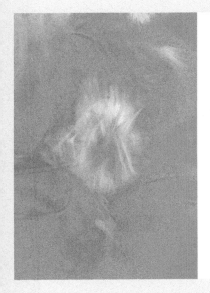

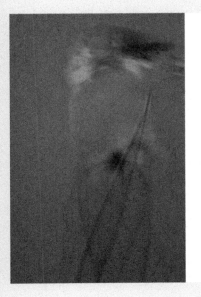

space \\'spās\ *n*

2 a: a limited extent in one, two, or three dimensions: distance, area, volume

4 a: a boundless three-dimensional extent in which objects and events occur and have relative position and direction

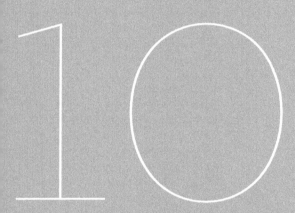

10

"I think that the ideal space must contain elements of magic, serenity, sorcery, and mystery."
LUIS BARRAGÁN (1902–1988), *Mexican, Architect*

Space is an essential design element in all visual communications. However, unlike other elements such as line, shape, form, color, and texture, space cannot be placed or located in a composition. Space refers to the distance or area between, around, above, below, or within other elements

The modulated page grid and the overall size of this brochure for Daycorp Property Development share the same proportional relationship that allows for the creation of related spatial compositions from page spread to page spread throughout the brochure. Additionally, the modulated structure of the brochure's custom letterforms, com-bined with regulated and consistent letterspacing and leading, creates uniform positive and negative spaces in each page composition.

VOICE
Adelaide, Australia

such as lines, shapes, forms, colors, textures, frames, and images in a composition. It can be two dimensional or three dimensional and described as flat, shallow, deep, open, closed, positive, negative, actual, ambiguous, or illusory.

The fundamental principle of space is an integral design element to be considered in any two-dimensional composition and can appear open, dense, compact, loose, empty, full, flat, or voluminous depending on how space is being used, organized, divided, or in other words—activated.

Describing Space

Space is usually identified as negative space or white space—terms that refer to the empty but often active areas of any visual composition that are void of the graphic elements. Space containing elements such as shapes, forms, images, and such is identi-fied as positive space. The varied degrees or amounts of negative or positive space in any composition can create an illusion of depth through the careful, established spatial rela-tionships of foreground and background or figure—ground relationships. When negative and positive space are equal, spatial depth is lacking and a more visually static composi-tion is created.

For example, think of compositional space as a room in your home. The room is a three-dimensional space containing your personal possessions—or compositional ele-ments. Is it cluttered or is there ample room to live, work, and relax? You design the room by filling it with objects on its walls, floors, and ceilings. The graphic designer does the same thing by creating a composition with shape, form, color, image, and type within a two-dimensional space.

(continued on page 106)

Boy and Girl on a Fence,
Rural Electrification Administration Series Two Poster
LESTER BEALL
New York, New York, USA

LESTER BEALL (1903–1969) was a twentieth-century American graphic designer notable as a leading proponent of modernist graphic design in the United States.

He was born in Kansas City, Missouri, and later moved to Chicago, where he studied at the University of Chicago and later at the Art Institute of Chicago. As a self-taught graphic designer, he initially designed exhibits and wall murals for the 1933 Chicago Century of Progress World's Fair. In 1935, he relocated to New York City and eventually opened his own design consultancy in Wilton, Connecticut.

Beall was deeply influenced by the European avant-garde and produced award-winning work in a minimalist, modernist style for clients such as the *Chicago Tribune*, Hiram Walker, *Collier's*, Abbott Laboratories, Time-Life, and International Paper. Throughout his work and career, he was known for utilizing angled elements, vibrant colors, iconic arrows, silhouetted photography, and dynamic shapes in an innovative and provocative manner.

Among his most recognized works are a series of public information posters that he designed for the U.S. government. The Rural Electrification Administration (REA) was one of the primary public improvement projects initiated by President Franklin Delano Roosevelt to revive a battered U.S. economy by building dams and hydroelectric power plants in rural areas of the country. The REA, a part of the U.S. Department of Agriculture, was responsible for promoting the use of electricity in rural areas throughout the United States. This now classic series of large-format posters received national and international attention. All three sets of six silk-screened posters for the REA were designed and produced over a four-year period. Their graphic simplicity and flat illustrative elements were appropriate for an audience with minimal reading skills and were reminiscent of the public posters designed by the Russian Constructivists twenty years earlier. Each poster is a thorough and thoughtful study in minimalist form and compositional space.

Boy and Girl on a Fence, a poster from Series Two, is considered one of the greatest American posters of all time. It features a young boy and girl smiling and looking to the future as they lean against a wood fence bordering their farm. Beall used flat, vibrant color, photomontage, and a juxtaposition of angled and orthogonal bands to further enhance an implied and active space in the poster's composition. It also conveys the strong, humanistic, and patriotic spirit of rural America. This poster series is also an early example of graphic design put to work for the public good.

In 1937, Lester Beall was the first American graphic designer to be honored with a one-man solo exhibition at the Museum of Modern Art in New York City.

Lester Beall and the REA Posters

This symbol for a real estate developer, LargaVista Companies, uses pictorial space to convey a three-dimensional volume or environment through an isometric projection of form contained within a six-sided trapezoid.

HINTERLAND
New York, New York, USA

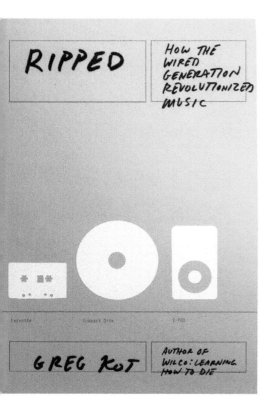

The open compositional space of this book cover for *Ripped: How the Wired Generation Revolutionized Music*, guides the reader's eye in immediately focusing on the three relevant music devices iconographically represented—tape cassette, CD, and iPod.

THE OFFICE OF
PAUL SAHRE
New York, New York, USA

Types of Space

In addition to the formal considerations of space as a compositional element, graphic designers can create specific types of compositional space to further enhance and strengthen any visual message:

Actual Space
The area that a visual composition physically occupies is identified as actual space.

Pictorial Space
The manipulation of flat surfaces to create a perception of depth, movement, or direction is called pictorial space. It relies on illusion to deceive the mind and eye of the viewer.

Psychological Space
A visual composition that influences the mind and eye of the viewer is called psychological space.

Physical Space
In this type of compositional space, the elemental, aesthetic, and functional requirements of space are critical physical considerations for any graphic designer, since they require an interface with the built environment. A wayfinding sign program for an airport, an exhibition of art and artifacts in a museum, or a large-scale display for an urban retailer are all representative examples of physical compositional space.

Characteristics and Techniques

Historically, artists and designers have created a number of methods to interpret and perceive spatial depth in a composition.

Compositional space in visual communications is essentially flat. It has height and width but not depth. However, the illusion of spatial depth and three-dimensional space in

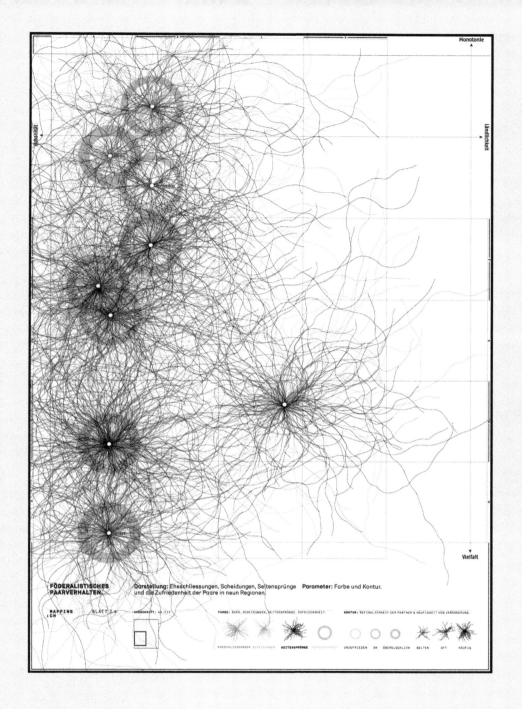

FÖDERALISTISCHES
PAARVERHALTEN.

Darstellung: Eheschliessungen, Scheidungen, Seitensprünge
und die Zufriedenheit der Paare in neun Regionen.

Parameter: Farbe und Kontur.

MAPPING
.CH

FARBE: EHEN, SCHEIDUNGEN, SEITENSPRÜNGE, ZUFRIEDENHEIT.

KONTUR: BEFINDLICHKEIT DER PARTNER & HÄUFIGKEIT VON VERÄNDERUNG.

EHESCHLIESSUNGEN   SCHEIDUNGEN   SEITENSPRÜNGE   ZUFRIEDENHEIT   UNZUFRIEDEN   OK   ÜBERGLÜCKLICH   SELTEN   OFT   HÄUFIG

These information-based posters use both positive and negative white space to create imaginary visual landscapes for the intersection and interplay of statistical data formulated in this study on people living in selected cities. Key cities are ranked according to their diversity and the degree to which they are rural or urban. Circles and spheres illustrate relationships between values and emotions—fidelity and infidelity, happiness and sadness. The different densities of colors suggest arbitrary ranking and proximity, implying that there is no simple explanation for this data.

LORENZO GEIGER
Bern, Switzerland

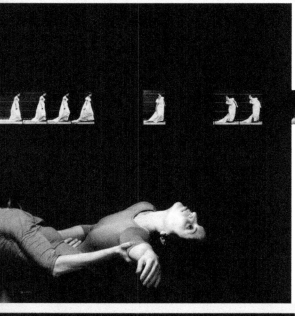

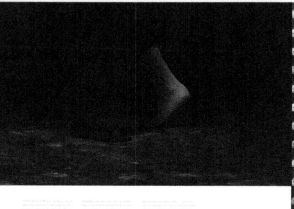

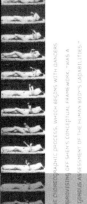

THE CHOREOGRAPHIC PROCESS, WHICH BEGINS WITH DANCERS IMPROVISING OFF SHEN'S CONCEPTUAL FRAMEWORK, "WAS A RIGOROUS ASSESSMENT OF THE HUMAN BODY'S [A]DABILITIES."

An effective use of compositional space is illustrated in these page spreads for *Dance* magazine. Reliance on extreme scale variations with compositional elements, such as photographic imagery, typographic blocks of text, repetitive patterns of images, and bands of flat color, further reinforces movement across the active and inactive spaces of each page.

LAURA GRALNICK, Student
RICHARD POULIN, Instructor
School of Visual Arts
New York, New York, USA

compositions can be achieved in the mind, as well as the eye, of the viewer through specific visual characteristics and techniques.

Relative size in spatial relationships is one of the easiest visual characteristics to create the illusion of space in a two-dimensional composition. A larger element will always appear closer in a composition than a smaller one.

Overlapping in spatial relationships is another way to suggest depth in a two-dimensional composition. When compositional elements overlap one another, they are perceived as if one is covering parts of the other so that one appears in the foreground and the other appears covered and in the background of the composition.

Location in spatial relationships refers to where an element is found vertically in a two-dimensional composition. The bottom of the composition is perceived as the foreground; the area nearest to the viewer and the top of the composition is perceived as its background—the area farthest from the viewer. The higher an element is placed in a composition, the further back in the composition it is perceived.

Types of Perspective
There are three types of perspective techniques that a graphic designer can rely upon to further enhance spatial depth:

Atmospheric Perspective
This type of perspective in spatial relationships is another visual effect that relies on elements such as color, tone, and contrast to create the illusion of space in a two-dimensional composition. When elements appear in the distance and farther away from the viewer, atmospheric haze can obscure their visibility. This effect can be achieved

This book cover for *The Language of Things* immediately focuses the reader's attention on the pristine white space that dominates the cover's overall composition. Small-scale, iconic-color halftone images and a black dialog box containing the title and author of the book are relegated to a secondary position and are set against this stark white space.

MOTHER DESIGN
New York, New York, USA

by changing or modifying the visual characteristics of the composition's elements—by lightening their value, lowering their contrast, softening their edges, minimizing their detail, or muting their color. For example, increasing the blue tone of an element also creates a sense of depth in a composition because cool colors appear to recede whereas warm colors appear to come forward.

Linear, or One-Point, Perspective
Parallel lines converging toward a single vanishing point located on a horizon line is called linear, or one-point, perspective. Perspective lines above a horizon line are drawn diagonally down toward the vanishing point; lines below this line are drawn diagonally up toward it. Vertical lines indicate height and horizontal lines indicate width; in both orientations the lines remain parallel. (see diagram on page 45)

This page spread utilizes effective and meaningful white space to create a visual immediacy with the free-form silhouette of the large-scale image as well as with the common intense red color found in each photograph.

MERCER CREATIVE GROUP
Vancouver, BC, Canada

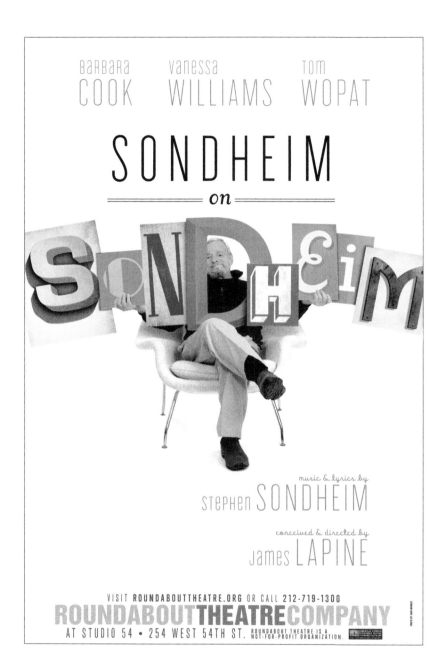

For example, if you see for miles along a straight road, the sides of the road in reality are parallel to one another; however they appear to draw closer and closer to one another and finally disappear at a vanishing point far off in the distance. It is one of the most common visual techniques to create spatial depth in two-dimensional compositions. This technique was first developed and used by Renaissance artists; they initially plotted perspective lines as a base to their compositions, using them to create realistic illusions of depth in drawings and paintings of architectural scenes.

Planar, or Two-Point, Perspective
In this type of perspective, the two visible sides of an element stretch away toward two vanishing points in the distance located on a horizon line. Vertical lines within the composition remain parallel to one another. The remaining lines that in reality appear parallel in the composition also appear to diminish diagonally toward one of the two vanishing points to either side of the horizon line. (See diagram on page 45.)

Using these visual characteristics and techniques, singularly or in combination with each other, will strengthen the illusions of depth and space in any visual composition.

While ample white space provides a visual anchor for its primary photographic image, typographic scale and weight variations used in this promotional poster for the theatrical production *Sondheim on Sondheim* create atmospheric perspective, which further reinforces an illusion of spatial depth in an otherwise flat, two-dimensional composition.

SPOTCO
New York, New York, USA

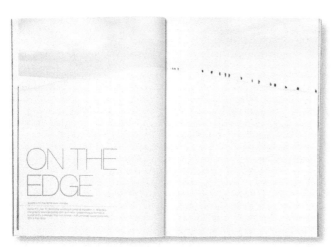

The effective use of ample pictorial or "white" space is apparent in these page spreads for Akzo Nobel's *A Magazine* and further shows how depth, movement, and direction can create dynamic and active compositions.

PENTAGRAM
London, United Kingdom

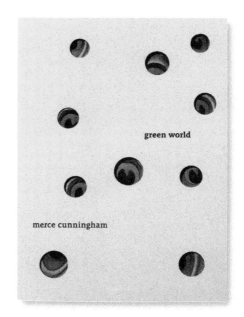

This brochure cover for Merce Cunningham's *Green World* effectively illustrates how location is a critical consideration in spatial relationships when wanting to achieve depth and perspective in a visual composition. In this example, the smaller die-cut circles located at the top of the composition appear farther away, or in the background, as opposed to the circles located toward the bottom, which appear closer to the reader's eye, or in the cover's foreground.

PENTAGRAM
New York, New York, USA

bal·ance \ˈba-lən(t)s\ *n*
6 a: an aesthetically pleasing integration of elements or harmonious or satisfying arrangement or proportion of parts or elements, as in a visual composition

balance

11

"What I dream of is an art of balance."
HENRI MATISSE (1869-1954), *French, Painter, Printmaker, Sculptor*

Balance occurs when visual elements within a composition are equally distributed and arranged to communicate a feeling of stability and harmony. This visual principle can be described as formal and symmetrical, dynamic and asymmetrical, or radial. Our response to balance is intuitively

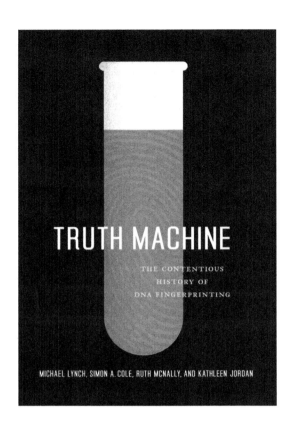

This book cover for *Truth Machine* reflects a well-resolved combination of symmetry and asymmetry that creates a unified balance to the overall composition. The large-scale compositional elements of image and typography are symmetrically, or formally, balanced, while the secondary title of the book is symmetrically composed but integrated to the overall cover, reflecting an asymmetrical or dynamic balance to the cover composition.

ISAAC TOBIN
Chicago, Illinois, USA

linked to taking our first steps as human beings. It is that essential need to stand, walk, and run that also relates to our fundamental, primal need to prefer balance in our lives, as well as in any composition.

Balance is achieved in a composition by arranging dissimilar elements with different visual characteristics.

Types of Balance

There are three types of visual balance:

Formal Balance
Symmetry, or formal balance, is the easiest type of balance to achieve in any visual composition. It is used extensively in architecture because it inherently conveys permanence and stability, as well as automatically provides a singular focus to whatever is placed in the center of a composition. It is also based on a mirror image. For example, if you draw a line down the center of a drawing of a gothic cathedral, elements on either side will appear as a mirror image.

Formal balance occurs when elements are arranged equally in a compositon, appear stable or static, and are identical and reflect one another.

(continued on page 117)

ARCTIC

ESTᴰ 1917

CLUB HOTEL

The logotype for Arctic Club Hotel, combined with a single spot-line illustration, creates a symmetrically, or formally, balanced typographic composition. This compositional balance is further maintained when this logotype is framed, contained, and applied to the hotel's advertisments, website, stationery, press kit folder, and guest collateral print materials.

URBAN INFLUENCE
DESIGN STUDIO
Seattle, Washington, USA

Charles Ross: Light Placed Poster
JACQUELINE CASEY
Cambridge, Massachusetts, USA

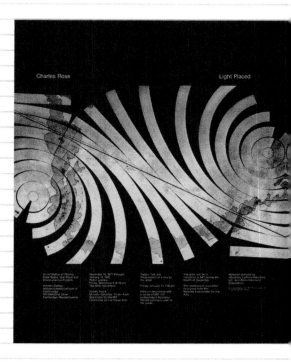

In 1955, JACQUELINE CASEY (1927–1991) started her professional career as a graphic designer when she joined the Office of Publications (Design Services Office) at the Massachusetts Institute of Technology (MIT) in Cambridge under the design direction of fellow classmate Muriel Cooper. When Cooper joined MIT's faculty in 1972, Casey took over as director, where she created a series of iconic promotional posters to publicize MIT events and exhibitions.

For over three decades, she was a woman working in a man's world, not only in the MIT Office of Publications but also in the environs of the entire MIT community that served as her sole client.

Born in Quincy, Massachusetts, she received a certificate of fashion design and illustration and a bachelor of fine arts degree from the Massachusetts College of Art in 1949. Following graduation, she worked in fashion illustration, advertising, interior design, and trade publications prior to her position at MIT.

Casey worked at MIT for over thirty years, during which time she developed a unique design philosophy, a memorable body of work, and a thought-provoking visual brand for the Institute.

In F. H. K. Henrion's 1983 book *Top Graphic Design*, Casey said, "Being a graphic designer at MIT continues to be a fascinating experience for me. My job is a constant learning experience. While MIT has its roots in tradition, the University represents all that is experimental, exciting, and future-oriented."

Her work was influenced by the modernist movement, the International Style, and by designers such as Karl Gertsner, Armin Hofmann, and Josef Müller-Brockmann. She developed a visual language that was purely her own but strongly connected to proportion, grid, and European san serif typography.

Balance also played a fundamental role in all of Casey's posters. They are humanistic visual metaphors—precise, clean, imaginative, engaging, and personal in tone and message.

Each of her posters contains a singular focal point or primary visual element that immediately attracts the viewer. In each case, a critical balance between visual and narrative form occurs, allowing the viewer to engage not only with his or her own imagination, but with their understanding of the poster's subject matter.

Casey's work engaged the intellect and curiosity of her academic audience because it was a seamless, balanced integration of type and image, as well as a memorable and powerful vehicle for storytelling.

Jacqueline Casey at MIT

This poster, titled *Rhythm Textures*, examines a series of selected quotes from Jack Kerouac's *On the Road* and uses formal balance to afford the reader ease and organization when accessing its dense and diverse content. The basic structure and tenor of each sentence or quote is graphically documented or mapped to further illustrate the writer's use of narrative rhythms and textures in the text, such as italicized words, commas, semicolons, dashes, colons, and question marks. Color classifies characters and themes within the text, such as blue for Dean Moriarity (protagonist), purple for travel, and brown for parties, drinking, and drugs. Each notation for each quotation is numerically coded for further reference with a specific number for part, chapter, paragraph, and sentence. All twenty quotes are listed at the bottom of the poster and cross-referenced with this numerical codification.

STEFANIE POSAVEC
London, United Kingdom

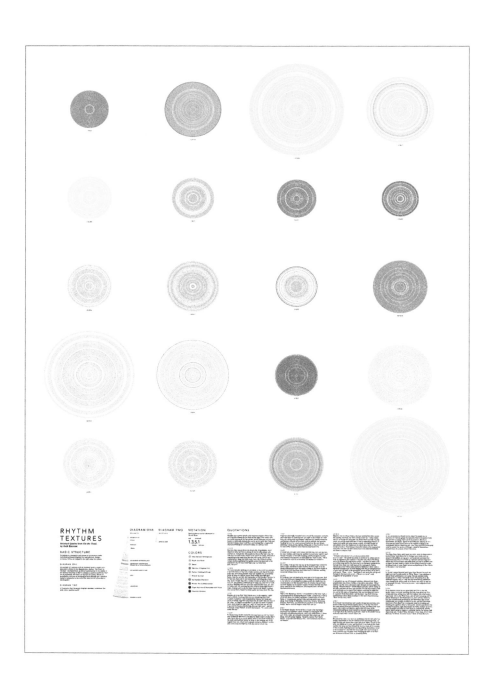

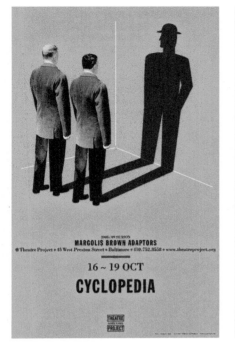

MARGOLIS BROWN ADAPTORS
Theatre Project • 45 West Preston Street • Baltimore • 410.752.8558 • www.theatreproject.org

16 ~ 19 OCT

CYCLOPEDIA

ELIZABETH HESS
Theatre Project • 45 West Preston Street • Baltimore • 410.752.8558 • www.theatreproject.org

30 APR ~ 10 MAY

LIVING OPENLY & NOTORIOUSLY

AMERICAN OPERA THEATER
Theatre Project • 45 West Preston Street • Baltimore • 410.752.8558 • www.theatreproject.org

25 SEPT ~ 5 OCT

LE CABARET DE CARMEN

Dynamic Balance
Asymmetry or dynamic balance is more interesting and more difficult to achieve. It occurs when elements are arranged deliberately unequally in a composition and appear random and dynamic. Here, the composition lacks balance and appears off-kilter. Although it has a more casual appearance, it requires careful planning to ensure that it always appears visually balanced.

Radial Balance
This type of balance is based on a circle and occurs when visual elements in a composition radiate out from a central, common point in a circular direction and their visual weight is equally distributed. Radial balance creates a strong focal point, always leading the eye to the center of the composition. Stars, watch faces, spokes of a wheel, and sunflowers are all prime examples of radial balance.

Degrees of Balance
Graphic designers can rely upon color, direction, location, shape, texture, value, and weight to emphasize a visual element to achieve a state of balance. Varied degrees of balance can be created in a composition through a combination of the following related design elements and principles:

Color
Our eyes are more drawn to color than to a neutral image. Small elements of vibrant color can offset larger elements of neutral color in a composition. Additionally, complementary colors visually weigh more than analogous colors.

Direction
Our eyes can be directed to a specific location in any visual composition based on its arrangement and composition of design elements. If elements are oriented in a specific direction, our eyes will also be led in that same direction.

Location
A smaller element located farther away from the center of a composition will always balance a larger element located closer to its center. Additionally, larger elements located on one side of a composition can be balanced by smaller elements located at the far end or on the other side of a composition. This is also the basis for asymmetry or informal balance.

Shape
Small, intricate shapes can balance larger, simpler shapes. Similarly, large uncluttered areas within a composition that have little or no detail can be balanced with small, irregular shapes, because the eye is usually drawn to the more intricate shapes.

Texture
Smaller areas containing textures, such as variegated, irregular, or random linear fluctuations, can balance larger areas with smoother, innocuous textures.

This promotional poster series for Baltimore's Theatre Project illustrates an effective use of formal compositional balance. Formal balance, or symmetry, is used to organize each typographic grouping consistently from poster to poster, while still achieving harmony and balance with the varied illustrations and photographic images used to ultimately communicate the theme, character, and message of each play.

SPUR DESIGN
Baltimore, Maryland, USA

Compositional balance of elements that are diverse in scale and visual character can create active and powerful asymmetrical, or informal, compositions, as shown in these promotional posters for the Guthrie Theater, Chicago, and the Roundabout Theatre Company, New York City.

SPOTCO
New York, New York, USA

Value
Value refers to the lightness or darkness of elements. Black against white has a much stronger contrast or visual weight than gray against white; therefore, small elements of high contrast can be used to balance larger elements of low contrast.

Weight
The perceived physical weight of an element in any composition contributes to its visual interest. For example, a visually heavier element has more visual interest than a visually lighter element of the same size.

This set of covers for various municipal publications is part of an overall branding and identity program for the city of Melbourne. In these examples, the diversity of visual content used in each of these covers—such as line art, illustration, photography, and typographic styles—still allows a visual unity and cohesiveness due to reliance on asymmetry or an informal balance to each and every cover composition within the overall program.

LANDOR
Paris, France

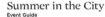

This eye-catching poster is part of an public awareness program that reintroduces classic literature to junior high school students. Its reliance on compositional balance through formal symmetry, as well as its use of iconic imagery, creates a provocative visual metaphor that is universal and appealing to a young audience.

MIKEY BURTON
Philadelphia, Pennsylvania, USA

Asymmetrical, or informal, balance is clearly evident in this promotional poster for a film screening of *Man on Wire* at the Cathedral Church of Saint John the Divine in New York City. This type of compositional balance combined with the simplicity of the photographic image and blacklettering creates a visual invitation that is both eye-catching and memorable.

PENTAGRAM
New York, New York, USA

Visual balance can be affected not only by the size of compositional elements but also by their intrinsic value such as lightness or darkness. This is also described as an element's visual weight. When compositional elements are of equal visual weight, they are in balance.

Visual balance is an essential requirement in all visual communications. Just as balance is a state of physical equilibrium where everything comes to a standstill, it is also a state of visual harmony in which all characteristics of a composition are mutually interconnected and interrelated.

Based on traditional Islamic arabesque patterning, this symbol for the Dubai Waterfront Canal District represents the entire city, as well as its eight distinct districts. Formal or symmetrical balance is used here as a primary compositional principle to integrate line, texture, color, and pattern in a cohesive, unified manner.

POULIN + MORRIS INC.
New York, New York, USA

In this atlas, formal and directional balance are used as primary organizational and compositional principles, helping the reader to access the analysis and comparison of 101 capital cities around the world. Dense information, organized in a series of horizontal bands of varied heights and containing different statistical data, shares a common leading system that unifies these variables from column to column, page to page, and spread to spread.

JOOST GROOTENS
Amsterdam, The Netherlands

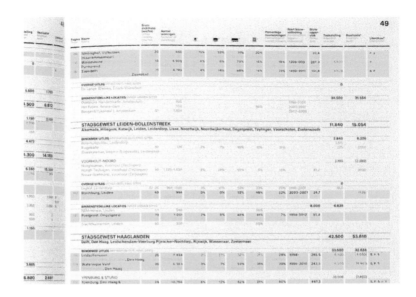

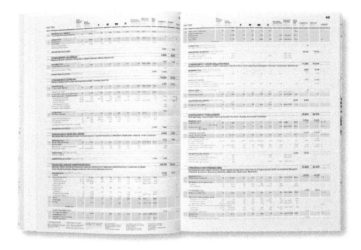

The balanced composition of this promotional poster for a student thesis exhibition at the School of Visual Arts relies solely upon one shared and common center point for the circular diagram and the justified, large-scale sans serif typography framing the upper and lower portions of the poster.

BRYAN FAREVAAG, Student
GENEVIEVE WILLIAMS, Instructor
School of Visual Arts
New York, New York, USA

sym·me·try \ˈsi-mə-trē\ *n*
1: balanced proportions;
also: beauty of form arising from
balanced proportions

12

"Symmetry is static–that is to say quiet; that is to say inconspicuous."
WILLIAM ADDISON DWIGGINS (1880-1956). *American, Book Designer, Calligrapher, Typographer*

Symmetry is a fundamental and timeless principle of visual perception. In visual communications, symmetry conveys balance, stability, and harmony. When visual elements are completely balanced or centered, they are in a state of equilibrium where all elements have equal weight. The result

L

LEO INGWER

EST. 1939

The visual integration of an uppercase *L* and *I* illustrate a strong symmetry, or balance, with this logotype for Leo Ingwer Jewelers, even if the combined letterforms are not truly symmetrical in graphic form. Additionally, the scale and typographic treatment of the company's name and year established further strengthens the symmetry of this typographic composition.

AND PARTNERS
New York, New York, USA

is a state of visual balance and is identified as symmetry. It is a compositional state where design elements are organized on the central axis of a composition (either its horizontal or vertical axis). A similar compositional state can be achieved when design elements are organized in relation to each other's central axes. A symmetrical composition is static, stationary, and balanced, with the negative spaces around its elements or the contours of its elements located around its central axis all appearing the same or of equal weight.

(continued on page 126)

The branding and identity program for Boney's Bayside Market, from packaging and advertisements to environmental graphics and shopping bags, uses symmetry combined with casual sans serif typography, hand-drawn letterforms, textural food photography, and quirky line illustrations to further communicate the feel, ambiance, and ultimate experience of shopping at a family-owned, neighborhood gourmet food market.

MIRIELLO GRAFICO
San Diego, California, USA

William Shakespeare: *The Tragedy of King Lear* Book Cover
JAN TSCHICHOLD
Engraved Shakespeare portrait by Reynolds Stone
London, United Kingdom

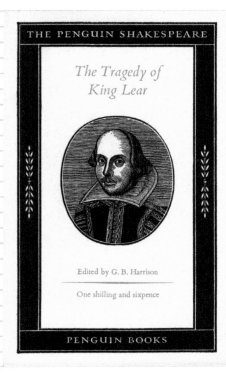

In 1947, JAN TSCHICHOLD (1902–1974) emigrated from Switzerland to Great Britain to accept a position at Penguin Books as its new design director. Founded in 1935, Penguin Books was one of the most commercially successful book publishers in Great Britain.

Prior to Tschichold's arrival in London, Penguin paperbacks were not produced with any specific design standards or production criteria. Their existing standards, dated and limited, were generic and inappropriate in comparison with the publisher's reputation and offerings. Tschichold quickly realized that a new and unique set of compositional rules and standards were needed at the publishing house.

Tschichold's redesign of Penguin books in the late 1940s not only revolutionized typographic conventions but also reintroduced compositional standards that had long been labeled out-of-date.

Tschichold developed a pragmatic look for Penguin Books that was extremely appropriate for a large number of book titles, while increasing a level of balance, consistency, and readability throughout their catalog. In his view, adherence to the tenets of classical typography—symmetry, legibility, a balance of type styles, wide margins, contrast, simplicity, and integrated rules and ornaments—were all integral to a book's timeless function.

Tschichold had begun to reject the rules of *Die Neue Typographie* (*The New Typography*) and functional Bauhaus principles while designing books in Switzerland between 1933 and 1946. He realized then that symmetrical and asymmetrical typographic treatments could equally accomplish the requirements and goals of successful book design.

While at Penguin, he established a new set of general design principles based on his broad vision of good design. These guidelines were documented in a four-page essay titled "Penguin Composition Rules," demanding that all Penguin designers follow these standardized rules for all aspects of book design and composition.

Tschichold also designed many book covers himself, including the Penguin edition of Shakespeare's *The Tragedy of King Lear*, released in 1949. While conventional in design, it is a clear and well-balanced composition that is immediately legible to the reader. Its solid black border is reinforced by inset hairline rules that provide a strong frame for the symmetrical typography set in Monotype's Perpetua. During his tenure, Tschichold standardized the design for Penguin's extensive book series, and *The Tragedy of King Lear* is a prime example of the basic compositional principles he devised for Penguin Classics, making them instantly recognizable to the consumer.

By raising the aesthetic level of a mass-market publisher of paperback books, Tschichold brought to life the timeless principle of symmetry that graphic designers still rely upon today. Tschichold later wrote, "We do not need pretentious books for the wealthy, we need more really well-made ordinary books."

Jan Tschichold and the Penguin Classics

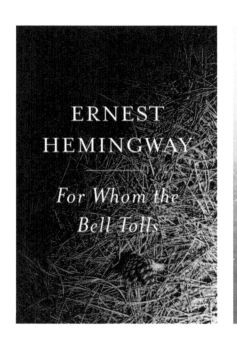

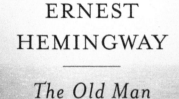

ERNEST
HEMINGWAY

*For Whom the
Bell Tolls*

ERNEST
HEMINGWAY

*The Old Man
and The
Sea*

ERNEST
HEMINGWAY

*To Have and
Have Not*

**In this monogram for Tiffany
& Co., the designer uses
ligature, as well as in-depth
knowledge of and intimacy
with letterform, to create
a unified, balanced symmetry
for an already simple idea.**

LOUISE FILI LTD.
New York, New York, USA

Symmetrical, or formal, balance is also
known as bilateral symmetry. It is achieved
by repeating the reverse of an image on the
opposite side of a vertical axis; each side
becomes the mirror image of the other side.
Symmetrical balance is considered formal,
ordered, stable, and quiet.

The compositional principle of symmetry has also long been associated with
physical beauty, natural or man-made. Symmetry can be found in virtually all forms of
the natural world, including the human body,
animals, and plants. Classical architecture
also combines symmetrical types, creating
unified, dynamic, and memorable forms.
Prime examples found in the man-made
environment are Notre Dame Cathedral, the
Eiffel Tower, and the U.S. Capitol.

Types of Symmetry
There are three types of basic symmetry:

Reflective
Horizontal and vertical symmetry are identified as reflective symmetry. This type of
symmetry is created by mirroring equivalent
elements around a central axis or mirror line.
Reflective symmetry can be achieved in any

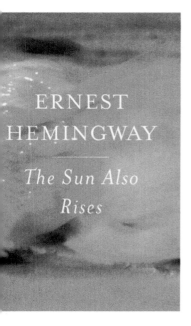

ERNEST
HEMINGWAY

The Sun Also Rises

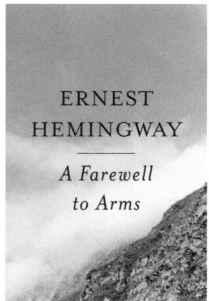

ERNEST
HEMINGWAY

A Farewell to Arms

This series of book covers for five Ernest Hemingway novels relies upon traditional symmetry combined with serif typography to celebrate these classic, seminal books. The use of textural images as visual metaphors allows the reader's imagination to further connect with the familiar themes of these iconic novels.

THE OFFICE OF
PAUL SAHRE
New York, New York, USA

orientation as long as its elements are the same on both sides of the mirror line. Forms found in nature, such as a monarch butterfly, exhibit reflective symmetry.

Horizontal symmetry is created with an imaginary horizon or a left-to-right line functioning as the divider of the composition, with the top and bottom sections mirroring one another. A landscape reflected in a still pond is an example of horizontal symmetry.

Vertical symmetry is created with an imaginary vertical or a top-to-bottom line functioning as the divider of the composition, with the left and right sections mirroring one another. A Rorschach inkblot is an prime example of vertical symmetry.

Each of the fourteen contained and framed blocks of typographic text in this cover for *Los Angeles* magazine is composed in a symmetrical manner, and collectively composed as one overall symmetrical composition, further illustrating the diversity and power of this guiding compositional design principle.

TIMOTHY GOODMAN
San Francisco, California, USA

Symmetry functions as the compositional guide for the typographic and line elements of this slipcase cover for a set of three novels by Thomas Mann—*Tristan*, *Death in Venice*, and *Gladius Dei*. While the trees are not truly symmetrical in the photographic composition, they are visually balanced and add a powerful metaphor to the title of this book set.

JOHN SURACE, Student
ANITA ZEPPETELLI, Instructor
School of Visual Arts
New York, New York, USA

This book cover for Sean McCloud's *Divine Hierarchies* illustrates how symmetry can create a state of visual equilibrium and balance through the effective and meaningful use of centered compositional elements, appropriate scale, color, value, and typographic style.

ROGERS ECKERSLEY DESIGN
New York, New York, USA

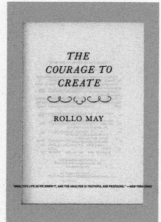

The typographic composi-
tions for Rollo May's *The
Courage to Create* and *Man's
Search for Himself* both
use symmetry as a guiding
compositional principle, combined with vibrant colored
frames and reviewer's pull
quotes to further reinforce
the dynamic, relational
balance between these two
book covers.

MOTHER DESIGN
New York, New York, USA

12

Symmetry

Rotative
Rotating equivalent elements in an outward
direction from a common center point while
drawing attention inward is identified as
rotative symmetry. This can occur at any
angle or frequency as long as its elements
share a common center point. Arabesque
and mandala patterns are examples of man-
made rotative symmetry. A sunflower is
an example of rotative symmetry found
in nature.

Translative
This type of symmetry is created by locating
equivalent elements in different areas of

a composition. Translative symmetry can
occur in any direction and over any distance
as long as the basic orientation of its design
elements is maintained. Continuous patterns
found in architectural surfaces such as
façades, friezes, and pediments are primary
examples of translative symmetry.

Aside from its aesthetic properties,
symmetry has other characteristics that are
potentially beneficial to graphic designers.
Symmetrical forms are seen as figure elements rather than ground elements in any
visual composition. They traditionally receive
more attention and are more memorable
than any other compositional organiza-

tions. Symmetrical forms are also simpler
than asymmetrical forms, which makes them
more immediate and recognizable in a visual
composition to the reader's eye.

This promotional poster for
the School of Visual Arts is
based on a common eye test
chart as well as the compositional design principle of
symmetry and was designed
to catch the attention of
prospective students as they
traveled the New York City
subway system.

MIRKO ILIĆ
New York, New York, USA

Bilateral symmetry is an integral compositional principle
used on this brightly colored,
triangular background
pattern as well as with the
decorative typographic and
line elements contained
within the larger triangular
frame used on these wine
labels for Tratturi Primitivo.

LOUISE FILI LTD.
New York, New York, USA

asym·me·try \(ˌ)ā-ˈsi-mə-trē\ *n*
1: lack of balance or symmetry

13

"Asymmetry is the rhythmic expression of functional design."
JAN TSCHICHOLD (1902-1974), *German-Swiss, Author, Book Designer, Educator, Typographer.*

Asymmetry is the opposite of symmetry. Asymmetrical balance, also called informal balance, means without symmetry. This definition by itself has nothing to do with balance. It means only that images within a composition do not mirror one another. The term, however, is usually used to

The symbol for Overture, a web search engine, is composed of a series of concentric *O*'s organized in an asymmetrical perspective that further conveys balance and movement, as well as referencing a target, informational hierarchy, and unlimited reach. This asymmetrical symbol also takes on an added visual dynamic when used as a greeting in reflected neon, cropped top and bottom, and interpreted as an environmental graphic wall mural.

C+G PARTNERS LLC
New York, New York, USA

describe a kind of balance that does not rely upon the principle of symmetry. With asymmetry, one dominant form or compositional element is often offset by smaller forms or compositional elements. In general, asymmetrical compositions tend to have a greater sense of visual tension than symmetrically balanced compositions.

References in Nature
Asymmetry in nature is uncommon and is a skill development trait identified as "handedness," a property of an object (such (continued on page 134)

J. Christopher Capital's business stationery is identified with a centered monogramlike logotype and organized within asymmetrical compositions for its letterhead, envelope, and business card.

HINTERLAND
New York, New York, USA

● vom 16. januar bis 14. februar 1937

kunsthalle basel

konstruktivisten

van doesburg
domela
eggeling
gabo
kandinsky
lissitzky
moholy-nagy
mondrian
pevsner
taeuber
vantongerloo
vordemberge
u. a.

JAN TSCHICHOLD (1902–1974) was born in Leipzig, Germany, the eldest son of a sign painter and calligrapher. He studied calligraphy, engraving, typography, and book arts at Leipzig's Academy for Graphic Arts and Book Production. Soon after establishing himself as a graphic designer, he became aware of the need for a new approach to typography.

At the time, typography was based on the principle of centered type or symmetry, using frame, border, and ornament to provide further texture, distinction, and individuality to each composition. Tschichold identified this approach as the "box block style" of typography, an approach that was predictable, uninteresting, and outdated.

In August 1923, he attended the first Bauhaus exhibition in Weimar and quickly started to assimilate this new design philosophy. Influenced and informed by the work of modern avant-garde artists and designers such as Herbert Bayer, Paul Klee, El Lissitzky, and Piet Zwart, Tschichold wanted to liberate visual form from its restrictive rules and provide designers with greater freedom and flexibility.

He believed that typographic information had to be purely functional and composed in a clear and precise manner, or else it would be ignored. Starting in 1925, he began writing a series of articles and publications proposing a revolutionary approach to a "new" typography—an approach strongly influenced by both the Bauhaus and the Russian Constructivists.

The major tenets of the New Typography were asymmetric compositions of elements based on their relative importance, the preference for sans serif type, and the creative use of white space. These tenets were ultimately summarized in Tschichold's treatise titled *Die Neue Typographie* (*The New Typography*, 1928) and in *Typographische Gestaltung* (*Asymmetric Typography*, 1935).

In 1926, he was appointed by Paul Renner to teach typography and lettering at the Munich Meisterschule fur Deutschlands Buchdrucker, and he continued to lecture there until 1933.

In 1933, Tschichold was arrested and accused by the Nazis of being a "cultural Bolshevik," creating "un-German" typography. Soon after his release, he and his family immigrated to Basel, Switzerland. In the later part of his life, Tschichold ultimately embraced principles of both symmetry and asymmetry, as well as the use of serif and sans serif typography in his work.

Jan Tschichold and *Die Neue Typographie*

as a living organism) that is not identical with its mirror image. This is fully evident in a person's tendency to use one hand rather than the other.

Other examples of handedness and left-right asymmetries in nature are the left dolphin lung that is smaller than the right to make room for its asymmetrical heart; a fiddler crab's different-size large and small claws; the narwhal's left incisor tusk, which can grow up to 10 feet (3 m) long and form a left-handed helix; the eyes of a flatfish, located on one side of its head so it swims with one side upward; and several species of owls whose size and ear position assists them in locating their prey.

Compositional Characteristics

Asymmetry is achieved when one side of a visual composition does not reflect the other side. Asymmetrical balance is a type of visual balance in which compositional elements are organized so that one side differs from the other without impacting the composition's overall harmony. Consequently, when an asymmetrical composition is disturbingly off balance, the result is jarring and disorienting.

As a compositional principle of visual communications, asymmetrical balance is more complex and more difficult to achieve than symmetrical balance. It involves organizing compositional elements in a way that will allow elements of varying visual weight

The asymmetrical balance of this page spread is achieved simply with the effective use of scale, proportion, and grid. Reliance on extreme large- and small-scale photographic images, a dynamic layout of typographic columnar text, and activation of a flexible page grid all add to the visual impact and kinetic qualities that can be achieved with an asymmetrical composition.

JOOST GROOTENS
Amsterdam, The Netherlands

This poster for promoting developing artists' films and videos throughout the United Kingdom relies upon the immediacy and power of pure typography and is organized in an asymmetrical composition to gain and hold the viewer's attention. An obvious hierarchy of typographic sizes and colors, as well as the use of horizontal, linear rules to highlight, group, and separate information, makes this poster easily and readily accessible to the reader.

FRASER MUGGERIDGE
London, United Kingdom

PICTURE THIS

WWW.PICTURE-THIS.ORG.UK

Developing artists' film and video through commissions, exhibitions and research

DOWN AT THE BAMBOO CLUB: FILM, PARTICIPATION AND RE-ENACTMENT
VICTOR ALIMPIEV   BARBY ASANTE
DAVID MALJKOVIC   MANDY MCINTOSH
IAIN FORSYTH   MARK WILSHER
& JANE POLLARD

BRISTOL MEAN TIME RESIDENCY
RACHEL REUPKE

VISUAL ARTISTS IRELAND RESIDENCY
LINDA QUINLAN

PRAYER PROJECT
DAPHNE WRIGHT

SLOW ACTION
BEN RIVERS

INTERNATIONAL FAUNA (A RELATIONAL COMMISSION FOR ANTI-BODIES)
MELANIE JACKSON

DIEGO GARCIA
AIKATERINI GEGISIAN

WAY OF THE GOAT
VARSITY OF MANEUVERS

THE NIGHT-TIME ROOM
RONNIE CLOSE

ASSOCIATE DANCE ARTIST
LISA MAY THOMAS

and a forthcoming project by
HITO STEYERL

Picture This

This 74-foot-high (22.6 m) sandblasted limestone tablet engraved with the forty-five words of the First Amendment is traditionally composed with serif all-cap letterforms in an asymmetrical organization, and located on the modernist, all-glass façade of the Newseum building, also in an asymmetrical manner. This treatment accentuates the large-scale typography as a bas-relief and permanently displays the first amendment as a timeless element set in a modern context.

POULIN + MORRIS INC.
New York, New York, USA

to balance one another around an axis or pivot point. This can be best visualized as a literal balance scale that represents visual weights in a two-dimensional composition. For example, it is possible to balance a heavy weight with a group of lighter weights on equal sides of a pivot point. In a visual composition, this might be a cluster of small elements balanced by a larger one. It is also possible to imagine compositional elements of equal weight but different mass (such as a large mass of feathers versus a small mass of stones), on equal sides of a pivot point. Unequal visual weights can also be balanced by shifting the pivot on this imaginary scale.

Maison Theatre's playful and childlike symbol is composed of two triangular, transparent color shapes layered on top of one another to create a third unique triangular shape. An all-cap treatment of the theater's name functions as a typographic base for this asymmetrically balanced symbol. To further appeal to a youthful audience, the symbol is applied to a variety **of print collateral materials with bright saturated colors, hand-drawn letterforms and script lettering, and triangular patterning—all active and dynamic asymmetrical compositions, reinforcing the unique, visual character of the theatre's overall message and brand.**

LG2BOUTIQUE
Montreal, Quebec, Canada

Perricone MD's branding campaign includes packaging, website, advertising, and promotional sales collateral that reflect a modern visual interpretation of a traditional apothecary—understated, small-scale serif typography; scientific photography; frosted amber glass containers—all organized and composed in an asymmetrical and balanced manner.

MONNET DESIGN
Toronto, Ontario, Canada

Asymmetrical balance is informal and generally more active and dynamic than symmetrical balance. While symmetrical balance is achieved through repetition, asymmetrical balance is completely dependent upon contrast and counterpoint in a composition. It results from combining contrasting design elements, such as point, line, shape, form, and color, evenly distributed along an axis of a composition.

Asymmetry is also a compositional state where elements are organized in a nonsystematic and organic manner to achieve visual balance. This type of visual balance relies upon the critical interaction and integrity of

The book cover for *The Good Men Project: Real Stories from the Front Lines of Modern Manhood* uses asymmetry to create visual tension, balance, and eye-catching recognition for the buyer and reader. These characteristics are further strengthened with the effective use of an iconic photographic image, bold typography, vibrant color, and distinctive proportions.

POULIN + MORRIS INC.
New York, New York, USA

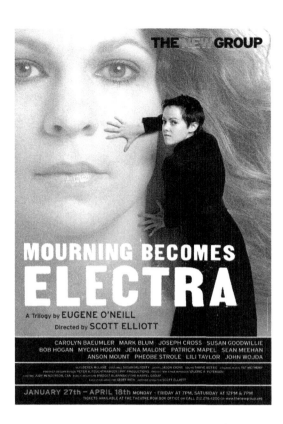

compositional elements and negative space, as well as their location and proximity to one another, to create tension, balance, and meaning in any visual communication.

These types of balanced compositions are inherently active and kinetic, and communicate the same to the viewer.

Asymmetrical compositions require a more disciplined and analytical eye due to their unique and ever-changing spatial requirements. Here the graphic designer has to constantly and consistently evaluate and assess potential compositional solutions based on spatial relationships varying from element to element and size to size, whether positive or negative, figure or ground.

In visual communications, the graphic designer's reliance on the principle of asymmetry in creating asymmetrical compositions increases the viewer's ability to organize, differentiate, and interact with a broad range of visual content.

Future Flight, a promotional poster for the Australian Graphic Design Association, functions as an announcement for a series of member programs and offerings. The immediacy and dynamic visual character of this poster is solely due to its asymmetrical composition. Additionally, the use of varied colors and scales of paper planes, as well as their illusive appearance of ascending and flying beyond the edges limitations of the poster, strengthens the asymmetry of this composition.

LANDOR
Paris, France

The asymmetrical composition and organization of this website's navigational elements for Mac Industries, a precision machining and fabrication company, allow the user to easily access various types of information, sections, and tools in a logical and easily understandable user-friendly sequence.

INFINITE SCALE DESIGN
Salt Lake City, Utah, USA

ten·sion \ˈten(t)-shən\ *n*
3 c: a balance maintained in artistic work between opposing forces or elements

14

"Tension is the great integrity."
RICHARD BUCKMINSTER FULLER (1895-1983), *American, Architect, Author, Inventor*

The principle of tension in visual communications is critical to effective graphic design. Tension is primarily a visual, as well as psychological, attention-getting device. It is also a tenuous balance maintained between opposing formal elements, often causing anxiety, stress, angst, or excitement,

Color and compositional placement are two key factors in creating a visual tension with this identity program for BPI, a lighting design consultancy. The lowercase, tri-letter acronym is always located at the lower edge of any print collateral so that the descender of the *p* can touch and bleed off the bottom edge. This visual tension is also reinforced with a vibrant fluorescent yellow used consistently throughout this program, whether figure or ground.

POULIN + MORRIS INC.
New York, New York, USA

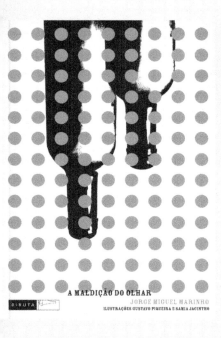

A MALDIÇÃO DO OLHAR
JORGE MIGUEL MARINHO
ILUSTRAÇÕES GUSTAVO PIQUEIRA E SAMIA JACINTHO

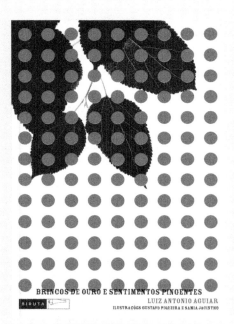

BRINCOS DE OURO E SENTIMENTOS PINGENTES
LUIZ ANTONIO AGUIAR
ILUSTRAÇÕES GUSTAVO PIQUEIRA E SAMIA JACINTHO

exuberance, and joy for the viewer. Tension and balance are interrelated principles in visual communications. Like balance, tension is an obvious and constant presence in our everyday lives. Unfortunately, we cannot experience one of them without the other. When something is out of balance in our life, we feel tense and anxious. For example, when we observe a daring feat, such as a high-wire act at a circus, it makes us feel uneasy and tense since there is always a potential for the performer to fall. The same experiences and emotions can be conveyed and ultimately felt in any visual message. (continued on page 145)

This set of book covers for Biruta, a Brazilian publishing house, uses visual tension as an eye-catching device. Each cover layers a high-contrast black-and-white photographic image turned and cropped in an unusual and jarring orientation with an over-scaled dot pattern. The effect is bold, dynamic, and relevant to each book theme, and full of compositional imbalance.

CASA REX
São Paulo, Brazil

Laga Company Advertisement
PIET ZWART
Amsterdam, The Netherlands

PIET ZWART (1885–1977), a Dutch craftsman, draftsman, and architect, was born in Zaandijk, an industrial area north of Amsterdam. From 1902 to 1907, he attended Amsterdam's School of Arts and Crafts, where he became interested in architecture. His early work involved designing textiles, furniture, and interiors in a style that showed his affinity for de Stijl.

Zwart was influenced by many of the modern, avant-garde movements of the early twentieth century, as well as Tschichold's *The New Typography*. He was one of the first modernist designers in Holland to apply the principles of de Stijl and Constructivism to commercial advertising during the 1920s.

From 1921 to 1927, Zwart worked for H. P. Berlage, the most influential Dutch architect of the era. While working in Berlage's office, he received his first typographic commission and designed the first of many advertisements for Laga Company, a Dutch flooring manufacturer.

These dynamic and arresting advertisements are early examples of Zwart's interest in typography, pure compositional form, and asymmetrical tension. Here, he mostly used found type and letterforms from various printers' cases. While photographs and photomontage were used sparingly, when he did rely on these forms, they were never used as embellishment or decoration. Every visual element, whether typographic or photographic, was used to collectively create a more meaningful and powerful message.

With this early work, Zwart rejected conventional symmetry and traditional typographic rules. He considered the design of a visual composition as a "field of tension" brought to life with a combination of asymmetrical balance, contrasts of size and weight of elements, and a dynamic interaction between positive and negative space.

Zwart synthesized two very distinct and contradictory points of view in his work—the Constructivist movement's visual playfulness and de Stijl's formal functionality. He ultimately created a unified language that has prevailed for the last eighty years and to this day strongly influences contemporary designers.

Piet Zwart and Laga Company

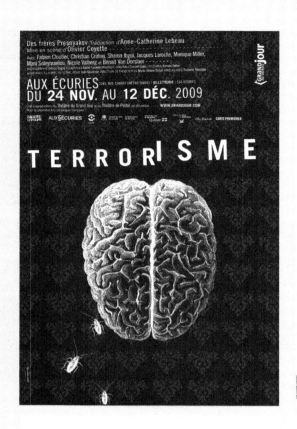

LAURENT PINABEL
Montreal, Quebec, Canada

Characteristics and Effects

Tension is a critical compositional element
that depends completely on opposing visual
forces. In the related fields of applied and
performing arts, such as architecture, music,
and dance, the same holds true. In architecture, monumental structure is juxtaposed
with curvilinear, natural form in the Eiffel
Tower and the Guggenheim Museum. In music, loud sounds compete with soft tones in
the compositions of Tchaikovsky and Philip
Glass. In dance, movement appears harsh
and irregular with fluid and gentle gestures
in the choreography of Martha Graham and
Merce Cunningham.

Tension can be realized through a wide
range of contrasts and imbalances—between
medium and message, form and content,
pattern and texture, scale and proportion. It
results from opposing forces and unresolved
relationships, not only in visual form but also
in narrative content.

It can also be achieved through the
compositional element of space. Varied proximity of elements can result in visual tension
that brings an apparent and dynamic interest
to a composition. Equal and regular spacing
creates visual static and uniformity.

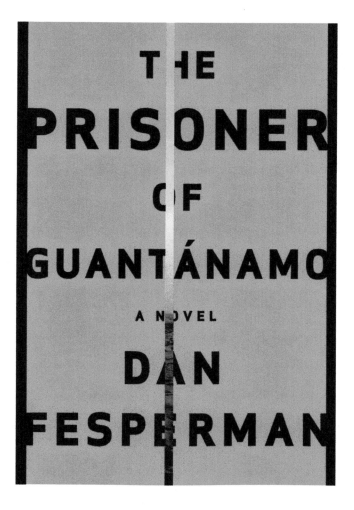

A simple, asymmetrically
placed graphic line not only
creates a palatable, visual
tension on this cover for *The
Prisoner of Guantanamo*, it
immediately communicates
the emotional, firsthand
experience of the novel. It
also represents the political,
emotional, conceptual, and
relevant spirit of the book's
narrative, as well as literally
illustrating what it looks like
to peer through the prison
gates toward the beaches
of Cuba.

JOHN GALL
New York, New York, USA

The John P. McNulty Prize, in association with Aspen Institute, supports extraordinary young leaders making creative, effective, and lasting contributions to their communities. The program's logotype is organized in three vertical bands anchored to the upper right-hand corner of any print collateral, creating a visual tension and excitement that is an essential character of the program. Color and typography are also used effectively and to further reinforce this compositional dynamic.

POULIN + MORRIS INC.
New York, New York, USA

For example, a space between two or more elements can affect not only their spatial relationship but also the perception of that relationship by the viewer. As these two or more elements move together, a visual tension can result. When they touch, a new shape or hybrid shape is created, and at some point, as they move apart, they become disassociated with one another. The graphic designer can think of tension as a conversation in which compositional elements communicate with one another. This conversation can be quiet and understated, or it can be loud and chaotic. The resulting dialogue can be affected profoundly by the position and number of elements in a composition. Proximity groupings can create patterns, a sense of rhythm, or other visual relationships that can elicit a response from the viewer. However, the graphic designer needs to keep in mind that this visual conversation should always be in support of the message's content.

Tension can also be created by the imbalance of design elements in a composition. With asymmetrical compositions, visual tension is in response to gravity and its obvious effect on the individual elements.

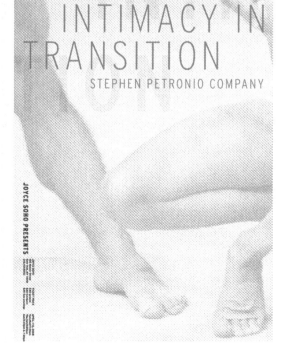

This poster series for the Stephen Petronio Company is a thorough study in spatial tension. Each composition is an integral representation of visual tension and balance, effectively using cropped photographic images contrasted with horizontal and vertical typographic elements, and varied layers of color and dot patterns— all collectively strengthening the tension between elements as well as the composition of each poster.

LAURA GRALNICK, Student
RICHARD POULIN, Instructor
School of Visual Arts
New York, New York, USA

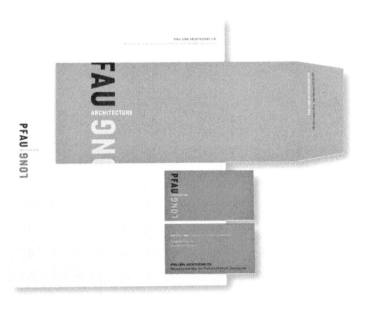

The intersection of two extremely different-size lines of typography, combined with their alternating direction and orientation, adds to the visual tension and distinctive visual character of this graphic identity program for Pfau Long Architecture. Saturated and muted colors also contrast with one another, creating another level of visual tension.

PUBLIC INC.
San Francisco, California, USA

It can create varied degrees and levels of excitement and visual tension depending on the degree of asymmetry.

Our lives are filled with opposites—happy, sad, angry, calm, crying, laughing. Effective visual communications echo these opposites in our lives, making us connect and engage with them in a much more immediate and meaningful way. This language of opposites is a language of tension, and it helps us understand so many things and experiences.

Visual tension speaks to the good and the bad, the easy and the difficult—in life, as well as in graphic design. Effective visual communications is often filled with tension.

A single vertical rule placed between the words *support* and *resist* in the title of this book creates a visual tension in a powerful and immediate way. This graphic rule also symbolizes the essence of the book's content, which celebrates design innovation in structural engineering.

THINK STUDIO
New York, New York, USA

These page spreads from the School of Visual Arts' *Senior Library* show how disparate, unrelated visual images can be cropped and paired to create a balanced, visual tension that ultimately provides unity and cohesiveness to the totality of each page spread, as well as to the overall book.

POULIN + MORRIS INC.
New York, New York, USA

clo·sure \ˈklō-zhər\ *n*
1: the process or ability to fill in missing parts of a visual stimulus; a Gestalt principle of visual organization holding that there is an innate tendency to perceive incomplete objects as complete

15

"Imagination is the beginning of creation. You imagine what you desire, you will what you imagine and at last you create what you will."
GEORGE BERNARD SHAW (1856-1950), *Irish, Playwright*

In visual communications, closure can basically be described as a visual illusion. Closure literally means the act of closing or the condition of being closed. It is also a definitive finish or conclusion. As human beings, we have an innate need to make sense of what we see; therefore, if we anticipate

In the identity, stationery, and website for the Max Protetch Gallery, the appearance of the *x* in the logotype is only partially closed and incomplete, bringing an additional visual nuance to the overall program. This form of closure provides an interactive engagement with the viewer, allowing them to fill in the blanks and ultimately create a visual conclusion.

LAURA GRALNICK, Student
RICHARD POULIN, Instructor
School of Visual Arts
New York, New York, USA

THE LANGUAGE OF GRAPHIC DESIGN

maxprotetch

STUART KRIMKO
Director of Exhibitions

511 West 22nd Street New York, NY 10011
T 212.633.6999 stuart@maxprotetch.com

511 WEST 22ND STREET NEW YORK, NY 10011
T 212.633.6999 F 212.691.4342 INFO@MAXPROTETCH.COM

a form we will always complete it. In human nature, we are constantly searching for resolution in everything we see and do. We have been taught to strive for the perfect balance in our lives. Even when we experience something incomplete or imperfect, we continually look for closure or a better-balanced sense of resolution.

In personal relationships we always expect a happy ending. When this doesn't occur, we feel unrest and disappointment. This is a example of our basic human need for resolution. In visual communications, closure is an equivalent visual resolution.

Precision and accuracy are the essential visual metaphors for this symbol identifying O'Shaughnessy Asset Management, a financial investment firm. A circular *O* letterform is pierced and interrupted by an arrowlike apostrophe pointing to its center. The viewer can immediately complete the full circular profile of the letterform; however, interrupting the letterform in this manner not only creates visual interest but also adds meaning to its overall message.

C+G PARTNERS LLC
New York, New York, USA

Historical References

A classic representation of closure in art history is in Michelangelo's *The Creation of Man* on the ceiling of the Vatican's Sistine Chapel. Here, God is reaching his pointed finger outward toward the finger of Adam's hand. In our minds, the fingers appear to touch, symbolically representing creation and birth. The fingers do not touch, yet they are perfectly positioned to imply such. If they were any farther apart, or conversely, if they were touching, the quality of this critical compositional relationship, as well as the visual perception of closure, would be lost.

Visual Characteristics

Closure is completely dependent upon spatial relationships in a composition. It is used to create visual interest for viewers because it engages them to complete the composition in their own mind's eye.

It is also dependent on the distance from one object or shape to another. When related objects are too far apart from one another, they have no immediate and apparent visual relationship. When related objects are composed in close relationship to one (continued on page 154)

1955

Theaterbau von der Antike bis zur Moderne
(Theater Construction in Antiquity and Modernity)
Exhibition Poster
ARMIN HOFMANN
Zurich, Switzerland

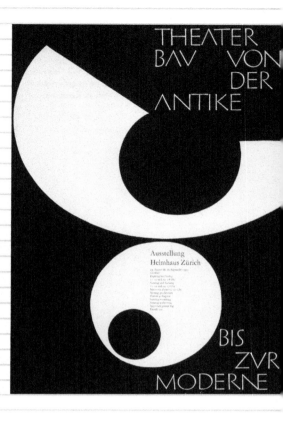

For over forty years, ARMIN HOFMANN (b. 1920) has devoted his life to teaching art, design, and the principles of visual perception and communications. His students' works are benchmarks of visual excellence, as well as the envy of students and teachers of graphic design worldwide.

In 1937, he studied foundation art at the Kunstgewerbeschule in Zurich; he also worked as a draftsman and lithography apprentice in Winterthur and as a lithographer and designer in various studios in Basel, Switzerland.

Hofmann began his career as an influential educator at the Allgemeine Gewerbeschule Basel School of Art and Crafts (later known as Schule fur Gestaltung or AGS) at the early age of 26. He followed Emil Ruder as the head of its graphic design department and was instrumental in developing the graphic design style known as the International Typographic Style or Swiss School.

His teaching methods and maxims were unorthodox and broad based, setting new standards that became widely known in design education institutions throughout the world. His independent insights as an educator, married with his rich and innovative powers of visual expression, created a body of work enormously varied—books, exhibitions, stage sets, logotypes, symbols, typography, sign systems, and most memorably, posters.

His exhibition poster titled *Theaterbau von der Antike bis zur Moderne* for the Austellung Helmhaus in Zurich is a simple, compositional study in black and white, figure–ground, and closure engaging the viewer with the compositional elements and principles of asymmetry, tension, contrast, and scale.

His posters are widely recognized for their contrasts in simplicity and complexity, representation and abstraction. They have a direct and immediate connection to the viewer's eye—engaging, challenging, and communicative. They pique interest and convey a clean and understandable message. Hofmann's posters are pure and symbolic visual statements. He has written that "a poster does more than simply supply information on the goods it advertises; it also reveals a society's state of mind."

Paul Rand, a close friend and longtime colleague of Armin Hofmann, has described Hofmann's contributions to the graphic design profession: "Few of us have sacrificed so much time, money and comfort for the sake of their profession as has Armin Hofmann. He is one of the few exceptions to Shaw's dictum, 'He who can, does; he who cannot, teaches.' His goals, though pragmatic, are never pecuniary. His influence has been as strong beyond the classroom as within it. Even those who are his critics are as eager about his ideas as those who sit at his feet. As a human being, he is simple and unassuming. As a teacher, he has few equals. As practitioner, he ranks among the best."

Armin Hofmann and the Austellung Helmhaus

The visual identity system for an exhibition titled *Graphic Design in China* relies solely on fluorescent light installations evident in each exhibition venue that spell out the names of each designer and disciplines represented in the exhibition. Custom letterform installations were photographed and used as primary visual elements in a series of promotional posters for the exhibition. These illuminated, stencil-like letterforms are another visual representation of the design principle of closure in graphic design.

SENSE TEAM
Shenzhen, China

another, they become meaningful and therefore related. They also become complements to one another, creating tension and engaging the viewer in a more immediate manner.

Closure is most successful when visual elements in a composition are simple and singular, recognizable patterns, such as geometric shapes. When shapes and patterns are not easily understood, they become unfamiliar; therefore, closure will not occur in the mind of the viewer.

Compositional Forms

The principle of closure refers to the condition of being closed. A form that is closed is fully described or complete. However, a form that is interrupted, partially closed, or incomplete can still be understood.

Closure is the recognition of meaning in an unclear or incomplete composition because the viewer has been able to draw on previous experiences to discover sufficient similarity between it and their own individual memories. It allows the viewer to bring something to an ultimate, visual conclusion.

By providing this opportunity in a composition, the graphic designer also creates an interactive experience for the viewer. They

Elements of this branding program for Bergen Street Studio, an architecture, planning, and interior design firm, rely upon the principle of closure to further engage the viewer. For example, the announcement card shows *bergenst* anchored to the right side of the card as if it continues off the page. On its reverse side, the word continues as *reet* as well as the full name of the firm. This compositional device is considered a form of visual closure, allowing the viewer to fill in the blank.

POULIN + MORRIS INC.
New York, New York, USA

scrap house

Stencil-like, typographic "scraps" or fragments give an unusual, hybrid appearance to these letterforms. The visually inconsistent characteristics of this logotype for Scrap House, a temporary demonstration home blitz-built using scrap and salvaged materials, provides visual interest and engages the viewer to complete this puzzlelike image.

MENDE DESIGN
San Francisco, California, USA

become engaged with the visual communication and therefore become more intimately involved with the visual process of assimilation, understanding, and memory.

Closure also provides us with balance and harmony. Visual closure gives the graphic designer the same results. Even if the goal of the designer is to create tension in a composition, closure is still part of the compositional equation.

This design principle enables graphic designers to reduce complexity and increase visual interest in a composition by relying upon simple and recognizable elements to communicate information. For example, a logotype composed of recognizable elements such as multiple, repetitive lines does not need to complete many or all of its lines and contours to be meaningful and effective. Reducing the number of lines in the logotype not only reduces the visual complexity of the logotype, it also makes it more engaging for the viewer to complete in their own mind.

Forms of Perception

Closure is a principle of visual perception where the eye tends to perceive a set of individual elements as a single, recognizable

Acquire New York, a licensed real estate brokerage firm, caters to affluent residential real estate buyers. Its logotype relies upon traditional serif typography, graphic patterning evocative of engraved currency and stock certificates, rich saturated colors, and fragmented linear brackets framing all of these elements into one cohesive unit. While a fully closed frame is not needed, it is implied through the visual principle of closure.

POULIN + MORRIS INC.
New York, New York, USA

whole as opposed to separate elements. It is also one of the principles of visual communication referred to as a "gestalt principle of perception," which means that we tend to perceive a single pattern so strongly that we will close gaps and fill in missing information to complete the pattern if necessary.

For example, when individual line segments are positioned along a circular path, they are first perceived holistically as a circle, and then as multiple, independent line segments. Our tendency to perceive information in this way is automatic and subconscious; it is most likely a function of an innate preference for simplicity over complexity, and pattern over randomness.

Many forms of visual storytelling rely upon closure in a similar way. For example, in film and in comic books, singular and discrete scenes are presented to the viewer, who in turn supplies what occurs in between each scene. Essential information is provided by the storyteller, and the remaining information is provided by the viewer.

By using this design principle effectively and creatively, a designer can enhance immediacy, interest, and understanding in any visual communication.

Coral Technologies is a systems software provider that bases their entire business on continuous communication and connection with their clients. Their symbol uses simple, stylized imagery to communicate this essential need for continuity with two separate and divorced icons. The viewer, however, perceives these icons immediately as a holistic whole before acknowledging that they are literally and visually distinct and separate.

TRIBORO DESIGN SOLUTIONS
Brooklyn, New York, USA

This acronym-based logotype for **BLT Architects**, a full-service architectural design firm, comprises a series of san serif monumental letterforms in two distinct weights and framed with two linear corner brackets. These two line elements imply a fully resolved, continuous, and articulated square frame; however, by using only partial fragments of the square, an illusion allows the viewer to close the frame in their own mind's eye.

POULIN + MORRIS INC.
New York, New York, USA

LA NUIT DE LA RADIO
À LA SCAM

MERCREDI 18 JUIN 2008
À PARTIR DE 19 HEURES

SCAM / SACD / INA
en collaboration avec
RADIO FRANCE

The large-scale, sans serif letterforms used in this poster for *La Radio dans le Noir* are of ample scale and familiarity to withstand the overlay of geometric forms that block and fragment their identity and reading. The viewer ultimately resolves each of these individual letterforms in their own mind, therefore retaining their identity and meaning as well as the overall visual impact and meaning of this powerful typographic composition.

CATHERINE ZASK
Paris, France

ex·pres·sion \ik-'spre-shən\ *n*
2 a: a mode, means, or use of
significant representation or symbolism;
esp: felicitous or vivid indication
or depiction of mood or sentiment

16

"All that is good in art is the expression of one soul talking to another; and is precious according to the greatness of the soul that utters it."

JOHN RUSKIN (1819-1900), *English, Art Critic, Artist, Poet*

Expression is a design principle fully dependent on the graphic designer's individual ideas, personal moods, sole emotional outlook on the world, and place within it. It is perceived visually, as well as psychologically, in any visual message. It is also a completely subjective principle and reflects

GAIL ANDERSON
New York, New York, USA

The central image of this promotional poster for the School of Visual Arts combines visual metaphor and narrative form with the graphic designer's personal point of view, interpretation, and ultimate expression of creativity defined here as an organic, evolving process requiring nourishment and constant care.

directly on the time and experiences in which the designer has lived. Expression cannot be taught; it is learned by each and every graphic designer. It is also a reflection of the designer's inner thoughts, dreams, fears, and passions. As a result, an inherent bias completely depends upon our separate experiences or realities. Dreams, fantasies, and imagination also influence a designer's creative process and choices.

In everyday occurrences and interactions, we hear someone say that they have "expressed their opinion." However, visual expression is something more concrete, more specific, and more intentional. Meaningful and memorable visual expression occurs when the fundamental elements and principles of graphic design are used selectively and collectively by a graphic designer to create a "visual experience" for the viewer.

Since the beginning of human development, we have had the desire, as well as the basic need, to express ourselves. While graphic design as a discipline has had a relatively short history, with the name *graphic design* first coined by William Addison Dwiggins in 1922, visual communication and visual expression has always been an integral (continued on page 164)

Utilitarian processes and found objects such as a photocopier, zippers, and a Dymo lettering machine are the designer's palette, so to speak, in expressing their point of view and interpretation of a "bad generation" for this CD cover.

ART CHANTRY DESIGN CO.
Tacoma, Washington, USA

1989

Les Noces Poster
BRUNO MONGUZZI
Lugano, Italy

BRUNO MONGUZZI (b. 1941) was born in the small town of Ticino in the southern lake district of Switzerland. He studied graphic design at the Ecole des Arts Decoratifs in Geneva, and then in London.

During this time, he was influenced by the work of modernist designers such as Carlo Vivarelli, Josef Müller-Brockmann, Herbert Bayer, Jan Tschichold, and Piet Zwart. Monguzzi began his career in 1961 as a designer with Antonio Boggeri at Studio Boggeri in Milan, Italy, and remained there until its closing in the early 1980s.

Now residing in the secluded town of Meride, in northern Italy, Monguzzi is also a renowned teacher of graphic design, first in Lugano and later throughout the world. In 1981, Monguzzi was the sole curator and designer of the Studio Boggeri retrospective at the Milan Trienalle. In 1983, in collaboration with Jean Widmer's Visuel Design studio, he won the international competition for Paris's Musee d'Orsay's identity and sign system.

Monguzzi is known as a thoughtful and thought-provoking designer and educator. His professional work, as well as his teaching, has always focused on the enrichment and betterment of the human experience through visual expression in graphic design. He has consistently created modern and timeless work that is as visually rich as it is diverse in design, content, and ultimate meaning. It is also devoid of any specific style.

Monguzzi's work and has been admired by many of his colleagues and described as "street communication at its most impressive. Informational, elegant, bombastic, and magnetic. Always a great light on any city thoroughfare . . . . It takes hold of your eye with an initial onslaught of beauty, then sense, then he hands you the gift of intellectual communication."

From 1987 to 2004, he was the sole designer for Museo Cantonale d'Arte in Lugano. His poster titled *Les Noces* for the Museo is an emblematic example of how he has realized visual form as a true form of expression—enlivening, enriching, and enlightening. It is clear from this work that he has a passion for form, craft, and function as well as for history, which allows him to integrate the past with the present.

For example, in this poster Monguzzi uses thirty-six letterforms—twenty-two letters are from Herbert Bayer's alphabets, which are mostly from his Bauhaus Universal type variations of 1925; one letter is from Theo van Doesburg's work, four letters are of his own assemblage, and three are from Schlemmer's *The Husband's Prayer*. All of these letterforms are in some manner or another historically and thematically connected to either Oskar Schlemmer or Igor Stravinsky. In this context he, has used expressive and historical-relevant typographic letterforms as a means to marry the past with the present.

He is a true poet of expressive form and function.

Bruno Monguzzi and Museo Cantonale d'Arte

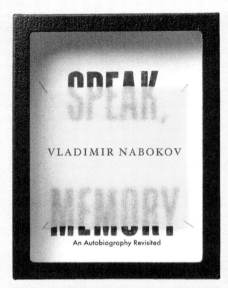

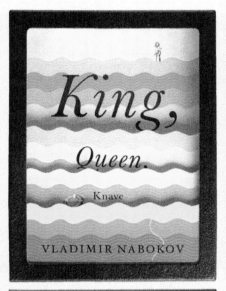

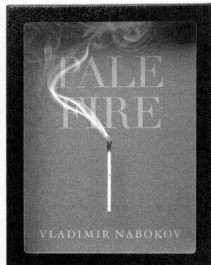

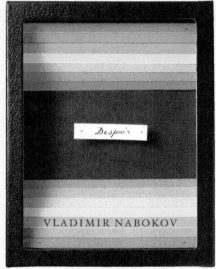

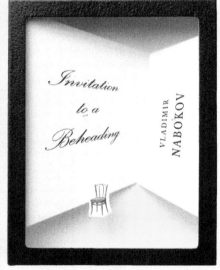

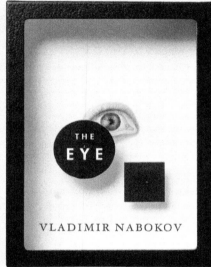

The redesign of a series of Vladimir Nabokov's book covers for Random House was a true exercise in collaboration and visual expression. Each cover was designed by a different graphic designer, whose sole requirement was to use the same black framed specimen box—the type used by collectors like Nabokov to display insects. Each box is then composed with paper, ephemera, insect pins, and the like, selected to evoke the book's content and theme. The designers represented here include Michael Bierut (*Speak Memory*), Peter Mendelsund (*King, Queen, Knave*), Stephen Doyle (*Pale Fire*), Barbara deWilde (*Stories*), Marian Bantjes (*Transparent Things*), Dave Eggers (*Laughter in the Dark*), Jason Fulford and Tamara Shopsin (*Despair*), Helen Yenthus and Jason Booher (*Invitation to a Beheading*), John Gall (*The Eye*), Chip Kidd (*Ada, or Ardor*), Carin Goldberg (*Pnin*), and Sam Potts (*The Real Life of Sebastian Knight*).

JOHN GALL
New York, New York, USA

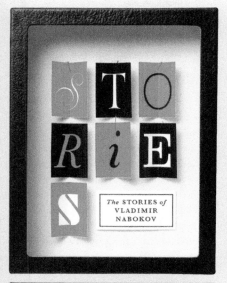

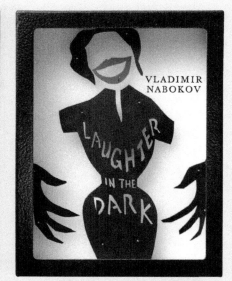

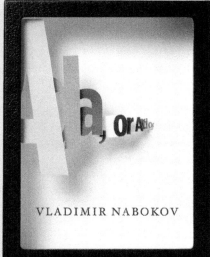

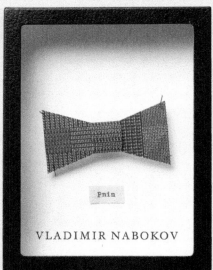

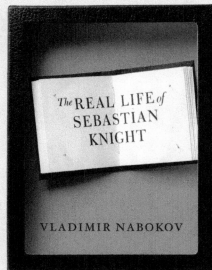

The duality of a playing card is the basis for this promotional poster celebrating "Amore y Arte" ("Love and Art") and the integral relationship between Frieda Kahlo and Diego Rivera, two of the most celebrated Mexican modernists of the 20th century.

CARBONE SMOLAN AGENCY
New York, New York, USA

part of our history. It is evident in the prehistoric cave paintings of northern Spain and southern France, in the Roman Forum's Trajan Column, in the illuminated medieval manuscripts of the Middle Ages, and in the mesmerizing neon signs of Times Square and Piccadilly Circus.

Expression is also a quality of inner experience or the emotions of the graphic designer communicated through other visual elements in a composition. Historically, this is evident in all forms of visual art, including painting and sculpture. The viewer cannot separate actual form and its integral expression when viewing memorable work such as Picasso's *Guernica*, the paintings of Jackson Pollock and Jean-Michel Basquiat, or the sculptures of Alexander Calder. Expression transcends all visual artists and graphic designers, as well as their own, individual personal experiences.

Visual communications provide a means for the graphic designer to "express" their imagination in ways that do not rely upon spoken or written language. Every element used in visual communications has the potential to express something. Although the explanation and ultimate use of design elements and principles may seem cut-and-dry,

In keeping with the themes and goals of this festival of used books in which attendees buy, sell, and exchange books, the designers decided to add value to old and used goods by reusing the remaining posters from last year's festival. The new promotional posters were now more visually expressive due to the evidence of tattered edges, repainted fronts accentuating visible old text, and hand lettering used in lieu of digital typography. This concept and theme was also used throughout the rest of the visual campaign, including recycled and reprinted sponsor T-shirts and shopping bags.

STUDIO SONDA
Porec, Croatia

Unusual, three-dimensional constructions representing de Stijl and Constructivism, a monochromatic "blanc" floral arrangement, animal fur, and kaleidoscopic colors all take on expressive meanings and messages when also representing the iconic black letter *T* of the *New York Times Style Magazine*.

JANET FROELICH
New York, New York, USA

THÉÂTRE
FRANÇAIS
2009-2010
WAJDI MOUAWAD
DIRECTION ARTISTIQUE
VIDÉO + PHOTOS
CNA-NAC.CA/TF

Une fête pour Boris

Thomas Bernhard / Denis Marleau
du 24 au 27 FÉV. 2010

AU STUDIO À 20 H
TEXTE DE THOMAS BERNHARD TRADUCTION DE CLAUDE PORCELL
MISE EN SCÈNE DE DENIS MARLEAU

AVEC SÉBASTIEN DODGE, CHRISTIANE PASQUIER ET GUY PION Conception, vidéo et scénographie : Stéphanie Jasmin et Denis Marleau Montage et diffusion vidéo : Pierre Laniel Musiques : Nicolas Bernier et Jérôme Minière Design sonore : Nancy Tobin Éclairages : Marc Parent Mannequins et poupées : Claude Rodrigue Costumes : Isabelle Larivière Maquillages et coiffures : Angelo Barsetti Un spectacle du du COMPAGNIE DE CRÉATION en coproduction avec le Festival d'Avignon, le Festival Transamériques, Pôche G, Le Manège Mons, la Maison de culture d'Amiens, l'Hippodrome du théâtre de Compiègne et Carrefour Doin

BILLETTERIE DU CNA   TARIFS DE GROUPE   BUZZ endirect   90.7   ticketmaster.ca
lundi-samedi 10 h à 21 h   613-947-7000 x384   613-755-1111

THÉÂTRE
FRANÇAIS
2009-2010
WAJDI MOUAWAD
DIRECTION ARTISTIQUE
VIDÉO + PHOTOS
CNA-NAC.CA/TF

Georg Büchner / Brigitte Haentjens

WOYZECK
du 9 au 13 FÉV. 2009

AU THÉÂTRE À 19 H 30
TEXTE DE GEORG BÜCHNER
ADAPTATION POUR LA SCÈNE DE BRIGITTE HAENTJENS, AVEC LA COLLABORATION DE LOUIS BOUCHARD, FANNY BRITT, STÉPHANE LEPINE ET MARIE-ELISABETH MORF
MISE EN SCÈNE DE BRIGITTE HAENTJENS

AVEC PAUL AHMARANI, CATHERINE ALLARD, MARC BÉLAND, RAOUL FORTIER-MERCIER, PIERRE-ANTOINE LASNIER, GAÉTAN NADEAU, SÉBASTIEN RICARD, EVELYNE ROMPRÉ ET PAUL SAVOIE Dramaturgie : Melanie Dumont Scénographie : Anick La Bissonnière Costumes : Yso Éclairages : Alexander MacSween Environnement sonore : Claude Cournoyer Maquillages : Angelo Barsetti Un spectacle de sive i icnes

BILLETTERIE DU CNA   TARIFS DE GROUPE   BUZZ endirect   90.7   ticketmaster.ca
lundi-samedi 10 h à 21 h   613-947-7000 x384   613-755-1111

du 10 au 14 NOV. 2009

THÉÂTRE
FRANÇAIS
2009-2010
WAJDI MOUAWAD
DIRECTION ARTISTIQUE
VIDÉO + PHOTOS
CNA-NAC.CA/TF

du 14 au 17 OCT. 2009

hedda gabler
HENRIK IBSEN
THOMAS OSTERMEIER

AU THÉÂTRE À 19 H30 – EXCLUSIVITÉ CANADIENNE
UN SPECTACLE DE LA SCHAUBÜHNE AM LEHNINER PLATZ (ALLEMAGNE) PRÉSENTÉ EN ALLEMAND AVEC SURTITRES FRANÇAIS ET ANGLAIS
TEXTE DE HENRIK IBSEN, TRADUCTION ALLEMANDE DE HINRICH SCHMIDT-HENKEL (HENSCHEL THEATER VERLAG, BERLIN)
MISE EN SCÈNE DE THOMAS OSTERMEIER

AVEC KAY BARTHOLOMÄUS SCHULZE, ANNEDORE BAUER, LARS EIDINGER, JÖRG HARTMANN, LORE STEFANEK ET KATHARINA SCHÜTTLER Scénographie : Jan Pappelbaum Costumes : Nina Wetzel Éclairages : Erich Schneider Musique : Malte Beckenbach Dramaturge : Marius von Mayenburg Vidéo : Sébastien Dupouey

BILLETTERIE DU CNA   TARIFS DE GROUPE   BUZZ endirect   90.7   ticketmaster.ca
lundi-samedi 10 h à 21 h   613-947-7000 x384   613-755-1111

HIPPOCAMPE
PASCAL BRULLEMANS / ERIC JEAN

AU STUDIO À 20 H
TEXTE DE PASCAL BRULLEMANS, EN COLLABORATION AVEC ERIC JEAN ET LES ARTISTES
MISE EN SCÈNE D'ERIC JEAN

AVEC DOMINIC ANCTIL, MURIEL DUTIL, ANNE-SYLVIE GOSSELIN, DOMINIQUE QUESNEL, ISABELLE LAMONTAGNE, GAÉTAN NADEAU ET SACHA SAMAR Scénographie : Magalie Amyot Costumes : Stéphanie Cloutier Éclairages : Étienne Boucher Conception sonore : Jean-François Pedno Maquillages et coiffures : Angelo Barsetti Un spectacle du THÉÂTRE DE L'UTOPIE

BILLETTERIE DU CNA   TARIFS DE GROUPE   BUZZ endirect   90.7   ticketmaster.ca
lundi-samedi 10 h à 21 h   613-947-7000 x384   613-755-1111

Hand-drawn, black letter-forms and line illustrations, dynamically cropped and composed, are extremely expressive visual elements communicating the intense, emotional, and araw power of each of these theatrical productions—*Une Fête pour Boris*, *Hedda Gabler*, *Hippocampe*, and *Woyzeck*.

LAURENT PINABEL
Montreal, Quebec, Canada

These unusual, unconventional, and highly expressive hand-built letterforms spell out the statement "Good Work" and are composed of drawing pencils—a clear and meaningful message for any designer who values the interconnection between the "medium and the message."

JASON TAM
Brooklyn, New York, USA

the quality of these elements and principles is perceived solely through the expression of the total message.

Imagery, such as photography and illustration, is the most powerful form of visual expression. When used in combination with typography, color, and other relevant design elements, it can create a distinct and memorable message that will always be associated with a specific human emotion. Understanding form, shape, line, space, and color is also essential to visual expression. With these tools, a graphic designer can fully embrace, as well as explore, new concepts, technologies, materials, and styles with confidence and assurance.

Unlike narrative form in which words are organized in a specific sequence to form sentences, visual expression provides a range of forms, symbols, and ideas with malleable meanings. It can help graphic designers achieve greater power and influence in their craft and discipline—a power to inform, educate, and/or persuade a single person or collective audience in a meaningful and memorable way.

A series of bold and expressive monochromatic textures are used as simple and unique visual metaphors for capturing the spirit and flavors of Mijovi and each of its products. Combined with bold sans serif lowercase typography and bright saturated colors, this packaging not only stands out among the overcrowded shelves of competing products but also communicates the essential brand message of this line of beverages. The imagery is metaphorically derived and symbolizes the spirit of individuality, energy, and ultimate self-expression.

POULIN + MORRIS INC.
New York, New York, USA

ab·strac·tion \ab-'strak-shən, əb-\ *n*

1: considered apart from concrete existence

2: not applied or practical; theoretical

3: having intellectual and affective artistic content that depends solely on intrinsic form rather than on narrative content or pictorial representation

17

"A designer knows that he has achieved perfection not when there is nothing left to add, but when there is nothing left to take away."

ANTOINE DE SAINT-EXUPÉRY (1900–1944), *French, Author*

Abstraction is independent of our visual world. It is an illusion of our own visible reality and solely a sensory experience. In graphic design, abstraction provides us with alternative ways of communicating visual messages containing specific facts and experiences. It is a visual language that does

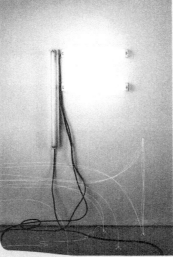

Simplification and distillation of letterforms using different light fixtures and bulbs is the primary visual metaphor for this promotional poster announcing an American Institute of Architects San Diego-sponsored conference. The conference title, "If Not, Then When?" spelled out in an abstract manner further conveys the theme of the conference, which explores how the practice of architecture is being transformed in the twenty-first century.

MENDE DESIGN
San Francisco, California, USA

not rely upon the literal nature of things—familiar and identifiable to us in our own world. Relying on an abstract visual language can reshape the familiar into the expressive. It is free from objective content, context, and meaning. It can be symbolic, interpretive, imaginary, impressionistic, nonrepresentational, nonobjective, or nonfigurative.

Historical References

Abstraction is not a twentieth-century phenomenon. It has been a part of our visual language since early mankind. From naïve (continued on page 173)

The abstract outline of a heart in this symbol suggests a human-centered approach to healthcare, beyond the traditional realms of science, chemistry, and manufacturing for the pharmaceutical company Kyorin. Continuing this human viusal metaphor, the center of the symbol is an "inner smile."

C+G PARTNERS LLC
New York, New York, USA

Nightwood Book Cover
ALVIN LUSTIG
New York, New York, USA

One of the most prolific collaborations between a graphic designer and client in twentieth-century American design was the one shared by ALVIN LUSTIG (1915–1955) and the progressive publisher New Directions Books in the 1940s and 1950s. During this time period, Lustig designed dozens of groundbreaking book covers and jackets for the Modern Reader and New Classics book series for New Directions.

A designer, writer, and educator in Los Angeles and New York City, Lustig was one of the first designers to approach his craft and profession in a nonspecialized manner. He believed that all design was a matter of form and content and that the role of the designer was that of a synthesizer, not of a style maker. His diverse work included books, book jackets, advertisements, magazines, trademarks, letterheads, catalogs, record albums, sign systems, furniture, textile design, interior design, product design, and architecture.

Lustig's first New Directions book covers began as an experiment with geometric patterns, but soon he was adapting forms familiar to him from his knowledge of modern painting. Within a few years, Lustig was incorporating biomorphic glyphs or what he called symbolic "marks" that recalled the work of abstract modernist painters such as Paul Klee, Joan Miró, Clifford Still, and Mark Rothko. His most striking and memorable book jackets combined modern typography with complex fields of line, shape, form, color, texture, and image.

He explained, "The primary intention in designing the book jackets of the New Directions series was to establish for each book a quickly grasped, abstract symbol of its contents that would be sheer force of form and color, attract and inform the eye.

Such a symbol is a matter of distillation, a reduction of the book to its simplest terms of mood or idea. The spirit of the book cannot be expressed by naturalistic representation of episodes or by any preconceived formal approach, but can only develop naturally from its own nature."

The reliance on modernist visual form was a means of communicating the book publisher's commitment to an intellectual literary tradition distinct from the mainstream—a new and sophisticated visual language that at once created and affirmed New Directions' place within a highly competitive and overcrowded market.

Lustig's visionary "distillation" of form and image developed into a complex, abstract, efficient, and resolutely modern visual language, simplified yet never simplistic, unique yet never forgettable.

Alvin Lustig and New Directions

This book cover series for a set of Irvine Welsh novels uses abstracted illustrations to further enhance the graphic design of each cover as well as convey the raw, emotional themes of each book. Saturated colors, bold sans serif, all cap letterforms, and textures collectively add power and impact to the expressive qualities of these cover compositions.

JAMUS MARQUETTE,
Student
KEVIN BRAINARD, Instructor
School of Visual Arts
New York, New York, USA

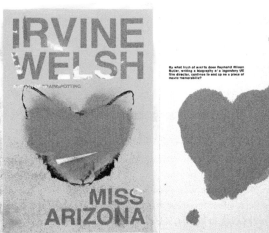

graphic gestures found in prehistoric cave paintings and stylized hieroglyphs in Egyptian funereal tombs to graphic emblems used in medieval science, heraldry, and religious rituals, abstraction is an integral design principle in all of these visual forms.

Levels of Abstraction

Abstract visual language is created by simplifying and distilling form and content. It depends solely upon its own intrinsic form rather than on narrative content or pictorial representation. A graphic designer who relies upon abstraction as a means to communicate a visual message also requires the viewer to connect immediately, intuitively, and emotionally with that same message.

There are different degrees or levels of abstraction in visual communications, from the least abstract to the most abstract.

For example, a photographic image (closer to a true representation than any other image type, such as illustration) has the lowest level of abstraction, since it only replicates the actual content or meaning of the actual image. Exact duplication of the reality represented in a photographic image is not possible because that reality is distorted as soon as the photographer takes

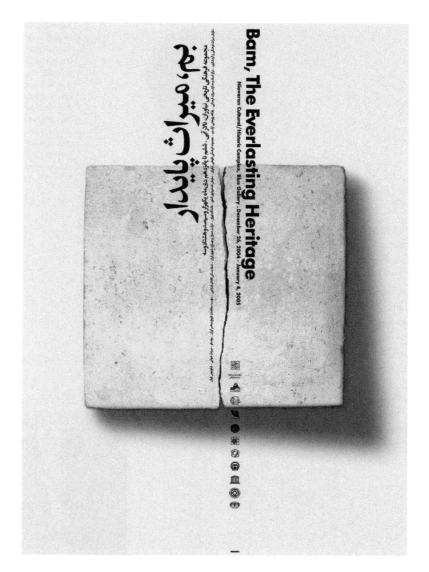

The cracked slab of limestone used in this poster is an abstract visual metaphor representing the legendary city of Bam and its citadel located in southern Iran, which was among the world's most famous architectural landmarks. In 2003, an earthquake destroyed the city and caused the death of more than 40,000 people. For the first anniversary of this earthquake, this promotional poster announced an exhibition and conference on the potential renovation of the city.

DID GRAPHICS INC.
Tehran, Iran

The mission of Amphibian Stage Productions, a theatrical production company, is to produce "innovative and engaging" theatrical works that challenge the way people see the world around them. This brand identity draws from abstract amphibian forms and patterns used to create a visual vocabulary appealing to all theatergoers —young and old.

ALFALFA STUDIO LLC
New York, New York, USA

the photo, as well as in the viewer's visual perception and interpretation of that photographic image.

The next level of abstraction is not based on reality or any recognizable form, but is represented by signs or something else to communicate a visual message. Letterforms, numbers, punctuation, and words are all signs—representations or visual expressions of written and verbal language.

The highest level of abstraction is evident in glyphs, pictograms, and symbols. These graphic forms are more abstract than signs because their meaning can be (contined on page 177)

The typography in this theatrical poster for a production of Shakespeare's *Macbeth* has been abstracted to a certain degree to imply a towering castlelike wall enclosing an environment that will have to be breached and broken down, but it still maintains an immediate identity for the title of the play. Color, typographic form, exaggerated scale, contrast, and proportion all add to the overwhelmingly dark and serious tone of this message.

CATHERINE ZASK
Paris, France

Meet Girls:

Approaching women is easy. Confidently walk up and say hi.

There's no need to be anxious or nervous, just be yourself and let

your bravado shine. Humor is always a great way to break the ice.

You Will Mingle:

Mingling at any party is easy and fun. You'll be pleasantly surprised

how interested others will be in you and what you have to say.

Just relax and go with the flow. Everyone is there to have a good time

and not to be judgemental.

Both of these posters, titled *You Will Mingle* and *Meet Girls*, use expressive abstractions of a person's eye and head to communicate the potential intensity and anxiety one can feel when considering these two natural yet uncomfortable social situations. Supporting typography functions as a narrative counterpoint to each visual representation.

JASON LYNCH, Student
WILLIAM MORRISEY,
Instructor
School of Visual Arts
New York, New York, USA

This series of stylized graphic variations for Alfred A. Knopf Publishers' classic Borzoi dog symbol uses visual simplification, interpretation, and levels of abstraction as a means to update and provide alternative graphic choices when incorporating the symbol on various book titles and spines.

TRIBORO DESIGN
SOLUTIONS
Brooklyn, New York, USA

An abstract human form made from found objects—threads and a button—and represented in a manner that is both lyrical and dancelike becomes a powerful and memorable figurative icon for this poster announcing a spring dance concert. Custom-drawn, lowercase letterforms identifying "open source" are also abstracted, evoking visual qualities similar to the reductive human form directly below this titling.

CHEMI MONTES DESIGN
Arlington, Virginia, USA

interpreted by the viewer on many levels. Symbols are not realistic in graphic form but represent concepts and ideas, which may be reflected spiritually, socially, politically, sexually, or culturally. For example, a triangle can represent inspiration, the gay-rights movement, or oppression in Nazi Germany during World War II.

Total abstraction bears no trace of any visual reference to anything recognizable. For example, color is completely free of objective representation and is a fully abstract visual form.

Using abstraction in visual communications provides the graphic designer with a broad palette of graphic form that has no concrete meaning yet can evoke powerful, memorable, and meaningful visual messages and responses.

In this promotional poster for an "orchestrated performance" by Henri Meschonnic, a French essayist, poet, and theorist of language, the primary image is of a man reduced and abstracted to a soft and illusive visual gesture. It appears figurative and, at the same time, not figurative. It is unfamiliar, yet engaging. Sans serif typography oriented on a vertical axis also acts as a strong counterpoint and frame for this image, giving it added strength and presence on the page.

CATHERINE ZASK
Paris, France

tone \ˈtōn\ *n*

7 a 1: color quality or value

7 a 2: tint or shade of color **b:** the color that appreciably modifies a hue or white or black

tone

18

"Every moment of light and dark is a miracle."
WALT WHITMAN (1819-1892), *American, Essayist, Journalist, Poet*

In visual communications, tone (also identified as value or shade) means the degree of lightness or darkness apparent on the surface of an object. Tone is also the relative degree of a color's lightness or darkness—its content of black or white. It can be characterized by the degree of light that

Muted tones of color, pattern, and typography are used as visual, figurative textures to further enhance the identity program for Ödün, a Mexico City restaurant featuring cuisines from China, Thailand, Japan, Vietnam, and other Asian countries. The overall identity, as well as its broad palette of tones, colors, and patterns, was inspired by a diversity of flavors, scents, and spirits found throughout Asian cultures.

BLOK DESIGN
Mexico City, Mexico

falls on an object and how it is then reflected, and ultimately perceived. It is also one of the most important principles in visual communication because it helps define an object's size, form, and position relative to orientation and composition.

Because the majority of our perceptible world is defined by color, it is critical that we understand its characteristics and effects.

Characteristics
Tone gives a composition unique characteristics that cannot be achieved with flat color. These visual characteristics are spatial depth, texture, and movement. Tone can also increase visual impact in a powerful and immediate way or create extreme visual restraint and nuance that is still obvious and palatable to the eye of the viewer.

Color is an absolute presence in our visual world; therefore, it is extremely difficult to extract the characteristic of chroma or hue from all of its other qualities.

Value
A tone (or shade) is a color to which black or another dark color or hue has been added to make it darker, thereby tending to make (continued on page 182)

Experimenta typographica
WILLEM SANDBERG
Amsterdam, Holland

WILLEM SANDBERG (1897–1984) was a Dutch typographer and graphic designer, as well as a unique presence in the Dutch cultural world during the 1940s and 1950s.

He was born in Amersfoot, Holland, and studied art at the State Academy of Art in Amsterdam. As a young man, he served as a printer's apprentice in Herrliberg, Switzerland. In 1927, he studied in Vienna and then at the Bauhaus in Dessau. Following his return to Amsterdam, he worked as a graphic designer until he was appointed deputy director of the Stedelijk Museum in Amsterdam in 1938.

His main sources of inspiration were Hendrik Werman and Piet Zwart, both groundbreaking Dutch typographers whose pioneering work abandoned the tenets of conventional symmetry. Sandberg also initially agreed with the "neue typographie" of Jan Tschichold and began to incorporate lowercase typographic characters and unjustified text in the majority of his work.

During World War II, Sandberg became a wartime hero as the only surviving member of a Dutch resistance group that in 1943 burned down Amsterdam's Municipal Office of Records in protest against the administration of the Nazi government.

After Europe's liberation in 1945, Sandberg became the director of the Stedelijk Museum. It was at the Stedelijk that he personally designed hundreds of its catalogs and posters, providing the museum with a unique brand and identity. As a designer, he produced innovative work characterized by the use of bold type, vivid colors, textured papers, and signature torn-paper forms.

From 1943 to 1945, while hiding from the Germans and working for the underground resistance, Sandberg produced the basis for *Experimenta typographica*, a series of print experiments in form, space, and tone presented in eighteen short, mostly handmade, books that were finally published in the 1950s and subsequently inspired his later work. These experiments included unjustified text settings and sentence fragments composed freely, with varying type weights and styles for visual interest or emphasis. They are void of symmetry and use bright colors, strong contrasts, and subtle tones for rhythm and pacing. Crisp sans serif typography is combined with large-scale, torn-paper, collaged letterforms with rough, irregular edges.

These sensitive explorations of compositional tone and space became enormously influential among a generation of graphic designers, as well as becoming the basis for many of Sandberg's later Stedelijk Museum catalogs, which were seen and then imitated around the world.

His body of work was a provocative marriage of the "neue typographie" combined with the expressive freedom of surrealism and the inevitable compromises of a wartime Europe.

Willem Sandberg and *Experimenta typographica*

In this series of brochures and posters for a regional theater and arts center, titled *Lux*, lighter, intense tints of color are used as tonal textures and patterns that provide a visually rich and animated series of background layers for the typographic information running throughout these collateral print promotions.

HELMO
Montreuil, France

ZERO
DECIBELS
THE
QUEST
FOR
ABSOLUTE
SILENCE
GEORGE
MICHELSEN
FOY

it more neutral in color. For example, black added to green creates a darker shade of green. Value changes in pure colors or hues are called shades and tints. This can be more clearly understood by viewing these variables on a color wheel.

Toning (or shading) shows changes from light to dark or dark to light in a composition by darkening areas that would be shadowed and by leaving other areas light. The blending of one value into another is also identified as feathering or gradient. Toning is often used to produce the illusion of dimension, volume, and depth.

The subtle, muted tone of the photographic image on this book cover for *Zero Decibels: The Quest for Absolute Silence* is used as a visual metaphor for silence, with an intent that it can be read and understood, but just barely. The added restraint of the serif typography, with its extreme thick and thin stroke nuances, adds a quiet presence to this message.

MOTHER DESIGN
New York, New York, USA

Graduated Color Wheel

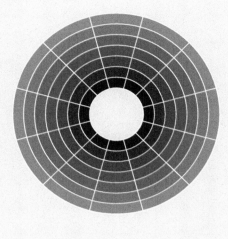

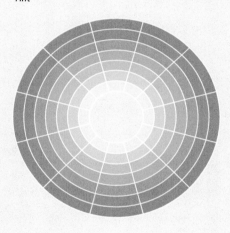

Graduated Color Wheel

Each hue is shown here in a progressive or graduated series of values (tints and shades). Note that the point of greatest saturation is the same for each hue. Yellow is of greatest intensity toward the lighter end of the scale, while blue is more intense in the darker zone. Use a graduated color wheel to look for combinations that are similar in value or saturation, and to build contrasting relationships.

Tone

These color tonal wheels demonstrate changes in saturation and value by adding or subtracting black, white, or gray. When white is added to a bright red, the value is lighter and the resulting color is less saturated. Adding black to a bright red results in a dark red closer to the neutral scale because of saturation changes. If gray is added, the saturation is lowered but the value is unchanged.

Saturation/Chroma

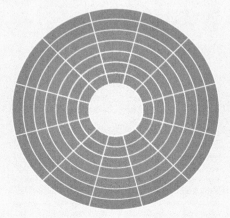

These three identity variations for the financial group Liquid Capital use a single color with related light and dark tones of that same color to further convey movement and diversity in their various organizations. Greens are used for markets, magentas for securities, and for the overall group—a range of oranges. This tonal concept is further reinforced and represented in the financial group's brand positioning photography—dynamic images that support the group's key brand messages.

JOG LIMITED
London, United Kingdom

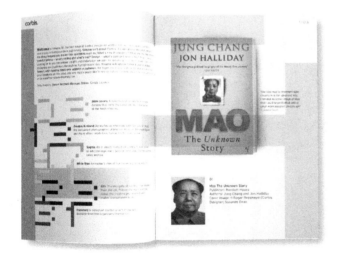

Volume magazine, a sales tool specifically designed for the image library, Corbis, to communicate with its book publishing clients, showcases recently designed book covers and publications using Corbis-based imagery. The visual diversity of this work is furthered accentuated by the framing and displaying of each cover or publication on a variety of background patterns. Each spread, activated with a different, distinct tone or shade, is actually an overscaled fragment of a customdesigned, pixilated letterform. These structured letterforms symbolize a digital age in which most publications are now designed and set electronically using pixels rather than picas.

JOG LIMITED
London, United Kingdom

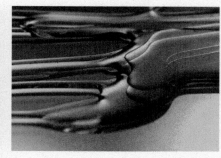

LIQUID CAPITAL
SECURITIES

LIQUID CAPITAL
MARKETS

LIQUID CAPITAL
GROUP

Types and Effects

In color theory, a tint is the mixture of a color with white, increasing its lightness, and a shade is the mixture of a color with black, reducing its lightness. Mixing a color with any neutral color, including black and white, reduces its chroma or colorfulness, while its hue remains unchanged.

A tone can also be gray or what is called a midtone. It is identified as achromatic and is mixed from black to white. Tones can range from light to dark values in a gray scale. Grays can flatten and minimize the brilliance of any pure color or hue. Darker grays also affect color or hue in a way similar

A variety of subtle tones are used in this promotional poster for a jazz ensemble performance titled "A Tribute to Kind of Blue" at American University. The poster's composition, as well as its use of different color tints and shades, reinforces the identity and meaning of jazz in American culture as a diverse, multifaceted, multilayered, musical experience.

CHEMI MONTES DESIGN
Falls Church, Virginia, USA

A range of light- and dark-colored tonal values and layers on these notebook covers provides a strong visual dynamic, spatial depth, and kinetic movement to these swirling, curvilinear color compositions.

ADAMSMORIOKA INC.
Beverly Hills, California, USA

Line illustration and hand lettering for this poster, *Les Aventures de Lagardére*, are further strengthened by the effective use of a monochromatic color palette—an intense, vibrant red paired with a darker tone of the same color. Here tone simulates the presence of another color, thereby adding volume and depth to the overall composition.

LAURENT PINABEL
Montreal, Quebec, Canada

to black; lighter grays affect color or hue in a way similar to white. For example, a tone mixed with yellow produces a rich, colorful, earth tone that resembles ochre and umber.

Monochromatic tone is a single color mixed with either a tint, shade, or tone. This type of color scheme can effectively simulate the presence of other colors or hues through use of tone and its effects on individual and distinct colors.

In theory, there are an almost infinite number of value gradations between true black and true white. The contrast between these two extremes is mitigated by midtones, from the palest to the darkest of grays.

It is due to these primary factors that tone is a valuable conceptual and compositional element in visual communications.

The identity and branding for the Microsoft Store, a square divided into four smaller squares, uses tones or tints of quadratic colors—red, green, yellow, and blue. This reliance on tints provides this symbol with depth, dimension, and visual activity. Variations on this same monochromatic theme of color and tone are used in environmental graphics and promotional elements, reinforcing the visual language of this program, as well as symbolizing the diversity of the company in a retail environment.

COLLINS
New York, New York, USA

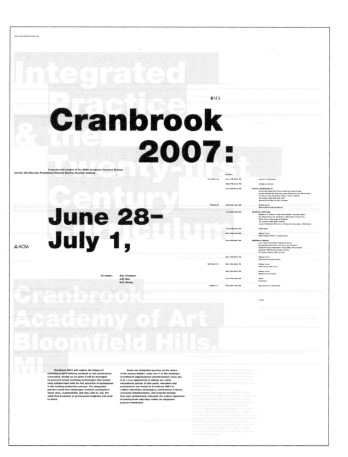

Intense color and tone is effectively used as a secondary informational layer to this poster announcing a series of educational programs at the Cranbrook Academy of Art. Sans serif typography set in various scales and contrasting colors, paired with figure-ground, allows the reader to change focus in an immediate manner, allowing easy access to layers of information.

JACK HENRIE FISHER
Brussels, Belgium

con·trast \'kän-,trast\ *n*
1 a: juxtaposition of dissimilar
elements (as color, tone, or emotion)
in a work of art

19

"There are dark shadows on the earth, but its lights are stronger in the contrast."

CHARLES DICKENS (1812-1870), *British, Author*

Contrast is a visual principle that fundamentally provides the eye with a noticeable difference between two things or objects—large and small, red and green, light and dark, or hot and cold. In visual communications, contrast is the perceptible difference in visual characteristics that makes

These notebook covers effectively use the design principle of contrast to present a graphic message that is powerful, and immediate. The bold use of pure geometric shapes, textures, figure–ground, and letterforms, further strengthen this concept.

ADAMSMORIOKA INC.
Beverly Hills, California, USA

an object (or its representation in an image) distinguishable and distinct from other objects in a composition as well as its surrounding background. Contrast in a composition is the opposite of visual harmony.

It can be achieved by exaggerating the visual differences in size, shape, color, and texture between compositional elements, thereby enhancing and making a message more immediate and understandable to a viewer. Contrast can draw and direct attention, create a mood or emotion, and create hierarchy and emphasis in complex information in any visual message.

(continued on page 192)

The extreme scale, cropping, and juxtaposition of these fluid, calligraphic letterforms, placed in counterpoint to formal serif typography and articulated in a stark black-and-white palette, provide dynamic contrasts that create tension, movement, and visual impact to each and every one of the spreads in this promotional brochure for Colour Cosmetica.

VOICE
Adelaide, Australia

Emil Ruder: Typography Book Cover
EMIL RUDER
Basel, Switzerland

EMIL RUDER (1914–1970) was a Swiss typographer, graphic designer, author, and educator instrumental in starting the Allegmeine Gewerbeschule (Basel School of Design), as well as developing the International Typographic Style or the Swiss School.

As a young man, he studied in Paris and trained as a typesetter in Zurich. In 1929, at the age of fifteen, he began a four-year compositor's apprenticeship and attended the Zurich School of Arts and Crafts.

In 1948, Ruder met the artist-printer Armin Hofmann, and they began a long period of collaboration and teaching that achieved an international reputation by the mid-1950s.

Ruder was also a writer and published a basic grammar of typography titled *Emil Ruder: Typography*, which was published in German, English, and French in 1967. This groundbreaking book helped spread and propagate the International Typographic Style and became a basic text for graphic design and typography throughout Europe and the United States.

The International Typographic Style was defined by sans serif typefaces and employed a rigorous page grid for structure that produced asymmetrical layouts. Its philosophy and tenets evolved directly from the de Stijl movement, the Bauhaus, and Jan Tschichold's New Typography.

In Ruder's work, as well as in his teachings, he called for all graphic designers to find an appropriate balance in contrasts between form and function. He believed that typography loses its function and communicative value when it loses its narrative meaning. He further believed that typography's primary role in any visual composition is legibility and readability. A careful and critical analysis of visual contrasts, or the contrast of macro and micro, was essential to understanding both of these parameters—the negative, or white, space of the page and the negative, or white, space of letter and word forms, such as counters, letter spacing, and word spacing.

Ruder stated, "Typography has one plain duty before it and that is to convey information in writing. No argument or consideration can absolve typography from this duty."

He also promoted an overall, systematic approach to the design of page layout and the use of complex, structured grids to bring all compositional page elements into a unified, cohesive whole while still allowing for contrasting variations in narrative and visual and content.

Emil Ruder and Typographie

These Eastern European-inspired labels and packaging for Slavko, an alcoholic beverage line, was created using contrasts in color, scale, typography, and graphic form. Bold, inline letterforms layered with high contrast, posterized imagery, and bright, saturated colors all give increased visual emphasis, weight, and prominence to this branding program.

LG2BOUTIQUE
Montreal, Quebec, Canada

Comparative Relationships

Contrast is the comparative relationship between light and dark. Many other types of contrast in visual communications refer to comparative relationships or juxtapositions between two or more compositional elements. These juxtapositions can be positive and negative, geometric and organic, organized and chaotic, smooth and rough, static and kinetic, and large and small.

Contrasting relationships can be further articulated by combining elements to achieve variety and unity. Here, the ultimate challenge is to create a composition made up of disparate elements that work together as one orchestrated whole. Contrasting size,

Contrast between black-and-white letterforms and hand-written script, as well as contrast in scale of graphic forms and textures, provides visual drama and excitement to this poster promoting a performance by the world-renowned mime Marcel Marceau. The emblematic use of a simple black-and-white palette, the dynamic cropping of the graphic hands as if they were moving beyond the edges of the poster, and the pure representation of the performer's face as a visual anchor and frame for the title of the performance all add to this series of visual contrasts found in this active and impactful composition.

TAKASHI KUSUI, Student
KEVIN BRAINARD, Instructor
School of Visual Arts
New York, New York, USA

weight, direction, value, color, texture, and form can all add effective and meaningful visual interest by allowing one element to contrast and complement the other.

For example, a serpentine curve appears more curvilinear when it is close to an extremely orthogonal and straight element. A color such as red will always appear redder when it is adjacent to or surrounded by its complementary color—green.

Characteristics and Functions

Contrast can create emphasis by establishing juxtaposition with compositional elements to stress their visual differences. For example, bright colors juxtaposed with dark colors,

Solid black fields layered over existing textural elements and intense colors of a tabloid newspaper create a highly distinctive contrast for this publication celebrating the ten-year anniversary of a contemporary art museum in Bregenz, Austria. Large-scale, sans serif letterforms and blocks of narrative text are knocked out of these black fields, allowing existing backgrounds of the newspaper to show through and provide ample contrast for immediacy and readability of specific information.

SAGMEISTER INC.
New York, New York, USA

angular shapes with curvilinear shapes, and minuscule elements with monumental elements can create visual excitement and emphasis, as well as direct attention to focal points in a composition and organize hierarchal orders in a visual message.

Contrast creates emphasis, importance, weight, or dominance for an element of a composition. A composition lacking contrast may result in visual monotony, neutrality, and even confusion.

Types of Contrast

Contrast effectively uses opposing design elements such as tone, color, and shape in a composition to produce an intensified, visual effect. For example, chiaroscuro (Italian for "light-dark") in fine art and photography is characterized by strong tonal contrasts between light and dark. It is also a technical term used by artists and art historians for using contrast of light and dark or tone to achieve a sense of volume in modeling three-dimensional form such as the human body.

Since we live in a world of color, using it as a contrasting force can immediately be understood by the viewer when conveying or emphasizing differences among visual

This logotype for Terence Higgins Trust's HIV campaign in the United Kingdom draws visual attention with the effective use of extreme contrast. A vibrant red symbolizing the potential nature of a person's HIV status is set against flanking monolithic black letterforms, creating a dramatic focus to the powerful impact of HIV throughout our society.

FELTON COMMUNICATION
London, United Kingdom

THIVK®

In this promotional poster for a symposium on "impure architecture" held at the Guggenheim Museum in New York City, the fundamental design principle of contrast is used as a conceptual and visual cue for the design and composition of the entire poster. An unconventional, angular axis is used to organize and display typographic information that varies in content, scale, character, figure-ground, alignment, and texture.

SUPERMETRIC
New York, New York, USA

Simple, obvious contrasts of large and small, black and white, and serious and playful are all evident in the interpretive graphics for a Tim Burton retrospective exhibition at the Museum of Modern Art in New York City. For example, Burton's hand lettering is juxtaposed with formal san serif typography used for an introductory career timeline, and a large-scale, spiraling floor graphic directs itself onto an introductory entry wall while simultaneously underlining the exhibition title Tim Burton, shown in his own smaller-scale, restrained hand lettering.

JULIA HOFFMANN
New York, New York, USA

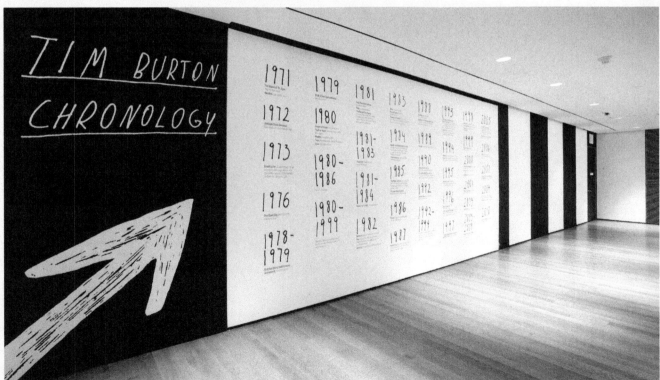

This memorable poster celebrating Fritz Gottschalk's seventieth birthday is a study in graphic simplicity, visual immediacy, and linear contrast. A segment of the crisp, evenly continuous outline of the universal cross symbol found in the Swiss flag is abruptly ragged and irregular, reconfigured to create a letterform. The designer literally tore off the left side of the cross and recomposed it into an *F* for Fritz. Here, the simple transformation of graphic form is further realized with contrasts in line, shape, color, and letterform.

CARBONE SMOLAN AGENCY
New York, New York, USA

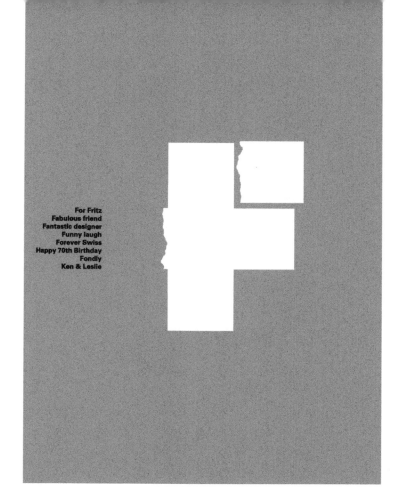

For Fritz
Fabulous friend
Fantastic designer
Funny laugh
Forever Swiss
Happy 70th Birthday
Fondly
Ken & Leslie

elements in a wide variety of messages and compositions. Distinct, contrasting shapes can also produce striking reactions from the viewer. For example, a conventional shape appears more conventional and normal when an irregular, nonconventional shape is present in the same composition.

Contrast can exist on many obvious and subtle levels in a composition. The human eye can simultaneously detect contrasts in scale, value, shape, direction, and surface. It can also clarify and strengthen any visual message by providing stability and clarity to the cohesiveness of a composition, draw the eye's attention to a specific area, and affect a figure–ground relationship by maximizing or minimizing its visual immediacy.

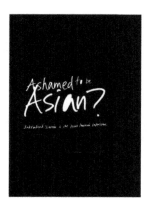

In this editorial spread titled "Ashamed to be Asian?" dynamic contrasts appear between its compositional elements—the figure–ground of black and white; the free-form character of letterforms and the sharp, cutout lines of illustrations; the intense and muted colors of the figurative illustration; and the scale of large and small elements.

TAMMI CHAN, Student
CHRISTOPHER AUSTOPCHUK, Instructor
School of Visual Arts
New York, New York, USA

fig·ure–ground \ˈfi-gyər ˈgraŭnd\ n
1 a: relating to or being the relationships between the parts of a perceptual field which is perceived as divided into a part consisting of figures having form and standing out from the part comprising the background and being relatively formless

f. figure–ground

20

"Everything we see hides another thing; we always want to see what is hidden by what we see."

RENE MAGRITTE (1898-1967), *Belgian, Painter*

Figure–ground is primarily the visual relationship between the foreground and background of a composition. This relationship between figure and ground is one of the primary principles of visual perception and visual communications. Related design elements of shape and contrast have a critical

The symbol for "Peace One Day," a public awareness campaign for global cease-fires and nonviolence, relies upon an ambiguous figure–ground relationship between a dove's wing and a profile of a person's face to further reinforce that we are directly connected to one another and ultimate peace in the world. In this compositional relationship, the symbol's positive figure—a silhouette of a dove with an outstretched wing—and its negative ground, a side profile of a person's face, are one and the same.

JEANELLE MAK
New York, New York, USA

direct effect on how a figure and its ground interact with one another. Figure–ground relationships also refer to the optical phenomenon that occurs when specific design elements in any composition appear to move forward or recede. For example, the page that you are currently reading contains typographic text and images that constitute "figure," and the book's white paper constitutes "ground." How and to what degree these two compositonal elements interact, creating either tension or harmony, is fully determined by the graphic designer and ultimately will contribute to the success or failure of this (continued on page 202)

This circular symbol for **APA Technologies,** a manufacturer of watches that monitor ultraviolet rays, uses figure-ground to create a dual visual effect. Lines radiate from the symbol's center representing the Sun, as well as create narrow triangular shapes that move inward bringing attention to the product name.

WINK
Minneapolis, Minnesota, USA

1931

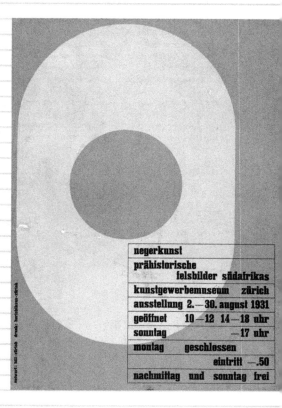

negerkunst
prähistorische
felsbilder südafrikas
kunstgewerbemuseum zürich
ausstellung 2.—30. august 1931
geöffnet 10—12 14—18 uhr
sonntag —17 uhr
montag geschlossen
eintritt —.50
nachmittag und sonntag frei

MAX BILL (1908–1994), born in Winterthur, Switzerland, was an architect, painter, typographer, industrial designer, engineer, sculptor, educator, and graphic designer.

Bill was initially a student at the Kunstgewerbeschule and apprenticed as a silversmith before beginning his studies in 1927 at the Bauhaus in Dessau, Germany, with teachers such as Wassily Kandinsky, Paul Klee, and Oskar Schlemmer.

He permanently settled in Zurich, Switzerland, in 1929, and in 1937 became involved with a group of Swiss artists and designers named the Allianz. The Allianz group advocated the concrete theories of art and design and included Max Huber, Leo Leuppi, and Richard Paul Lohse.

In 1950, Max Bill and Otl Aicher founded the Ulm School of Design (Hochschule fur Gestaltung-HfG Ulm) in Ulm, Germany, a design school initially created in the tradition of the Bauhaus and that later developed a new design education approach integrating art and science. Bill served as the school's director from 1951 to 1956. Ulm is notable for its inclusion of semiotics, the philosophical theory of signs and symbols, as a field of study. Faculty and students included Tomas Maldonado, Josef Albers, Johannes Itten, John Lottes, Otl Aicher, Walter Zeischegg, and Peter Seitz.

Bill was the single most decisive influence on Swiss graphic design or the International Typographic Style, beginning in the 1950s with his theoretical writing and progressive work. He said, "It is possible to develop an art largely on the basis of mathematical thinking."

From 1967 to 1971, he was a professor at the Staatliche Hochschule fur Bildende Kunste in Hamburg and chair of environmental design.

As a graphic designer, he fully and enthusiastically embraced the tenets and philosophical views of this modernist movement. The majority of his graphic work is based solely on cohesive visual principles of organization and composed of purist forms—modular grids, san serif typography, asymmetric compositions, linear spatial divisions, mathematical progressions, and dynamic figure–ground relationships.

His powerful use of figure–ground relationships is never more evident than with his exhibition poster, designed in 1931, for the Kunstgewerbemuseum in Zurich, Switzerland. The poster's figure–ground is its primary compositional principle; its bright white figure is asymmetrically located and set against a muted-tone background. The pure geometry of the figure's inner circle is a powerful focal point further offset by the pure linear square containing information on the exhibition.

Max Bill and Swiss Modernism

This assignment is a study of unit, structure, pattern, and figure–ground created in the repetition of a single, cropped letterform. Students start with a basic compositional exercise involving a black letterform on a white surface, cropping away pieces of the letterform within a 20 cm (7.8-inch) square. These initial letterform compositions are used to generate patterns of four and then sixteen units within a predetermined grid system. Attention is given to the complexity of figure–ground relationships within each pattern. Color is introduced in the final stage of the assignment as students explore further means to enhance pattern, rhythm, and figure–ground relationships.

ERINI FAHIM, SEHYR AHMAD, OMAR MOHAMED, Students
AMIR BERBIC, RODERICK GRANT, Instructors
American University of Sharjah
Sharjah, United Arab Emirates

chapter, as well as the reader's interaction with and understanding of this narrative and visual information.

Definition of Elements

Design elements in any composition are perceived as either figure (objects or focus) or ground (the remaining background or the rest of the perceptual compositional field).

It is also critical to remember that ground, or the space surrounding a figure, is also a shape. Shapes can exist independently as well as overlap each other, depending on the specific figure–ground relationship of a composition.

Figure is also considered a positive compositional element, while the space, or ground, around it is considered opposite and a negative compositional element. Each is dependent upon the other—it is impossible to change one without affecting the other. Creating dynamic relationships between positive and negative is the cornerstone of well-resolved visual compositions.

Figure is a compositional element to which we pay attention. It is also identified as a positive shape in a visual composition. It is defined as the outline, form, or silhouette of

an object. It refers to an active, positive form revealed against a passive, negative ground. In the simplest visual compositions there may be only one figure that the viewer needs to pay attention to. In more complex visual compositions, there may be multiple figures. Familiar, figurative, and representational objects are easy to see and assimilate as figure.

Ground is the surrounding space of an object or compositional element. It is also defined as the negative space in a composition, as well as everything else that is not a figure. As attention shifts from figure to figure, the ground also shifts so that an object can go from figure to ground and back.

Types of Figure–Ground
There are three basic types of figure-ground compositions and relationships:

Simple
A simple figure–ground can be created when a coherent, independent object is juxtaposed in a space that functions as its surrounding ground. The ground can be compressed or shallow, or convey an illusion of depth. In a simple figure–ground composition, the figure is positive and active, whereas its ground is always negative and passive. In this compositional relationship, the figure is clearly visible and separate from its background.

This set of arboreal-based letterforms is the outcome of a student's thorough photographic exploration of letterforms found in nature. It is also a primary representation of a simple figure-ground relationship, one in which the figure's, or in this case the foreground's, darker branches and limbs are positive and active, whereas its ground, or in this case the background's, green textures in the surrounding woodlands are negative and passive.

TAKASHI KUSUI, Student
JI LEE, Instructor
School of Visual Arts
New York, New York, USA

This public awareness campaign's logotype for Terence Higgins Trust's HIV Program in the United Kingdom— "Get It On"—uses the exaggerated negative space or counter of its lowercase *n* for the figure-ground reversal of a symbolic condom.

FELTON COMMUNICATION
London, United Kingdom

This promotional poster, titled *Stealth* and developed for New York City's Studio Museum in Harlem, is an exploration of identity through the use of figure-ground, visual texture, and three-dimensional form. Despite the poster's ultimately becoming a dynamic physical object, its essential message is revealed in its form and is based on a quote from Ralph Ellison's *Invisible Man*—"I am invisible, understand, simply because people refuse to see me." When flat, it reveals this almost invisible typographic statement through the illusion of figure-ground. When folded, the poster's form is evocative of a stealth bomber (hence its name).

THE MAP OFFICE
New York, New York, USA

Reversal

A figure–ground reversal can be created when a figure functions as a ground and ground as figure. This graphic inversion is caused by shapes that form in the spaces located between the parts of the figure, creating the reversal. This type of figure–ground composition can be a dynamic means to activate neutral white space in a visual composition. In a simple figure–ground composition, the borders are perceived as limitless, whereas a figure–ground reversal bounds and limits an image.

This symbol, based on a simple figure-ground relationship, clearly illustrates green trees and brown mountains. However, when arranged as shown, the symbol's white "negative" space framed by the upper and lower "positive" figures create a negative or ground that reads as a *w* for Mountain Woods, a community in rural Colorado.

WINK
Minneapolis, Minnesota, USA

Bold, all-cap sans serif letterforms juxtaposed with delicate handmade letterforms composed of branches and flowers create a dramatic and memorable composition, as well as a simple figure-ground reversal for this brochure cover for the Fort Worth Opera Festival.

THE MATCHBOX STUDIO
Dallas, Texas, USA

Ambiguous

An ambiguous figure-ground composition is created when the graphic relationship between a composition's figure (or object) and ground (or space) is undetectable, yet fully comprehensible. With this type of figure-ground relationship, a pair of objects share the same edge or profile. A classic example of an ambiguous figure-ground relationship is Rubin's vase, developed by psychologist Edgar Rubin. In this image, the black positive space forms two profiles of a human face that appear to be ready to kiss, and the inverse negative space forms a vase. Visually, the eye's concentration on either the black or white alternates between the faces and the vase.

Characteristics

The principle of figure-ground is one of the most basic in visual communications because it refers to our ability to visually separate elements based on contrast—dark and light, black and white, and positive and negative. In the simplest terms, the figure is what we notice and the ground is everything else we tend to not notice.

FORT WORTH OPERA FESTIVAL 2009

This circular symbol for Girard Management, a residential property management company, uses the principle of figure-ground to combine the cap letter *G* with a lockset.

WINK
Minneapolis, Minnesota, USA

An effective and perceptible figure–ground relationship occurs when the eye can identify a figure as an object distinct and separate from its ground or compositional background. This perception is dependent solely on the design principle of contrast.

A composition's figure–ground relationship is clear and stable when the figure receives more attention and immediacy than the ground. When a figure–ground relationship is unstable, the relationship is ambiguous; therefore, the compositional elements can be interpreted in different ways.

Balanced and effective figure–ground relationships animate any composition, adding visual impact and power to its message.

However, when a figure dominates its ground, the effect can be clear but potentially boring. Locating a clearly defined object in the center of a composition leaves no doubt about the subject, but its presentation may lack visual nuance and power.

Ultimately, figure–ground is one of the most important design principles to consider when creating any visual communication. In doing so, graphic designers can further guarantee that the work they are producing will be effective, communicative, memorable, and highly meaningful to the viewer.

This wall mural is an integral storytelling element of the overall visitor exhibit experience at the WTC Tribute Center located fewer than 50 feet (15 m) from Ground Zero directly across from the World Trade Center (WTC) site. Most New Yorkers remember how extraordinarily blue the sky was the morning of 9/11. This 80-foot (24 m) long wall begins as an expanse of blue, appearing like the sky that day, then gradually filling with missing-person posters, stretching from floor to ceiling at the far end of the gallery. This collagelike figure–ground treatment invokes the iconic image of walls all over lower Manhattan covered with posters for weeks after the disaster, as families looked for their missing loved ones.

POULIN + MORRIS INC.
New York, New York, USA

This series of book covers for Albert Camus' *The Stranger*, *The Plague*, and *The Fall* are seminal studies in simple figure–ground relationships fully articulated using fundamental design elements such as point, line, and shape, as well as a stark black-and-white color palette.

JOHN GALL
New York, New York, USA

frame \\'frām\ *n*

1: a closed, often rectangular border of drawn or printed lines

21

"Art consists of limitation. The most beautiful part of every picture is the frame."
G. K. CHESTERTON (1874-1936), *British, Author, Essayist*

In basic terms, a frame is an enclosure to a visual image. It is a fundamental element of visual com-munications and can be used to separate, organize, unify, contain, and distinguish, as well as increase visibility and immediacy in any visual message. Like an actual picture frame, it can take various

The graphic identity for the Toledo Museum of Art uses frame as a graphic representation for the institution as well as an icon that has been an integral element to the presentation and viewing of fine art for centuries. The four words that make up the museum's name help define the edges of the frame's form. The frame also provides views inside the institution by serving as a visual stage for its collections, exhibitions, and cultural activities. Typography anchors and activates the inside perimeter of the frame and is knocked out of it to create a stronger visual dynamic and figure-ground when incorporating and framing other visual elements such as fine art details or images of the exhibitions. The sign system uses the logotype's frame to focus attention on either landmark historic and contemporary architecture or sculpture.

C+G PARTNERS LLC
New York, New York, USA

graphic forms and can be found virtually everywhere. In the familiar world, a frame can set off a work of art from the wall on which it is being displayed and simultaneously bring visual attention to it. In the broadest definition of the word, a frame can be many things and have many functions. It can be a proscenium stage for a theatrical event, an exhibition vitrine for displaying an artifact, or an architectural molding surrounding an entrance door. Frames can be obvious or implied. They can be realized as a border to a page or as an inset solid surface within a page composition.

Characteristics and Functions

As a compositional element, a frame can have a variety of visual characteristics and functions. It can appear simple or decorative, subtle or obvious, flat or modeled. It can be a container for another element as well as act as a transition element from active compositional space to passive compositional space. Its presence in a composition can be subtle, thereby becoming more integrated to its visual content, or it can have extreme graphic presence, ultimately setting content apart in a composition.

(continued on page 212)

A fluid, serpentine linear frame, evocative of ornamental ironwork, captures the fluid hand lettering on this wine label for Calea Nero d'Avola, vintage 2007. The integral graphic relationship of frame to letterform in this composition creates a visual unity that further strengthens the delicate, subtle graphic quality of this wine's brand and identity.

LOUISE FILI LTD.
New York, New York, USA

1955

The Man with the Golden Arm Poster
SAUL BASS
Los Angeles, California, USA

SAUL BASS (1920–1996) was a graphic designer and Academy Award–winning filmmaker who received global recognition for his work in graphic, film, industrial, and exhibition design but was best known for his animated film-title sequences.

During his forty-year career, he worked with some of Hollywood's greatest filmmakers, including Alfred Hitchcock, Otto Preminger, Stanley Kubrick, and Martin Scorsese. His work included the epilogue for *Around the World in Eighty Days* (1956), his direction and editing of the racing sequences for *Grand Prix* (1966), the shower sequence for *Psycho* (1960), and the prologue for *West Side Story* (1961).

Among his most famous film-title sequences are the kinetic typography racing up and down a high-angle view of the United Nations building façade in *North by Northwest* (1959) and the disjointed typography that raced together and then pulled apart for *Psycho*. His later work for Martin Scorsese allowed him to move away from conventional optical techniques he had pioneered earlier and work with computerized titles for films such as *The Age of Innocence* (1993) and *Casino* (1995).

Bass was born in New York City and studied at the Art Students League and then at Brooklyn College with Gyorgy Kepes. He initially began his time in Hollywood designing print advertisements for the film industry, until he collaborated with director Otto Preminger on the design of the poster for the film *Carmen Jones* (1954).

Preminger was so impressed with Bass's work, Bass was asked to produce the title sequence for the film as well. This was Bass's first opportunity to design more than a conventional title sequence and to create something that would ultimately enhance the audience's experience and further contribute to the mood and theme of the film.

Bass was one of the first designers to realize the creative potential of the opening and closing credit sequences of a film, all contained within a fundamental design element—frame. He believed that film-title sequences could "set the mood and the prime underlying core of the film's story, to express the story in some metaphorical way. I saw the title as a way of conditioning the audience, so that when the film actually began, viewers would already have an emotional resonance with it."

His first popular success, for which he became widely known, was with Otto Preminger's film *The Man with the Golden Arm* (1955). The film was about a jazz musician's struggle to overcome heroin addiction, a taboo subject in the 1950s. Here he uses the addict's arm, jagged and distorted, as the central, iconic image. The film's poster is a study on how a frame can be used to bring focus, tension, contrast, and balance to an image that is extremely dynamic and powerful. The film's title sequence featured an animated, black-paper cutout of the same arm used for the poster. As expected, the sequence caused a sensation and became a memorable benchmark for the design of future title sequences.

Saul Bass and The Man with the Golden Arm

A continuous, bold, magenta frame surrounding this poster for the National Theatre School of Canada maintains a visual order and focus to the varied, free-form, and highly expressive illustrative elements used in its composition.

LAURENT PINABEL
Montreal, Quebec, Canada

A frame typically functions as a containment element for an image, setting it apart from its background to give the image more prominence, as well as increase its visibility within a composition. It can also have other functions, such as dividing, cropping, fragmenting, and distorting elements.

In either extreme, a frame can be used effectively to emphasize or deemphasize the content of any visual message.

Related Forms and Functions

A frame can be considered as a margin in a traditional page layout, such as in a book or magazine. Margins influence the way a reader interacts with narrative and visual content of a page, such as a block of typographic text or a group of photographic images, by providing passive or open space around these compositional elements. A more pronounced margin provides visual emphasis and immediacy to images or a block of typographic text. The opposite result occurs when a margin is minimal and narrow, creating an effect where images or blocks of text appear larger than they actually are, as if they were expanding beyond the limitations of the compositional page.

A simple frame surrounding the title *Mao* and articulated in the same line weight or stroke thickness as the title's three letterforms brings this book cover literally into focus, while the overall image remains out of focus.

MUCCA DESIGN
New York, New York, USA

A consistent-weight linear frame that matches the stroke thickness of the "Heath" typography further unifies this logotype, especially when it is integrated and layered with other visual elements such as stationery, sales catalogs, brochures, website, and advertising.

VOLUME INC.
San Francisco, California, USA

Multiple graphic framing of this project name and location, "Prospect New Orleans," creates a structured, integrated pattern similar to brick coursing, further communicating strength, connection, teamwork, and community.

PURE + APPLIED
New York, New York, USA

In this poster, frame is used
to contain and accentuate the
film festival title—Japanese
Cinema Festival '09—as well
as separate and organize in
individual graphic frames a
wide range of information
such as programs, screenings,
dates, times, and locations.
As a visual metaphor, frame is
this context is also evocative
of film frames, shoji screens,
and tatami mats.

RYOTA IIZUKA, Student
SIMON JOHNSTON,
Instructor
Art Center College of Design
Pasadena, California, USA

Another form of frame—in this case,
margin—also provides a "safe" area in a composition, such as a publication, for specific
elements such as folios (page numbers),
headers, and footers. While these page
conventions are usually located in a nominal
space, a page margin can also be more pronounced to contain other elements such as
images, captions, and sidebars, when needed.

A frame can also act as a border. A border clearly and concisely demarcates where
an image ends and its surrounding background begins. It can be an obvious edge to
an image or composition that may lack a
definitive perimeter or outline, or it can be
used to visually emphasize an outer edge, or
frame, as well as separate a section of an image or information within an overall composition. A border can be graphically articulated
with line, shape, and texture, realized with
simple and restrained visual characteristics or
more detailed and complicated ones.

The framing of elements in a composition is called cropping. Cropping can alter
the size and shape of any image, as well as
directly impact an image's content and
meaning. For example, a vertical image can
be cropped to become a square, circle, or

such, each time taking on new proportions and potential meaning. Cropping in on a specific element or detail of an overall image can alter the focus of that image, giving it a new identity and visual presence.

The visual representation of a frame is not limited to compositional elements such as line, shape, color, texture, or tone. It can also be articulated with type and letterform.

Even in the virtual world of websites and electronic interfaces, a frame is a ubiquitous element with a multitude of appearances and functions. It is the literal and physical frame around a computer monitor, and it appears on a computer's desktop on

A singular graphic frame, equal in visual prominence and weight to this public awareness campaign's logotype for Darfur, allows this typographic element to stand apart and maintain its visual immediacy when layered on a variety of photographic images and graphic textures.

VOLUME INC.
San Francisco, California, USA

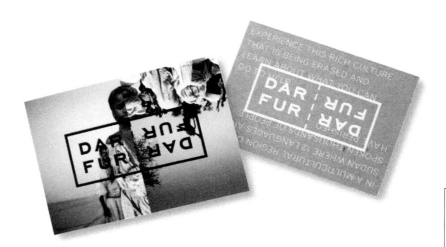

A subtle, tinted frame is used to bring immediate attention to this restaurant's restrained, sans serif logotype "SĪNO," an Asian-inspired Chinese restaurant and lounge. When layered on a variety of different color fields, textures, and images, this frame maintains a visual immediacy and focus to this identity program.

PUBLIC INC.
San Francisco, California, USA

The cookbook cover has a sophisticated visual character, capturing the warmth, personality, and elegance of the restaurant Chanterelle, while at the same time communicating the gracious service found in this family-run establishment. The composition of the cover is also evocative of a fine art book, with a centered white field framing the book title's classic serif typography as well as bridging and connecting the two distinct photographic images, further unifying the cover as a cohesive whole.

MUCCA DESIGN
New York, New York, USA

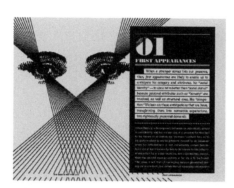

numerous windows that contain a hierarchy of information such as controls, icons, and other types of navigational information.

A frame can be a functional, as well as an aesthetic element within a composition. It can strengthen and reinforce the viewer's understanding of information as well as appear solely as a decorative element. With either of these functions, it is the responsibility of the graphic designer to determine the appropriate use of frame.

Graphic variations on a literal frame and bracket are used extensively throughout this branding program and annual report for "The 1%." A bold, effective use of color, proportion, and figure–ground all enhance depth and dimension without illustrating the literal nature of these visual qualities and characteristics.

MENDE DESIGN
San Francisco, California, USA

Frame takes on a series of varied graphic forms throughout *This Book Is Not Pink*, as represented in these spreads, which maintains a consistency and continuity for the reader as a means to bring further focus and grounding to the varied visual elements and narrative content of each spread.

ANDREW LIM, Student
MICHAEL IAN KAYE, Instructor
School of Visual Arts
New York, New York, USA

pro·por·tion \prə-ˈpȯr-shən\ *n*
3: the relation of one part to another or to the whole with respect to magnitude, quantity, or degree

22

> "Without proportion there can be no principles in the design of any temple; that is, if there is no precise relation between its members, as in the case of those of a well-shaped man."
>
> VITRUVIUS (80-70 BC), Roman, Architect, Author, Engineer

Proportion is the systematic relationship of one thing to another in any given composition. In visual communications, it is an essential design principle defined as the integral relationship of sizes within a composition. These integral relationships are transparent and function as an underlying

Good design makes choices clear.

framework for all compositional elements. Proportion also represents the critical relationship between one part of a composition and another or between the whole of a composition and its size, quantity, or degree. Generally the goal of any proportional system is to produce a sense of coherence, harmony, and integrity among the elements.

Historical References
Proportion has shaped our visual world throughout history—it is an intrinsic part of the Parthenon, da Vinci's *Mona Lisa*, and Michelangelo's *David*.
(continued on page 222)

This poster, sponsored by AIGA and promoting the get-out-the-vote campaign for national elections, presents a simple, evocative, and intriguing image and message. Posed in front of bold, sans serif typography that spells "vote," an enigmatic figure is wrapped and bound, ultimately raising questions about freedom, identity, self-expression,

change, and power—and their opposites. The vertical proportion of this poster's format, married with the monumental proportion of the wrapped, bound figure and its vertically proportioned letterforms, further creates a seamless and integrated visual composition.

ALFALFA STUDIO LLC
New York, New York, USA

This book's proportional format, as well as its interior layout, is derived from the Brooklyn Botanic Garden's overall plan designed by the Olmsted Brothers and based on the golden section or rectangle. This proportional formula is also graphically articulated as a continuous series of hairline borders and frames that contain, isolate, and highlight a wide range

of photographic, illustrative, and narrative content throughout the book.

POULIN + MORRIS INC.
New York, New York, USA

1957

Univers Family of Typefaces
ADRIAN FRUTIGER
Paris, France

				39 univers

45 univers	46 *univers*	47 univers	48 *univers*	49 univers

53 univers	55 univers	56 *univers*	57 univers	58 *univers*	59 univers

63 univers	65 univers	66 *univers*	67 univers	68 *univers*

73 univers	75 univers	76 *univers*

83 univers

ADRIAN FRUTIGER (b. 1928) is one of the most prominent typographers of the twentieth century and the designer of one of the most notable typeface families ever to be created—the sans serif Univers.

As a young boy, he experimented with invented scripts and stylized handwriting as a negative response to the formal, cursive penmanship being enforced at the Swiss school he was attending. At the age of sixteen, he began a apprenticeship as a compositor with an Interlaken printer. During this apprenticeship, he also learned woodcutting, engraving, and calligraphy.

Between 1949 and 1951, Frutiger studied at the Kunstgewerbeschule (School of Applied Arts) in Zurich. In 1952, Charles Peignot recruited Frutiger for Deberny & Peignot, one of the world's foremost type foundries in Paris. At that time, Deberny & Peignot was using a new phototypesetting process and wanted Frutiger to adapt typefaces for it, as well as design a large, matched typeface family of different weights. During this period, he began to design the Univers family.

The twenty-one variations of the Univers typeface family have five weights and four widths. At its center is Univers 55, the equivalent of a standard "book" weight. Frutiger also proposed to abandon imprecise terms such as *condensed, extended, light, bold, roman, and italic,* and instead use a reference numbering system that illustrated the proportional relationships between each variation. At the time, it was a revolutionary concept of how typefaces and their related families could be described.

He also created a visual "periodic table" for the Univers family—its vertical axis identifies different weights, and any variation beginning with the same number is of the same weight. Its horizontal axis identifies perspective shifts, from extended to condensed with italic variations. Any weight ending with an even number is italic. Roman variations are designated with an odd number, oblique variations with an even number.

With the design of Univers, Frutiger also started a trend in type design toward a larger x-height with lowercase letters proportionally more similar to their ascenders, descenders, and capitals. The sizes and weights of its capitals are also closer in size and weight to its lowercase letters, ultimately creating a page of text with visual harmony and ease for the reader.

The Univers family of typefaces is known for its remarkable visual uniformity, which enables a graphic designer to use all twenty-one fonts together as a flexible, integrated typographic system.

In 1986, Adrian Frutiger was awarded the Gutenberg Prize for technical and aesthetic achievement in typography.

Adrian Frutiger and Univers

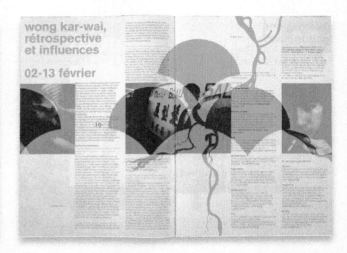

The three-column page grid of this publication for Lux, a regional theater and arts center in southern France, is fully integrated to, as well as based on, the proportional design principle of the golden section. The use of this proportional page relationship further guarantees visual cohesiveness and continuity throughout this publication, as well as related posters, announcement cards, and collateral print material that is diverse and varied with narrative and visual content.

HELMO
Montreuil, France

Euclid, the famous Greek mathematician, was the first to put the theory of proportion into words and images. He divided a line into two sections in such a way that the ratio of the whole line in relation to the larger part is the same relationship as the larger part is to the smaller.

Vitruvius defined proportion in terms of unit fractions, the same system used by the Greeks in their orders of architecture.

One of the most universal images representing the visual theory of proportion is Leonardo da Vinci's famous drawing *Vitruvian Man*, which first appeared in the 1509 book, *Divina Proportione*, by Luca Pacioli. It was here that daVinci attempted to codify proportion based on his studies of the human form, as well as his numerous observations and measurements of proportions for all its parts. He referred in these notebooks to the works of Vitruvius. Many artists of the Renaissance subsequently used proportion as a primary design principle in their work.

In the fifteenth century, Albrecht Dürer determined what characteristics of the human body were visually balanced and beautiful by accurately measuring and documenting the proportions of its parts.

Basic Relationships

Not obvious, and not hidden, the principle of proportion can be simply conveyed. In Priya Hemenway's *Divine Proportion: Phi in Art, Nature, and Science*, she states, "The whole is to the larger in exactly the same proportion as the larger is to the smaller." Proportion lends insight into the process of design and gives visual coherence to composition through visual structure.

In basic proportional relationships, the outer dimensions determine the format of a two-dimensional design and are its most basic proportion. A square, a vertical rectangle, and a horizontal rectangle are all formats with unique proportions that affect particular characteristics of a composition. Outer proportions or dimensions can have an integral relationship to internal divisions and alignments. Outer dimensions affect the viewer's orientation and are often dictated by the composition's ultimate proportion.

The relationship between outer dimensions and internal divisions also provides the graphic designer with a system for managing design decisions. Proportional systems have been used for centuries in architecture and art, and are based on ratios—a comparison of one set of sizes with another. Although ratios are commonly expressed in mathematical terms, they also can be expressed as visual relationships. For example, the golden section or rectangle is a ratio that dates back to the ancient Greeks, and its proportional properties have both aesthetic beauty and structural integrity.

The Golden Ratio

The golden ratio is the ratio between two segments or elements of an object such that the smaller (*bc*) segment is to the larger

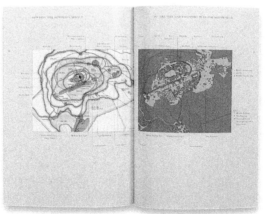

The format and page design of *Assuring the Jefferson Legacy: The Site and Facilities Plan for Monticello* is fully influenced by the design and planning principles used by Thomas Jefferson in all of his work. These visual principles are reflected in the book's layout, typography, and color palette. They are also evident in the overall proportion of the book, which is based on the golden ratio, furthering Jefferson's ideal of harmony found in nature as well as in the built environment.

POULIN + MORRIS INC.
New York, New York, USA

The cover of this promotional brochure for a commerical photographer uses a series of proportional frames or "stages" to further symbolize the creative process undertaken by a photographer in realizing their work, as well as the conventional format of a photographic image.

MERCER CREATIVE GROUP
Vancouver, BC, CANADA

The relationship of form and content is an obvious influence in the design of this monograph for Kruno Vrgoc, a Croatian artist and sculptor. The extreme vertical proportion of this monograph's format is directly reflective of the artist's use of similar extreme proportions in his sculptural work. This monumental format is furthered enhanced and strengthened by a textural wood detail on the cover with its grain oriented on the same vertical axis as the book, as well as the use of a singular column of justified typographic text.

STUDIO SONDA
Porec, Croatia

segment (*ab*) as the larger segment (*ab*) is to the sum of the two segments (*ac*), or *bc/ab* = *ab/ac* = 1.618.

It can be found throughout nature, as well as throughout the history of visual and applied arts. This proportional ratio is evident in natural forms such as pinecones, nautilus shells, seed patterns in the center of sunflowers, and the human body. It is constructed through a series of extended relationships with a strong aesthetic harmony, since the interior proportions relate in scale to the proportions of the original square and its extensions.

The golden ratio can also be extended to construct the golden rectangle, which the Greeks used as the basis for the majority of their city planning and architecture, including the Parthenon. Renaissance artists used it to create overall harmony and balance in works of painting and drawing. Stradivarius used it in the design and construction of his violins. It has also been used in the planning and design of the Great Pyramid at Giza, Stonehenge, Chartres Cathedral, the LCW chair designed by Charles Eames, and the Apple iPod. Even today, contemporary graphic designers use the golden ratio as an optimal format for print and digital media. This proportional relationship has also been identified in many other ways over the centuries, including the golden mean, golden number, golden section, golden proportion, divine proportion, and section aurea.

Visual communication is partly an experience of visual balance—of the relationship of parts to the whole. Perceiving it as anything else is missing its most fundamental component. Painting, sculpture, architecture, music, prose, or poetry are also organized and methodically balanced around a hidden sense of true proportion.

Most of what we perceive as pleasing to the eye, as well as balanced and harmonious, has some relationship and connection to the rules of proportion.

**How to Construct the
Golden Section Rectangle**

Step One

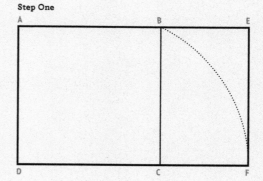

Step Two

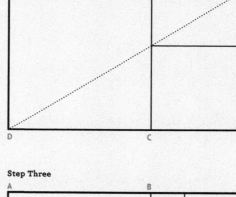

Step Three

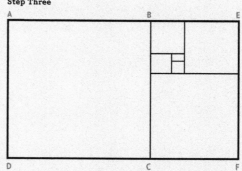

Step Four

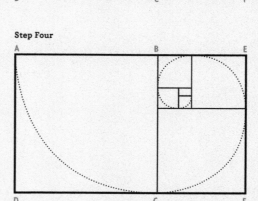

Step One
Draw a perfect square,
ABCD.

With the midpoint of
DC as a center, draw an
arc with a radius equal
to the length of a line
drawn from the midpoint
of *DC* to *B.*

Step Two
Draw a line from *D* to *E*
to divide the rectangle
into smaller divisions.

Step Three
To continue, draw a
line between opposite
corners of the rectangle.
For example, a line from
F to *B.*

Step Four
This is the proportion
recognized as the golden
section or rectangle.

A golden rectangle is
one whose side lengths
are in the golden ratio,
$1:\frac{1+\sqrt{5}}{2}$ or 1:1.618.

im·age \\'i-mij\\ n
2 b: a visual representation of something:
as (1): a likeness of an object produced
on a photographic material (2): a picture
produced on an electronic display
(as a television or computer screen)
6: a vivid or graphic representation
or description

"A picture is a poem without words."
HORACE (65-8 BC). *Roman, Poet*

An image is an artifact usually defined as a two-dimensional picture, idea, or impression of a person or physical object. A powerful and memorable image can make or break any visual communication. Photography, illustration, and other types of image forms can communicate a specific idea or

emotion, gain a viewer's attention, further a reader's imagination, and ultimately enhance and enrich any visual message.

Characteristics

In visual communications, a graphic designer can consider numerous forms and methods when undertaking the act and process of image making—glyph, pictogram, symbol, drawing, illustration, painting, photography, and even typography can all be described as forms of image. While they all have distinct and varied visual characteristics and functions, they also have potential as meaningful and obvious counterpoints to narrative form. (continued on page 230)

A variety of illustration styles is used in provocative and meaningful ways, creating a memorable and highly communicative series of covers for these public awareness brochures for the Scripps Research Institute.

MIRIELLO GRAFICO
San Diego, California, USA

This singular photographic image of a rich, lush landscape is used to communicate a series of performances titled *Promenades* at a regional theater and arts center located in southern France. The subtle, yet dynamic, use of a figurative cutout from the same background image and then juxtaposed is eye-catching and extremely engaging. The incorporation of hand-drawn lettering is secondary and supportive of this powerful photographic composition.

HELMO
Montreuil sous Bois, France

Common Sense and Nuclear Warfare Book Cover
IVAN CHERMAYEFF
New York, New York, USA

In the 1960s, American paperback book publishers and American graphic designers started working together for the first time with a collective, creative objective. At the forefront of this new collaborative movement was a group of visual pioneers and designers such as Paul Rand, Alvin Lustig, Roy Kuhlman, Rudolph de Harak, Tom Geismar, and Ivan Chermayeff.

IVAN CHERMAYEFF (b. 1937), with his partner, Tom Geismar, have created some of the most memorable and recognizable images of the twentieth century.

In his formative years, Chermayeff worked as a record album cover designer as well as an assistant to Alvin Lustig in the early 1950s. He studied at Harvard University, Illinois Institute of Technology (IIT), and Yale University School of Art and Architecture. Following his graduation in 1960, Chermayeff and fellow classmate Geismar moved to New York City to join with already-established Robert Brownjohn to start their own design consultancy firm.

It was during the early 1960s that Brownjohn, Chermayeff, and Geismar established themselves as one of the few progressive and innovative groups of image makers in American graphic design. They were masters in combining their background and training in modernist ideals with the streetwise visual language of the times. Their early work explored a remarkable integration of type and image combined with expressive, intelligent, and literate storytelling. Their numerous book covers produced at the time combined images and symbols to further convey and brand the essence of a book's subject matter. They were powerful signs that grabbed the attention, as well as sparked the imagination, of the reader.

Chermayeff's cover design for Bertrand Russell's *Common Sense and Nuclear Warfare* is a high-contrast, photomontage of two black-and-white photographs—a mushroom cloud superimposed on the back of a man's head. These powerful visual metaphors act as a counterpoint and provide the reader with an unnerving and fearsome idea about mankind's vulnerability to nuclear war, even before opening the book. It is a seminal example of the marriage of image, symbol, and word to create powerful and meaningful visual communications.

He says, "Great images, to be great, must be original and memorable. Occasionally a designer recognizes a commonality between two separate visual images and pins them together, making one new, powerful, and provocative form. Finding connections, large and small, is what the design process is all about."

Ivan Chermayeff and Thomas Geismar were awarded the prestigious American Institute of Graphic Arts (AIGA) Gold Medal in 1979.

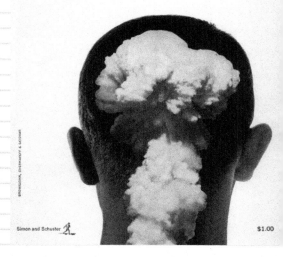

Bertrand Russell
Common Sense and Nuclear Warfare

BROWNJOHN, CHERMAYEFF & GEISMAR

Simon and Schuster

$1.00

Ivan Chermayeff and the Modern American Paperback

09 soulpepper

THE GUARDSMAN
FERENC MOLNÁR
TRANSLATED BY FRANK MARCUS
AUGUST 31 — OCTOBER 24

416.866.8666
SOULPEPPER.CA

09 soulpepper

AWAKE AND SING!
CLIFFORD ODETS
JUNE 6 — JULY 31

416.866.8666
SOULPEPPER.CA

09 soulpepper

CIVIL ELEGIES
DENNIS LEE
CREATED BY MIKE ROSS & LORENZO SAVOINI
ORIGINAL MUSIC BY MIKE ROSS
DECEMBER 3 — 24

416.866.8666
SOULPEPPER.CA

09 soulpepper

WHO'S AFRAID OF VIRGINIA WOOLF?
EDWARD ALBEE
AUGUST 29 — OCTOBER 24

416.866.8666
SOULPEPPER.CA

09 soulpepper

TRAVESTIES
TOM STOPPARD
FEBRUARY 12 — MARCH 21

416.866.8666
SOULPEPPER.CA

09 soulpepper

GLENGARRY GLEN ROSS
DAVID MAMET
APRIL 2 — MAY 9

416.866.8666
SOULPEPPER.CA

Character-driven themes, such as for these three plays— *The Guardsman*, *Travesties*, and *Glengarry Glen Ross*, provide any graphic designer with a multitude of image challenges and opportunities. This poster series for the Soulpepper Theatre uses dynamic and provocative imagery that is composed of photography, illustration, line art, and a layering combination of styles. All provide a highly interpretive and communicative visual story directly related to each of the play's themes.

SANDWICH CREATIVE
Toronto, Ontario, Canada

An image can be two-dimensional or virtual, such as a photograph, an illustration, or a screen display; or it can be three-dimensional, such as a sculpture or statue. An image can be captured by an optical device such as a camera, mirror, lens, telescope, or microscope, as well as by natural objects and phenomena such as the human eye or the reflective surface of water.

The word *image* is also used in the broader sense of any two-dimensional figure such as a map, graph, pie chart, or abstract painting. Images can be rendered manually, such as through drawing, painting, or carving, or rendered automatically through conventional printing or digital technology.

Classifications

Images vary greatly in media and content. The extensive choice of image types available today can be organized as follows:

Volatile

A volatile image exists only for a short period of time. This image type may be a reflection of an object in a mirror, a projection of a camera obscura, or a scene displayed on a cathode ray tube or video monitor.

Fixed

A fixed image, also called a hard copy, is an image that has been recorded on a material or object, such as paper or textile, by a photographic or digital process. A laser print, photographic print, and a large-scale digital wall mural are all types of fixed images.

Still

A still image is a single static image, as distinguished from a moving image. This term is used in photography, visual media, and the digital world.

Moving

A moving image is typically a movie (film) or video, including digital video. It can also be an animated display such as a zoetrope. In addition to conventional film, moving images can be captured with digital cameras, laptops, webcams, and cell phones.

Graphic Forms

An image is a potentially powerful element in visual communication because it is one of the few forms that can represent an emotional experience and be immediately understood and embraced by the viewer.

The Penguin Classics imprint is more than a half-century old and is recognized around the world for its offerings of world-class literature. In the these three book covers for Robertson Davies' novels, four-color photographic imagery is used as bold, iconic storytelling vehicles for each of the book's fictional themes. The imagery also has distinct, memorable, and relevant characteristics from each narrative due to the unconventional and unorthodox vantage points and interpretations taken with each photograph.

SOAPBOX DESIGN COMMUNICATIONS
Toronto, Ontario, Canada

This set of book covers is part of an branding campaign based on the illustrative reinterpretation of classic book covers directed toward junior high school students. Dynamic, textural, and highly emotional line illustrations engage the young reader, giving them an immediate and meaningful connection to each book and its themes. Vibrant and intense color palettes, hand-drawn letterforms, and reductive and representational visual elements are collectively used to unify this diverse series.

MIKEY BURTON
Philadelphia, Pennsylvania, USA

Images can be stylized and take many graphic forms, such as an icon, sign, symbol, supersign, or logotype. Photography and illustration are forms of image that are broad based in content, compositions, and style, each affording the designer a specific visual language or dialect. Both forms can be realistic representations or interpretive expressions depicting a wide range of visual narratives. Each of will have a direct impact and influence on the ultimate meaning in a visual message.

Type (letterform, narrative form) is also a form of image that can have meaningful qualities for effective visual communications.

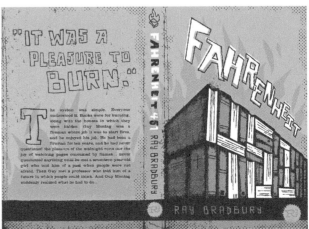

This class assignment is an exploration of addition, subtraction, transformation, and substitution relationships created with photographic form. Students start with two photographic images—one of architecture and one of a landscape. These images are first printed, then cut to a 4 cm (1.5-inch) grid and flush mounted to black kraft paper. This process involves a substitution of sixteen landscape squares into the architecture image, and then sixteen architecture squares into the landscape image. The goal is to achieve the greatest transformation with each substitution. This process is also informed by the composition of each image, not only in terms of the overall arrangement of visual elements, but also in the formal qualities of each unit in the imposed structure or grid. The substitution is defined and governed by such design principles as contrast, continuity, rhythm, juxtaposition, similarity, and difference. The ultimate objective is for each student to develop new relationships of photographic form that did not exist previously.

SARAH AL GROOBI. Student
AMIR BERBIC,
RODERICK GRANT,
Instructors
American University of Sharjah
Sharjah, United Arab Emirates

The presentation and representation of any image can span a broad spectrum defined at one end by realism and at the other end by abstraction. Between these two visual extremes are a myriad of possibilities for the graphic designer to choose from—the more realistic, the more direct and immediate the image; the more abstract, the more restrained and interpretive the image.

Functions

Images can function in a multitude of roles within any visual communication. They can provide a meaningful counterpoint to narrative text, engage the reader with enhanced visual interest, bring clarity and organization to complex information, and communicate emotions grounded in the human experience.

They can visually represent a specific person, place, event, or reference in narrative text, as well as provide a counterpoint to it. An image can be literal, representational, metaphorical, or abstract. They can also immediately alter the meaning of words, just as words can change the meaning of any image.

Combining image and narrative form is challenging for any graphic designer. These distinct visual forms can be combined

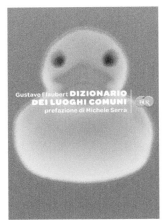

to establish more meaningful relationships or contrasting counterpoints between the two forms and simultaneously strengthen the collective message.

When deciding to use photography versus illustration, a graphic designer needs to consider that the most people will respond and engage more immediately with a photograph because they perceive this image type as the closest form of their own objective reality, as opposed to illustration that is traditionally seen as an artist's (or designer's) visual inter-pretation of a subjective reality. One form is immediate, intuitive, powerful, and persuasive; the other, less so.

The juxtaposition of line art and photography, scale and texture, horizontal and vertical orientation all provide additional visual impact and presence to the figurative images used on this cover for the *Visual Arts Journal*, a bi-annual publication featuring work from School of Visual Arts students and alumni, as well as perspectives on the latest art trends.

VISUAL ARTS PRESS
New York, New York, USA

Bright, saturated colors and iconic photographic images with an out-of-focus appearance create a visual power and immediacy for each of these book covers. Additionally, bold, sans serif typography combined with open-space kerning allows the typography to be visually perforated, creating more immediacy and connection for the viewer.

MUCCA DESIGN
New York, New York, USA

The visual immediacy of this book cover for *Killing the Buddha* is solely dependent on the fundamental element of image. The calming soft blue sky with a white cloud combined with an iconic, overscaled red *X* implies the violence of this book's theme and cover concept without relying on literal typography or imagery.

THE OFFICE
OF PAUL SAHRE
New York, New York, USA

Ultimately, there are many methods to communicate meaningful messages and ideas with image. The possibilities are endless for any graphic designer to create rich, communicative, and memorable visual experiences for the viewer. The only limitation is the graphic designer's imagination.

pat·tern \ˈpa-tərn\ *n*
3: an artistic, musical, literary, or mechanical design or form

24

"Pattern, the fruit of design, can be seen as the measure of culture."
WILLIAM FEAVER, *British, Art Critic, Author*

Like texture, pattern is a fundamental design principle that helps define the visual quality of surface activity. The visual characteristics of any pattern help us see distinctions between one object and another. Pattern is a specific type of visual texture and is traditionally derived from a defined and

Soft, muted tones of color, pattern, and typography are used as figurative textures to further enhance the identity program for Odun, a Mexico City restaurant featuring Asian cuisines. The overall identity, as well as its array of tones, colors, and patterns, was inspired by a diversity of influences, flavors, scents, and spirits found throughout Asian cultures.

BLOK DESIGN
Mexico City, Mexico

repeated compositional structure always appearing in an organized and regimented graphic manner.

The visual elements of point, line, and shape are the basis for creating pattern throughout history. Combining pattern with the organizational design principle of the grid, graphic designers can create an infinite variety of end results. By utilizing a singular element in different organizations, configurations, and compositions, patterns can be realized with endless variations either subtle or obvious, all built around a singular common graphic denominator.

(continued on page 240)

AZUERO
EARTH
PROJECT

A carefully composed pattern of natural leaf forms, varied in scale, color, profile, and orientation, creates the fluid form and body of a monkey symbolizing the Azuero Earth Project. Its mission is to preserve the ecosystem of the Azuero Peninsula, protect biodiversity, and promote healthy 'green' communities.

SAGMEISTER INC.
New York, New York, USA

1911

Hermann Scherrer Poster
LUDWIG HOHLWEIN
Munich, Germany

LUDWIG HOHLWEIN (1847–1949) was trained and practiced as an architect until 1906, when he became interested in graphic design and the visual arts.

During the 1890s, he lived in Munich, where he was part of the United Workshops for Arts and Crafts, an avant-garde group of artists and craftsmen dedicated to the tenets and principles of the Arts and Crafts movement. Hohlwein moved to Berlin in 1911 and started working as a graphic designer primarily designing advertisements and posters for the men's clothing company Hermann Scherrer.

Hohlwein's most creative phase of work and a large variety of his best-known posters were created between 1912 and 1925. It was during this critical period that he developed his own unique visual style. By 1925, he had already designed 3,000 different advertisements and became the best-known German commercial artist of his time.

Poster historian Alain Weill comments that "Hohlwein was the most prolific and brilliant German posterist of the twentieth century... Beginning with his first efforts, Hohlwein found his style with disconcerting facility. It would vary little for the next forty years. The drawing was perfect from the start, nothing seemed alien to him, and in any case, nothing posed a problem for him. His figures are full of touches of color and a play of light and shade that brings them out of their background and gives them substance."

Hohlwein's work relied mostly on strong figurative elements with reductive qualities of high contrast, intense flat color, and bold patterns of geometric elements. This is evident in his iconographic poster for Hermann Scherrer. The figurative element of the man is optically centered in the field of the poster with no apparent horizon line. The well-dressed gentleman and his riding accessories, as well as his pure-bred dog, are all represented in a reductive, stark manner combined with vivid color and an abstract, black-and-white checkerboard pattern. Here, Hohlwein treats this distinctive pattern as a two-dimensional plane. It is in extreme contrast to the surrounding three-dimensional compositional elements, creating a strong and memorable focal point for the poster.

His adaptation of photographic images was based on a deep and intuitive understanding of visual design principles. His creative use of color and architectural compositions dispels any suggestion that he used photographs as the basis of his creative output. Additionally, his use of high tonal contrasts, interlocking shapes, and distinctive graphic patterns made his work instantly recognizable and memorable.

Aside from Lucian Bernhard, Ludwig Hohlwein was one of the most successful and celebrated designers of the Plakatstil and Sachplakat modes or "poster" and "object poster" styles in Germany during this time period.

Ludwig Hohlwein and the Hermann Scherrer style

The branding program for Nizuc, an upscale resort and residential community in Mexico, was inspired by the site's Mayan history. The project's figurative symbol, also evocative of Mayan carvings and bas-reliefs, is the base element of graphic patterns used throughout this visual program.

CARBONE SMOLAN AGENCY
New York, New York, USA

Historical Influences

Throughout history, an abundance of pattern making has occurred in practically every culture around the world. Patterns have been evident not only in the graphic arts, but in fine and applied arts, such as textiles, pottery, wallpaper, apparel, furniture, interiors, metalwork, ceramic tiles, mosaics, and stencils, as well as new and innovative digital experiments by contemporary artists and graphic designers.

Artists and graphic designers have also developed a wide range of styles, forms, and motifs. For example, early twentieth-century innovators of pattern making include William

The Street Sweets graphic identity and branding program uses a combination of pattern, typography, and color. For example, a dense arrangement of verbs and adjectives such as *delightful*, *bliss*, *love*, *fresh*, and *delicious* form a dynamic, structurelike pattern that is used as a typographic backdrop in a variety of large and small-scale applications—business cards, food packaging, shopping bags, and food truck graphics.

LANDERS MILLER
New York, New York, USA

Morris (British), Koloman Moser (Austrian), Anni Albers (German), Fortuny (Italian), Alvin Lustig (American), Ray Eames (American), and Alexander Girard (American) up to contemporary designers such as Richard Rhys (British).

In the early 1900s, with the advent of the modernist movement in the visual and applied arts, a preference for minimalist surfaces and textures became the norm; ornate patterning and overtly decorative surfaces were avoided. This trend has now been tempered, and a far wider palette of choices is now evident and appreciated worldwide.

Basic Structures and Forms

A pattern can be a theme of recurring events or objects, sometimes referred to as elements of a given set. These events, objects, or elements always repeat themselves in a predictable and organized manner.

Pattern has a strong relationship to geometry, since it is an organized and regimented texture in which singular elements are composed on a defined and repeated structure. It is due to this underlying structure that patterns are always synthetic, manmade, and mechanical, and never organic.

TCHO is a San Francisco-based luxury chocolate manufacturer and uses a broad palette of pattern as functional and interpretive elements in its visual branding program. Its graphic influences are derived from Aztec culture, where chocolate was used as a form of currency. Contemporary line variations on currency patterns, representing the six

flavor-driven product lines—chocolaty, nutty, fruity, floral, and citrus—are used as decorative product identifiers. Each pattern is framed within a square and is the base element connecting all packaging, collateral, and visual communication material. The brand's color palette extends from dark brown to bright magenta, orange, and yellow, reflecting

the flavors as well as the high-tech modernist values of the product line.

EDENSPIEKERMANN
Berlin, Germany

This assignment requires students to analyze the potential of pattern in relationship to color and composition. Using abstract shapes and fundamental graphic elements, students initially develop a 10 X 10-inch (25.4 X 25.4 cm) square complex pattern based on an assigned piece of music. The final pattern is to visually represent the music (or a portion of it) in some visual manner. This pattern is then modified into seven color variations—black and white, monochromatic, analogous, complementary, split complementary, triadic, and tetradic.

ALETA CORBOY, Student
ANNABELLE GOULD, Instructor
University of Washington
Seattle, Washington, USA

Brown, Juana Francisca's Kitchen is a confectionery located in Bogotá, offering a delicate selection of gourmet sweets. Their packaging system uses kraft board boxes, a series of preprinted tag cards, and rubber stamps with decorative motifs and patterns that carry information about what's inside the box. The repetitive dot and line motifs and patterns are evocative of decorative icing used on confections and small baked goods.

LIP
Bogotá, Colombia

The most basic patterns are composed through repetition and are considered a repeat of any visual element such as point, line, shape, form, or color. A single element is combined with duplicates of itself without change or modification. For example, a checkerboard is a simple pattern based on alternating squares of black and red.

Patterns can also be based on familiar elements, such as in simple decorative patterns of stripes, zigzags, and polka dots. Other patterns can be more visually complex and can be found in nature, art, and the built environment. These include arabesques, branching, circulation, fractals, helixes, lat-

This entrance to Brooklyn Botanic Garden comprises two 12-foot (4 m) high curved walls rising on both sides of the entrance and sheathed in stainless steel with an etched cherry tree leaf pattern. The actual entrance gates are the same material; however, the leaf pattern here is water-jet cut, creating a stainless steel grille for viewing into the garden when it is closed.

POULIN + MORRIS INC.
New York, New York, USA

Decorative geometric patterns are layered in vellum; the outer layer represented graphically in stark black and white, the other revealing the same pattern in a rich, vibrant, multicolored palette. This pattern layering device is a metaphor for the dual undertone themes of these classic Jane Austen novels—*Sense and Sensibility* and *Emma*.

ISABELLE RANCIER, Student
TRACY BOYCHUK, Instructor
School of Visual Arts
New York, New York, USA

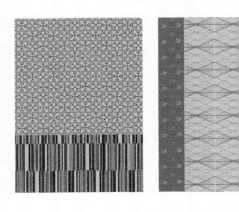

Kinetic and energetic line
patterns are used for a series
of notebook covers
developed, designed, and
marketed by this California-
based design firm. The
juxtaposition of two patterns
for each notebook, and the
use of a broad range of intense, vibrant color palettes
throughout, add a visual
power and vibrancy to each of
these cover combinations.

ADAMSMORIOKA INC.
Beverly Hills, California, USA

tices, meanders, nests, polyhedra, spheres,
spirals, symmetry, volutes, and waves. A
recurring pattern in fine art and architecture
is referred to as a motif.

Moirés are also a form of pattern
first used after World War II, when graphic
designers began to exploit and experiment
with the conventional methods and attributes
of process reproduction and offset printing.
Moiré patterns revealed to the viewer the
layered tints and enlarged halftones of these
processes, creating dynamic and unexpected
visual effects of color and texture that had
not been visually experienced before this
time period.

Today, digital software is an easily accessible and immediate means by which the
same visual pattern effects can be achieved.

Both labels for "Il conte" use
a common base pattern
comprising geometric form
triangles and vine leaf
elements that function as a
frame and iconic backdrop
for each wine name—
Montepulciano d'Abruzzo and
Pinot Grigio. This pattern is
further enhanced and articulated with color, red or warm
white, depending upon which
wine type is identified.

LOUISE FILI LTD.
New York, New York, USA

ty·pog·ra·phy \tī-ˈpä-grə-fē\ *n*
2: the style, arrangement, or appearance of typeset matter

25

"Typography at its best is a visual form of language linking timelessness and time."

ROBERT BRINGHURST (B. 1946), *Canadian, Author, Poet, Typographer*

Typography is designing with type. Type is the term used for letterforms—alphabet, numbers, and punctuation—that when used together create words, sentences, and narrative form. The term *typeface* refers to the design of all the characters mentioned above, unified by common visual

Bold, sans serif letterforms, slanted back in perspective to imply movement, speed, and direction, are the primary visual characteristics of the new logotype for the Van Nuys FlyAway, a part of the Los Angeles World Airports' system of regional satellite bus depots that service Los Angeles Airport (LAX) via a park-and-ride bus system. As part of the recent renovation and expansion of the facility, the new logotype was designed to look and feel like an extension of a modern airport and applied extensively to architectural and wayfinding signs, environmental graphics, and bus fleet graphics.

SUSSMAN/PREJZA
& COMPANY
Culver City, California, USA

elements and characteristics. Typography is also a unique principle in a graphic designer's vocabulary because it has dual functions. It can function on its purest level as a graphic element such as point, line, form, shape, and texture in a visual composition. However, its primary function is verbal and visual. It is to be read. When typography has a relationship only to its verbal meaning, its communicative character can lack visual impact. When typography reflects a treatment that enhances both its verbal and visual meaning, it is perceived on multiple levels, not only intellectually but also sensually and emotionally.

Typography, of course, is all around us. In graphic design, the goal of the designer is not to just place typography on a page but rather to understand and use it effectively in visual communications. The selection and choice of typography, size, alignment, color, and spacing all are critical.

Historical References

Since the beginning of mankind, we have needed to communicate our lives to our fellow man. Before we learned to "speak" verbally, we spoke "visually" by leaving crude (continued on page 250)

1974

U&lc cover
HERB LUBALIN
New York, New York, USA

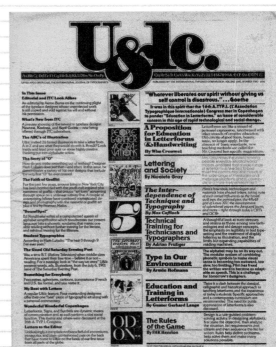

HERB LUBALIN (1918–1981) was a legendary art director, designer, and typographic master who brought humor, sensuality, and a modernist flair to every letterform and typographic element in his work.

Born in Brooklyn, New York, he attended Cooper Union, where he began his love affair with calligraphy, letterform, and formal typography. Immediately following his graduation in 1939, he joined the advertising agency of Sudler & Hennessey (later Sudler, Hennessey & Lubalin) as an art director.

In 1964, he left the agency to start his own design firm, where he ultimately worked in a broad range of areas including advertisements, editorial design, trademarks, typeface design, posters, packaging, and publications.

During this time, he became discontent with the rigid limitations of metal type and began to experiment with cutting and reassembling his own type proofs. Here, he was able to explore typography in a detailed and intimate manner that he had never experienced before. He manipulated type by hand—compressed it into ligatures, enlarged it to extreme sizes, and ultimately transformed it by giving it added meaning. It was also during this period that he produced some of the most memorable and dramatic typographic work of the decade.

In 1970, Lubalin joined with phototypography pioneer Edward Rondthaler and typographer Aaron Burns to establish the International Typeface Corporation (ITC). From 1970 to 1980, ITC designed, produced, and licensed thirty-four fully developed typeface families and approximately sixty display typefaces. Characteristics of ITC type families included an emphasis on large x-heights as well as short ascenders and descenders, allowing for tighter line spacing—a prevalent typographic style of the time.

During this same period, ITC published a typographic magazine, *U&lc*, which showcased its various type families and display typefaces to the design community. Because of its extraordinary combination of typographic design, illustration, and editorial content celebrating the virtues of well-designed typography, it was avidly read by type enthusiasts worldwide. Lubalin, as design director, gave this tabloid-size newsprint publication a complex, dynamic, and expressionistic style that had a major impact on publication design of the 1970s.

Throughout his career, he always considered space and surface his primary visual communication tools. One designer noted that Lubalin's work reminded him of a Claude Debussy quote that said "music is the space between the notes."

Lubalin embraced typographic characters as both visual and communicative forms—forms that were meant to invoke, inform, and ultimately engage the viewer. Rarely have complex typographic arrangements been so dynamic and so unified. The traditional rules and practices of typography were always abandoned for a more nontraditional and humanistic approach that made him a typographic master.

Herb Lubalin and *U&lc*

Bold, black, oversized letterforms are used on this set of textbook covers for *Written Language and Power* and *Introduction to Linguistics* to create iconic, singular, and immediate identifiers for each publication.

CASA REX
São Paulo, Brazil

Linguagem, escrita e poder
Maurizio Gnerre

Introdução à lingüística textual
Ingedore Grunfeld Villaça Koch

marks on walls and surfaces. From prehistoric cave paintings and Egyptian hieroglyphics to Roman inscriptions and medieval crests, communicating experiences to one another has been a common human denominator for telling our stories at any given time. Man has discovered how to make the word and the image become one. As our world has become more complex, so has the means by which we communicate those stories in their many forms. The most universal means throughout our collective history has been, and will continue to be, typography.

Anatomy of Letterforms
To better understand and recognize the similarities and differences between typefaces, an effective graphic designer needs to be familiar with the anatomy of letterforms. Each typeface has a distinct appearance with fundamental characteristics and features that provide distinguishing details to group or set typefaces apart from one another.

Form Variations
Typographic form varies only in case, weight, contrast, posture, width, and style. The extensive choices of individual typefaces or

fonts, available today share the following six common characteristics with only subtle alteration and variation:

Case
Each letter in any alphabet comprises two case forms—uppercase and lowercase.

Weight
The weight of a letterform is defined by the overall thickness of its stroke in relation to its height. Common weight variations include light, book, medium, bold, and black.

Contrast
The contrast of a letterform is determined by the degree of weight change in its stroke.

Posture
The posture of a letterform is its vertical orientation to a baseline. Upright and perpendicular letterforms to a baseline are roman; slanted or angled are italic.

Width
The width of any letterform is based on how wide it is in relation to its height. A letterform's standard width is based on a square

A f M g R x

K b s fj Q o

Labels on letterforms:
- Apex
- Ascender
- Crossbar
- Bracket
- Vertex
- Ear
- Counter
- Descender
- Stem
- x-height
- Leg
- Joint
- Serif
- Cap height
- Baseline
- Arm
- Spur
- Terminal
- Spine
- Ligature
- Vertical Stress
- Inclined Stress
- Tail

Apex
The outer point where two diagonal stems or strokes meet, as at the top of an *A* or *M* or at the bottom of an *M*.

Arm
A projecting horizontal or upward diagonal stem or stroke not enclosed within a character, as in an *E, K,* or *L.*

Ascender
The stem or stroke of a lowercase character located above the x-height, as in *b, d,* or *k.*

Baseline
A line on which the bottom of characters without descenders sit or align.

Bowl
A curved stem or stroke that encloses a counter, as in a *b, p,* or *O.*

Bracket
A curving joint between the serif and a stem or stroke; also known as a fillet.

Cap height
The distance from a baseline to the top of a capital character.

Cicero
A European typographic unit of measurement approximately equal to the British or American pica, or 4.155 mm.

Counter
An area enclosed by a bowl or a crossbar.

Crossbar
A horizontal element connecting two vertical or diagonal stems or strokes, or crossing a stem or stroke, as in an *A, H, f,* or *t;* also known as a bar or cross stroke.

Descender
The stem or stroke of a lowercase character located below the baseline, as in a *g, p,* or *y.*

Ear
A small projecting stroke sometimes attached to the bowl of a *g* or the stem of a *r.*

Joint
The angle formed where two strokes meet or intersect, as is a *K* or *R.*

Leg
A projecting diagonal stem or stroke extending downward, as in a *R* and *K;* also known as a tail.

Ligature
A stem or stroke that connects two characters together creating a ligature or tied character.

Link
The stem or stroke that connects the bowl and the loop of a *g.*

Loop
The descender of a *g* when it is entirely closed.

Pica
A typographic unit of measurement where 12 points equal 1 pica (1/16 inch or 0.166 inch) and 6 picas equal 1 inch (0.996 inch).

Point
The smallest unit of typographic measurement; one point is equal to 1/72 inch or 0.0148 inches or 0.351 mm.

Serif
The beginning or end of a stem or stroke, arm, leg, or tail drawn at a right angle or at an oblique to the stem or stroke.

Shoulder
The portion of a curved stroke, but not the hairline, connecting two vertical strokes or stems.

Spine
The diagonal portion or main curved stroke of an *S* or *s.*

Spur
A small, pointed projection from a stem or stroke, sometimes found on the bottom of a *b, t,* or *G.*

Stem (or Stroke)
The principal vertical or oblique element(s) of a character, as in an *A, B, L,* or *V;* except for curved characters where they are called strokes.

Stress (or Axis)
The inclination suggested by the relationship of thin and thick stems or strokes in a character, which can be an inclined or vertical stress or axis.

Swash
A flourished terminal, stem, or stroke added to a character.

Tail
The short stem or stroke that rests on a baseline, as in a *K* or *R;* or extending below a baseline, as in a *Q* or *j.* In a *K* and *R,* also known as a leg.

Terminal (or Finial)
A stem or stroke ending other than a serif.

Vertex
The angle formed at the bottom of a character where the left and right strokes meet or intersect, as in a *V* or *x.*

x-height
The distance from the baseline to the top of lowercase *x.*

The graphic and packaging design for Mrs. Meyer's Clean Day, a line of aromatherapeutic household cleaners, uses no-fuss, no-frills, utilitarian, sans serif typography that is functional with a subtle hint of visual style, character, and flair. This typographic approach is appropriate in this context since the product line is designed to represent the same work ethic.

WERNER DESIGN WERKS
St. Paul, Minnesota, USA

proportion. Exaggerated widths with narrower proportions are identified as condensed or compressed; ones with wider proportions are identified as extended or expanded.

Style
The style of letterforms refers to the two basic categories of serif and sans serif, as well as its historical context and classification.

While there have been many different approaches to typographic design over the centuries, whether driven by societal needs or technological advances, basic typographic characteristics such as the ones referenced above are still used today. Well-designed typographic forms transcend history, culture, and geography.

Descriptions and Classifications
How does a graphic designer decide, among the thousands of typefaces available, which font or font family might fulfill a specific design need? While most typefaces are classified into three categories, namely serif, sans serif, and script—it is a limited and somewhat shortsighted classification system. One method for familiarizing yourself with typefaces and their unique characteristics and

This series of theatrical production posters for Edward Albee's *The Goat, or Who Is Sylvia?* uses typographic overlays as interpretive representations of the play's themes and explorations of morality and identity. The effective use of bold typographic forms and collage, as well as the overlay blocking, fragmenting, and revealing of alternative representations of "Goat" and "Sylvia," forces the viewer to immediately question and further consider who these two characters are.

ADRIANA URIBE, Student
PAUL SAHRE, Instructor
School of Visual Arts
New York, New York, USA

attributes, as well as understanding their historical development and potential applications, is to use a more detailed and accurate system of typeface classification.

The following classification system is a simplified, practical reference tool for any graphic designer:

Old Style
Typefaces classified as Old Style are primarily based on roman proportions. They do not have strong contrasts in stroke weights, the stress of curved strokes is noticeably oblique, a smaller x-height defines their lowercase letters, terminals are pear shaped, and lowercase counters are small. Bembo, Centaur, Garamond, Jenson, and Goudy are Old Style typefaces.

Transitional
Typefaces classified as Transitional primarily have greater stroke contrast in comparison to Old Style typefaces. Their serifs are sharper, a larger x-height defines their lowercase letters, and the stress of curved-stroke letterforms is vertical or nearly so. Baskerville, Bell, Bulmer, Fournier and Perpetua are Transitional typefaces.

Perricone MD's branding campaign includes packaging, website, advertising, and promotional sales collateral that reflect a modern visual interpretation of a traditional apothecary—understated, small-scale serif typography, scientific photography, frosted amber glass— all organized and composed in an asymmetrical, balanced manner. In this application, asymmetrical serif typography, while restrained and small-scale in relationship to the detail photograph of the bottle, is clean, crisp, immediate, and highly visible.

MONNET DESIGN
Toronto, Ontario, Canada

The purity and simplicity of these all-cap letterforms used in this identity program for the retailer Walrus creates a strong and impactful visual message that is immediate, direct, and memorable due to the sensitive and effective use of sans serif typography.

MERCER CREATIVE GROUP
Vancouver, BC, Canada

Modern

The most prominent characteristic of Modern typefaces is their extreme contrast in stroke weights. Serifs are thin and completely flat, displaying little if any bracketing. The stress of Modern typefaces is almost invariably vertical. Bodoni, Didot, Melior and Walbaum are classified as Modern typefaces.

Sans Serif

The distinguishing feature of sans serif typefaces is their lack of serifs (sans means "without" in French). Stroke weight is even and uniform, and their stress is vertical. The italic versions of san serif typefaces often appear as slanted romans or obliques. Akzidenz Grotesk, Franklin Gothic, Futura, Meta and Univers are classified as sans serif typefaces.

Slab Serif

Slab serif typefaces are uniform in stroke weight and their stress is vertical. Their serifs are usually the same weight as the stem of the letterforms. Slab serif typefaces are also identified as Egyptian. Cheltenham, Clarendon, Egyptienne, Lubalin Graph, Memphis, Rockwell, Serifa and Stymie are classified as slab serif typefaces.

Graphic

This category of typefaces includes unique and idiosyncratic type families that have graphic and illustrative characteristics such as script, cursive, brush, display, decorative, and blackletter.

The graphic character of any typeface communicates a purely visual message as well as a narrative one. It may have a distinct physical presence on the page and also convey obvious or implied meanings such as young or old, feminine or masculine, aggressive or timid. While everyone may not understand or connect with the designer's intent with any given typeface used, it is the sole responsibility of the graphic designer to carefully evaluate his or her own typographic decisions in the context of the message and the audience.

Optical Issues

The graphic character of a typeface also has a direct relationship to the perception of its size. For example, a typographic line set in the same point size with two visually distinc-tive type styles will appear to be different sizes. This optical discrepancy is due to a graphic, as well as measured, difference

How Can Graphic
Design Help Save
The Planet?
Designer
Dinner #3
Deus Ex Machina
Opening Doors
Colour Trends
Ken Cato
Designer
Dinner #4
David Pidgeon
Xmas Party

AGDA

AUGUST
SEPTEMBER
OCTOBER
NOVEMBER
DECEMBER

Trivia
Designer
dinner #1
Inspired by design
Business focus
Tobias
Frere-Jones
Designer
dinner #2
The other forty
one minutes
Inspirational
spaces

AGDA

MARCH
APRIL
MAY
JUNE
JULY

Both of these promotional posters for the Australian Graphic Design Association function as an announcement for a series of member programs and offerings. The visual power and dynamic character of typographic form—in this case, Futura—is used as a visual common denominator in both poster compositions. Left and right justification of each program listing, as well as the use of horizontal hairlines located between each listing, further organize and isolate information reinforcing a visual hierarchy. Bold, graphic contrast with black and white and saturated colors of red and yellow are used effectively to further engage the viewer.

LANDOR
Paris, France

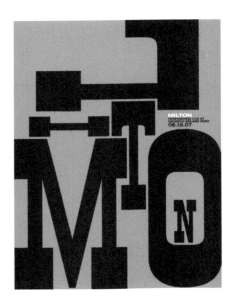

Old, wood-type, slab serif
letterforms are the inspiration, as well as the primary
imagery, for these posters
promoting the band Milton's
public concert in Madison
Square Park in New York City.
This bold, black typography
is organized in a playful
composition and set off by
vibrant color backgrounds.

STEREOTYPE DESIGN
New York, New York, USA

between the actual x-heights of both type
styles. Sans serif x-heights tend to be larger
in relationship to their cap heights than
serifs, which tend to be smaller in relationship to their cap heights. The difference in
graphic and measured sizes can vary as much
as two to three points, depending on the
typeface. For example, a sans serif typeface
such as Frutiger or Gill Sans may be legible
and comfortable to read at 8 points, but an
Old Style typeface such as Bembo or Garamond at the same size will be illegible and
impossible to read with any level of comfort
or ease.

Alignment Formats

Typography can be organized in several
different compositional formats called alignments. A flush left alignment is set so that
multiple typographic lines (or text) begin
at the same point along a left-hand vertical
edge. A flush right alignment is set in the
same manner with all text beginning at the
same point along a right-hand vertical edge.
A centered alignment is set so that all text
shares the same center axis with the width
of the paragraph. Additionally, there are two
alignment options with a centered composi-

tional format. A centered alignment is set so
that all text lines are varied lengths, centered
above one another, and share the same
center axis with the width of the paragraph.
A justified alignment is set so that every text
line is the same length and aligning on both
the left- and right-hand vertical edges. A justified alignment is the only alignment where
all text lines are the exact same length.

When text is set flush left, flush right,
or centered, the varied lengths of these text
lines create an uneven textural edge(s) called
a "rag."

Alignments also can have an effect on
typographic spacing within a body of text.
When text is set flush left rag right, word
spacing is uniform and even. The same effect occurs with flush right rag left and
centered alignments. In a justified alignment,
word spacing varies because the width of the
paragraph is fixed and the words on every
line need to align with both vertical edges,
no matter how many words are on each line.

With justified alignments, variations in
word spacing are the most challenging issue
for any graphic designer to resolve properly
and effectively. The result of ineffective
justified alignments is an overabundance of

The textured letterforms used in these two posters for UCLA School of Architecture's "Double Edge" lecture series function as visual metaphors and identifiers for each architect's style, aesthetic, and individual approach to their discipline and craft. A two-column grid provides maximum scale and visibility, allowing the viewer to immediately connect with the subtle visual nuances appearing in each typographic treatment. Color, contrast, and figure-ground also reinforce these subtle textural distinctions and characteristics in both posters.

THE MAP OFFICE
New York, New York, USA

This logotype for Brawer & Hauptman Architects is unified and singular in appearance due to the use of layered and integrated letterforms—a ligature created with the ampersand and *c* in the word *Architects*, and the lower serif of the *A* in *Architects* registered with the crossbar of the *e* in *Brawer*.

PAONE DESIGN
ASSOCIATES, LTD.
Philadelphia, Pennsylvania, USA

This visual identity system for an exhibition titled Graphic Design in China relies solely on the fluorescent light installations evident in each exhibition venue that spell out the names of each designer and disciplines represented in the exhibition. These custom, stencil-like letterforms used in the exhibition, as well as in smaller-scale, print applications such as this promotional poster, are all derived from lines representing fluorescent tube fixtures used throughout the light installations.

SENSE TEAM
Shenzhen, China

"rivers"—arbitrary negative spaces that occur and visually connect from line to line within the body of the typographic text. One of many methods to solve this issue is to identify the optimum flush-left alignment width for the type size being used prior to creating a justified alignment.

Typographic Color

Typography is a reality as well as an abstraction in visual communications. While we think of typography primarily as elements used together to form words and sentences, it also has an inherent function purely as a visual form. As such, typography can function in the same way as other basic graphic design elements such as point, line, shape, form, color, texture, contrast, and pattern in any visual composition.

It has rhythmic, spatial, and textural characteristics, identified as typographic color. Typographic color is similar to a color's hue—such as yellow, red, or blue—as well as its variations in density, contrast, texture, and value. Effective typographic color in any visual communication is determined by variations in weight, spacing, kerning, leading, mass, and texture.

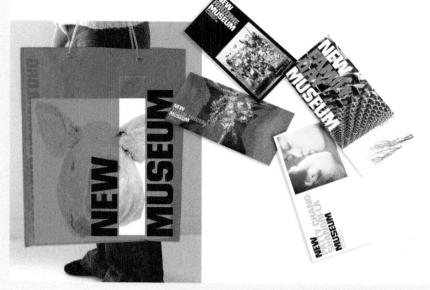

A change in typographic color immediately influences not only the spatial and textural appearance of typography but, more importantly, its meaning. A typographic color change allows a designer to highlight structure and invigorate a page. An effective use of typographic color in graphic composition and verbal clarity is directly related to the success of any visual communication.

Ultimately, a graphic designer's use of typography as an effective and communicative design element is solely dependent upon their technical expertise and historical knowledge, as well as a thorough understanding of the functional and aesthetic characteristics of letterform and typographic composition.

NEW
235 BOWERY
NEW YORK NY
10002 USA
MUSEUM

New York City's New Museum of Contemporary Art is the city's only museum dedicated exclusively to showcasing contemporary art. Its branding program, as well as its bold, sans serif logotype, is based on the premise of "new art and new ideas" as well as the act of self-renewal. The designer's first step with this program was to simplify the institution's name to "New Museum" and to loosen up the visual feel of the museum itself. The logotype changes and takes on new visual forms when used in a variety of print and digital applications that rely upon a full spectrum of colors, images, and other related visual elements.

WOLFF OLINS
New York, New York, USA

grid \'grid\ *n*
2 b: a network of uniformly spaced horizontal and perpendicular lines (as for locating points on a map)

26

"The grid system is an aid, not a guarantee . . . . But one must learn how to use the grid; it is an art that requires practice."
JOSEF MÜLLER-BROCKMANN (1914-1996). *Swiss, Author, Designer, Educator*

Fundamentally, a grid is composed of a series of horizontal and vertical lines that provide alignments and intersections for the graphic designer to use in an obvious or subtle manner. It is a primary design principle for all visual communications. Similar to many other design elements and

principles in this book, a grid's functions are limitless. It can provide order and visual unity as well as enhance the rhythm and pacing of any visual message. A typographic page grid is a two-dimensional organizational framework used to structure content. It is an armature for the graphic designer to organize narrative and visual content in a rational, aesthetic, and accessible manner.

Historical References

Whenever there has been a need to build an object, divide an area, or decorate a flat surface, some form of a grid has been used. The (continued on page 264)

A three-column page grid, based on a square planning module, is used as an effective organizational tool for the layout and design of this annual report for Media Trust, an organization that works in partnership with the media industries throughout the United Kingdom in building effective communications for charities and nonprofit organizations. This type of page grid provides maximum flexibility and continuity, allowing for a variety of types of narrative and visual information to be treated in a meaningful and accessible manner for the reader. Different-scale typographic elements and blocks of narrative text are set flush left, ragged right, and hang from a set of integral grid datums throughout the report, giving it a more active and varied presentation yet still providing a unified visual voice.

FORM
London, United Kingdom

1971

The Herald Newspaper
MASSIMO VIGNELLI
New York, New York, USA

In 1960, after completing his architectural studies in Milan and Venice, MASSIMO VIGNELLI (b. 1931) moved to the United States as cofounder and design director of Unimark International, at the time one of the largest design-consulting firms in the world. During the 1960s, Unimark and Vignelli designed many of the world's most recognizable corporate identities and public information systems for clients such as American Airlines, Ford Motor Company, and Knoll International, as well as the iconic sign program for the New York City subway system.

Unimark's philosophy was based on a disciplined and systemized approach for creating effective and rational mass communications for their clients; solutions that provided the means by which an individual could implement any aspect of a program in an efficient and effective manner.

The primary tool for achieving this objective was the grid, ultimately standardizing graphic communications for the majority of their corporate clients including Alcoa, JCPenney, Memorex, Panasonic, Steelcase, and Xerox.

In 1971, following the closing of Unimark's New York offices, Vignelli cofounded Vignelli Associates with his wife, Lella. It is a multidisciplinary design consultancy firm whose philosophy and approach is firmly grounded in the modernist tradition and on simplicity through the use of fundamental elements and principles in all of their work. The firm's broad range of work and interests, including furniture, tableware, apparel, showrooms, interiors, posters, publications, and corporate identity programs, is based on a simple belief, Vignelli says: "If you can design one thing, you can design everything."

While Vignelli's typographic range expanded beyond the sole use of Helvetica for Unimark's clients to now include classical typefaces such as Bodoni, Century, Garamond, and Times Roman, he retained and strengthened a rational use of grid systems and an emphasis on clear, precise, and objective visual communications.

One primary example of this philosophy was evident in the early 1970s with the design of the *Herald* newspaper. Prior to this time, newspapers and tabloids were one of the most neglected areas of visual communication. In 1971, Vignelli Associates was given the opportunity to design the *Herald*, a new weekly newspaper for the New York City tristate area. the *Herald* was structured on a page grid of six columns with sixteen modules per column. One typeface, Times Roman, was used throughout the publication, with one type size for all running, narrative text, two type sizes for titles and subtitles, and italic for captions and decks. Every page or two constituted a section of the whole paper, and all pages were structured with clear horizontal bands, which provided a strong, easy-to-read accessibility to the paper's editorial content. Reliance on a fully articulated page grid, as well as a unified set of design specifications, further indicated that the paper would be equipped for fast production and quick turn-around.

Unfortunately, the newspaper folded in less than a year due to union and distribution problems. However, use of the grid as an organizational, design, and production principle proved to be successful and was subsequently used by designers and publishers as an effective tool for the redesign of numerous newspapers and tabloids in the coming years.

Massimo Vignelli and *The Herald*

The Shape of **News**

This information-based data poster titled *The Shape of News*, documents the designer's analysis of newspaper title pages and their various content. The overall composition is arranged according to the U.S. states and provides the viewer with insight into the way public opinion was formed during the Iraq War. This study uses various colors to express a multivariate mapping of news interests and coverage such as local, national, and international; the wars in Iran and Afghanistan reveal the tenor of regional reporting over a period of two months. The actual use of newspaper page grids as the poster's primary communication device further conveys the use and type of information in a familiar manner.

CHRISTINA VAN VLECK
Lexington, Massachusetts, USA

grid has been relied upon as a guiding organizational principle by Renaissance artists as a method for scaling sketches and images to fit the proportion of murals, by cartographers in plotting map coordinates, by architects for scaling drawings and plotting perspective views, and by typographers in the design of letterforms and the printed page.

Prior to the invention of movable type and printing by Johannes Gutenberg in the fifteenth century, simple grids based on various proportional relationships were also used to arrange handwritten text on pages. While the grid evolved and developed over the next five hundred years, it primarily remained the same in structure and use.

Evolution of the Modern Grid

In the early 1950s, European designers such as Emil Ruder and Josef Müller-Brockmann, influenced by the modernist tenets of Jan Tschichold's *Die Neue Typographie (The New Typography)*, began to question the relevance and use of the conventional grid.

The result was the development of the modern typographic grid that became associated with the International Typographic Style or Swiss Design, which provided

CITY OF MELBOURNE

designers with a flexible system for achieving variations of the printed page. A seminal reference book on this subject, *Grid Systems in Graphic Design*, written by Müller-Brockmann, helped propagate the use of the modern page grid, first in Europe, and later throughout the world.

Functions

Visual communication carries its message and meaning through the organization and arrangement of disparate design elements. The clarity and immediacy of any message is further achieved with visual unity by the use of the grid. It is a useful and purposeful tool for any graphic designer. A page grid provides a framework for composition through its network of horizontal and vertical intersecting lines that organize and divide the page into field and interval, thereby creating a guide for establishing proportional relationships between the composition's design elements.

The grid is an invaluable principle of a graphic designer's vocabulary, as well as an essential tool that can be used in the increasingly complex production of print-based and digitally based visual communications.

The identity and branding program for the city of Melbourne is based on a triangular grid and fully expresses the multifaceted spirit of the city as a creative, cultural, and sustainable urban center. An iconic *M* is the central element of this program and has been constructed from the same triangular element of the program's organizational grid.

This grid's triangular base module is also used as an interpretive visual element that is articulated in a diverse palette of colors, patterns, textures, and images.

LANDOR
Paris, France

The inventive use of a flex- grid, while a thoughtfully
ible, four-column page grid considered hierarchy of type
with alternating narrow and weights and sizes contributes
wide columns, when needed, to a unified whole.
provides Yale's "A Guide to
Yale College" with a rhythmic
pacing and unexpected varia- PENTAGRAM
tion from spread to spread. New York, New York, USA
Full color, photographic
images of different scales are
allowed to invade columns
and bleed beyond the de-
lineated format of the page

It can be used to compose, organize,
separate, enlarge, reduce, and locate visual
elements. Grid construction can be loose and
organic or rigorous and mechanical. When
used correctly and appropriately, a grid provides simplicity, clarity, efficiency, flexibility,
economy, continuity, consistency, and unity
to any visual communication.

A grid, like any other element in the
design process, is not an absolute. It should
be used with flexibility and, when necessary,
be modified or even abandoned for a more
intuitive solution. It can be developed as
a simple framework that has an obvious and
integrated relationship to its narrative and
visual content or it can be composed of more
complex forms and proportions that provide
more varied and nuanced results.

Müller-Brockmann maintains that "the
grid system is an aid, not a guarantee. It
permits a number of possible uses, and each
designer can look for a solution appropriate
to their own personal style. But one must
learn how to use the grid: It is an art that requires practice." As a counterpoint, Charles-
Édouard Jeanneret-Gris (aka Le Corbusier),
a pioneer of modernist architecture and the
International Style, in his comments about his

An asymmetrial columnar
grid provides clear organization, flexibility, and
compositional diversity for
the navigation, narrative
information, and photographic elements of this website
for Gotham Construction,
a New York City–based
construction company.

SUPERMETRIC
New York, New York, USA

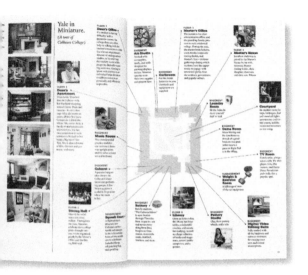

grid system called "Le Modulor" points out: "I still reserve the right, at any time, to doubt the solutions furnished by the Modulor, keeping intact my freedom which must depend on my feelings rather than my reason."

The use of an underlying organizational grid can enhance the clarity, legibility, and balance of any visual communication. When multiple pages are involved, as in a book or website, it guarantees continuity and unity.

Applications

A grid can be used to solve a wide range of design problems and is an effective organizational framework for newspapers, magazines,

A purely utilitarian, organizational grid used in this poster is composed of forty-eight equally proportioned modules and functions as a visual identity for this water table communicating the effects of Hurricane Katrina in the Gulf of Mexico. Stenciled letterforms are used solely to identify each of the neighboring states—Mississippi, Alabama, Louisiana, and Florida—that were affected by flooding, intermittently interrupted by the letters SOS as a further identifier for the urgency of the message. The contrast of warm and cool colors further reinforces the seriousness of this message.

STEREOTYPE DESIGN
New York, New York, USA

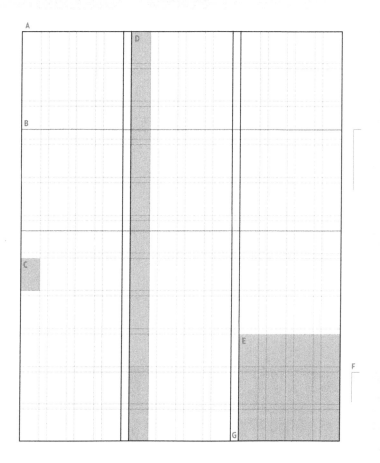

A

Margins are the borders or negative spaces surrounding the page's format and content. They define the live area of the page where type and image are located and composed. Proportions of margins are also a critical consideration since they assist in establishing the overall balance and tension in the page composition. Margins are also used to bring focus and attention to content, create respite for the reader's eyes, and function as an area for supporting page information.

B

Flow lines are horizontal alignments that organize content into defined areas, assist in guiding the reader's eyes across the page, and used to imply additional start and stop points for type or images on the page.

C

Modules are individual units of space within the grid separated by regular intervals that, when repeated across the page, create columns and rows.

D

Columns are vertical alignments of type that create horizontal divisions between the page margins. There can be any number of columns; sometimes they are all the same width or are different widths corresponding to specific types of information.

E

Spatial zones are groups of modules that form distinct fields on the page for containing or displaying similar or alike information, such as groups of images or multiple columns of text.

F

Markers are graphic indicators for supporting page information, such as running headers or footers, folios or page numbers, or any other element that occupies only one location on a page or spread.

G

Gutters, also known as alleys, are vertical spaces located between columns of type.

* The page grid illustrated here is the page grid used throughout this book.

books, annual reports, brochures, catalogs, sign systems, corporate identity and branding programs, and websites.

As a flexible compositional tool, a grid can assist the graphic designer in creating either static, symmetrical compositions, or active, asymmetrical ones. The construction of any grid can be orthogonal, angular, irregular, and circular. It can be an invisible and functional layer of a composition or it can be an obvious and active visual element of a composition.

The structure of a grid should always be based on a thorough understanding and analysis of the visual and narrative material to be used. This will allow a considerable degree of flexibility when composing and arranging disparate elements, such as typographic text and images, on a grid and ultimately the page, be it two-dimensional, three-dimensional, or virtual.

A grid can be visible or invisible, an implied framework or an obvious design element. It is also an essential design principle for organizing and presenting complex, multifaceted information in a systematic manner. Publications, websites, sign systems, advertising campaigns, and corporate communica-

Both of these informational data-based posters use the same articulated grid to organize and structure relational statistics in a meaningful and informative manner. Imaginary visual landscapes are built from the intersection and interplay of data formulated in both of these studies on people living in selected cities.

LORENZO GEIGER
Bern, Switzerland

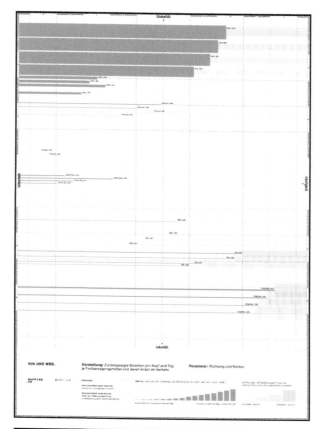

tions are all made up of multiple pages—each requiring a slightly different composition due to their varied content.

If a grid is well planned and conceived, it provides the graphic designer with an efficient way to create multiple layouts while maintaining visual consistency, continuity, and cohesiveness.

The development of the grid has been an evolutionary process. No one artist or designer can be identified as its sole creator or inventor; however, many creative minds have contributed to its development and will continue to influence its further refinement over time.

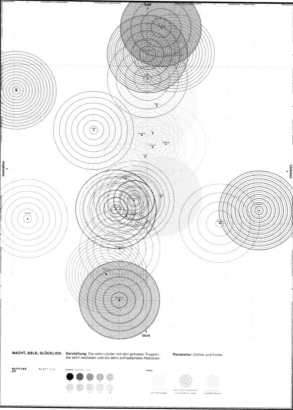

abstraction
the visual simplification, distortion, or rearrangement of a recognizable image

analogous colors
colors created from adjacent colors on a color wheel, with minimal chroma differences

apex
the outer point where two diagonal stems or strokes meet, as at the top of an *A* or *M* or at the bottom of an *M*

arm
a projecting horizontal or upward diagonal stem or stroke not enclosed within a character, as in an *E*, *K*, or *L*

art nouveau
French for "new art"; also known as Jugendstil, German for "youth style"; an international movement and style of art, architecture, and applied art that was popular from 1890 to 1905 and characterized by organic, floral, and plant-inspired motifs

Arts and Crafts movement
an international movement that originated in Great Britain during the late 1800s through the writings of William Morris (1834–1896) and John Ruskin (1819–1900) and was characterized by simple form and a medieval style of decoration

ascender
the part of a lowercase letter that rises above the body of the letter, or x-height, as in a *b*, *d*, *f*, *h*, *l*, and *t*

asymmetry
a state of visual balance (also known as informal or dynamic balance) in which compositional elements are not identical but are perceived as visually balanced

axonometric
a drawing projection method where a form is viewed from a skewed direction to reveal more than one of its sides in the same picture plane

balance
a state of equilibrium in which visual forces of equal strength pull in opposite directions

baseline
a line on which the bottom of characters without descenders sit or align

bowl
a curved stem or stroke that encloses a counter, as in a *b*, *p*, or *O*

bracket
a curving joint between the serif and a stem or stroke; also known as a fillet

cap height
the distance from a baseline to the top of a capital character.

chiaroscuro
a technical term for achieving strong contrasts of light to create a sense of volume in modeling three-dimensional objects

chroma
the amount of colorant in a pigment

cicero
a European typographic unit of measurement approximately equal to the British or American pica, or 4.155 mm

closure
a principle of visual perception in which the human eye visually completes an unfinished shape or form through the memory of that shape or form

color
a visual property of an object that depends on a combination of reflected and absorbed light from the spectrum, as well as inherent hues found in light and pigment

column
vertical alignments of type that create horizontal divisions on a page grid

complementary colors
any two colors found directly opposite one another on a color wheel

Constructivism
an art movement, originating in Russia in 1919, that rejected the idea of "art for art's sake" in favor of art as a practice directed toward social purposes and needs

contrast
a visual principle in which differences in light, value, texture, and color create the illusion of depth

counter
an area enclosed by a bowl or a crossbar

crossbar
a horizontal element connecting two vertical or diagonal stems or strokes, or crossing a stem or stroke, as in an *A*, *H*, *f*, or *t*; also known as a bar or cross stroke.

cubism
a twentieth-century avant-garde art movement, pioneered by Pablo Picasso and Georges Braque, characterized by objects that are broken up and reassembled in abstract forms

descender
the part of a lowercase letter that falls below the body of the letter or baseline, as in *g*, *j*, *p*, *q*, and *y*

de Stijl
a Dutch art movement (also known as neoplasticism) founded in 1917 and characterized by pure abstraction, as well as essential reduction of form and color

ear
a small projecting stroke sometimes attached to the bowl of a *g* or the stem of an *r*

expression
a principle of visual perception concerning the emotional, cultural, and social content of a visual message

figure-ground
the relationship of foreground and background in a two-dimensional composition

figure-ground reversal
a visual effect where a figure can function as a ground and a ground as a figure

flow line
horizontal alignments that organize content into defined areas on a page grid

form
three-dimensional derivatives of basic shapes, such as a sphere, cube, or pyramid

gestalt
the perception of the whole image as opposed to its individual parts or elements

glyph
a simplistic form or element of writing

golden ratio
also known as the divine proportion, golden section, and golden rectangle; proportional relationship defined as the whole compared to a larger part in exactly the same way that the larger part is compared to a smaller one; its mathematical expression is the number 1.618

grid
a module system composed of a set of horizontal and vertical lines used as a guide to align type and image and create a uniform composition

gutter (or alley)
vertical spaces located between columns of type on a page grid

hierarchy
an arranged, established visual order of importance, emphasis, and movement given to elements in a composition

hue
a fundamental property of color defined in its purest form

International Typographic Style
a graphic design style developed in Switzerland in the 1950s and characterized by clean, readable, asymmetric layouts and use of the page grid and san serif typefaces; also known as the Swiss School

isometric
a drawing projection method where three visible surfaces of a form have equal emphasis, all axes are simultaneously rotated away from the picture plane at 30 degrees, all lines are equally foreshortened, and angles between lines are always at 120 degrees

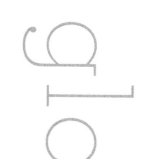

joint
the angle formed where two strokes meet or intersect, as is a *K* or *R*.

leg
a projecting diagonal stem or stroke extending downward, as in an *R* and a *K*; also known as a tail

ligature
a stem or stroke that connects two characters together creating a ligature or tied character

light
electromagnetic radiation of wavelengths visible to the human eye and used to create contrast, depth, brightness, and illumination

line
a fundamental element that consists of a number of points located next to one another in one direction

link
the stem or stroke that connects the bowl and the loop of a *g*

loop
the descender of a *g* when it is entirely closed

margin
border or negative space surrounding a page's format, grid, and content, and defining the live area of the page where type and image are located and composed

marker
graphic indicators for supporting page information, such as running headers or footers, folios or page numbers, or any other element that occupies only one location on a page or spread

module
individual units of space within a page grid separated by regular intervals that, when repeated across, create columns and rows

monochromatic colors
colors with varying values of a single color, created by adding white or black to a color

movement
a principle of visual perception that moves the viewer's eye through a two-dimensional space

pattern
the combination of lines, shapes, and/or colors in a consistent, orderly, or repetitive motif

pica
a typographic unit of measurement where 12 points equal 1 pica (1/16 inch or 0.166 inch) and 6 picas equal 1 inch (0.996 inch)

Plakatstil
an early poster style of art that began in the early 1900s and originated in Germany

point
an abstract phenomenon indicating a precise location; also defined as the smallest typographical unit of measure; one point is equal to 0.0148 inches

primary colors
yellow, red, and blue are pure in color composition and cannot be created from other colors

proportion
a comparison of two ratios; includes an indication of how the two ratios are related

quadratic colors
created from colors located in the corners of a square or rectangle juxtaposed on a color wheel

radial balance
a state of visual balance (also known as rotative symmetry) in which visual forces of equal strength radiate or extend out from a central point

rhythm
an alternating repetition of shape and space or a planned movement of visual elements in a composition

saturation
a fundamental property of color defined by intensity, or the brightness or dullness of a color

scale
the relationship of size or a composition of size from one element to another

secondary colors
colors created by combining two of the three primary colors

semiotics
the study of sign processes or the significance and communication of signs and symbols

serif
the beginning or end of a stem or stroke, arm, leg, or tail drawn at a right angle or at an oblique to the stem or stroke

shade
a fundamental property of color defined by the amount of black in a color

shape
the external outline or contour of an object, figure, or mass

shoulder
the portion of a curved stroke, but not the hairline, connecting two vertical strokes or stems

space
an element of design that indicates area and depth on a two-dimensional plane

spatial zone
groups of modules that form distinct fields on a page grid for containing or displaying similar or alike information, such as groups of images or multiple columns of text

spine
the diagonal portion or main curved stroke of an *S* or *s*

spur
a small, pointed projection from a stem or stroke, sometimes found on the bottom of a *b*, *t*, or *G*

stem (or stroke)
the principal vertical or oblique element(s) of a character, as in an *A*, *B*, *L*, or *V*; except for curved characters where they are called strokes

stress (or axis)
the inclination suggested by the relationship of thin and thick stems or strokes in a character, which can be an inclined or vertical stress or axis

Suprematism
a Russian abstract art movement that focused on fundamental geometric forms such as the circle and the square

swash
a flourished terminal, stem, or stroke added to a character

symmetry
a state of visual balance (also known as formal balance or reflective symmetry) in which compositional elements are identical, equally balanced, and can be divided into two equal parts that are mirror images of each other

tail
the short stem or stroke that rests on a baseline, as in a *K* or *R*; or extending below a baseline, as in a *Q* or *j*. In *K* and *R*, also known as a leg

tension
a principle of visual perception in which the forces of balance or imbalance, stress, action, and reaction exist between the elements of any composition

terminal (or finial)
A stem or stroke ending other than a serif

tertiary colors
colors created by combining one primary color with one secondary color

texture
a design element that creates or implies the tactile quality and characteristics of a surface

tint
a fundamental property of color defined by the amount of white in a color

tone
a visual characteristic, also known as value or shade, based on the degree of light or dark apparent on the surface of an object

triadic colors
colors created from other colors that are equidistant from one another on a color wheel

typography
the arrangement and aesthetics of letters and letterforms

value
a fundamental property of color defined by the lightness and darkness of a color

vertex
the angle formed at the bottom of a character where the left and right strokes meet or intersect, as in a *V* or *x*

x-height
the height of the body of lowercase letters, exclusive of ascenders and descenders

Books

AdamsMorioka and Stone, Terry. *Color Design Workbook: A Real-World Guide to Using Color in Graphic Design*. Beverly: Rockport Publishers, 2006.

Albers, Josef. *Interaction of Color*. New Haven: Yale University Press, 1963.

Arnheim, Rudolf. *Art and Visual Perception: A Psychology of the Creative Eye*. Berkeley: University of California Press, 1971.

Arntson, Amy E. *Graphic Design Basics*. New York: Rinehart and Winston, 1988.

Blackwell, Lewis. *20th Century Type*. New Haven: Yale University Press, 2004.

Bringhurst, Robert. *The Elements of Typographic Style*. Vancouver: Hartley and Marks, 2005.

Cohen, Arthur A. *Herbert Bayer: The Complete Work*. Cambridge: MIT Press, 1984.

Dondis, Donis A. *Primer of Visual Literacy*. Cambridge: MIT Press, 1973.

Drew, Ned, and Sternberger, Paul. *By Its Cover: Modern American Book Cover Design*. New York: Princeton Architectural Press, 2005.

Eason, Ron, and Rookledge, Sarah. *Rookledge's International Directory of Type Designers*. New York: The Sarabande Press, 1994.

Elam, Kimberly. *Geometry of Design: Studies in Proportion and Composition*. New York: Princeton Architectural Press, 2001.

Elam, Kimberly. *Grid Systems: Principles of Organizing Type*. New York: Princeton Architectural Press, 2005.

Elam, Kimberly. *Typographic Systems*. New York: Princeton Architectural Press, 2007.

Eskilson, Stephen J. *Graphic Design: A New History*. New Haven: Yale University Press, 2007.

Evans, Poppy, and Thomas, Mark A. *Exploring the Elements of Design*. New York: Thomas Delmar, 2008.

Gertsner, Karl. *The Forms of Color: The Interaction of Visual Elements*. Cambridge: MIT Press, 1986.

Goethe, Johann Wolfgang Von. *Theory of Colours*. Cambridge: MIT Press, 1970.

Heller, Steven, and Fili, Louise. *Stylepedia*. San Francisco: Chronicle Books, 2006.

Hemenway, Priya. *Divine Proportion*. New York: Sterling Publishing Co. 2005.

Hofmann, Armin. *Graphic Design Manual: Principles and Practice*. Switzerland: Niggli Verlag, Sulgen, 1965.

Igarashi, Takenobu. *Igarashi Alphabets*. Zurich: ABC Verlag Zurich, 1987.

Igarashi, Takenobu. *Igarashi Sculptures*. Tokyo: Robundo Publishing, 1992.

Itten, Johannes. *The Art of Color*. New York: Van Nostrand Reinhold, 1970.

Jute, Andre. *Grids: The Structure of Graphic Design*. Mies, Switzerland: RotoVision, 1996.

Kandinsky, Wassily. *Point and Line to Plane*. New York: Dover Publications, 1979. Originally published in 1926.

Kepes, Gyorgy. *Language of Vision*. Chicago: Paul Theobold, 1944.

Kirkham, Pat, ed. *Women Designers in the USA: 1900–2000*. New Haven: Yale University Press, 2000.

Klanten, Robert. *Data Flow: Visualising Information in Graphic Design*. Berlin: Gestalten, 2008.

Krause, Jim. *Color Index*. Cincinnati: How Design Books, 2002.

Kurlansky, Mervyn. *Masters of the 20th Century: The ICOGRADA Design Hall of Fame*. New York: Graphis, 2001.

Leborg, Christian. *Visual Grammar*. New York: Princeton Architectural Press, 2004.

Lupton, Ellen. *Thinking with Type: A Critical Guide for Designers, Writers, Editors, and Students*. New York: Princeton Architectural Press, 2004.

Lupton, Ellen, and Miller, J. Abbott. *The ABC's of The Bauhaus: The Bauhaus and Design Theory*. New York: Princeton Architectural Press, 2000.

Lupton, Ellen, and Phillips, Jennifer C. *Graphic Design: The New Basics*. New York: Princeton Architectural Press, 2008.

Maier, Manfred. *Basic Principles of Design*. New York: Van Nostrand Reinhold, 1978.

McLean, Ruari. *Jan Tschichold: A Life in Typography*. New York: Princeton Architectural Press, 1997.

Meggs, Philip B. *A History of Graphic Design*. New York: John Wiley & Sons, 2005.

Moholy-Nagy, Laszlo. *Vision in Motion*. Chicago: Paul Theobold, 1947.

Mount, Christopher. *Stenberg Brothers: Constructing a Revolution in Soviet Design*. New York: Museum of Modern Art, 1997.

Mouron, Henri. *A. M. Cassandre*. New York: Rizzoli International Publications, 1985.

Müller-Brockmann, Josef. *The Graphic Artist and His Design Problems*. Teufen AR, Switzerland: Verlag Arthur Niggli, 1968.

Müller-Brockmann, Josef. *Grid Systems in Graphic Design*. Niederteufen: Verlag Arthur Niggli, 1981.

Books (*continued*)

Rand, Paul. *Paul Rand: A Designer's Art*. New Haven: Yale University Press, 1985.

Remington, R. Roger. *Lester Beall: Trailblazer of American Graphic Design*. New York: W. W. Norton & Co., 1996.

Remington, R. Roger, and Hodik, Barbara J. *Nine Pioneers in American Graphic Design*. New York: W. W. Norton & Co., 1989.

Resnick, Elizabeth. *Design for Communication: Conceptual Graphic Design Basics*. Hoboken: John Wiley & Sons, 2003.

Ruder, Emil. *Typography*. New York: Hastings House, 1971.

Samara, Timothy. *Design Evolution: Theory into Practice. A Handbook of Basic Design Principles Applied in Contemporary Design*. Beverly: Rockport Publishers, 2008.

Samara, Timothy. *Making and Breaking the Grid: A Graphic Design Layout Workshop*. Beverly: Rockport Publishers, 2002.

Samara, Timothy. *Typography Workbook*. Beverly: Rockport Publishers, 2004.

Spencer, Herbert. *Pioneers of Modern Typography*. Cambridge: MIT Press, 1983.

Spiekermann, Erik, and Giner, E. M. *Stop Stealing Sheep and Find Out How Type Works*. Mountain View: Adobe Press, 1993.

Vignelli, Massimo. *design: Vignelli*. New York: Rizzoli International Publications, 1990.

Von Moos, Stanislaus, Mara Campana, and Giampiero Bosoni. *Max Huber*. London: Phaidon, 2006.

William Purcell, Kerry. *Josef Müller-Brockmann*. New York: Phaidon, 2006.

Wong, Wucius. *Principles of Two-Dimensional Design*. New York, John Wiley & Co., 1972.

Periodicals

Doubleday, Richard B. "Jan Tschichold at Penguin Books—A Resurgence of Classical Book Design," *Baseline*, No. 49, 2006, pg. 13–20.

Friedman, Milton, ed. "LA 84: Games of the XXIII Olympiad," *Design Quarterly 127*, 1985

Heller, Steven. "Paul Rand Laboratory: The Art of Bookjackets and Covers," *Baseline*, No. 27, 1999, pg. 17–24.

Heller, Steven. "When Paperbacks Went Highbrow—Modern Cover Design in the 50s and 60s," *Baseline*, No. 43, 2003, pg. 5–12.

Nunoo-Quarcoo, Franc. "Bruno Monguzzi—Master Communicator," *Baseline*, No. 30, 2000, pg. 25–32.

Page numbers in italic indicate figures.

About the Author

Richard Poulin is cofounder, design director, and principal of Poulin + Morris Inc., an internationally recognized, multidisciplinary design consultancy located in New York City.

His work has been published in periodicals and books worldwide, is in the permanent collection of the Library of Congress, and has received awards from the American Institute of Architects, American Institute of Graphic Arts, *Applied Arts*, *Communication Arts*, *Creative Review*, *Graphis*, *ID*, *Print*, Society for Environmental Graphic Design, Society of Publication Designers, Type Directors Club, and the Art Directors Clubs of Los Angeles, New York, and San Francisco.

Richard is a fellow of the Society for Environmental Graphic Design (SEGD), the organization's highest honor for lifetime achievement; and past president and board member of the New York Chapter of AIGA, He is also a recipient of a research grant in design history from the Graham Foundation for Advanced Studies in the Fine Arts.

Since 1992, he has been a faculty member of the School of Visual Arts in New York City and was formerly an adjunct professor at The Cooper Union. He has also taught and lectured at Carnegie-Mellon University, Maryland Institute College of Art, Massachusetts College of Art, North Carolina State University, Simmons College, Syracuse University, University of the Arts, and University of Cincinnati.

He lives in New York City and Clinton Corners, New York, with his partner of twenty-one years.

DEDICATION

This book is dedicated to the two most important and influential people in my life:

Muriel Poulin, who has always inspired me and taught me "to know is nothing at all . . . to imagine is everything."
—*Anatole France, French Novelist, 1881.*

And, above all, to

Doug Morris, for giving me the time, freedom, love, and support to pursue my dreams.

ACKNOWLEDGMENTS

This book would not have been possible without the support and contributions of all the designers who shared their work with me. Going through this process has truly reminded me of the incredible community that I am a part of and the great work my colleagues are producing all around the world. A special thanks to Sean Adams, Michael Bierut, Ivan Chermayeff, Richard Doubleday, Steff Geissbuhler, Allan Haley, Takenobu Igarashi, Bruno Monguzzi, Roland Mouron, Deborah Sussman, Massimo Vignelli, and Catherine Zask for their assistance, cooperation, and contributions to this book.

To Steve Heller for recommending me to Rockport Publishers as a potential author for this volume.

To everyone at Rockport Publishers, especially Winnie Prentiss, publisher, and Emily Potts, acquisition editor, for their encouragement, enthusiasm, and support, as well as to David Martinell, Betsy Gammons, and Cora Hawks for collaborating with me on this book.

To AJ Mapes and Erik Herter, two of my colleagues at Poulin + Morris Inc. who have helped design this volume with a level of detail and nuance that I did not fully realize when we started this project. Their invaluable contributions and insights to the design of this book are deeply appreciated and have made it one of the truly memorable and enjoyable experiences of my career.

And to my students—past, present, and future.

COLOPHON

The Language of Graphic Design was designed and typeset by Poulin + Morris Inc., New York, New York. Digital type composition, page layouts, and type design were originated on Apple Macintosh G5 computers, utilizing Adobe InDesign CS3, Version 6.0.5 software.

The text of the book was set in Verlag and Archer, two typefaces designed and produced by Hoefler & Frere-Jones, New York, New York.

DEFINITIONS

All definitions used in this book are from *Merriam-Webster's Collegiate Dictionary*, Eleventh Edition, 2009.

CPSIA information can be obtained
at www.ICGtesting.com
Printed in the USA
LVOW05s2142261015

459792LV00008B/10/P

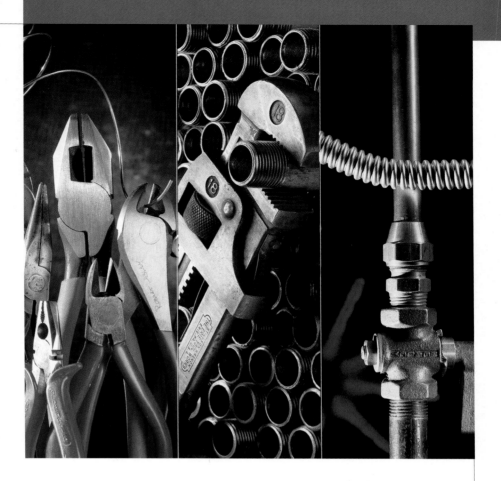

ORTHO'S HOME REPAIR PROBLEM SOLVER
MECHANICAL EDITION

Created and Designed by the Editorial Staff of Ortho Books

Writers
Robert J. Beckstrom
Jeff Beneke
Matt Phair
Naomi Wise

Project Editor
Sally W. Smith

Illustration Manager
Cyndie C. H. Wooley

Designers
Barbara Ziller and John Williams, Barbara Ziller Design

ORTHO BOOKS

Publisher
Robert B. Loperena

Editorial Director
Christine Jordan

Manufacturing Manager
Ernie Tasaki

Managing Editor
Sally W. Smith

Editor
Robert J. Beckstrom

Prepress Supervisor
Linda M. Bouchard

Editorial Assistants
Joni Christiansen
Sally J. French

Editorial Coordinator
Cass Dempsey

Copyeditor
Elizabeth von Radics

Proofreader
David Sweet

Indexer
Debbie Baier

Separations by
Color Tech Corp.

Lithographed in the USA by
Banta Company

Special Thanks to
Maja Beckstrom
Deborah Cowder
David Van Ness

Photographers
Laurie A. Black
Saxon Holt
Kit Morris
Ortho Library
Brent Lindstrom
Stephen Marley
Geoffrey Nilsen
Joyce OudkerkPool
Kenneth Rice
Sepp Seitz/Woodfin Camp

Art Director, Cover
Barbara Ziller

**Design Director,
Special Edition**
Beth Ann Edwards

Technical Consultants
Dan Fuller
Michael Hamman
Redwood Kardon

Illustrators
Edith Allgood
William Barrett, William Barrett
    Design
Jonathan Clark, Dart
Wayne S. Clark
Deborah Cowder, Indigo Design
    & Imaging
Tim Graveson, Pandion
    Productions
Dillon Riley
Hal Lewis and Andrew Richards,
    Apple-day
Elizabeth Morales and Jim Roberts
Jenny Page and George Vrana,
    Illustrious, Inc.
Cyndie C.H. Wooley

Address all inquiries to:

Meredith Corporation
Ortho Books
1716 Locust Street
Des Moines, Iowa 50309-3023

If you would like more information on other Ortho products, call 800/225-2883 or visit: www.ortho.com

ISBN 0-89721-493-5

UPC 071549058937

EAN 9780897214933

ORTHO'S
Home Repair Problem Solver
Mechanical Edition

Special Edition for
Handyman Club of America

Handyman Club Library™
Handyman Club of America
Minneapolis, Minnesota

Before taking any other steps to make your home comfortable, beautiful, and problem-free, learn what to do in an emergency. In addition to the information and prevention tips presented in this chapter, you will find tips throughout the book for working safely as you make repairs around the home.

SAFETY FIRST

▶ House is on fire.

Get everyone out fast. Crawl if there is smoke. Call from a neighbor's house (or grab the cordless phone on your way out). Don't go back in; let firefighters handle rescues. Fire spreads through a home astonishingly fast. The biggest danger is smoke asphyxiation.

Evacuating the house

Phoning fire department

▶ Chimney has fire.

A chimney fire makes a loud, roaring sound and is incredibly hot (2,000° F or more). It is probably visible from the street. Evacuate the house. After calling the fire department from a neighbor's house, hose down the roof.

Some experts recommend, if you have time, closing the damper of a woodstove or smothering the fireplace fire with a fire extinguisher or huge amounts of coarse salt; never douse it with water.

Don't use the fireplace or woodstove again until you have the chimney inspected and cleaned.

▶ Roof is on fire.

Evacuate everyone and call the fire department.

▶ Smoke is emerging from around chimney area.

Extinguish the fireplace fire or close the woodstove damper. Call the fire department. The smoke may be from the fireplace, escaping through cracks in the brick chimney, or it may be from smoldering framing that could erupt into flames. Evacuate if you see flames. Do not reuse the fireplace until the chimney is inspected and repaired.

▶ Clothes are on fire.

Drop and roll. Do not run. If possible, smother fire with a blanket.

Dropping and rolling

Using a blanket

▶ House has small fire.

Get everyone out of the house. Call the fire department. If you can do it safely, return and use a Class-ABC fire extinguisher, aiming toward the base of the fire. Stay between the fire and a safe exit. If you don't extinguish the fire immediately, get out.

Using a fire extinguisher

▶ Oven has fire.

Turn off heat. Leave it alone. Don't open the oven door until the oven has cooled down. Keep watch.

Tip *With your entire family, plan escape routes ahead of time, especially from bedrooms. Establish a meeting place, usually the front of the home, and designate a person to notify neighbors and call for help.*

Tip *Chief causes of home fires: (1) cooktop flare-ups, (2) falling asleep while smoking, (3) fireplace, woodstove, or kerosene heater, (4) playing with matches, and (5) faulty electrical system or equipment.*

▶ Cooktop has grease fire.

Turn off heat. Smother fire quickly with a large lid, use a Class-B fire extinguisher, or throw baking soda or salt on the fire (*never* water, flour, or sugar). Call for help if you don't extinguish the fire immediately.

Smothering a range-top fire

Oven mitt

▶ Electrical appliance or receptacle is smoking, sparking, or on fire.

If it's only sparking or smoking, unplug the appliance or turn off the circuit breaker. Have it repaired before using it again.

If the appliance is on fire, evacuate the house, call the fire department, and use a Class-C fire extinguisher. *Never* use water—it could conduct electricity to you.

Extinguishing an appliance fire

▶ Fire has damaged house.

Secure the house (board up windows, repair the roof). Remove debris. Store damaged but salvageable items in a safe place. Protect the plumbing system against freezing. Inspect the electrical system before using it. Clean up. Air out carpets and furnishings damaged by water. Take smoke-tainted clothes and fabrics to a dry cleaner with an ozone chamber. Place smoke-tainted books and valuable papers in a freezer until a time when you can have them professionally cared for. Open up walls and other covered areas where water may have caused hidden damage. It's necessary to air them out to prevent rotting. Often, more damage is done by water inside walls than from the fire itself, so make every effort to dry out the house thoroughly, including pumping the basement or crawl space.

Cleaning up after a fire

Clean walls

Plywood

Pump

Wallboard removed

Tip   *When phoning 9-1-1 or other emergency numbers, don't hang up until told to do so. You may be asked for additional critical information.*

Tip   *Do not empty ashtrays into wastebaskets. Use a metal trash can, a container of water, or other nonflammable receptacle for this purpose.*

SAFETY FIRST

Fire safety equipment.

■ Smoke detectors: At least one for each floor. Critical areas are kitchen, rooms with fireplaces, hallway near sleeping rooms, and top of basement stairs. Combination of "hard-wired" and battery-operated types is recommended.

■ Extinguishers: Have several (kitchen, basement, shop, smoking areas, each floor). Locate near the room's <u>exit</u>, so you can grab it on your way back <u>into</u> the room after evacuating the house. For all-around use, keep a Class-ABC on hand. For specific uses:

   Class-A: paper, wood, cloth, rubber, dry materials

   Class-B: oil, grease, gasoline, flammable liquids

   Class-C: electrical

■ Emergency lights: Place flashlights with fresh batteries by beds, in kitchen, in basement, and in other areas of house. You may also want to get lights that stay plugged into electrical receptacles and which go on only in a power failure.

■ Escape ladder (chain ladder that hangs from a windowsill): Locate in any upstairs bedroom that does not have two easy escape routes.

■ Sprinklers: Consider them if you are planning a remodeling project, especially if your household includes small children or elderly persons.

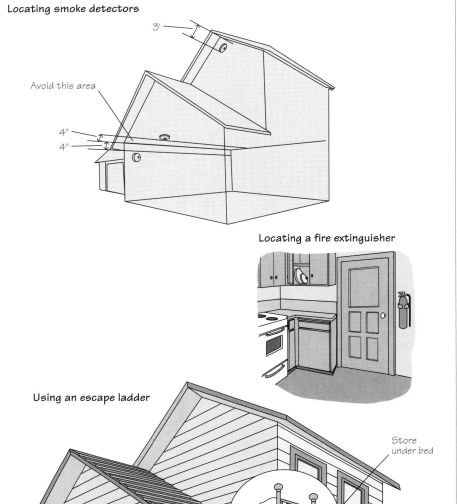

Locating smoke detectors

3'

Avoid this area

4"
4"

Locating a fire extinguisher

Using an escape ladder

Store under bed

Tip   Most fires start at night during sleeping hours. Rooms where most fires start: (1) kitchen, (2) bedrooms, and (3) heater closet or room. Rooms where most deaths occur by fire: (1) living/family room and (2) bedroom. At greatest risk are children under 10 and adults over 65.

▶ *House has gas odor.*

Very dangerous. Evacuate the house immediately, leaving doors open as you go. Call the gas company or 9-1-1 from a neighbor's house.

If odor is only slight, turn off gas at meter. Open windows and doors. Do not light a match, use the phone, switch on lights, or do anything that causes sparks or friction. Get out. Call the gas company or 9-1-1 from a neighbor's house.

If the gas is bottled propane (LP), it is heavy and will settle to the floor or basement area; things will seem normal at nose level. Do not reenter the house—and especially don't relight pilots—until you are sure the gas has dissipated. Bottled gas ignites more readily than natural gas and is much more explosive.

Turning off natural gas

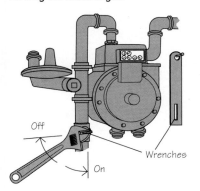

Off

Wrenches

On

Turning off liquid gas

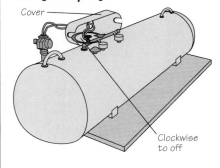

Cover

Clockwise to off

▶ *You smell fumes.*

It's probably improper venting or backdrafting of a gas appliance (in backdrafting, flue gases are forced back down the flue because of unbalanced air pressure, a common occurrence with tightly insulated homes). Although not an immediate problem unless it is highly concentrated in a confined area, this condition is still a serious safety hazard. (The most dangerous component, carbon monoxide, is odorless.) For immediate relief, ventilate the house. Don't operate exhaust fans (such as a kitchen hood or bathroom fan) without opening a window or door first; it will only exacerbate the problem.

For a long-range solution, make sure every gas appliance has a flue to the outdoors and an adequate supply of fresh combustion air. Test by holding a smoking match or incense next to the flue intake while the appliance burner is on; the smoke should be sucked up the flue. If it isn't, have a combustion

Testing for backdrafting

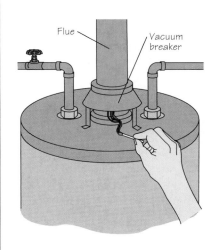

Flue

Vacuum breaker

air duct installed to provide a continuous supply of fresh air, even when the house has negative air pressure. Also consider purchasing a carbon monoxide detector.

▶ *House has a sewerlike odor.*

Pinpoint the source—usually a bathroom fixture, laundry sink, or drain. Most likely the water has drained out of the trap of that fixture. Pour water into it and monitor it for several weeks to see if the smell resumes. If so, have a plumber inspect it. If you can't pinpoint the source, inspect under the house for a broken or leaking drainpipe. It could even be underground, so check along the ground above the house sewer line. If you don't know where the line runs, locate the point under the house where the main drain goes under or through the foundation and project a line from that point to the street. A cleanout plug outside the foundation may provide a clue. Dig to expose the suspected source, or call a plumber.

▶ *You smell ammonia or refrigerant.*

This sharp, strong, acrid smell is caused by gases leaking from an air-conditioning compressor, refrigerator, or freezer. It is dangerous. Evacuate the house and then call the fire department from a neighbor's house.

Tip If you have bottled gas (LP), have the control valve inspected by a professional. Many defective valves made by various manufacturers have been recalled since 1977. If your local supplier, heating contractor, or plumbing contractor is not aware of particular recalls, contact the Consumer Products Safety Commission (look in the phone book under "U.S. Government" listings).

▶ Electricity goes off in whole house.

Provide emergency lighting (candles, flashlights, backup lights). You need to check the main disconnect to see if it is tripped. As you approach it, examine the immediate area for loose or dangling power lines. If you see some, call the utility company. If there are no dangling wires, check the disconnect, being careful not to stand on damp ground; wear gloves. If the breaker is tripped, call an electrician. If it is a cartridge fuse or other device besides a breaker, you will need to have an electrician test it for you.

If the breaker is not tripped, see if the power for the rest of the neighborhood is also out. If so, turn on a portable radio for information. If the phone works, report the outage to the utility company. Turn off any large appliances that were on,

so there won't be a heavy demand when electricity is restored. Turn off TVs, computers, and other electronic equipment that could be damaged by a power surge. Don't open the refrigerator or freezer.

In cold weather, if power will be off for more than two or three days, drain the water system and/or put antifreeze in P-traps, appliances connected to the plumbing system (such as washing machines), and plumbing fixtures that have standing water. Steps for draining the water system: (1) turn off main valve, (2) turn off inlet valve (cold water) to water heater, (3) open faucets at the highest point of system, (4) open faucet or disconnect pipe at lowest point, and (5) drain water heater by attaching a hose to the drain valve, running it outdoors, and turning on the valve.

▶ Electricity goes off in part of house.

Blown circuit. Turn off appliances and light switches in those rooms. Reset circuit breaker (or replace fuse). If electricity goes back on, test all the fixtures and receptacles one by one until you discover the one that caused the short. (Turn off each fixture before turning on the next one.) Remove the defective appliance. If none is defective, the problem was probably too many turned on at once. Reduce the load. Eventually, you may have to add a new circuit. See page 60.

▶ Finding solutions to other emergencies.

Pipe is burst or leaking.
    See page 12.
Pipe is frozen.
    See page 16.
Faucet won't shut off.
    See page 30.
No hot water.
    See pages 25-27.
Hot water is scalding.
    See page 22.
Toilet is clogged.
    See page 49.
Drain is clogged.
    See page 17.
Heat is off.
    See page 96.
Smoke detector goes off frequently.
    See page 90.

Locating main disconnect

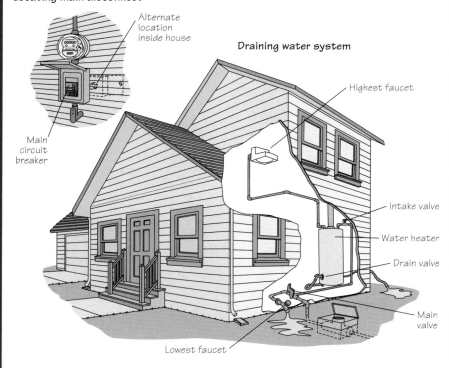

Alternate location inside house

Main circuit breaker

Draining water system

Highest faucet

Intake valve

Water heater

Drain valve

Main valve

Lowest faucet

Tip *The National Fire Protection Association estimates that as many as 33 percent of all residential smoke detectors have missing or dead batteries and are therefore inoperable. Push the test button on your smoke detector to make sure the battery is working.*

The plumbing system in most homes moves water and waste so efficiently that it's easy to take the system for granted. Problems do occur, however, and are often urgent. This chapter covers 130 plumbing problems that you can either solve yourself or diagnose well enough to know when to call for help.

SOLVING PLUMBING PROBLEMS

▶ Plumbing leak is coming from unknown source.

To fix a leak, you have to find the source. Sometimes this can be a frustrating search, but be persistent and don't dismiss the impossible (for example, water flowing uphill, pipes having invisible cracks, and tile installations not being waterproof). Start your detective work by considering sources other than a leaking pipe. Water that splashes around sinks often works its way down walls or into cabinets. A sink may also have a crack or loose drain fitting that dribbles a hidden stream of water. Tubs and showers are likely sources of leaks, especially at joints along the floor, at joints between the tub rim and walls, and at tiled corners inside a shower stall or tub surround. All of these areas, as well as joints between sinks and walls and around sink faucets, should be sealed with flexible caulk specified for tubs or bathrooms. To apply, first remove old caulk and loose debris; then dry out the joints with a hair dryer or portable heater and apply the caulk according to the manufacturer's instructions. (See page 43.)

If those aren't the sources, and clues point toward a leaky pipe, look for a pattern in the telltale drips, water stains, or musty smells. A steady leak, especially when plumbing fixtures aren't used, is almost certainly from a water supply line and should be repaired immediately (see right). A leak that fluctuates between a trickle and a gush is probably from a leaking drainpipe. You can temporarily stop this type of leak by not using the fixture(s) served by the pipe. If moisture appears only when certain fixtures are used or if the leak dries up when you're away on vacation, the problem is most likely a leaking drain pipe or water being regularly splashed on the floor.

If you still can't verify whether the leak is from a drainpipe or supply line, turn off the main water valve, open faucets in the house to relieve pressure, and let the area around the leak dry out for a while. Then close all faucets and open the main valve. If signs of leakage reappear, you can figure that you have a supply leak because you haven't let any water into the drain system or used any fixtures. You can also detect a supply-line leak, especially one that you may not be aware of (for example, in an underground pipe), by turning off all faucets in the house and then monitoring your water meter for a while (don't forget to turn off an automatic ice maker and other appliances hooked directly to water pipes).

To verify a drainpipe leak: Fill some buckets with water, shut off the main water supply, wait a while, then pour buckets of water down drains near the suspected pipe; watch for signs of leaking after each pour. For ambiguous leaks (such as water on the sidewalk that could be from your drain or your neighbor's), add fluorescent tracer dye (available from plumbing suppliers) to the water before pouring it down drains.

▶ Supply pipe leaks.

To temporarily fix a pinhole leak, jam a toothpick into it or tighten a piece of rubber over it with a hose clamp; for cracks or larger holes try wrapping the pipe with electrical tape or resin-coated fiberglass cloth. Another quick fix is a repair clamp. Buy the same size as the leaking pipe (usually ½ inch or ¾ inch), lay the rubber gasket over the leak, and tighten the clamp onto it.

For permanent repairs replace the pipe or fitting or, if it's a small hole, patch it with a dresser coupling. To install a dresser coupling, turn off the water and cut through the pipe at the leak with a hacksaw. If there's no "give" in the pipe you will have to make two cuts—far enough apart to slip the coupling onto one of them but close enough for the coupling body to bridge the gap. Separate the pipes enough to slip the disassembled coupling components, in sequence, onto the cut ends of the pipe. Align the pipe and center the coupling body over the cut(s); then snug the gaskets and retainers into place, screw the nuts onto the coupling body, and tighten them with two wrenches. If you find a leak in a buried pipe, you may be able to patch it, but it could be a sign that it's time to install a new line.

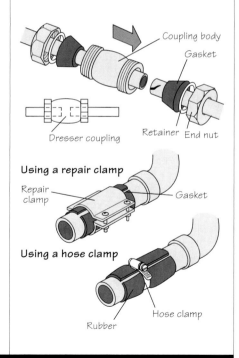

Using a dresser coupling

Coupling body
Gasket
Retainer   End nut
Dresser coupling

Using a repair clamp

Repair clamp
Gasket

Using a hose clamp

Hose clamp
Rubber

Tip   *Pipes in the drain-waste-vent (DWV) system are 1½, 2, 3, and 4 inches ID (inside diameter). At one time virtually all DWV pipes were cast iron or galvanized steel. More recently, copper pipes were used for the smaller sizes (1½ and 2 inch). Now almost all systems use plastic pipes, either ABS (black) or PVC (white or beige).*

Tip   *Supply pipes, which bring hot and cold water to fixtures, are easy to distinguish from drainpipes because they are smaller (usually ½ inch or ¾ inch ID). The hot-water and cold-water pipes are often (but not always) installed parallel to each other, about 8 to 12 inches apart, and don't have to slope downward on horizontal runs as drainpipes do.*

▶ *Drainpipe leaks.*

Drainpipes can be frustrating to repair because of difficult access, bulky materials, and rigid pipes with no "give" to them. However, the advent of plastic piping and no-hub couplings eases much of the work, and you can take your time because you don't have to shut off the water (although nobody can use fixtures affected by the leak). After you've found the leak (most drainpipe leaks are in joints), remove any ceiling or wall materials necessary to gain full access to it; then warn everyone in the house not to use fixtures that drain into the leaking pipe. If you trace the leak to a bathtub drain, see page 44.

For temporary repairs, seal a leaky joint in cast iron or steel pipe with plumber's epoxy putty (available at plumbing-supply stores). Follow label directions carefully and wear gloves. Use the same putty to patch cracks and small holes in pipe, or cover the hole with a rubber patch cut from an inner tube or similar material. Wrap a piece of sheet metal over the patch and secure it with hose clamps. Seal a leaking joint in plastic pipe with epoxy putty or the bonding solvent used to join plastic pipes. First dry the pipe with a hair dryer or heat lamp. Use solvent specified for the type of plastic—ABS (black pipe) or PVC (white or beige pipe)—and follow directions on the label. Apply a thick layer and press it into the joint with a toothpick. Work quickly and wear gloves.

For permanent repairs, cut out the leaky section of pipe or fittings and replace it with new pipe and fittings. Make cuts where exposed pipe ends will be accessible and will leave room for new pipe to be jockeyed into place. For cutting plastic pipe use a carpenter's handsaw; for

copper, a hacksaw; for steel, a reciprocating saw with bimetallic blade; and for cast iron, a pipe snapper (which you can rent) or circular saw with metal-cutoff blade. Make cuts square (mark by wrapping a piece of paper around the pipe and tracing along one edge). After cutting out the leaky section, carefully examine the remaining pipe ends for cracks. If an end is cracked, cut off more pipe (make sure the stub is long enough to fit into the new fitting or coupling).

When measuring for the new pipe and fittings, allow for a ⅛- to ¼-inch gap at each end. To join plastic pipe to fittings, see page 14. To join steel or cast-iron pipe, or to join plastic pipe to either one (or itself), use a no-hub coupling. It has a stainless-steel sleeve with a neoprene gasket inside and tightening bands around the outside, and comes in 1½-, 2-, 3-, and 4-inch diameter sizes. Make sure the coupling is specified for the type of pipe you are joining (cast iron, steel, plastic, or copper), which all have different wall thicknesses even though the nominal pipe size is the same. Use a transition coupling for joining two different types of pipe. Tighten any coupling to 60 foot-pounds of pressure (rent or borrow a plumber's torque wrench).

Before positioning pipes for the last joint, slide the stainless steel sleeve of the coupling onto the old pipe; then slip the neoprene gasket onto the pipe until it is halfway on, and roll the loose end back over itself (like rolling a sock inside out). Position the new pipe and secure it at the other end. Then unroll the gasket onto the new pipe and center it over the joint. Slide the sleeve over the gasket and tighten the bands.

If wet spots in your yard make you suspect that you have a leaking sewer line, or perhaps a hole in your septic tank, pick up a bottle of

tracer dye at a local plumbing-supply store. Flush some down the toilet and watch for signs of the dye in the yard. If it shows up, you will need to have repairs made on your sewage system right away.

Using epoxy putty

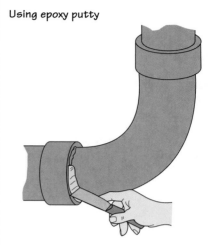

Cutting cast-iron pipe

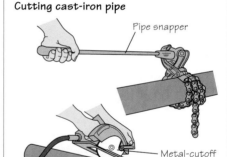

Pipe snapper

Metal-cutoff blade

Using no-hub connectors

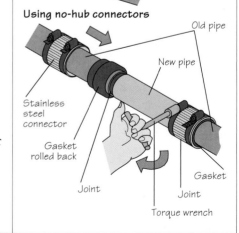

Old pipe

New pipe

Stainless steel connector

Gasket rolled back

Joint

Gasket

Joint

Torque wrench

Tip *Terminology for drain-waste-vent (DWV) fittings may seem confusing but is really quite logical. Couplings join two pipes of the same size. Adapters join fittings and pipes of different sizes or materials. Elbows, called ells or bends, are named by their angle or by the fraction of a full circle they turn (for example, a 90-degree bend or quarter bend, a 45-degree bend or eighth bend). Tees (T shaped) and wyes (Y shaped), which have three openings, are referred to by the size of their openings as well as type of fitting (for example, 2-inch wye). If the opening sizes vary, they are listed in this order: downstream outlet, upstream inlet, branch inlet (for example, a 3X3X2 wye or 2X1½X1½ sanitary tee).*

▶ *Steel pipe needs replacing.*

Turn off the water supply. Cut through the damaged section and unscrew both sections of cut pipe. Take them to the hardware store or plumbing supplier and buy a union fitting, one short nipple, and a threaded section of pipe long enough so that the new assembly, when tightened, will be the same length as the original section of pipe. If you can't find threaded pipe the right length, you will need to have one cut and threaded. You can rent pipe threaders, but you should be able to get it threaded at a hardware store, at a plumbing supplier, or by a cooperative plumber.

Before screwing a pipe into a fitting, coat the male pipe threads with pipe joint tape or compound. (Do not coat the male half of the union fitting that the ring nut tightens onto.) To assemble, tighten the two halves of the union onto the new pipes. Then slip the ring nut onto the pipe that has the non-threaded union half on it, with the threads of the ring nut facing the union fitting. Screw each pipe into one of the fittings in the water line. You'll have to push the first pipe over slightly to get the second one in; be careful not to loosen any joints. Tighten each joint with two wrenches (one on the pipe, one on the fitting for opposition).

Once the pipes are in place, align them so the union halves mate without binding, spin the ring nut onto its corresponding half of the union, and, with two wrenches, cinch it tight.

Replacing leaking pipe

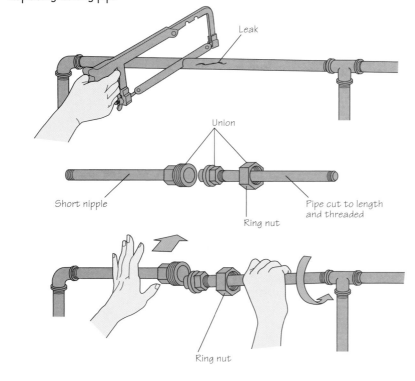

Leak

Union

Short nipple

Ring nut

Pipe cut to length and threaded

Ring nut

▶ *Plastic pipe needs replacing.*

Shut off the water (if a supply pipe) or warn people not to use upstream fixtures (if a drainpipe). You will need to cut out the leaky section of pipe; use a carpenter's handsaw for plastic drainpipes, a hacksaw for supply pipes (smaller diameter). Locate cuts where the remaining pipe ends will be accessible and will allow you to jockey the new pipes into place. On large pipes, to be sure cuts are square, mark cut lines by wrapping a piece of paper around the pipe and tracing along one edge. When measuring between fittings to cut new pipe to length, include the full depth of each hub in your measurement, less ⅛ inch per hub, to make sure "slip-in" dimensions are included. After cutting, sand off any burrs or rough spots.

If the assembly includes bends or tees, dry-fit the pieces together before gluing them to make sure everything aligns. If you're dry-fitting ABS (black) pipe, the pipe will slip only about halfway into each hub when dry (it goes all the way when cemented), so make allowances. PVC (white or beige) pipe will slip into hubs the full distance, with or without solvent cement. With pipes aligned, use a nail to scratch a line across each joint so you can quickly align the pipe and fitting when you glue them together.

When you are sure everything will fit, pull the pieces apart and glue the assembly together, joint by joint. If you are joining PVC pipe, coat each mating surface with primer first, then solvent cement (both specified for PVC pipe). For joining ABS pipe, use just ABS solvent cement (no primer). Use the applicators attached to the can lids and follow all label directions. After coating the outside of the pipe and

Tip　*DWV fittings differ from water supply fittings in two important ways. First, fittings that change the direction of flow allow for the slope that horizontal pipes must have. For instance, a 90-degree bend turns slightly more than 90 degrees. Using this fitting to change the direction of flow from vertical to horizontal gives the horizontal pipe a slight downward slope away from the vertical pipe. Using the same fitting to change direction of flow from horizontal to vertical allows the horizontal pipe to slope toward the fitting. The second difference is that tee fittings have the direction of flow built into them: The two openings that form the straight "through" part of the fitting are an inlet and an outlet and must be oriented accordingly. (Vent tees are an exception and can be installed either way.)*

the inside of the fitting hub with cement, insert the pipe into the fitting and turn it so the scratch marks align; then shove the pipe so it bottoms out in the fitting and hold it until the cement sets. Work quickly; setup time is less than 10 seconds.

If there's not enough flexibility in the drain line to separate pipes far enough to slip them into fittings, use no-hub couplings, at least for the last joint you make (see page 13).

Joining plastic pipe

Marking alignment

Applying solvent cement to pipe . . .

. . . and fitting

Joining pipe

Alignment marks

▶ *Soldering copper pipe may present fire hazard.*

The flame from a propane torch can ignite wood framing in a matter of seconds. Be prepared! Keep a fire extinguisher or a spray bottle filled with water close by. Whenever possible, prefabricate assemblies by soldering joints before putting the assembly in place. When soldering joints in place, protect all flammable surfaces with a piece of sheet metal—a double thickness of standard flue pipe works well. You can also buy fireproof pads at a hardware or plumbing-supply store. Make sure you can access the back of the joint as well as the front, and bend the solder into a curve or hook to reach those awkward areas before you start the flame.

▶ *Copper pipe needs replacing.*

For an assured permanent repair to a leaking copper pipe, replace it with new copper tubing. First turn off the water supply or, for a drainpipe, stop upstream usage. Cut out the leaking section with a tubing cutter or hacksaw. Cut a new piece of the same size tubing to length; include the hub depths of both fittings in your measurement (hub depth equals the nominal size of the pipe—for example, ½ inch or ¾ inch). Using the appropriate fittings, such as a straight coupling or an elbow, dry-fit the assembly to make sure all the pieces fit. If it is a complex DWV assembly, use a nail to scratch a line across each joint so it will be easy to align when you solder it.

To prepare a joint for soldering, shine both mating surfaces so the copper has no oxidation (discoloring) marks: Use sand cloth to shine the end of the tubing, and a fitting brush to scour the inside of the fitting. To be successful, soldering must be done on dry tubing. If

there is any water remaining in the pipe, plug the pipe with a piece of white bread or a dissolvable plug made for this purpose. The bread or plug will disintegrate and pass out of a faucet (you might want to remove aerators until it does).

To solder, spread a small layer of flux on the mating surfaces and assemble the joint. Light a propane torch and heat the fitting uniformly. As you heat, touch the solder against the joint. It will melt and be drawn into the joint when the metal is hot enough; when it starts to melt, remove the flame and run the solder all around the joint, forming a continuous bead. Let the joint cool before touching it or turning the water back on.

Joining copper pipe

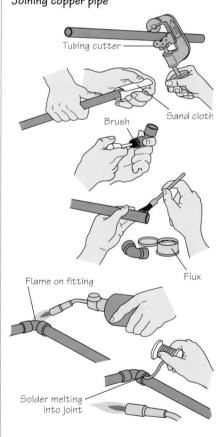

Tubing cutter
Brush
Sand cloth
Flux
Flame on fitting
Solder melting into joint

Tip *Gas lines are always steel, so when you work on a steel water pipe you want to be sure it's not a gas line. The best way to tell is to trace the pipe to a fixture or other known component of the plumbing system. If that's impossible, you certainly know it's a water pipe if water is leaking from it. If there are no active leaks, look for rusty spots near joints. If the pipe is black (ungalvanized) or coated uniformly with rust, it is probably a gas line. However, note that gas lines may have galvanized fittings and even galvanized pipe for short runs. Finally, pipes in pairs indicate water piping for hot and cold water.*

Tip *Solder with lead in it cannot be used for making plumbing joints. Buy lead-free solder.*

▶ Pipe is frozen.

Shut off the water supply to the pipe. Open the nearest faucet to allow melting ice and steam to escape. Using a hair dryer or, on a metal pipe, a propane torch, apply heat to the frozen pipe, starting at the open faucet and working back. (Be careful not to overheat the pipe.) Alternatively, wrap the pipe with electrical heating tape or a securely tied towel and pour hot water on the tape or towel. Once the ice has melted, turn on the water supply, then close the faucet after water flows freely. If freezing persists, insulate the pipe or permanently wrap it with electrical heating tape.

Thawing a frozen pipe

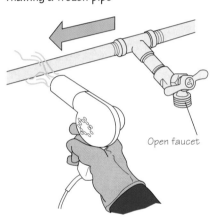

Open faucet

▶ Fixture has no vent pipe.

Plumbing codes require that every fixture drain within a specified distance of the fixture trap (P-trap) be connected to a vent pipe that terminates above the roof. The vents have two purposes: to vent sewer gases from the drain/waste system and to equalize pressure in the drain system so water won't siphon out of the fixture trap every time a fixture is used, thereby admitting sewer gases into the house.

If a sink or other fixture drains slowly or periodically releases sewer gas through the drain, it is probably not vented properly. You can tell for sure only by inspecting the drain line behind the wall or under the floor; it should have a vent pipe that branches off from it and eventually terminates above the roof. Consult a plumber to see if a vent pipe is needed and to have one installed. There are strict code requirements governing vents—where and at what angle it should connect to the drain line, what size pipe is required, what fittings are allowed, whether the same pipe can be a vent for one fixture and a drain for another ("wet vent"),

and what type of pipe is allowed if exposed to sunlight and weather.

If you have experience with rough plumbing and want to install a vent yourself, the most difficult part of the job is finding a pathway for a vent configuration that satisfies code requirements. The easiest vent to install is an individual pipe from the fixture all the way to the roof, one size smaller than the drain pipe size, but there may be windows and other obstacles in the way. Look for closets and corners where the pipe could be boxed in. Limit horizontal runs to half the total vertical rise. Horizontal runs should slope ¼ inch per foot back toward the drain. Some local codes

Venting fixtures

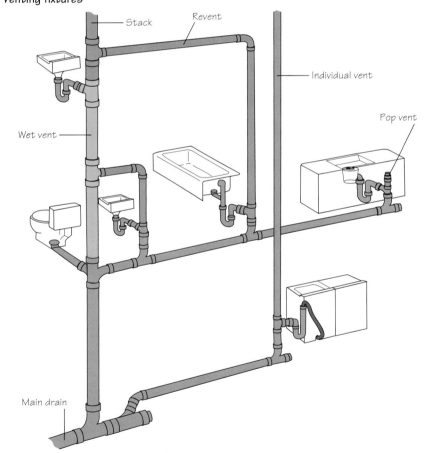

Stack

Revent

Individual vent

Pop vent

Wet vent

Open faucet

Main drain

Tip   *An important part of the venting system is the trap that every fixture must have, which functions as a seal to keep sewer gases out of the house. The trap is a semicircular section of pipe that retains a small amount of water after each use of the fixture. Most traps have a horizontal outlet and are thus shaped somewhat like the letter P—hence the term "P-trap." Some, such as sink traps, are visible. Tub and shower traps are located under the floor. Washing-machine traps are located inside the wall above floor level. Toilet traps are integrated into the fixture. Double traps (two traps serving one fixture—for instance, if a trap is plumbed into the waste outlet of a toilet) are prohibited.*

allow vents to be run outside the house. If an individual vent is unworkable and wet-venting is allowed, is there a stack (main vent for house, usually 4-inch pipe) close by that you can tie into? If not, can you "revent" by tying the new vent pipe into a stack above the point where its highest branch drain connects to it? Some codes allow the use of indoor vents, sometimes called "pop vents." These can save you the trouble of having to run a vent up through the roof. Check with the local building-inspection department about these and other requirements before you begin.

▶ Pipes are corroded on outside.

If old galvanized-steel or iron pipe looks corroded but is not leaking, poke at it with an awl or a small screwdriver to see if the walls seem solid. If the pipe seems strong, there's probably no reason to take any remedial action—just keep an eye on the pipes from time to time. If you detect severe corrosion, you can cover the damaged area with plumber's epoxy or a clamp (see page 12), or you can cut out the old pipe and replace it with new (see page 14).

Copper tubing is unlikely to corrode unless the water supply is particularly acidic. If this is the case, keep an eye on the pipes—especially joints—and be prepared to replace leaky copper pipes with plastic supply pipes (PVC for cold water, CPVC for hot) as the need arises. Consult a plumber about replacing all the pipes at once and other remedies.

▶ Vent pipe is frozen or clogged.

As water vapor from draining hot water exits a vent pipe and contacts frigid air, it causes frost and ice to form. On small-diameter vent pipes (1½ and 2 inches), it can build up enough to form ice across the opening. If you can get on the roof, dig out the ice with a stick or chipping tool; if not, look for a cleanout or use the closest plumbing fixture to run a drain auger up the vent. To prevent the problem in the future, have vent "reducers" (they actually enlarge the vent size) installed at the top of small vents. Other clogs, such as bird nests or leaves, should be cleaned out by hand (barbecue tongs work well for reaching down the pipe). Then flush the pipe using a garden hose.

▶ Drainpipe is clogged.

First locate the blockage by noting which fixtures are backing up and tracing the drain system from there. If only one fixture is clogged, the blockage is probably very close to it. First try clearing it with a plunger. If it's a sink or tub, remove the strainer or stopper, and plug the overflow opening with a wet rag. Make sure there's at least a couple of inches of water in the bottom. Coat the bottom of the plunger with petroleum jelly, plunge vigorously, wait, then plunge some more.

The traps on sink drains often have a cleanout plug. If the plunger fails to open the drain, place a bucket under the trap and remove the plug. Use a piece of wire to try to detect a clog in the trap and if so, to break it up.

If the problem persists, try "snaking" the pipes with a drain auger. Push the auger down into the drain until it meets resistance. Tighten the thumbscrew on the crank handle so it's about 1½ inches from the drain hole; rotate

the handle back and forth while pushing it down, until you can push the handle all the way to the drain with no resistance. To determine whether the auger tip broke up the clog or merely turned a tight corner, turn on the water to see if it drains quickly. If so, remove the auger and flush the drain. If not, plunge onward by releasing the thumbscrew and reeling out some more auger until you meet resistance again. Repeat the process until water flows. On tub drains, remove the overflow plate and run the auger down the overflow opening.

If all fixtures are blocked, the clog is probably in the main drain. If upstairs fixtures are blocked and downstairs fixtures aren't, the clog is probably located in an upper portion of the soil stack. Look for a cleanout plug near the affected fixtures. Cleanouts are located at the upstream ends of horizontal runs, usually where a branch drain connects to the main drain. Even if you can't find exposed drainpipes, you may find an exposed cleanout protruding from an exterior wall, in a stairwell, or behind a laundry area. Remove the cleanout plug and try to open the drain using an auger. Have buckets, rags, and newspapers handy. If there is no cleanout near the fixtures, run the auger down the vent pipe or down the drain of the fixture that is farthest downstream of all the affected ones.

Chemical drain cleaners should be used only as a last resort. They are potentially dangerous to the user and if on the first try they don't dissolve the blockage completely, it may harden and won't dissolve again. They work best for periodic cleaning or for clearing pipes that are only slightly blocked. If you must use one, follow directions carefully, and avoid using a

Tip   When buying and installing DWV fittings, pay attention to the direction of flow built into tee and wye fittings. Unlike supply fittings, which are reversible, DWV fittings can be installed backward by mistake.

plunger on a drain after you have dumped chemical drain cleaner down it.

If all of this fails to remove the clog, call a plumber or drain-cleaning service. (See also entries for specific fixtures: sink, page 34; bathtub, page 45; toilet, page 49.)

Using a drain auger in a sink

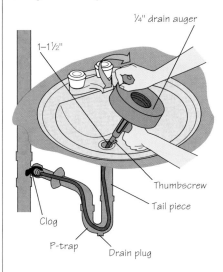

Drainpipes are noisy.

Drainpipes located inside walls and ceilings can transmit the sound of rushing water into adjacent rooms, especially if the pipes are plastic and the walls thin. The remedies are drastic—you will have to open up the walls and either replace the plastic pipes with cast iron or wrap them in sound-absorbing insulating material. It also helps to isolate pipes from the framing with sound-deadening pipe hangers or with cushioning material packed around the holes where they penetrate the framing. Also check any drains where the noise is noticeable

to see if they are properly vented (see page 16). If so, check the vent opening on the roof to see if it is clogged. If that doesn't fix the problem, consult a table of drain and vent sizes to make sure that the drainpipes and connections are properly sized (see page 152).

Supply pipes are noisy.

All water pipes create a certain amount of sound when the water is on; it's usually a low murmur (different from the sudden sloshing sound of drainpipes) that is easy to get used to. When pipes are in direct contact with the house framing, this sound is magnified and may become annoying. If so, trace as many water pipes as you can and look for the straps and hangers that secure them to the house framing. Remove old hangers and secure the pipes with plastic or plastic-coated straps and hangers. Where pipes go through holes drilled in the framing, force pieces of insulation, rubber matting, rubber gloves, or other sound-deadening material between the pipe and wood.

Supply pipes make another sound that is much more annoying: "water hammer," a loud hammering noise whenever a faucet is turned off, especially automatic valves in a dishwasher or washing machine. To reduce the sound, first insulate the pipes from the house framing with insulated straps and hangers, and pack insulation between pipes and wood framing. If that doesn't fix the problem, install air chambers at each offending fixture. These are devices installed on the hot- and cold-water pipes that function as shock absorbers to cushion the sudden change in water pressure created by a faucet being turned off. You can make air chambers from pipe one size larger than the supply pipes you are

muffling. Turn off the main water supply and drain the pipes. On a horizontal section of each supply pipe near the fixture, cut out enough pipe to install a tee fitting, pointing up. Attach a short nipple, a reducing coupling, and a 12- to

Insulating pipe from framing

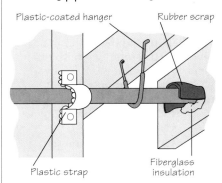

Installing an air chamber or shock absorber

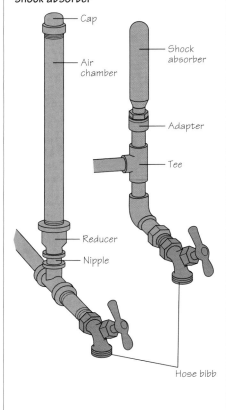

Tip *It is normal for hot-water pipes to knock and groan, even when water is not running through them. Changes in temperature cause the pipes to expand and contract.*

18-inch length of larger-diameter pipe (this is the air chamber) to the tee. Cap the pipe.

You can also buy water-hammer arresters, or shock absorbers, at a plumbing-supply house. One type is connected to the supply piping, the same way as an air chamber. The other type, which is more expensive but much easier to install, fits between the washing-machine hose and hose bibb. If several fixtures have water-hammer problems, it is due to high water pressure throughout the house. Rather than install several air chambers, a better solution would be to install a pressure-reducing valve near the water meter (see right).

▶ *Pipes bang even after air chambers have been installed.*

Air chambers act as shock absorbers in pipes. They rely on a cushion of air that is in contact with water under constant pressure. Eventually, the air cushion dissolves into the water. To restore air to the chamber, turn off the main water supply to the house and open all faucets. When the pipes have completely drained, turn off the faucets and turn the water supply back on. If you want to avoid this chore, replace the air chambers with water-hammer arresters, which can't become waterlogged (see opposite page).

▶ *Water flow is restricted.*

If the problem is not due to chronic low water pressure (see right), check any aerators at the affected faucets to see if they are clogged. If not, and if the fixture has a shutoff valve, turn off the valve, disconnect the supply riser (rigid or flexible tube that connects the shutoff valve to the faucet) from it, and temporarily connect a flexible riser that can be aimed into a bucket. Turn on the shutoff valve and observe the flow of water into the bucket. Test both valves. If water pressure is low, pipes supplying water to the affected fixture are undersized or clogged. They should be at least ½ inch in diameter. If they are old galvanized-steel pipes, they are probably clogged and should be replaced. If the whole house has been hit suddenly with low pressure, suspect a leak in an underground supply line (see page 12).

▶ *Water pressure is too low or too high.*

If low pressure is a problem throughout the house, it may be completely unrelated to the plumbing in the house. Have the water company come out and check the pressure at the meter. If it tests normal (30 to 55 psi), the problem is in the supply pipes for the house. It could be caused by an undersized feeder pipe from the meter or by clogged pipes. The supply pipe should be at least ¾ inch in diameter, 1 inch if your house is upslope from the street. If you have galvanized-iron water pipes, and especially if your water is "hard," the pipes may be clogged by scale and rust. In this case consider replacing the clogged pipes with copper tubing, which won't clog up like galvanized, and/or upsizing the main supply line. Replacing the pipes involves digging a trench from the water meter to the house foundation, turning off the meter, removing the old pipe, installing new pipe in the trench, and connecting it to the meter and house piping inside the basement or crawl space. If you use copper pipe, check with your local building department to see if Type L or Type K is required, and if underground connections must be made using different soldering techniques from those used above ground. (Silver solder or brazing may be required.)

If the low pressure exists at only one fixture or in one wing of the house, see left.

If the water pressure is too high, it can damage pipes and fixtures. Telltale signs are banging and chattering pipes, spurting water when you turn on a faucet, and excessively forceful water from a faucet only partially opened. To reduce pressure, install a pressure-reducing valve on the house side of the main shutoff valve. Turn off the water supply, cut the pipe, and install the valve as you would a replacement pipe (see page 14). However, you will probably not need to install a union fitting because the valve has coupling nuts at each connection. After you install it and turn on the water, adjust the pressure to between 30 and 55 psi, or until clanging noises in the pipes cease.

Installing a pressure-reducing valve

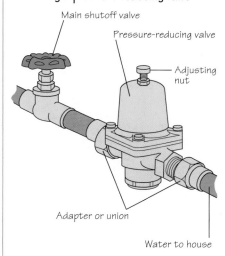

Main shutoff valve

Pressure-reducing valve

Adjusting nut

Adapter or union

Water to house

Tip *After you repair or replace a water pipe, let water run through a nearby faucet for several minutes to flush out any debris that may have been dislodged into the pipes. Remove the aerator from the faucet first.*

▶ *Basement lacks a below-grade drain.*

If you want to install a new bathroom or plumbing fixture in a basement with no drain below the floor, install a sewage ejector or sump pump. Check local code for your exact needs. Normally, a sump pump will be sufficient to dispose of gray water (the waste water from a sink or bath). If the bathroom contains a toilet, you will need a sewage ejector, which is designed to pump solids as well as liquids. In either case the pump requires a pit under the basement floor into which you install an airtight tank. Then run a waste line from the bathroom to the tank, venting it properly, and a discharge pipe from the tank to the sewer line. This line is plumbed differently from ordinary waste lines because it's under pressure; it must also have a check valve to prevent the waste from flowing back into the tank.

In addition to digging a hole through the basement floor for the sump, you will need to dig a trench for a 4-inch drainpipe. Cutting through concrete will probably require a jackhammer or concrete-cutting saw. Because of the scope of this project and the unusual plumbing requirements, you should consult a plumber before attempting the installation yourself.

Installing a sewage ejector

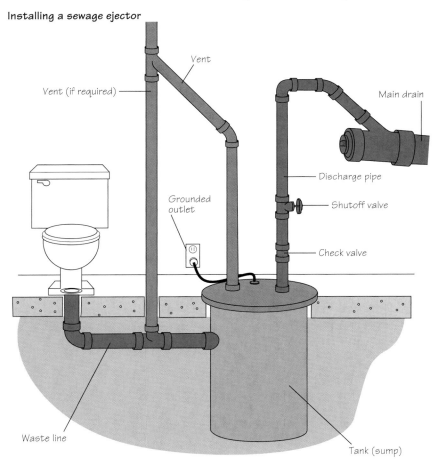

Vent

Vent (if required)

Main drain

Grounded outlet

Discharge pipe

Shutoff valve

Check valve

Waste line

Tank (sump)

▶ *Gas lines emit fumes.*

If you notice a strong gas odor or if your gas detector is going off, open some windows and doors and evacuate the house. Turn off the main gas supply, which should be near the meter on a natural-gas system or on the propane (LP) tank. Call the gas supplier or 9-1-1 from a neighbor's house.

If the gas smell you notice is faint and seems to be limited to certain rooms, check the valves and pipe joints around that area by spraying them with a soapy-water solution. If you find some bubbling, carefully tighten the connection with two wrenches, then retest. If the main supply has been turned off recently, it may be that some pilot lights weren't relit and are emitting gas. Check the pilots in all the gas appliances and, after ventilating the room, light any that are off, following instructions on the appliance.

If you have any gas appliances in your house, you should have a gas detector as well. It operates like a smoke detector and will alert the household to a dangerous concentration of natural gas, propane, or carbon monoxide. Contact your gas company for a supplier in your area.

▶ *Gas line has flexible connector in the middle of a run.*

Flexible connectors are generally permitted only at the end of a run to connect an appliance directly to the gas piping (some codes won't allow any flexible gas lines). If you have a flexible line anywhere else, have it replaced with rigid pipe. There are strict requirements for gas piping regarding type of fittings (no unions), size of pipe, length of runs, changes of direction, and the use of certain materials, so have the work done by a qualified professional.

Tip *If you aren't sure whether a pipe is a gas line or water pipe, have someone run hot and cold water at the nearest faucet. Listen to the pipe, holding an empty can or other small container against it to magnify the sound. If it's a water pipe, you should be able to hear running water in it very clearly.*

▶ Gas line has manual shutoff valve in middle of a run.

Gas valves (or cocks) are generally allowed only at the end of a line serving an appliance (except the main valve located at the gas meter). If you have one anywhere else, it should be removed because it presents the possibility of gas being inadvertently turned on and off. Also, valves are not entirely leakproof and become a weak link in an otherwise reliable run of rigid gas piping. To replace a fitting in the middle of a run of threaded pipe means working backward and unscrewing all the connections to that point, or cutting the adjacent piece of pipe to unscrew the valve, then replacing the valve and cut pipe with new fittings. However, plumbing and mechanical codes prohibit the use in gas piping of a union normally used to join threaded water pipes in the middle of a run; a left/right nipple and coupling must be used instead. Because gas piping has stricter requirements than water pipes, have the work done by a qualified professional.

▶ Gas lines are corroded.

Gas lines are most often run with black iron pipe, not galvanized pipe (some fittings and nipples may be galvanized, but pipe for long runs cannot be because the inside has a rough surface that inhibits the smooth flow of gas). Black pipe is susceptible to a little surface rust, which isn't necessarily a problem unless the pipe is in direct contact with the ground. Poke the corrosion with a sharp point; if the corrosion is thick and the pipe seems less than sound, call the gas company or a plumber.

▶ Gas line for a new appliance needs installing.

This work should be done by an expert. Gas lines need to be sized properly. If you were to simply tap into an existing branch line to serve the new appliance, you might overload the line, which could result in the other appliances on that line not working safely. A new line will normally be run from the large-diameter trunk line, but if the trunk line isn't large enough, it will have to be run from the gas meter.

In most areas, homeowners are not allowed to run or service gas lines. Plumbers are permitted to do gas piping in some areas, but not in others. Your gas supplier should be able to inform you.

▶ Gas line is in the way of other work.

If gas piping interferes with some other work (carpentry, plumbing, wiring), try to find some way to re-route the new job. Having to reroute threaded iron pipe, which is what gas piping most often is, can be intensive work. If it is not possible to avoid the piping and it has to be disconnected temporarily or rerouted permanently, the work should be done by a professional. Codes have strict rules for running gas lines; for instance, they usually won't allow gas piping to run through air ducts, laundry chutes, dumbwaiters, or vents.

All concealed gas lines must be rigid pipe and solid fittings. If you decide to conceal piping that was previously accessible, rather than move it, make sure it is rigid pipe and has no unions, fittings, couplings, bushings, or flexible connectors.

For tying into existing gas lines, there are some restrictions that differ from what is allowed with water piping. For example,

vertical branches run from horizontal pipes should connect to the top of the pipe, not the bottom. A branch that is taken from the side must run at least 6 inches horizontally before dropping from an elbow. Also, if you need to add offsets to the piping to get around an obstacle, it should be made with 45-degree elbows, not 90-degree elbows. This provides for less friction in the gas flow. Other requirements must be observed, but these three examples are most often overlooked, even by professional plumbers.

Changing direction of gas piping

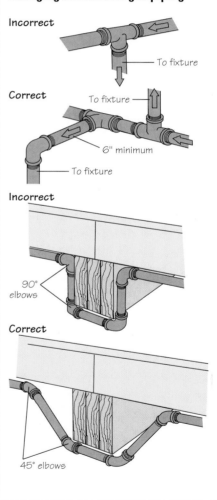

Incorrect

To fixture

Correct

To fixture

6" minimum

To fixture

Incorrect

90° elbows

Correct

45° elbows

▶ Scalding water or steam comes out of faucet.

Water heaters are pressurized tanks that can explode. Leave the faucet open to relieve pressure. Immediately turn off the main gas valve for the house (if water heater is gas) or main circuit breaker (if water heater is electric) and get out of the house. Wait at least 15 minutes to re-enter. Shut off the faucet that was steaming. Before restoring gas or electricity to the rest of the house, turn off the gas valve or circuit breaker for the water heater and the shutoff valve on the cold-water inlet pipe above the tank. Then repair or replace the unit, depending on the age of the water heater and type of problem.

With a gas water heater, the scalding water, steam, and excess pressure indicate that the thermostat wasn't turning off the burner. Replace the water heater or have a plumber install a new control unit. Get an estimate first; buying and installing a new tank yourself may be cheaper. With an electric unit, the heating elements didn't shut off in time. The problem could be a faulty upper thermostat and high-temperature cutoff; replace it (see page 29). For either type of heater the TPRV should also be replaced; it should have released steam and scalding water through the discharge pipe before they had a chance to build up in the pipes and faucets (see right).

▶ Temperature-pressure relief valve (TPRV) leaks.

The TPRV is supposed to open in an emergency—that is, when the temperature and/or pressure in the water heater gets dangerously high. If the valve is constantly dribbling water, the thermostat may be set too high. For a gas unit, turn down the temperature knob on the control unit near the bottom of the heater; for an electric unit, turn down the dial or small screw on the side of the heater. If water still dribbles from the TPRV, it may be stuck open slightly. To loosen it, lift the lever on top of the valve several times and let some water run out (the discharge pipe should direct it to a sink, drain, or outside). If the problem persists, replace the valve.

To replace a TPRV, first buy a new one that matches the BTU and pressure rating of the original. Shut off the electric power or gas supply and close the cold-water inlet valve. Drain about 10 gallons out of any hot-water faucet. Remove the discharge pipe from the valve and, with a pipe wrench, loosen and remove the valve from the water heater. Coat the male threads of the new valve with pipe joint tape or compound and screw it tightly into the tank. Reattach the discharge pipe (coat the male threads first). Turn on the inlet valve and restore power.

Installing a TPRV and discharge pipe

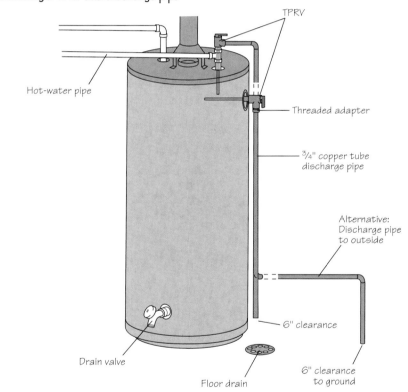

Hot-water pipe

TPRV

Threaded adapter

¾" copper tube discharge pipe

Alternative: Discharge pipe to outside

Drain valve

6" clearance

Floor drain

6" clearance to ground

Tip *In a home with young children or elderly adults, set the water-heater thermostat to 120° F to prevent accidental scalding.*

Tip *Test the TPRV every six months by lifting the lever and letting some water run out. If, when you lift the lever, no water comes out, tap on the valve lightly with a hammer and try again. If that doesn't fix the problem, replace the valve right away. Water heaters lacking TPRV valves or with nonfunctioning ones have been known to explode, sending the tank up through the roof like a rocket.*

▶ Tank leaks.

To find the source of the leak, check and tighten all connections (cold- and hot-water pipes, drain valve, anode rod, TPRV, thermostat, heating elements). If a leaking drain valve is brass, replace the stem washer or packing washer (see page 170). If it is a plastic doughnut-shaped knob, replace the valve (see next paragraph). For leaks at threaded fittings, remove the fitting, clean it, wrap it with pipe joint tape, and then reinstall. If the threads appear damaged, replace the fitting or pipe (see page 154).

To replace the drain valve, the tank doesn't have to be drained but the pressure must be removed from the tank. Close the cold-water inlet valve and open any hot-water faucet just long enough to let water flow. Shut it off and make sure no one uses any water while you work. Turn off electric power or turn the gas control to *Pilot*. Place a pan under the valve and unscrew it. Wrap pipe joint tape around the nipple on the water tank, then screw on the new valve.

If water is leaking through the tank itself, pronounce the tank dead and replace it as soon as possible.

▶ Tank hasn't been drained in six months.

A water heater should be drained regularly to prevent sediment from accumulating on the bottom of the tank, which shortens the life of the heater. One good strategy is to drain off 1 gallon every month. Some recommend that the tank be completely flushed every six months; this requires turning off

the inlet valve and draining the tank completely, then turning on the inlet valve while the drain hose is connected and running water through the tank at full force.

To drain a heater tank, shut off the cold-water inlet valve and the source of power—for an electric heater shut off the circuit breaker; for a gas heater turn the burner control to *Pilot*. Open the hot-water faucet that is at the highest level in the house, and leave it open. Screw a garden hose onto the drain valve at the bottom of the water heater and run it outside or to a drain. Open the valve. If the heater is in a basement and there is no drain, you will have to drain it off one bucket at a time.

To flush the tank after it's drained, keep the drain valve open and open the cold-water inlet valve for a couple of minutes to give the bottom of the tank a good flushing.

Close the drain valve and let the tank fill; keep the upstairs faucet open until water comes out of it for a few minutes to purge all the air from the pipes. Turn off the faucet and start up the water heater.

If sediment buildup is a common problem with your heater or in your neighborhood, replace the straight dip tube in the heater with a curved one. This will force the incoming water to swirl around the bottom of the tank, flushing it out when the drain valve is opened. To replace the tube, turn the control knob to *Off*; shut off the cold-water inlet valve and drain off a few buckets of water from the drain valve. Then disconnect the pipe or fitting from the cold-water inlet and pull out the plastic dip tube. Replace it with a curved one, then reassemble the inlet fitting. There

are also chemical products that can help remove certain kinds of sediment. Check with the water-heater manufacturer for recommendations.

Replacing a dip tube

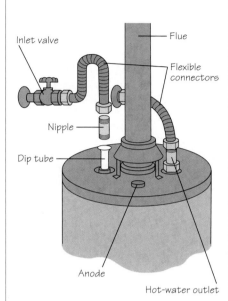

Inlet valve — Flue — Flexible connectors — Nipple — Dip tube — Anode — Hot-water outlet

▶ Hot water is rusty.

There are several possible causes. First check the water coming into the tank by closing the inlet valve, disconnecting the pipe from the tank, and capturing a few buckets of water from the inlet pipe. If it's rusty, the problem is rusty water supply lines; have them replaced. If the water is slightly rusty but not as much as the hot water is, the anode in the water heater may have deteriorated and is no longer able to clear mineral deposits from the water. Check it and, if it is worn, replace it (see page 14). If the water is still rusty, the glass lining in the

---

Tip *If water is leaking from a plastic drain valve—a common occurrence—consider replacing it with a ³⁄₄-inch ball valve or hose bibb, which will assure you of a sound fit and easier maintenance.*

Tip *A clue that sediment has accumulated in an electric water heater is if the lower heating element burns out. A clue for a gas heater is if the burner remains on for excessively long periods of time; the sediment creates a barrier between the water and the flame, which slows down heating.*

tank may have deteriorated—especially if the water heater is quite old. To check, drain a few buckets of water from the drain valve and compare it with hot water from a faucet. If the tank water is as rusty as, or more rusty than, the faucet water, the tank lining has worn through; replace the water heater. If the tank water is less rusty than the faucet water, and the hot-water pipes are galvanized steel, the pipes are probably deteriorating and need to be replaced. Finally, certain bacteria ("iron bacteria") in the water can also give it a rusty appearance. Have the water tested.

▶ Hot water has a strange odor or taste.

If there is a taste of plastic in the water, it may be due to a deteriorating plastic dip tube; replace it. Another cause might be sediment accumulating on the bottom of the tank. If you suspect this, drain and clean the tank (see page 23).

▶ Hot water takes too long to reach faucet.

First make sure that the hot-water pipes are thoroughly insulated.

If the problem is confined to a single bath or shower located far from the water heater, the best solution is to have a small 4- to 10-gallon electric heater installed at the point of use. A 120-volt heater can be plugged into normal household current, and it will supply hot water where you want it, when you want it.

If there are several remote locations, it might be more cost-effective to have a recirculating loop installed that constantly runs hot water to the remote locations and back to the water heater, or have a plumber run small-diameter pipes directly to each point of

use rather than a main line with branches. This will reduce the volume of water in the plumbing and speed up the arrival of hot water. Consult a plumber about these options.

▶ Recirculating system is using too much energy.

A recirculating system provides instant hot water at the faucets. It eliminates water waste, but it requires the water heater to heat water more often, and most systems have a small circulating pump that runs constantly. You can control energy usage by installing a timer to shut the pump off when it's not needed and/or a thermostat to control water temperature in the loop. Consult a plumber.

▶ Water heater uses too much energy.

First turn the thermostat down to 120° F. If your dishwasher requires 140° F, consider installing a small point-of-use water heater for the dishwasher. Note that many newer dishwashers are sold with their own built-in water heaters, allowing you to keep the household water heater at a lower temperature. Next drain the tank if that hasn't been done in six months or more, and check the pipe connections and bottom of the tank carefully for leaks.

Insulate the water heater and the hot-water pipes. Ready-made blankets are sold to fit over water heaters

specifically for this purpose. Insulate pipes with closed-cell foam insulation, which can be bought preslit and is easy to install. Just make sure you get the right size for your pipes; most are ½ inch or ¾ inch.

Add low-flow showerheads and faucet aerators.

If you have an electric heater, you can install a timer, which will run it during less expensive, off-peak hours. Check with the local electric company for details.

If you use a lot of hot water at a point far from the heater, install a point-of-use water heater there, or have a recirculating loop installed if it can be done efficiently.

Next time you have to replace your water heater, buy an energy-efficient unit. Study the labels on the sides. If you buy a tank that has been insulated to R-16 or more, you won't have to add an insulation blanket after it's installed. If your water comes from a well, consider installing a holding tank, in which the water can warm up before going to the heater.

Installing insulation on a gas water heater

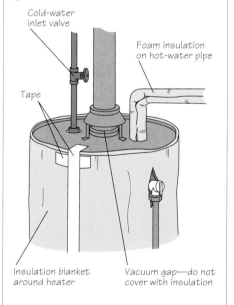

Cold-water inlet valve

Foam insulation on hot-water pipe

Tape

Insulation blanket around heater

Vacuum gap—do not cover with insulation

Tip *Check the anode rod of your water heater every three or four years—more often if you have particularly hard, softened, or acidic water. This is a "sacrificial" rod that is intended to deteriorate over time so that the tank doesn't. If the anode is corroded, replace it by shutting off the power, closing the water inlet valve, draining a few gallons of water from the tank, unscrewing the rod from the top of the tank, and screwing in a new one.*

Tip *When insulating a gas water heater, consult the manufacturer's recommendations. Some prohibit the use of insulating blankets on certain models. In all cases, never cover the vent on the top, the air intake on the bottom, or the temperature-pressure relief valve.*

▶ *Pilot light won't light or goes out.*

If it won't light, check the gas supply (valves are open, propane tanks aren't empty). If there is no supply problem, the pilot line may be clogged. To check it, turn off the gas supply, remove the pilot burner assembly, and run a thin wire through the line. If the pilot still won't light, the problem is in the gas supply line or the automatic control valve. Call a plumber.

If you can light the pilot but, when you release the gas control valve after holding it down for at least one minute, the pilot doesn't stay lit, the thermocouple is not transmitting heat to the automatic valve that regulates the flow of gas to the pilot light and burner. First see if the tip of the sensor is completely surrounded by the pilot flame. If not, with pliers bend the bracket that holds the sensor so that it is centered in the pilot flame. If the pilot still won't stay lit, replace the thermocouple.

First turn off the gas supply. With two wrenches, unscrew the nuts that hold the thermocouple to the burner bracket and the control unit (you may have to remove the whole burner assembly to access the burner bracket). Remove the thermocouple and install the new one in the same way; make sure it's the right one for your water heater. Light the pilot while pushing on the pilot button (see right). Then check that the thermocouple is properly aligned with the flame. After a minute or two, release the pilot button and turn the gas control valve from *Pilot* to *On*.

If you can light the pilot successfully but it goes out frequently, check for drafts along the floor and seal them off. There may also be dirt in the thin tube that supplies gas to the pilot, causing the pilot flame to burn low and go out easily. Clean out the blockage with a thin wire, as described. A low flame may also be caused by insufficient pressure in the gas lines. The gas company should be called to check this.

Clearing pilot supply line

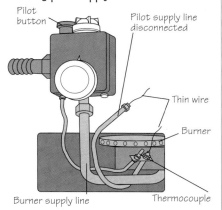

Pilot button | Pilot supply line disconnected | Thin wire | Burner | Thermocouple | Burner supply line

Replacing thermocouple

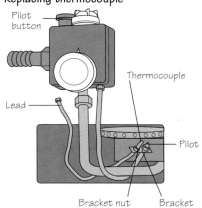

Pilot button | Thermocouple | Lead | Pilot | Bracket nut | Bracket

▶ *Gas burner will not fire.*

Make sure the pilot is lit, then turn the temperature knob to the highest setting. If the burner does not fire, the gas supply doesn't have enough pressure to activate the automatic control valve, or the thermostat is defective. Make sure the gas shutoff valves for the water heater and the house are fully open (handles parallel with pipes). If they are, the gas flow may still be impeded by dirt in the burner line or orifices. Shut off the gas, remove the burner, and clean out the supply tube and orifices with a piece of soft copper wire (see page 27). If the burner still doesn't fire, the thermostat in the control valve is probably not functioning. Call a plumber and get an estimate; it may be more economical to replace the whole water heater than to have it repaired.

▶ *Gas water heater isn't heating the water.*

First see if the pilot light is lit. If not, relight it following the instructions on the tank. (For models with electronic ignition, see below.) If you can't get a flame at the pilot light, check the gas shutoff valve for the water heater and the main shutoff valve for the house to be sure they are open (the handles should be parallel to the pipes). If gas supply is propane, check the gauge on the tank to make sure it isn't empty. If the pilot won't stay lit, the orifice may be clogged. Turn off the pilot, let it cool, and carefully clean out the tip with a toothpick, old toothbrush, or thin wire. If that doesn't fix the problem, replace the thermocouple (see left).

If the pilot light is on and the water doesn't heat up, check to make sure that the control knob is turned to *On*, not *Pilot*. Also turn up the temperature-control knob. If neither of these start the burner, the burner supply line or ports may be clogged (see left), or the thermostat in the automatic control valve may be faulty (call a plumber).

If the gas heater has electronic ignition instead of a pilot light

Tip *Newer, more efficient gas water heaters have electronic ignition devices instead of pilot lights. You can tell by looking inside the burner compartment (use a flashlight): a pilot light has a small fan-shaped hood that emits a steady flame; an electronic ignition device is contained in a small box with electrical wires attached.*

Tip *The temperature settings on thermostats aren't always accurate. The best way to measure how hot the water is getting is to run hot water out of a faucet near the water heater, fill a glass, and then quickly test the temperature with a thermometer that goes up to 180° F, such as a meat or confection thermometer.*

(which you can identify by a conspicuous box-shaped device on the side of the tank or in the burner chamber, or by checking the printed instructions to make sure there is no mention of lighting a pilot), you will have to have the unit replaced. Call a plumber.

Identifying water heater components

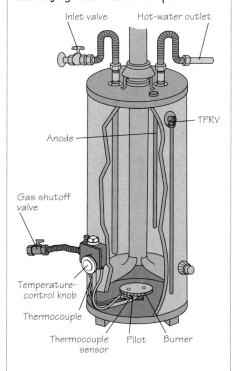

Lighting a pilot light

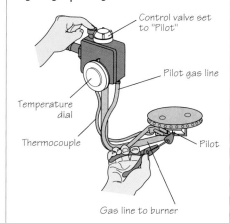

▶ Gas water heater makes water too hot or too cool.

Turn the temperature-control knob higher or lower to adjust the temperature. Experiment with slight increments over the course of several days. For most conditions 120° F will be adequate. If you want the water hotter but it fails to reach at least 140° F, even at the highest setting, the tank may have sediment on the bottom or the water may be cooling off in the pipes because of inadequate insulation or excessively long runs (see page 24). Also make sure that all valves to and from the water heater are open fully. If the tank is located outdoors or in an unheated space, it should have an insulating blanket and insulated pipes (unless it's a newer model that should not be covered by a blanket).

Adjusting temperature knob

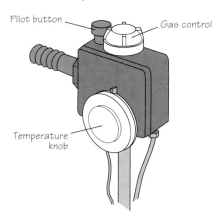

▶ Gas water heater doesn't provide enough hot water.

Check the temperature knob or measure the temperature of the hot water (see page 25). Perhaps a setting of 120° F is too low, in which case set the temperature to 130° F or even 140° F. Check the holding size of the water heater. A 40-gallon gas heater will satisfy the requirements of most families, but large households or unusually high hot-water needs may require a larger tank. Also make sure that hot-water pipes are well insulated, especially on long runs.

Perhaps you are just wasting too much hot water. Make sure that you don't have any leaking hot-water faucets. The dip tube may have fallen or corroded. This plastic tube hangs down inside the tank directing the incoming cold water to the bottom of the tank so that it doesn't mix with (and thereby cool) the heated water at the top of the tank. Many a water heater has been replaced simply because this inexpensive element was broken. To check, shut off the cold-water inlet valve and then disconnect the inlet below the valve. Remove the dip tube (or what is left). If it's not intact, replace it with a new plastic one, or have your plumber make a more durable copper dip tube by flaring one end so it will seat in the inlet opening and not fall through the hole. See page 23.

The burner may not be burning at full capacity due to clogged orifices. Observe the burner in operation. If you see weak or broken flames, shut off the heater, wait for it to cool (or wear oven mitts), and

Tip *If gas is turned off for the entire house, all the pilot lights will have to be relit when it is turned on again, otherwise gas will escape from unlit pilots. Whenever you turn off the gas, call the gas company to turn it back on.*

clean out the clogged orifices with a thin wire (you may have to remove the burner); or call the gas company for service.

If you get your water from a well, the problem may be due to a very cold source of water, which forces your water heater to work overtime and perhaps fail to keep up with household demand. If this is the problem, you can install a holding tank between the well and the water heater inside the house that allows the water to warm up before it reaches the water heater.

Cleaning burner orifices

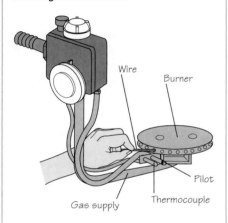

▶ **Gas water heater makes strange noises.**

Sizzling or popping noises are caused by drops of water falling on the burner. First check the sides of the tank for condensation; it can form on the outside of a tank if the water is cool enough, such as when the tank fills rapidly after all the hot water has been used. This is a temporary condition that will stop after the water heats up. If the sound persists, check for leaks (see page 23).

If the water heater sounds as if rocks are being shattered inside when it fires up, the bottom of the tank has a layer of minerals and sediment that have accumulated and hardened over the years. Although the sediment buildup has an insulating effect that compels the burner to stay on longer, the problem is not as serious as it is loud, and there is little you can do about it. When sediments have built up to this extent, they are too solid to be flushed out. You can, however, slow down the natural buildup by flushing out the water heater every six months (see page 23). When you replace the tank with a new one, it will have an anode that also helps to control sediment buildup.

▶ **Gas water heater emits fumes or strange odors.**

The flue may be clogged or broken. While the water heater is on, hold a smoking match or candle near the vacuum gap (draft diverter or flue hat) on the water heater. If smoke is drawn into the flue, the flue is fine; the fumes are most likely caused by inefficient operation of the burner due to low air supply or low gas pressure. Call the gas company. But if smoke is pushed away, the flue is not drawing properly and fumes are being backdrafted into the house. The flue may be blocked or

have too many turns—have it inspected by a heating contractor; or the house has negative air pressure due to tight insulation and poor ventilation (see pages 116 and 117).

If you smell fumes around a gas water heater, coat the connections with soapy water; you will see bubbles if there is a gas leak. If there is a leak, carefully tighten the connection with two wrenches and check again, until no bubbles form. If tightening doesn't stop the leak, shut off the gas at the water heater valve or house shutoff valve, depending on where the leak is. Disconnect the pipes and coat the male threads with pipe joint compound specified for gas lines; then reassemble and tighten the connections. If you turned off the gas at the heater, turn it back on. If you turned it off at the main house valve, call the gas company to turn it back on. If there are no leaks, light the pilot. *Note:* Do not coat pipe threads of compression fittings, which are part of flexible gas connectors and consist of a brass coupling nut that tightens onto a threaded brass fitting with a rounded tip.

Testing for backdrafting

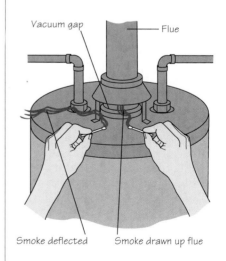

Tip *The shutoff valve for natural-gas service usually requires a wrench to turn the handle. You can obtain an inexpensive wrench for this purpose from a hardware store or home center. Store it near the gas meter where you can reach it quickly if you have to turn off the gas.*

Tip *If the main gas valve is shut off for any reason, contact the gas company to turn it back on. The service representative will be able to perform safety checks and light pilots.*

▶ Electric water heater makes strange noises.

Scale buildup on electric heating elements can cause noise. Check and clean the elements, if necessary, by turning off the power to the heater, draining the water, removing the elements, soaking them in vinegar, and removing the scale with a soft brush. If the noise is a chattering thermostat, replace the thermostat. For other noises, see page 27.

▶ Electric water heater doesn't provide enough hot water.

Check the size of the tank; a 50-gallon electric heater will satisfy the requirements of most families, but large households or unusually high hot-water needs may require a larger tank.

If you suddenly start running out of hot water sooner than you used to, the cause may be a burned-out lower heating element due to sediment piling up around it in the tank. This can and does happen even on tanks that are "glass lined." You will have to drain the tank and replace the heating element. (See page 29.)

▶ Electric water heater makes water too hot or too cool.

Most electric heaters have two thermostats, an upper and a lower, controlling two heating elements. On some newer heaters, the upper thermostat can't be adjusted; instead it is preset at 120° F and will shut down if water exceeds 190° F. Once shut off, it can be reset by pushing the reset button. If it keeps kicking off, the heater is consistently overheating the water; the upper thermostat is defective and should be replaced. If the water is getting much too hot, perhaps with steam coming out of the faucet, see page 22.

If water is not hot enough, first check all valves to and from the water heater to make sure that they are fully open. Then try adjusting both thermostats to a higher temperature. On a dual-element water heater, one of the heating elements may be defective. If the water won't heat up sufficiently, the upper is probably at fault; if it heats up but not for long, the lower is at fault. See right for instructions for testing and replacing an element or for replacing a thermostat.

Scale from mineral deposits may also build up on heating elements, causing them to overheat. If you remove the elements and find some scale on them, soak them in vinegar and use a soft brush to remove the scale. Scale buildup on the elements can indicate that you need a new anode. (See pages 23 and 24.)

Adjusting a thermostat

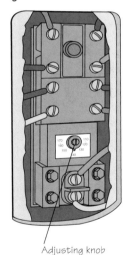

Adjusting knob

▶ Electric water heater isn't heating water.

First check for a tripped circuit breaker or blown fuse; if that is the problem, reset the circuit breaker or replace the fuse. If the breaker trips or fuse blows again, have an electrician determine the cause.

If the power is OK, push the reset button on the water heater, which cuts off power when the temperature exceeds a certain limit, usually 190° F. To gain access to this button you may have to remove the cover panel and push insulation aside. If so, *turn off the power first!* Wire terminals will be exposed, with the potential of a 240-volt shock if the two feeder terminals are touched simultaneously.

If the heater works somewhat but not at full capacity, one of the two heating elements has failed. If there is no heat, the water heater is most likely an old style with a single heating element that has failed. In either case the heating elements need to be tested and, if necessary, replaced. If the heater works temporarily, then shuts off again, the thermostat is defective and should be replaced (see opposite page).

To test the heating elements, turn off power to the heater. Remove the panel cover and push aside any insulation to expose the thermostat and heating-element terminals. *Avoid touching wires or screw terminals until you have tested all combinations—especially the two wires at the top of the upper thermostat—with a voltage tester to be absolutely certain that power is shut off.* To locate the heating-element terminals, look for the large tightening nut (some models have four small bolts instead) with two wire terminals attached. Disconnect

Tip *An electric water heater is a 240-volt appliance and can deliver a fatal shock from exposed wires. Be absolutely certain that the power is off before you work on it. Post a warning sign on the circuit breaker or lock the breaker panel box so somebody won't inadvertently reset the breaker.*

the wires from the terminals and, with a continuity tester or volt-ohmmeter (set at 4 × 1 ohms resistance), touch the probes to the two terminals of each element, in turn. If an element shows no electrical continuity, replace it. If it shows continuity, repeat the test (with the ohm setting at 4 × 1000), this time touching one probe to the tank side or a bolt attached to the tank, and the other probe to each terminal, in turn. If there *is* continuity on this test, the element has a short and should be replaced.

To replace an element, drain the tank (see page 23). Unscrew the tightening nut with a pipe wrench (or remove the bolts securing a mounting flange) and pull out the element carefully. The replacement should be identical. Coat the new gasket on both sides with pipe joint compound; carefully thread the new element through it, and tighten the bolt (or bolts) to the tank. Connect the wires, set the temperature, restore the power and the water supply, and press the reset button.

To replace a thermostat, make sure the power and water are shut off; then remove the panel cover and push the insulation out of the way. Remove wires from the screw terminals. Loosen the bracket bolts and lift the thermostat out of the bracket, or clip. Slip the new one into the clip and reconnect the wires. Then set the temperature, turn on the water, restore power, and press the reset button.

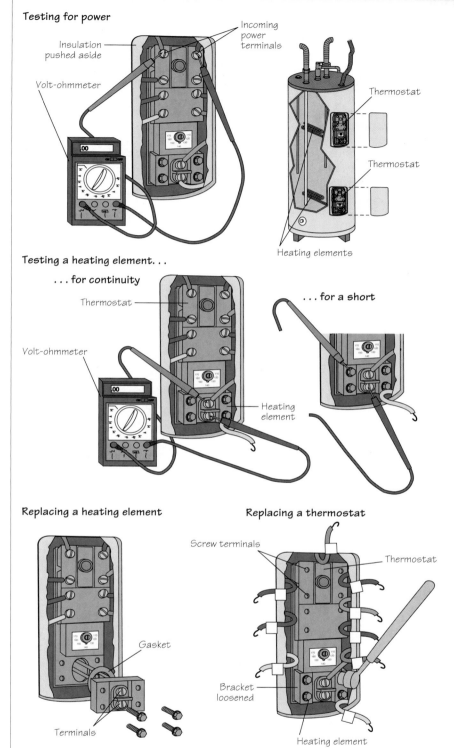

Testing for power

Insulation pushed aside

Volt-ohmmeter

Incoming power terminals

Thermostat

Thermostat

Heating elements

Testing a heating element. . .

. . . for continuity

Thermostat

Volt-ohmmeter

. . . for a short

Heating element

Replacing a heating element

Gasket

Terminals

Replacing a thermostat

Screw terminals

Thermostat

Bracket loosened

Heating element

Tip   *Before disconnecting any wires, draw a color-coded sketch of which wires go where and use the sketch to assist you in reconnecting the wires.*

SOLVING PLUMBING PROBLEMS

▶ *Faucet drips or won't shut off.*

Different types of faucets require different repair techniques (see right). Buy replacement parts and kits for only your specific brand and model. Many repair kits will contain specialized tools needed to disassemble the faucet. The kit will probably include more parts than you intend to replace, such as washers and gaskets; always replace all parts included in the kit. If you take the faucet apart before buying any replacement parts, take the assembly with you to the hardware store or plumbing supplier.

Begin by closing both shutoff valves (also called angle stops) below the sink. Some water will remain trapped in the faucet and supply risers, so have a bucket and rags available before you start to work. Cover the drain and clear off enough counter space so you can set down the parts in order. Work slowly and study how each part is positioned before you disassemble it; if you don't trust your memory, make a sketch of each part as you remove it. When using metal tools on a polished surface, protect the surface with a rag or several layers of tape. Remove all grit and debris from faucet parts as you work.

▶ *Faucet leaks around handle stem.*

This problem is restricted to compression (washer-style) faucets. Depending on the specific type, replace the packing washer, O-ring, or packing string wrapped around the stem. See below.

▶ *Compression (washer-style) faucet drips or won't shut off.*

First see left. Remove the handle screw (it may be hidden under a decorative cap or behind the handle), and pull the handle off the valve stem. If it is stuck, don't force it off by prying; use a faucet handle puller, available from a hardware or plumbing store. Next, with an adjustable wrench or pliers, unscrew the nut or nuts holding the valve stem and lift the stem out. Replace the washer and screw at the end of

Repairing a compression faucet

Cap
Screw
Handle
Retaining nut
Packing washer or O-ring
Washer
Stem
Packing string
Screw
Seat

the stem; tighten the new screw firmly. If the holding cup (recessed end of valve stem that holds the washer) is broken, buy a replacement valve stem or file off the cup and buy an appropriate replacement assembly. Before reassembling the faucet, feel the valve seat for pits, cracks, and wear. If it is damaged, remove the seat with a valve-stem wrench or allen wrench and replace it. Reassemble the valve. The spout may still drip until the washer has had a few days to work in. *Note:* Some compression faucets have a cartridge assembly that contains the washers and moving parts. Simply replace the whole assembly.

▶ *Ball faucet drips or won't shut off.*

First see left. With an allen wrench loosen the setscrew on the handle and remove the handle. Slightly loosen the adjusting ring on top of the dome-shaped cap to relieve pressure from the internal ball mechanism (a special wrench is provided with the manufacturer's repair kit). Unscrew the cap (with the adjusting ring still attached), remove the plastic cam holding the ball in place, then the gasket and ball. Use needle nose pliers to gently lift out the small rubber seals and springs that were under the ball. Remove any loose debris and put replacement springs and sleeves back into the seats. While you're at it, lift off the spout and replace the two O-rings. Remove the old rings with a sharp knife, being careful not to scratch the metal faucet body; apply a light coating of valve grease to the new rings before installing them. Reassemble the faucet and tighten the adjusting ring just enough to prevent leaks with-

Tip *To drain water out of a faucet before working on it: (1) shut off the main house valve, (2) open both the hot and cold sides of the faucet, (3) find another nearby faucet lower than the faucet you're working on, (4) open the other faucet for a short time to allow the faucet you're working on to empty, (5) shut off all faucets, (6) close the shutoff valves below the sink, and (7) turn the main house valve back on. Now you're ready to work.*

Tip *While you're at it, replace the washers for the other side (hot or cold) of the faucet.*

out making the handle difficult to operate. Leave the handle half open and turn the shutoff valves (angle stops) back on. Let the water run for a few seconds before shutting off the faucet.

Repairing a ball faucet

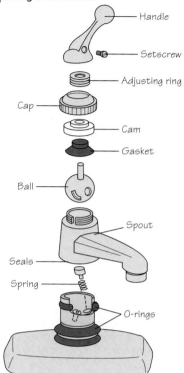

- Handle
- Setscrew
- Adjusting ring
- Cap
- Cam
- Gasket
- Ball
- Spout
- Seals
- Spring
- O-rings

▶ Cartridge faucet drips or won't shut off.

First see opposite page. Pry off the handle cap with a small screwdriver. Remove the exposed screw, handle, and handle assembly, then remove the spout (you may first need to remove a retaining nut or retaining ring with pliers). If the faucet has a sprayer, there will be a collar-shaped diverter beneath the spout housing; remove it. Next use needle nose pliers to pull out the horseshoe-shaped clip that holds the cartridge

in place. Remove the cartridge by pulling up on it firmly with pliers (you may need a special puller made by the faucet manufacturer, often included in the replacement kit). Flush out any debris from the faucet body, then apply a light coat of valve grease (included with the repair kit) to the new cartridge and push it into the faucet body firmly, compressing any trapped air. Make sure the notch in the stem faces the sink. Use the retaining clip to secure the cartridge. While you're at it, replace the faucet O-rings with new O-rings provided in the kit. Remove the old rings by cutting them with a sharp knife (don't scratch the metal faucet body). Then reassemble the faucet.

Repairing a cartridge faucet

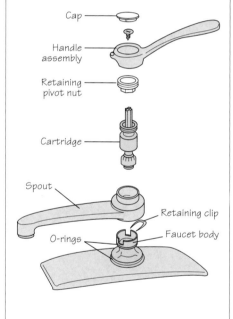

- Cap
- Handle assembly
- Retaining pivot nut
- Cartridge
- Spout
- Retaining clip
- O-rings
- Faucet body

▶ Ceramic-disk faucet drips or won't shut off.

First see opposite page. Although this type of faucet has a replaceable disk assembly that may become worn, the cause of most leaks is worn rubber (neoprene) seals located under the disk assembly. Find the setscrew in the handle, which may be hidden under a cover, loosen it, and lift off the handle. Remove the escutcheon, cap, or retainer ring. Then remove the disk assembly as a unit by unscrewing the mounting screws and pulling it out; turn it over and remove the rubber seals. Clean the inlet holes and filter cones (if included), flush out all debris, install new seals, and reassemble the faucet. Leave the handle half open when you turn the angle stops back on and let some water flow before turning off the faucet. If the faucet still leaks, replace the disk assembly with a new one.

Repairing a ceramic-disk faucet

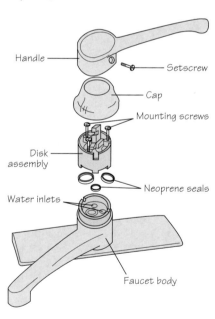

- Handle
- Setscrew
- Cap
- Mounting screws
- Disk assembly
- Neoprene seals
- Water inlets
- Faucet body

Tip   *If you aren't sure which type of faucet you have, here's how to tell: If the faucet has separate handles for hot and cold, it is compression or ceramic disk. Compression faucets require several turns of the handle and tighten gradually. Ceramic-disk faucets, which are more modern, require only a quarter turn and shut off abruptly. Single-handle faucets are cartridge, ball, or ceramic disk. Cartridge faucet handles slide outward as well as rotate to the right or left. Ball and ceramic-disk handles rotate but don't slide. Handles of ball faucets usually have a wider range of travel than ceramic-disk handles. Once you remove the handle, you can tell the difference immediately. Single faucets, such as hose bibbs, are the compression type.*

▶ Faucet is noisy.

Whistling, rattling, or vibrating noises that you can trace to the faucet itself are caused by loose or misaligned parts. Disassemble the faucet (see pages 30 and 31) and restore or replace any loose parts. Noises not from the faucet itself, such as banging that occurs when you shut off the faucet or loud humming within the walls or floor, are caused by poorly secured or insulated pipes, excessively high water pressure, the absence of air chambers near the suspect faucets, or air chambers that have become waterlogged (see page 18).

▶ Water flow is restricted.

Make sure the shutoff valves (angle stops) below the sink are open. If they are, the problem is probably a clogged aerator. Unscrew the aerator from the spout; to get a grip on it, use rubber gloves or pliers (with tape or a rag around the jaws to protect the finish). Run the faucet without the aerator to see if the pressure is adequate. If it is not, you will need to investigate further. In either case flush out the aerator parts; be sure to keep the parts in order. Remove all debris, using a fine needle if necessary. If the parts look damaged or hopelessly clogged, buy a new aerator.

If a clogged aerator wasn't the problem, get under the sink with a flashlight and inspect the bottom of the faucet. Some models have copper inlet tubes that constrict easily if they are kinked. If a tube is kinked, close the shutoff valve (in case the tube comes loose as you work on it) and carefully straighten the kink with your hands. Then squeeze the sides of the kink with pliers to restore the tube to full roundness. Turn the water back on and check.

If the problem was not kinked tubing, check for blockage within the faucet itself. Close the shutoff valves and disassemble the faucet (see pages 30 and 31). Look for trapped debris or misaligned parts, make adjustments, and reassemble the faucet.

Finally, if none of the above works, the problem is blockage within a shutoff valve, supply tube, or pipe. If the problem is restricted to just hot water or just cold water, close that shutoff valve and place a bucket under it. Remove the supply tube and check it for blockage. Then attach a flexible supply tube (not all tubes are flexible; use the old one if it is, or buy one) to the shutoff valve and aim it into the bucket. Open the shutoff valve enough to check whether it has full force. If not, call a plumber. If it does, the problem is in the supply tube or faucet; replace them.

▶ Brass surface is tarnished.

Most brass faucets have a clear protective coating to prevent tarnishing. Once the coating is scratched or begins to peel off, the brass tarnishes rapidly. Recoating is difficult and seldom satisfactory. Instead peel off all of the coating with your fingernails or a toothpick and either let the brass age gracefully or polish it regularly with brass cleaner. A paste of lemon juice and salt works well. Avoid scouring pads and abrasive powders.

▶ Chrome surface is tarnished.

Remove stains by rubbing with ammonia or a paste of baking soda and water. Avoid abrasive scouring pads and powders, salt, harsh metal cleaners, and acids such as vinegar. Polish with silver polish, rinse, and dry immediately.

▶ Faucet wobbles or is separating from sink.

With a helper centering the faucet while you work, crawl under the sink with a flashlight. If there is no rubber gasket between the sink and faucet to prevent water from seeping between them, apply silicone bathroom caulk or plumber's putty under the outside edge of the sink base. You may first need to loosen the faucet-mounting locknuts to be able to lift the faucet base high enough to inject caulk under it. Now tighten the locknuts, using a basin wrench to reach up into the awkward cavity behind the sink. Be sure to tighten the locknuts (the ones snugged up to the sink bottom), not the coupling nuts that connect the water supply tubing to the faucet.

Tightening faucet under sink

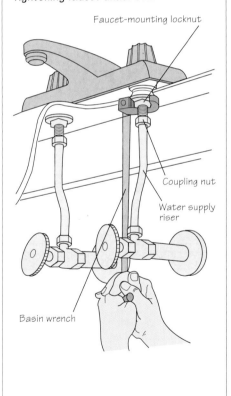

Faucet-mounting locknut
Coupling nut
Water supply riser
Basin wrench

Tip   If you're replacing an old faucet with a new one, be sure the faucet fits the hole configuration of the sink. If the sink holes are spaced 4 inches apart, buy a centerset faucet for 4-inch centers. If the sink holes are spaced 8 inches apart, buy a wideset faucet or a faucet with handles separate from the spout. Kitchen sinks often have extra holes for sprayer attachments and other accessories.

Tip   If you need a light while working under a sink, use a flashlight. It could be dangerous to work on water pipes or plumbing fixtures with a light, cord, or appliance that's plugged into the electrical system.

▶ *Shutoff valve is hard to turn.*

To get a good grip, use channel lock (tongue-and-groove) pliers, but don't force a stuck valve. The packing around the valve stem may have dried and can crack, causing a leak. To lubricate it, place a few drops of light machine oil on the valve stem next to the nut. Next loosen the nut one turn, then tighten it finger-tight. Wait for the packing to absorb oil, then try turning the valve handle. If it works, tighten the packing nut; if not, repeat the process.

▶ *Shutoff valve leaks.*

Dry it off and inspect it carefully to pinpoint the leak. If water comes from the compression nut at the top of the valve, tighten the nut. Use two wrenches, one for the nut and one to hold the valve (channel lock pliers also work). If the leak persists, turn off the valve, unscrew the compression nut, slide the tubing away from the valve, and wrap pipe joint tape around the brass ferrule (ring) at the base of the tubing. If it's an older style of valve with a slip-joint connection (rubber cone washer instead of a brass ferrule), replace the washer, then reassemble, using two wrenches to tighten the nut.

If water leaks from behind the valve where it is connected to the water pipe, tighten that compression nut with two wrenches. If the valve is an older style without a compression nut, the leak is due to a loosened valve or a badly corroded joint. You can try tightening the valve, but at the risk of breaking off a corroded connection or loosening pipe joints behind the wall. Call a plumber, unless you are willing to open up the wall and replace the valve altogether if necessary.

If water leaks from around the handle stem, see left. If water leaks from a crack in the valve body, call a plumber; the valve needs to be replaced.

Stopping a leak in a shutoff valve with compression connections

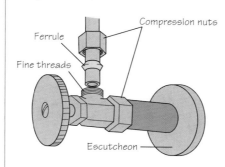

Compression nuts

Ferrule

Fine threads

Escutcheon

Stopping a leak in a shutoff valve with slip-joint connections

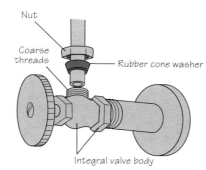

Nut

Coarse threads

Rubber cone washer

Integral valve body

▶ *Outdoor faucet (hose bibb) leaks.*

Close the main shutoff valve, then open the faucet to drain water from the nearby pipes. Use the same repair technique as for a compression faucet (see page 30), or, because hose bibbs are inexpensive, simply unscrew the entire faucet and replace it. Apply pipe joint tape or compound to the male threads before screwing on the new bibb.

▶ *Outdoor faucet (hose bibb) is hard to reach.*

If shrubs or other obstacles block a faucet, have a new one installed in a better location, or "extend" it temporarily by mounting a second faucet in a more convenient place, such as elsewhere on the house or on a sturdy post driven in the ground. Since there won't be a rigid pipe to help support the faucet, buy one with "ears" (mounting flanges with holes drilled through them for screws) so it's easy to attach. If the faucet has no ears, secure it to the house or post with a pipe clamp or plumbing strap. After it's mounted, connect the two faucets with a short, heavy-duty garden hose, using a hose-to-pipe adapter to attach the male end of the hose to the inlet side of the new faucet. To prevent leaks, insert new washers in the hose couplings, apply pipe joint compound to the threads, and tighten all joints securely. Inspect the connections periodically and turn off the original faucet during the winter and when you go on vacation. Most hardware stores carry complete kits for this project.

▶ *Outdoor faucet (hose bibb) freezes.*

Replace it with a freezeproof bibb. This type of faucet has a longer shank than ordinary bibbs, so you will have to cut back some of the water pipe that the old bibb is connected to. You will need access to the pipe, which is probably located in the floor joist cavity above the crawlspace or basement ceiling. To mark where the pipe should be cut, measure the shank of the freeze-proof bibb and transfer that distance onto the pipe, measuring from the outside face of the house

Tip   *When loosening nuts around faucets and sinks, you may find one or two that are corroded and difficult to turn. Instead of forcing the wrench, spray some penetrating lubricant onto the threads around the nut. Let it soak in for a few minutes before you try to loosen the nut.*

Tip   *When sealing the joint between a faucet and marble sink, don't use plumber's putty; it will deteriorate the marble. Use silicone bathroom caulk instead.*

siding. Mark where you need to cut the supply pipe, allowing for whatever transition fittings or threaded nipples are needed. If necessary, your local hardware store can cut and thread a short piece of iron pipe to replace the existing one. (If a shutoff valve was installed on the water pipe to protect the old bibb from freezing, it won't be needed with the freezeproof bibb; don't worry if you have to cut it out.)

Before cutting the pipe make sure you have all of the pipe and materials you'll need. Then shut off the main house valve, cut the pipe, and remove the old bibb. Insert the new bibb through the same hole and solder or thread the bibb, fittings, and pipe together. Coat all threaded joints with pipe joint tape or compound. Seal any openings in the wall with caulk and attach the bibb flange to the wall with brass screws. If the freezeproof bibb is the type with a vacuum breaker next to the valve, make sure the bibb is level when you connect it.

Installing a freezeproof outdoor faucet

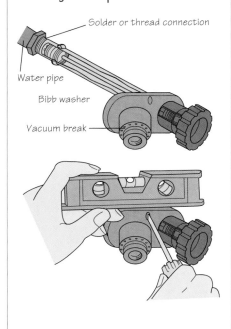

Solder or thread connection

Water pipe

Bibb washer

Vacuum break

▶ *Drain is clogged or drains slowly.*

If the sink has a pop-up stopper, lift it out of the drain hole to see if the clog might simply be hair and other debris trapped by it. If the stopper won't lift out, release it by unscrewing the retaining nut under the sink that holds the stopper pivot arm in place, and sliding the arm out of the drain fitting (see page 36). Since this may release water from the stopped-up sink, be sure to place a bucket under the drain first. If removing the stopper doesn't clear the drain, leave the stopper out, replace the pivot arm and retaining nut, and proceed.

Next try clearing the drain with a plunger. For the plunger to work effectively, you must first seal off the overflow hole and second drain (if it's a double sink) by holding a wet rag over each opening (you may need a helper). If the sink has a disposer with a dishwasher hose attached to it, seal the hose to the air gap shut with two woodblocks squeezed in a C-clamp. Next lightly coat the rim of the plunger cup with petroleum jelly and place the plunger over the drain. The drain should be covered by 1 to 2 inches of water to provide a tight seal. Over a period of two or three minutes, work the plunger up and down vigorously 10 to 12 strokes at a time.

If plunging isn't successful, look for a clog in the P-trap. First place a bucket under the trap to catch water. If the trap has a cleanout plug, remove it and poke around the trap with a wire to find and remove any clogs. If it doesn't have a cleanout, you will have to disassemble the trap. With channel lock pliers loosen the slip nuts; then, holding the trap with your free hand, unscrew the nuts, remove the trap, pour out the water, and remove any debris.

If the trap wasn't clogged, leave it off and run a drain auger into the drainpipe (see page 17). After clearing the obstruction, reassemble the trap, tighten the slip nuts with a quarter turn of channel lock pliers, and run hot water down the drain for five minutes to flush away scum and residue from the clog.

Locating drain components of a kitchen sink

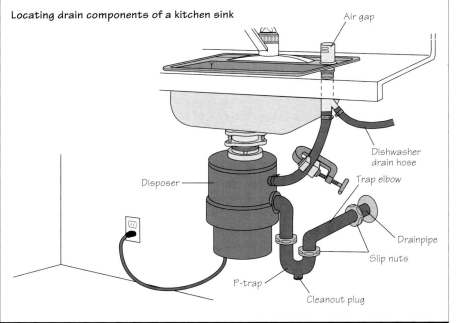

Air gap

Dishwasher drain hose

Disposer

Trap elbow

Drainpipe

Slip nuts

P-trap

Cleanout plug

Tip *The space under a sink is awkward and often underutilized. There are many types of pull-out shelves, storage containers, and trash receptacles designed for under-sink use that will help you keep the space organized. These are widely available at home centers and other hardware outlets. To make choosing components easier, bring along a sketch of the area under your sink, with accurate measurements. Choose components that are easy to move out of the way in case you need access for repairs.*

▶ *Water puddles under the sink.*

To find the source of the leak, fill and then drain the sink. If the leak seems most apparent during filling, the leak is probably on the supply side. Look closely at the shutoff valves (angle stops) and faucet connections under the sink. Dry off any wet areas and observe them. If leaking occurs around a loose connection, tighten it (use two wrenches, not just one). For faucet leaks, see page 30. If no leaks occur until you drain the water, check the drain assembly (see right).

If the leak is in a sink with a garbage disposer, run the water and disposer while you investigate for the source. Vibration from the disposer can loosen slip nuts on the drain connections; these can be tightened.

Water may also be seeping under the faucets or through gaps along the wall or around the edge of the sink. If a faucet is loose, get under the sink with a basin wrench and tighten the mounting locknuts (not the coupling nuts that connect the faucet to the supply risers). If this doesn't help, loosen the locknuts enough that you can raise the faucet and apply silicone tub caulk around the bottom of the faucet base; have a helper center the faucet as you tighten the locknuts. On rim-type sinks and on self-rimming stainless steel sinks, the cause may be loose or missing hold-down clips. These are located under the countertop around the edge of the sink and can easily be tightened or replaced. Make sure that the sink is sealed under the rim with plumber's putty or caulk. If not, loosen all of the hold-down clips enough to raise the rim and apply a bead of silicone tub or bathroom caulk under it; then retighten the clips.

On sinks that have been set in mortar, water may be leaking through the grout. Apply a grout sealer to the joints, according to manufacturer's instructions, and seal the gap around the sink with caulk specified for tile. A permanent solution may require resetting the tile, using an epoxy grout. Consult an experienced tile setter.

▶ *Water leaks from the drain.*

For bathroom sinks, if water is leaking from around the drain fitting where it's connected to the bottom of the sink, either the putty seal under the sink flange inside the bowl has failed, or the rubber gasket on the underside of the sink has deteriorated. Replace both. First disconnect the P-trap, then loosen the locknut that holds the drain assembly against the bottom of the sink. Unscrew the flange above the sink while holding onto the tailpiece below the sink (you may need a helper; loosen the flange with a strainer wrench or a woodblock shoved into the drain hole). With the drain disassembled, remove the rubber gasket and take it to the hardware store to buy an exact replacement (along with a supply of plumber's putty).

To reassemble, first clean off the bottom of the drain flange and apply a fresh bead of plumber's putty to it. Thread the body of the drain fitting up through the sink hole and screw the flange down onto it as far as possible without rubbing off the putty. Slip the new gasket (and fiber or brass friction washer, if included) over the drain fitting from below the sink and screw the locknut onto the fitting to force the gasket up against the sink. Tighten the locknut while holding the flange steady from above with a strainer wrench or woodblock shoved into the drain hole. Reassemble the P-trap.

Pop-up assemblies can leak at the connection between the drain and the pivot rod. Tighten the retaining nut. If this doesn't stop the leak, unscrew the nut, spread some plumber's putty onto the threads, and tighten it again; or replace the washers or gaskets surrounding the pivot-ball assembly (see page 36).

If a kitchen sink drain (called a basket strainer) leaks, try tightening the large locknut under the sink with channel lock pliers (some basket strainers have a retainer with setscrews; tighten them with a screwdriver). If the fitting is tight but still leaks, replace the gasket between the sink and locknut (or retainer). The procedure is the same as for a bathroom sink, except that the entire strainer body lifts out of the sink hole from the top.

The locknut on a basket strainer may be too large for any wrench you own. You could buy a spud wrench for the job, or large channel lock pliers if you have other uses for them around the house; otherwise you can usually loosen the nut by tapping on it with a hammer and a small woodblock. To hold the body of the strainer in place from above, strainer wrenches are available, or you can stick the handles of a pair of pliers (held upside down) into the strainer and wedge a screwdriver between the handles for leverage.

Leaks can occur in the P-trap assembly. Before working on one, have a bucket handy to catch water in case you have to disassemble the trap. If there is a cleanout plug at the bottom of the trap, make sure it is tight. Loose slip nuts should be tightened. If a slip nut is tight but still leaks, loosen the joint and inspect the washer. If it is cracked, stiff, or deformed, replace it. If the new washer still leaks, coat the inside of the slip nut with plumber's

Tip   *Use mechanical means to clear a drain before resorting to chemical drain cleaners. Avoid using a plunger on a drain after dumping chemical drain cleaner down it; it may spatter caustic material around. Chemical cleaners work best for periodic cleaning or for clearing pipes that are only slightly blocked. If the pipe is fully blocked and the chemicals don't dissolve the blockage completely, the clog can harden and become impossible to remove, requiring replacement of the blocked section of pipe.*

putty. If you overtighten a slip nut and strip the threads, or if the trap is cracked, replace it (wrapping the trap with waterproof tape may stop the leak temporarily). When buying a new trap, be sure to get the right size—traps in bathroom drains are usually 1¼ inches in diameter (with a 1½-inch outlet); in kitchens, they are always 1½ inches.

Replacing a drain gasket in a bathroom sink

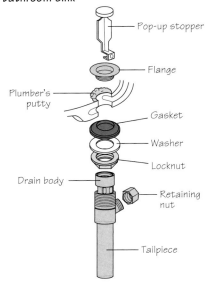

Pop-up stopper
Flange
Plumber's putty
Gasket
Washer
Locknut
Drain body
Retaining nut
Tailpiece

Tightening a kitchen sink drain locknut

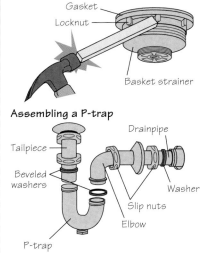

Gasket
Locknut
Basket strainer

Assembling a P-trap

Tailpiece
Drainpipe
Beveled washers
Washer
Slip nuts
Elbow
P-trap

▶ Stopper leaks and doesn't hold water.

If it's a rubber stopper, it may be dried and cracked; buy a new one (make sure it's the right size). If it's the pop-up stopper of a bathroom sink, see if the stopper is dropping all the way down into the drain. If not, lower the stopper by adjusting the linkage under the sink (see below), or by removing the stopper and rotating an adjusting nut that regulates the length of the stopper. If the stopper covers the drain hole but still leaks, replace the O-ring on the stopper; take the stopper with you to the hardware store when you buy the new ring. If the stopper still leaks, the drain hole or stopper may be slightly out of round or have a crack or burr on it. Inspect carefully and replace any damaged parts.

If the basket strainer of a kitchen sink leaks, check the rubber seal on the bottom. If it appears worn, buy a new strainer. You can also buy a flat disk stopper that covers the strainer completely.

▶ Pop-up stopper is out of alignment.

If a stopper wobbles, doesn't travel far enough, or comes to rest in a cockeyed position, you can make adjustments to bring it back into alignment. First make sure that the stopper is correctly engaged with the pivot rod. This will depend on the type of stopper you have. Some simply lift out, others must be twisted on and off the pivot rod, and a third type requires that the pivot rod be threaded through a hole in the bottom of the stopper. If it's not attached, you have to remove the pivot rod by unscrewing the retaining nut, then insert the rod through the hole at the bottom of the stopper before tightening the nut again.

With the stopper resting firmly on the pivot rod, or securely connected to it, push the lift rod up and down to see if the stopper opens and closes far enough. To raise the stopper higher, loosen the screw that secures the clevis strap to the lift rod (you may need pliers); slide the strap farther down the rod and tighten the screw. To lower the stopper, slide the clevis strap farther up the rod. If adjusting the stopper one way limits it the other way, increase the total distance (range) the stopper can travel by moving the clevis strap down the pivot rod, closer to the drain fitting. To do this, simply squeeze the spring clip and slide the strap along the rod. Finally, by tightening or loosening the retaining nut you can adjust the stiffness, or resistance, of the stopper mechanism so that it glides more smoothly.

Adjusting a pop-up assembly

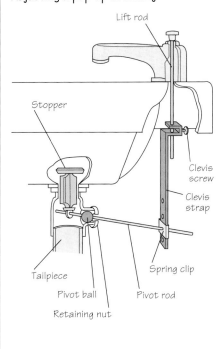

Lift rod
Stopper
Clevis screw
Clevis strap
Spring clip
Tailpiece
Pivot ball
Pivot rod
Retaining nut

Tip   *When disassembling a sink trap, stuff a rag into the trap arm or drainpipe to prevent sewer gas from escaping.*

Tip   *To maintain the beauty of a sink, clean it daily. Use mild cleaning powders or paste cleaners, not heavy-duty abrasive cleaners. Avoid steel wool; scour with a nylon brush or cleaning pad. Rinse with clear water.*

▶ Wall-mounted sink is coming loose from the wall.

Look under the sink for visible screws anchoring the sink to the wall. If there are some, tighten them. If there are none, or if the sink is still loose, you will have to remove it to tighten or replace the support bracket. Close the shutoff valves under the sink and disconnect the supply risers from the valves by unscrewing the compression nuts. Disconnect the P-trap by unscrewing the slip nuts (have a bucket of water handy to dump the water from the trap). Stick a rag into the drainpipe to block sewer gas. If the sink has been screwed to the wall, remove the screws. If the gap between the sink and the wall has been caulked, cut the caulk with a utility knife.

Now carefully lift the sink straight up until it clears the wall bracket; set it aside on its back. If the bracket is loose, tighten the screws; if the bracket is worn or corroded, you will need to replace it with an exact duplicate (contact a reputable plumbing-supply house or the sink manufacturer).

If the screws won't tighten, you will have to open up the wall and install new blocking to support the bracket. First measure the height of the bracket above the floor, then remove it. Remove a swath of wall covering the same width as a 2x6 and long enough to expose two studs; it should be at the same height as the bracket. Cut notches in the studs to recess a 2x6. Screw the 2x6 to the notched studs, then repair the wall and screw the bracket into the 2x6 blocking. Carefully position the sink on the bracket, tighten anchor screws through the sink into the wall (if the sink back has holes for them), and reconnect the water supply and drain.

An easier solution in some cases might be simply to install leg supports under the front corners of the sink; the legs must be the right type for your sink. Attach them according to manufacturer's instructions.

Removing sink to expose wall bracket

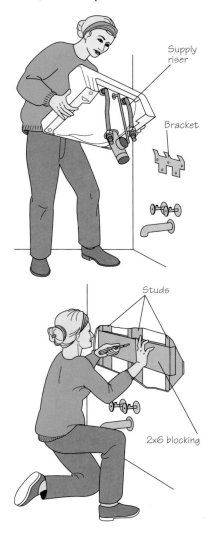

Supply riser

Bracket

Studs

2x6 blocking

▶ Sink surface is chipped or scratched.

If the sink is cast iron (heavy, with thunking sound) or enameled steel (lightweight, with tinny sound), you can repair the porcelain enamel surface with compounds or repair kits available at hardware stores. However, they work best on parts of the sink that are not frequently wet. You can mix the compound with alkyd paint to match the color of the sink. To repair, first carefully smooth the area around the chip or scratch by sanding it with emery cloth (medium grit); then clean it with a cloth dampened with rubbing alcohol. After it dries, apply the compound, according to label directions. Using a small putty knife or razor blade, keep it flush with the enamel surface. Let it dry thoroughly and then smooth the surface using a cotton swab and some fingernail-polish remover. These repairs are not likely to last long if the damage was in the basin itself, where it is regularly exposed to water. In this case you may want to find a professional refinisher (check in the Yellow Pages under "Bathtub Refinishing"), or replace the sink.

Scratches in a stainless steel sink are almost impossible to remove. You can try polishing the sink with automotive polishing compound to restore the overall sheen.

▶ Sink made of solid-surface material is cracked.

Some sinks, known by various brand names, are made from synthetic materials such as cast or compression-molded modified acrylic. Some are continuously molded into one piece as a sink and countertop; others are just the sink and are installed in a conventional countertop. It is best to call a professional

Tip *If you plan to replace the kitchen sink, consider the wide range of materials, sizes, and configurations available to you. Besides cast iron, stainless steel, and enameled steel, sinks are manufactured from solid-surface synthetic materials and lightweight composites. The most common size is 22x33 inches, but you can get narrower sinks to utilize more counter space, or wider sinks that have multiple compartments. Consider where the deck is located for mounting a faucet on the sink, and how many holes will be needed for the faucet, sprayer, and other accessories. Finally, if you have an awkward space where the sink will be placed, or want to take advantage of a corner window, consider a double-bowl sink that wraps around the inside corner of two intersecting counters, allowing you easy access to both bowls.*

to repair these sinks. If the crack is at the drain hole, the sink may have to be replaced, but other cracks can be repaired with plugs and/or joint adhesive.

▶ Stainless steel sink is too noisy or bouncy.

Get underneath the sink and, with a screwdriver, tighten the screws on the clips holding the sink to the rim or counter. If there is a garbage disposer in the sink, tighten its connections as well. Lighter sinks, which are made from 22-gauge steel, are prone to be noisy and show scratches, dents, and stains. Higher-quality sinks are made with thicker steel (20 and 18 gauge) and have an undercoating applied to the bottom that retains heat and reduces noise. If you have a persistent problem, consider replacing the sink.

▶ Sprayer hose leaks or is stiff and cracked.

Buy a new sprayer kit, or, if the spray head is working fine, replace only the hose with a new nylon-reinforced vinyl one. First close the shutoff valves under the sink. Then with a basin wrench loosen the nut connecting the sprayer hose to the bottom of the faucet. You might find it easier to cut the hose first to get it out of the way. Then remove the spray head by unscrewing it from the coupling. Take the head and the old hose to the hardware store to make sure the new hose will fit; also pick up a new washer for the spray head.

To install the new hose, start at the attachment under the faucet. Wrap some pipe joint tape on the male threads, then screw on the hose coupling nut and tighten it

with a basin wrench. Bring the other end of the hose up through the hole in the sink and slide on the coupling, retaining ring, and washers (or plastic rings). Apply pipe joint tape to the male threads of the sprayer head and attach it to the coupling ring on the hose. Restore the water supply and test the sprayer.

Attaching a new sprayer hose

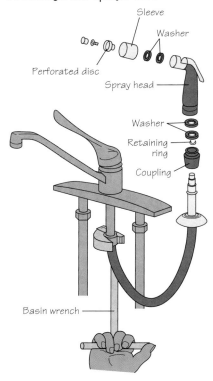

Sleeve
Washer
Perforated disc
Spray head
Washer
Retaining ring
Coupling
Basin wrench

▶ Sprayer head leaks.

Close the shutoff valves under the sink. If the sprayer head leaks where it is connected to the hose, unscrew the head from the hose coupling and replace the washer in the head (there may be two). Also make sure that the retaining ring that holds the coupling onto the hose is properly seated in the groove on the fitting at the end of the hose.

If the leak is from the nozzle, remove the nozzle from the head. On some models you pry off a small cover over the screw; on other models the whole nozzle housing screws onto the head. Carefully remove the parts. You should find either a standard washer (or washers) or a flexible seat. Replace these and reassemble.

▶ Sprayer won't spray.

If you have hard water, the head may be clogged with minerals. Wrap a rubber band around the handle to keep it in the open position, and drain all the water from the hose. Fill a small glass with a solution of equal parts vinegar and water. Let the spray nozzle soak in the solution for a couple of hours. Then, with hot water, try to use the sprayer. If the clog remains or the spray is inconsistent, take the nozzle apart and examine the perforated disc. Remove any debris with a pin or small wire. Reassemble the nozzle and test the sprayer again.

If it is still clogged, the problem is probably in the diverter valve under the spout. Turn off the water supply and remove the spout (see pages 30 and 31). Most often you'll need to remove a nut at the base of the spout (double-handled faucets) and unscrew the diverter from the top; or you will have to remove the spout sleeve (single-handled faucets) and pull the diverter out from the side of the assembly. Use a wire to clean debris from the inlet holes, or soak the assembly in a solution of 1 part vinegar to 1 part water. Reassemble. If the cone on the diverter is loose, replace the diverter.

Tip *Always retract a sprayer hose back into its housing after use. Leaving it in the sink subjects the water supply to potential contamination, especially if there is standing water.*

▶ Disposer won't start and makes no sound.

If the disposer suddenly shuts off while running, wait a few minutes and then press the reset button, usually on the bottom of the disposer. If it won't start, try the on-off switch in both positions. If it does not start in either position, check the circuit breaker or fuse. If none of the switches or breakers is off, check the instruction booklet that came with the disposer. Call a plumber or electrician for more-involved repairs.

Locating disposer switches under sink

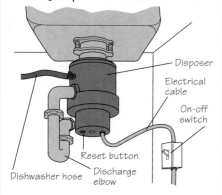

▶ Disposer makes a humming noise but won't grind.

Most likely something is stuck between the impeller (a rotating plate at the bottom of the waste chamber) and the grind ring (a stationary collar). Turn off the electric power at the on-off switch or at the circuit breaker or fuse box. Most disposers today are sold with a wrench that fits into the bottom of the disposer, allowing you to turn the motor back and forth until it is free. An alternative method is to carefully insert a dowel or broom handle into the disposer and rotate the impeller until it spins freely. Remove the material that jammed the impeller, restore power, push in the reset button on the bottom of the

disposer, and let it run for a few minutes with the cold water on.

Freeing a jammed impeller

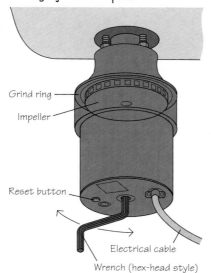

▶ Disposer runs slowly.

Turn off the electric power at the circuit breaker. Remove the rubber shield from the sink drain and look for undisposed material in the drum. If you find some, remove it and see if that solves the problem. If the problem persists, the impeller may be damaged or the cutting edges on the grind ring dulled. Replace them according to manufacturer's instructions, or call a plumber.

▶ Disposer makes strange or excessive noise.

Turn off the electric power and check for undisposed material in the drum. Also examine the impeller; if it is broken, replace the turntable, following manufacturer's instructions. If the problem persists, the motor bearings may be worn or damaged. You may find that it costs

you little more to replace a malfunctioning disposer than it does to repair it.

▶ Disposer smells.

Foul odors from a garbage disposer often indicate that you are letting food sit in the drum too long before turning on the disposer. To remove the smell, grind up some raw potatoes or citrus rind. For a preventive treatment, when replacing the box of baking soda in your refrigerator, pour the old soda down the drain rather than throwing it away. Always use only cold water when running the disposer; hot water will liquefy grease, allowing it to cling to surfaces. Grinding a handful of ice cubes from time to time will congeal any greasy buildup and allow it to be carried away.

▶ Disposer leaks at sink flange.

From under the sink tighten the mounting flange that attaches to the sink drain and holds the disposer in place. Some models have a large ring that can be turned with a spud wrench or channel lock pliers, or can be tightened by hammering a woodblock held against it; others have three setscrews that you can tighten with a screwdriver. If tightening the flange doesn't fix the problem, replace the gasket or gaskets.

First shut off power to the disposer by turning off the circuit breaker or by unplugging the unit. Then disconnect the P-trap from the disposer outlet and the dishwasher drain hose from the inlet located on the disposer body. While supporting the disposer with one hand, loosen it from the mounting bracket under the sink by turning the locking collar with a screwdriver or hex-head wrench provided with the disposer; lower the disposer to the cabinet floor (it may be heavy; use a helper). With the mounting flange

Tip *Before turning on a disposer, check for silverware, scrubbers, and other items that may jam it. Avoid putting stringy or fibrous materials into the disposer, such as onion skins, banana peels, artichoke leaves, or celery. Don't put large bones, pits, or grease into the disposer (but do put small bones, such as chicken bones, into the disposer; they clean out the chamber with a scouring action).*

exposed, disconnect it from the sink drain by loosening the lockring or setscrews and remove the gasket. Replace it with a new one. Apply a fresh bead of plumber's putty under the sink flange before you insert it into the sink drain hole (see below). Then reassemble the disposer in the same order as you removed it.

Detaching the disposer

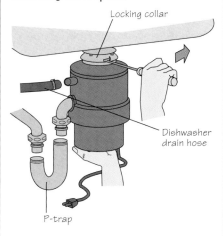

Locking collar

Dishwasher
drain hose

P-trap

Disconnecting the mounting flange

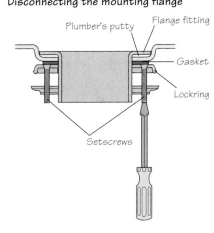

Plumber's putty   Flange fitting

Gasket

Lockring

Setscrews

▶ *Disposer needs replacing.*

Turn off the electricity at the circuit breaker or fuse. Make sure that the electrical wiring is sound (see page 60) and up to code (a garbage disposer should have its own circuit with a switch wired into it). Disconnect the wiring by unplugging the disposer from the wall receptacle, or by removing the cover plate on the bottom of the disposer and disconnecting the cable connector and cable from the unit. Disconnect the P-trap or other drain fitting from the disposer outlet pipe, then disconnect the dishwasher drain hose from the disposer. Remove the disposer from the mounting flange by loosening the locking collar with a screwdriver and lowering the disposer to the cabinet floor (see page 39). Remove the mounting flange by loosening the lockring or setscrews that secure it to the sink. Remove the sink gasket, any hardware securing the mounting plate to the sink, and the sink flange.

Reverse the process to install the new unit. First install the mounting flange. Apply a bead of plumber's putty underneath the flange and lower the fitting through the drain opening. From under the sink, place the gasket, mounting ring, and any other mounting hardware onto the body of the sink flange extending down through the sink hole (different models of disposers have different parts). Tighten the screws on the mounting ring to seat the flange and then remove excess putty from the sink.

Remove the electrical cover plate from the bottom of the disposer. Attach the feeder cable (armored conduit, nonmetallic cable) or power cord that was attached to the old disposer to a cable connector (connector for attaching electrical cable to the knockout hole of an electrical box). Run the wires into

the junction box through the knockout hole and secure the connector to the disposer. Connect the wires (white to white, black to black) using electrical wire connectors. Attach the ground wire to the green screw. Replace the cover plate.

If a dishwasher drain hose will be attached to the disposer, remove the plug from inside the dishwasher inlet tube on the side of the disposer. Attach the drain fitting (usually an elbow) to the disposer. Lift the disposer up to the mounting flange, turn it so the drain fitting will line up with the P-trap, and secure the mounting hardware. Attach the P-trap to the drain fitting and connect it to the drainpipe in the wall. Turn on the electricity, press the reset button, and test the disposer.

Making electrical connections

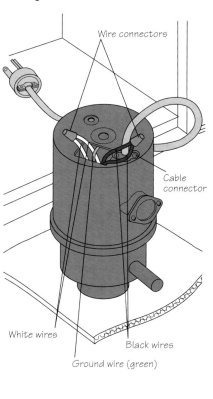

Wire connectors

Cable
connector

White wires

Black wires

Ground wire (green)

Tip *Scrape small amounts of waste into the disposer; don't pack it in. Always turn on a strong flow of cold water before you start the disposer. Let it run another minute or two after grinding to be sure all waste is flushed away.*

Tip *If food is stuck in a disposer, turn off the power at the circuit breaker and remove the food by hand or with tongs. Avoid clearing a disposer with chemical drain cleaners containing lye or acid.*

▶ *Tub or shower faucet drips.*

Tub and shower faucets (called valves) have either separate handles for hot and cold water, or a single handle. Two-handled faucets have a compression washer or a ceramic-disk operating mechanism in each handle. You may be able to tell which side is leaking by the temperature of the dripping water; but for a compression faucet, at least, you should repair both sides while you're at it.

To repair a compression faucet, first turn off the water supply (at shutoff valves behind an access door behind the wall or under the floor, or at the main house valve). Next remove the setscrews that hold the handles onto the stems (they may be under decorative caps) and pull off the handles (you may need to use a handle puller, or pry carefully on each handle with two screwdrivers from opposite sides). If there's an escutcheon (collar) block-

ing the stem, remove that. Remove the packing nut (if it's recessed too far for an ordinary wrench to reach, use a bonnet wrench or a deep socket wrench). You may have to chip away some tile with a hammer and cold chisel to gain access. With the nut off, rotate the valve stem out of the valve body. Replace the washer and screw at the end of the stem, and any O-rings elsewhere on the stem (take the stem with you to the store and buy replacements for the stems on both faucets). Examine the holding cup (recessed end of valve stem that holds the washer) and the valve seat. If the holding cup is broken, buy a replacement valve stem or file off the cup and buy an appropriate replacement assembly. If the valve seat is damaged, remove the seat with a valve-stem wrench or allen wrench and replace it. As you reassemble the valve, wrap some packing string

around the stem a few times before threading the packing nut back on.

A single-handled faucet will be of cartridge, ball, or ceramic-disc design. Obtain a replacement kit for the type you have. The repair procedure is the same as for a sink faucet, except that there is no spout attached to the faucet for you to remove (see pages 30 and 31).

▶ *Faucet leaks around stem.*

Turn off the water supply to the tub or shower, then remove the handle and escutcheon (or stem cover). You may have to pry a cover plate off the handle to gain access to the screw. Two-handled faucets will be either a compression or a ceramic-disk type. On a compression faucet tighten the packing nut, using an adjustable wrench if you can, or a deep socket wrench or bonnet wrench if the nut is recessed. You may have to chip away some tile with a hammer and cold chisel to gain access. Now turn on the water. If the leak persists, turn off the water and remove the packing nut. Unscrew the stem and replace any O-rings it has and, while you're at it, the stem washer (see page 30). Screw the stem back in and wrap some packing string around the top (two to four wraps should do) before threading the packing nut back on.

A two-handled ceramic-disk faucet, or a single-handled faucet, will very rarely leak around the handle. If it does, the problem is probably a worn O-ring or gasket under the retaining cap or escutcheon. Buy a replacement washer kit for the model of faucet you have. Turn off the water, remove the handle, and loosen the screws or retaining ring holding the cover in place. Remove it to expose the gasket or O-ring. While replacing it, look for scratches around the gasket seat or loose grit

Identifying the parts of a . . .

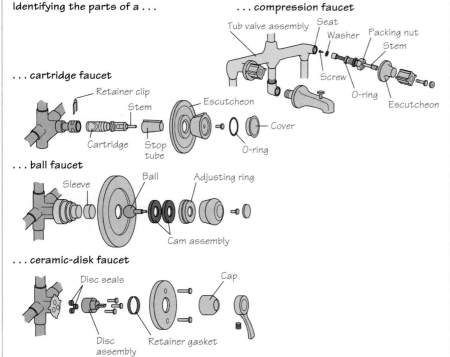

. . . cartridge faucet
Retainer clip
Stem
Escutcheon
Cartridge
Stop tube
Cover
O-ring

. . . compression faucet
Tub valve assembly
Seat
Washer
Packing nut
Stem
Screw
O-ring
Escutcheon

. . . ball faucet
Sleeve
Ball
Adjusting ring
Cam assembly

. . . ceramic-disk faucet
Disc seals
Cap
Disc assembly
Retainer gasket

Tip *A shower valve, tub valve, and combination tub/shower valve are essentially the same. Some combination tub/shower valves have diverter handles built into them to divert the water to the spout or showerhead, but valves without this feature can be used interchangeably. These valves have two outlets—one on the bottom for a tub spout and one on the top for a showerhead. Either or both can be used.*

that may prevent a tight seal. Flush away any grit and smooth rough edges around scratches. Apply valve grease to the seat and reassemble the faucet.

▶ Tub spout drips when shower is turned on.

If the shower is turned on and water still dribbles from the tub spout, the diverter mechanism is not working properly. For some tubs, the diverter is located in the tub spout and is operated by pulling up on a knob. To fix this type of diverter, replace the entire spout with a new diverter spout. To remove the old spout, unscrew it from the nipple hidden in the wall behind it. If it doesn't loosen by hand, insert the handle of a hammer, wrench, or large screwdriver into the spout for leverage (you may first need to loosen a setscrew under the spout with an allen wrench before the spout will turn). After removing the spout, look inside to see if the diverter is blocked by grit or debris and remove it; if this doesn't solve the problem, replace the spout. Make sure that the

Loosening tub spout

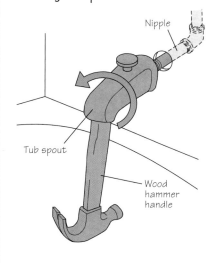

Nipple

Tub spout

Wood hammer handle

threaded inlet hole on the new spout is in the same position and of the same diameter as the one in the old spout. Before screwing on the new spout, fill the gap between the wall and nipple with caulk, and apply a thin bead of caulk to the back edge of the spout.

If the shower flow is controlled by a diverter knob that is part of the faucet, remove the handle and packing nut, and replace washers, O-rings, and packing. If the leak persists, the entire faucet may have to be replaced. This is a major job, probably not equal to the nuisance caused by a dribbling tub spout.

▶ Scalding water sometimes comes out of spout or showerhead.

Either turn down the water-heater control to 120° F or less (see page 26), or install an antiscald faucet. Two types are available: One contains a built-in control that will prevent the water temperature from rising to a dangerous level; another type allows the user to choose the desired temperature, which the valve will maintain within a very close range.

▶ Showerhead wastes water.

Install a low-flow showerhead. Look for one with a maximum flow of 2½ gallons per minute or less, with a built-in on-off button. Unscrew the old showerhead, apply pipe joint tape or compound to the threads of the shower arm, and carefully thread on the new head.

▶ Showerhead is at an inconvenient height.

You can alter the height by installing a shorter or longer shower arm. To raise the height of the showerhead significantly, get an S-shaped arm. These easily thread into the

fitting in the wall. If you want to be able to change the height of the showerhead, get an adjustable arm, which allows as much as 20 inches of height flexibility. You can also install a handheld sprayer, either as an addition to your regular showerhead, by placing a diverter valve between the shower arm and head, or as an addition to the tub spout, by replacing it with one that has a side outlet. Both allow the water flow to be directed to either the showerhead or the handheld unit. Be sure to apply pipe joint tape or compound to the male threads.

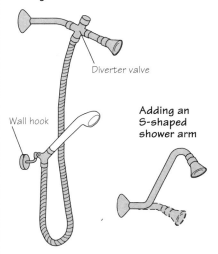

Adding a handheld showerhead

Diverter valve

Wall hook

Adding an S-shaped shower arm

▶ Showerhead drips.

If the faucet is turned off completely and the showerhead drips, the valve in the faucet doesn't seal properly and needs to be repaired (see page 41). If the shower is on and water drips from around the knurled tightening nut, creating a nuisance, remove the showerhead and replace the washer in the nut. Apply pipe joint tape or compound

Tip Many single-handled shower or tub faucets have shutoff valves built into them. After removing the handle and escutcheon or cover plate, look for a setscrew on each side of the valve near the connection to the cold- and hot-water supply pipes. Tighten both screws to shut off the water supply. You can also regulate the rate of flow with these screws.

Tip Fixtures with chrome finishes can be restored by rubbing with ammonia or a paste of baking soda and water. Avoid abrasive scouring pads and powders, harsh metal cleaners, salt, and acids such as vinegar. Polish with silver polish, rinse, and dry immediately.

to the threads on the shower arm. Replace the showerhead. If water dribbles out of clogged spray holes, see below.

▶ Showerhead seems to be clogged.

Remove the showerhead and, if possible, disassemble it. Rinse out loose debris and clean out water holes with a pin. If you find mineral deposits, soak the showerhead overnight in a solution of equal parts water and vinegar. Reassemble and reinstall the showerhead, using pipe joint tape or compound on the threads. If it's too difficult to remove the showerhead, you can mix the solution in a heavy plastic bag and strap the bag over the showerhead so it can soak in the solution overnight.

▶ Enamel tub surface is stained.

First scrub with a household cleaner. To remove mineral deposits, use a solution of equal parts of vinegar and water. Special cleaners are available to remove lime buildup. Iron stains may require a rust dissolver or a cleaner containing oxalic acid. Mildew should be removed with a solution of chlorine bleach and water, mixed according to label recommendations.

▶ Enamel tub surface is chipped or scratched.

Compounds and repair kits for enamel surfaces are available at hardware stores. Be sure to read the product information carefully; some may not work on areas that get submerged or that are frequently exposed to water. They may need to be mixed with paint to match the surface (check product recommendations for the type of paint; most work with alkyd). The area around the chip or scratch must be cleaned and carefully sanded with emery cloth. Apply the compound according to label directions, using a small putty knife or razor blade to keep it flush with the enamel surface. Let it dry thoroughly and then smooth the surface using a cotton swab and some fingernail-polish remover. For repairs that will get wet repeatedly, or for large scratches, you may want to find a professional refinisher (check in the Yellow Pages under "Bathtub Refinishing").

▶ Tub bottom has adhesive from old antiskid appliqués.

If the tub is enameled steel or cast iron, carefully remove the adhesive with a single-edged razor blade. Alternatively, buy a cleaner that is formulated to remove sticky residue, checking to be sure it is compatible with the surface to which you will be applying it.

▶ Enameled-steel tub is too noisy and cools the bathwater too fast.

If you can gain access through the wall behind the tub or through the floor from under the tub, install fiberglass insulation around the underside of the tub.

▶ Tub is leaking at tile joint around rim.

Remove the old caulk or loose grout from the joint with a small putty knife or screwdriver, being careful not to damage the tiles or tub surface. Clean the area with rubbing alcohol, which removes soap residue, and wipe away the cleaner with a dry paper towel before it evaporates. Dry the joint thoroughly using a heat lamp, or leave it to dry over several days.

For a crisp caulk line, mask off the joint with masking or transparent tape. Using caulk specified for bathtub and tile installations, apply a fresh, continuous bead of caulk to the joint. Cut the nozzle on the caulking tube to create a bead of caulk the same size as the joint, so the caulk will make contact with both sides of the gap and the bottom (three-point adhesion) and will fill the joint completely in one pass. Smooth the caulk with a plastic spoon moistened in soapy water. For a straight joint, cut the end of a flat stick (a paint stirrer works well) to a point with two 45-degree cuts, then square off the end of the point so it has a straight edge exactly the same width as the joint. Moisten it, then smooth the caulk by dragging it along the joint corner. Clean off excess caulk from around the joint as soon as possible, before it can set. For best results stand in the tub while caulking, or fill the tub with water; the extra weight will open the joint to its maximum size.

Applying caulk

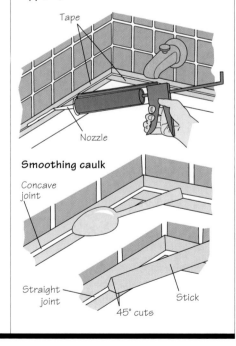

Tape

Nozzle

Smoothing caulk

Concave joint

Straight joint

45° cuts

Stick

Tip If the bathtub or shower stall finish is acrylic, fiberglass, gelcoat, or a similar product, avoid using abrasive cleansers on it. Contact the manufacturer for recommended cleaning products and procedures and for use specifications, such as avoidance of bath oils and other products.

Tip Soap film and mildew can usually be removed from a shower curtain by scrubbing it with full-strength vinegar and a wet sponge. The curtain can also be washed in a washing machine (put a bath towel in the load at the same time). Add a cup of white vinegar to the rinse water. Be sure to remove the curtain hooks before washing.

SOLVING PLUMBING PROBLEMS

▶ Acrylic or fiberglass tub has a crack.

Buy a repair kit from the manufacturer or a local supplier of acrylic fixtures. Most repairs will require you to enlarge the crack and then mix and apply a filler compound. Pigment can be added to match the color of the tub. Once the compound has set, sand with progressively finer grits of sandpaper. Then apply a gel-type polish or some car wax and buff. If you want to be certain of a repair that blends in perfectly with the tub, call a professional bathtub refinisher.

▶ Shower pan made from synthetic material has stains.

Some pan materials, such as solid-surface synthetics, are the same color and texture throughout, and you can sand out the stain with emery cloth or fine sandpaper (according to manufacturer's recommendations). Other materials, especially older cast polymer (cultured marble) pans, have only a thin color veneer and must not be abraded in any way. For these materials, to remove mineral deposits from hard water mix ½ cup ammonia, ¼ cup vinegar, and ¼ cup baking soda with ½ gallon hot water. Wearing rubber gloves, apply the solution with a sponge to a small area first to make sure it does not harm the finish. If it causes no damage, apply it to the stained surface. After five minutes, rinse well.

For darker stains, try placing a cotton rag soaked with hydrogen peroxide on the stain for several hours. Rinse with cold water.

▶ Stopper won't hold water.

Tub drains are usually one of two designs. A trip-lever stopper seals by dropping a brass plunger into a seat in the overflow tube. Wear on the plunger, which causes it to leak, may be overcome by lengthening the linkage. Remove the screws in the overflow plate and lift out the whole assembly. To lengthen it, loosen the locknut and turn the threaded rod in the desired direction. Make only a small adjustment, counting the rotations, and then reassemble the mechanism and test.

On a pop-up drain, the stopper is visible in the drain hole. First check the O-ring on the stopper by opening the drain and pulling out the stopper and connected linkage; replace the O-ring if it appears worn. If the stopper isn't dropping far enough into the drain, remove the overflow plate and adjust the linkage as for a trip-lever stopper.

Adjusting a pop-up stopper

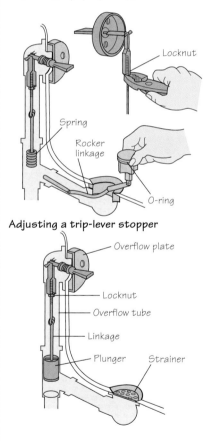

Locknut

Spring

Rocker linkage

O-ring

Adjusting a trip-lever stopper

Overflow plate

Locknut

Overflow tube

Linkage

Plunger   Strainer

▶ Tub drain leaks.

Get below the tub and inspect the joint between the tub and waste arm (L-shaped drain fitting). If water leaks from this joint, replace the gasket. (You may need a helper so one person can work below the tub, another above.) First, from above, remove the stopper. Then insert a strainer wrench or a wedge-shaped woodblock into the drain hole and, with large pliers, turn it counterclockwise to loosen the fitting; unscrew it and pull it out. From below retrieve the gasket. Buy a new one and slip it into place. Then, from above, screw the drain fitting back in, first putting pipe joint tape or compound onto the threads of the fitting and plumber's putty under the flange. Tighten it snug but do not distort the alignment of the waste outlet.

If the leak is at the tee fitting where the horizontal waste arm joins the vertical overflow pipe, loosen the slip nuts and take the unit apart (to pull the assembly apart you may have to detach the overflow fitting from the tub; do this from above). Then reassemble the tee joint, applying pipe joint tape or compound to the male threads of the overflow pipe and installing new 1½-inch washers under the slip nuts. (Some plumbers solder the overflow pipe to the tee to ensure a leakproof joint.) When you reattach the overflow fitting to the tub, make sure the wedge-shaped rubber gasket is sound and seals completely around the overflow hole of the tub. If the leak persists, try taking the tee apart again and applying a ring of plumber's putty inside each slip nut, where it engages the washer. If this doesn't work, the problem is probably a crack or a leaking joint caused

Tip   *Tub joints and corners are the places in a tile installation most vulnerable to water penetration; make sure they are sealed with flexible caulk. Replace the caulk periodically whenever it gets dried or cracked.*

Tip   *Make sure your tub or shower drain has a strainer to keep out hair and debris.*

by the deformed end of a tube. Install a new waste and overflow assembly.

Disassembling a waste and overflow assembly

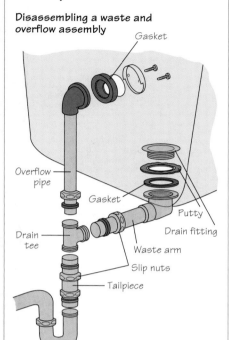

First try a plunger to clear the clog. Remove the drain strainer and run a little water into the tub. Hold a wet rag over the overflow hole (a helper makes this much easier), then begin pushing the plunger up and down. Start slowly, and gradually increase the speed of plunging; continue for several minutes.

If this fails, run an auger down the drain. In a tub, snake the auger down the overflow pipe. To gain access, remove the stopper linkage by unscrewing the cover plate and then pulling the assembly out. Check to see if the plug is covered

▶ Water drains slowly or not at all.

with hair or other debris that could cause slow drainage. Then work the auger into the overflow hole and through the pipes until it contacts the blockage (see page 17). If the auger can't reach or break up the clog, the problem may be deeper in the drain piping (in this case, other fixtures may be backing up as well). If possible, follow the drain from the tub or shower (ideally in a basement or crawl space) to the nearest cleanout plug. Remove the plug and try the auger again. If you still can't remove the clog, call a professional drain-cleaning service.

Old bathtubs often had drum traps located next to the tub. These function as P-traps and can be the source of a clog. Take off the cover (you may need a hammer and cold chisel to unscrew it) and remove any visible clog, or probe with an auger.

Clearing a tub drain

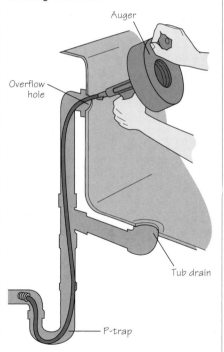

▶ Drain emits odor.

If it smells like sewer gases are coming out of the drain, the P-trap does not have enough water in it to seal them out. Run some water into the drain and see if the odor dissipates after a short period. If so, the water in the P-trap probably evaporated out; perhaps the tub or shower had not been used for several weeks. Otherwise the P-trap might have a leak, or the vent system for that trap is not functioning properly. Inspect the P-trap from under the tub (see left). If it has a leak, replace it. This is fairly easy if the P-trap has slip-joint connections; just loosen the slip nuts and remove it. If the trap is connected with pipe joints, it will have to be cut out and new piping installed; call a plumber. If the trap is sound, but the odor problem persists, a malfunctioning vent system is allowing water to be siphoned out of the trap when the tub is drained; call a plumber.

▶ Bottom is slippery.

Stick-on appliqués can be applied to the bottom of tubs and showers to prevent slipping, but they often begin peeling off and looking ugly after a while. For a tub, a better solution may be to purchase a replaceable rubber mat. A soapy buildup can create a particularly slippery surface. Clean the tub or shower regularly with a household cleaner (for acrylic or similar surfaces, consult the manufacturer's recommendations for cleaning).

Tip   Not all tub drains are easily accessible. If there's no access panel below the floor or behind the wall, you will have to cut into the downstairs ceiling or the back of the wall behind the tub drain. After you cut the hole and make repairs, fit the opening with an access panel. Glue molding around the edge of it to conceal the joint, and screw the panel to the framing around the cutout.

▶ Water in tub doesn't flow toward drain.

The tub is probably not level. With a carpenter's level and long straight-edge, check whether the tub rim is level in several places, lengthwise and across the width. Measure discrepancies so you will know how far the foot end of the tub must be lifted and shimmed to level it. This seems like a major job because a bathtub is locked into place by the wall and floor finish materials, but the work is done in small increments and most of it involves just patching and repair work. However, there is no way to estimate how involved the work will be until you get into it. Ironically, the process is easier with a heavy cast-iron tub than a lightweight tub because the heavier tub is probably not attached to the walls with screws (its weight keeps it in place). In either case the joints between the tub and walls must be opened, some of the wall tile or other finish material around the rim must be removed, and the joint between the tub and floor must be opened. If the tub is nailed or screwed to the wall, the fasteners must be removed along the side and back, after the tile or other backing is removed to expose them. Then, with a pry bar or other lever, slightly raise the foot end of the tub and slip metal shims under the feet and between the tub rim and any ledger boards attached to the walls. After the tub is level, the wall and floor must be patched and the joints caulked.

If the tub is level to begin with, you may have a slightly deformed tub (from a less-than-perfect casting, for example). If shims can't make the water drain better, the tub should be replaced.

▶ Old tub is too large to remove through the doorway.

If you plan to discard the tub, break or cut it into pieces. A sledge-hammer will be needed on a cast-iron tub, whereas a reciprocating saw should do the trick on a steel or plastic tub. If you want to keep the tub in one piece, you will have to lift it and then turn it on its side. If it is a cast-iron tub, you will need several helpers. One trick for moving a heavy tub is to place it on several 24-inch rollers cut from 1½-inch plastic drainpipe.

▶ Tub is difficult to get in and out of.

Install grab bars. The recommended standard is four horizontal grab bars around a typical tub: one on each wall at a convenient height to use while showering, and a lower one along the side (long) wall. The bar at the foot of the tub can be omitted if the tub has a built-in transfer seat. Some individuals may prefer slight modifications, such as a vertical bar at the end of the tub.

Grab bars, which are available in a wide variety of colors to match bathroom decors, must be carefully selected and installed. Because they must be able to support a force of 250 pounds in any direction, they should not be attached to existing stud walls without first providing some blocking for reinforcement. If you are adding them to a finished wall, you can either open the wall and add blocking between studs, or you can install exposed reinforcement in the form of a wood cleat over the wall, bolted securely through the wall material into the studs. The wood must be of a durable species and sealed or painted thoroughly. Use stainless-steel screws and bolts. Check the local building-inspection department for further requirements.

A tub seat also makes it easier to enter and use a tub. Some move back and forth and are removable. Built-in seats are safer and more stable; install according to the manufacturer's instructions.

Locating grab bars in a tub

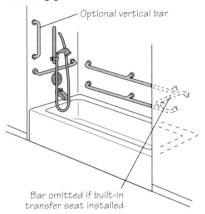

Optional vertical bar

Bar omitted if built-in transfer seat installed

Installing grab bars

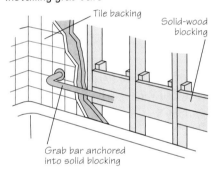

Tile backing

Solid-wood blocking

Grab bar anchored into solid blocking

▶ Shower stall is mildewed.

Clean with a solution of 3 tablespoons chlorine bleach to 1 quart water; follow label precautions carefully. You may need to increase the ratio of bleach for stubborn stains. If mildew is a persistent problem, fill a squirt bottle with the solution and keep it in the bathroom. On a weekly basis, spray the spots where mildew appears, then rinse.

Tip *To prevent water from seeping behind a tub spout into the wall, be sure the spout fits tightly against the tile behind it. If there is a gap, unscrew the spout and replace the pipe with one slightly shorter. Seal the space between the pipe and wall hole with a generous application of caulk. When you screw the spout back onto the pipe, apply caulk to the back of the spout along the top edge and sides, so it fills any gaps between the wall and spout.*

▶ Sliding glass door is hard to move.

Clean the tracks. Pour white vinegar into the tracks and let it stand for five minutes; then rinse carefully. Repeat as necessary, scraping away crusty material with a sharp stick (avoid screwdrivers or other metal objects that might scratch the finish). Use tweezers to remove any debris. If the door slides on wheels in the upper part of the frame, clean the wheels with a solution of equal parts vinegar and water and make sure that they are riding in their tracks.

▶ Shower leaks but source is hard to detect.

Don't use the shower for a few days, giving it a chance to dry out. Then remove the showerhead and screw on an adapter that will allow you to attach a garden hose to the shower arm. (On some units, you may have to remove the arm completely and install a long nipple to connect with the hose adapter.) Now run the hose out a window or into a different drain and turn on the water (hot and cold). If the leak reappears, you will know that it is coming from the valve assembly or piping (see page 41).

If no signs of a leak appear, insert the hose into the shower drain and run some water. If this produces the leak, you will know that the source is in the drain assembly (see page 44).

If you still haven't found the leak, start investigating all corners in the shower and other joints along the floor, walls, and shower door; apply new caulk to joints where it is missing, dried, or cracked (see page 43). Water often leaks over the shower curb or edge of a tub when the shower is on. This can be cured either by replacing the shower curtain with one that provides better coverage, or by installing a small dam to block the water. This can be a simple bead of caulk, or you may be able to find an adhesive-backed product at a home center designed specifically for this problem.

▶ Shower-door frame has come loose from the wall.

Tighten the screws securing the frame to the wall. If the screws aren't holding well enough, use longer ones or enlarge the hole for a hollow-wall fastener. If that doe not fix the problem, you can create new screw holes in the track. First, drill a hole into the wall through the track, then install the screws. If the frame is glued rather than screwed to the wall, you should remove the door or doors, then pry off the frame. Scrape the mating surfaces clean and smooth, and rinse with rubbing alcohol to remove soap residue. Wipe it dry with a clean cloth and apply a suitable waterproof sealant to both surfaces. Carefully reinstall the frame.

▶ Shower-door glass needs replacing.

Tempered glass and safety glass are labeled near one of the edges. If your shower-door glass is not so labeled, replace it immediately with acrylic or safety glass—don't wait for it to break. If you already have an acrylic door but it has become scratched, it is easy to replace. First take the door off its hinge. Remove the screws in the corner and gently tap the corners to separate them. Carefully remove the gasket, and clean it and the frame with a household cleaner and rag. Using 1/8-inch acrylic, cut a new piece to match the size of the old door. Most hardware stores will cut it to size for you, or you can carefully scribe a cut line with a utility knife (make several passes), then break the acrylic over a dowel or broom handle. Put the gasket around the new acrylic, reassemble the frame, replace the screws, and rehang the door.

Disassembling a shower-door frame

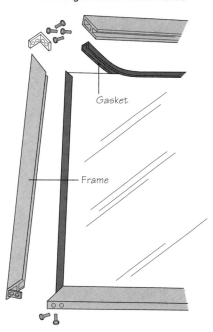

Gasket

Frame

Tip   If you have a shower door that is safe but lacks visual appeal, look for a stained-glass or window shop in your area that offers stained-glass appliqués. Some you can apply yourself; for others you may have to bring the door into the shop and leave it for a few days.

Tip   If the curtain rod is falling off, tighten the screws on the flange holding the rod. If the screws are loose and don't grab, try longer screws; if they don't grip, rotate the flange 45 degrees and drive the screws in the new location. If there is no backing behind the wall, use hollow-wall fasteners behind the screws.

▶ *Water runs constantly.*

Tap the handle a few times. If this works but the problem frequently recurs, there may be a mineral buildup on the handle mechanism. Take the cover off the tank, loosen the handle nut on the inside of the tank, and scrub the threads with some vinegar and a small brush with brass or nylon bristles (an old toothbrush might work in a pinch).

If jiggling the handle doesn't work, look for water flowing into the top of the overflow tube. If it is, the mechanism for adjusting the water level is set too high. If there is a float ball on the end of an arm, carefully bend the arm to force the float downward by placing both hands near the middle of the arm; try not to apply pressure to the float or ball-cock valve. After bending it, test by flushing. The float is correctly positioned when the water level stabilizes about ½ inch below the top of the overflow tube.

If your tank has a floating-cup ball cock, adjust the water level by squeezing the clip located on its side and moving the ball cock up or down.

If water is not flowing into the overflow tube, carefully lift the float a bit. If this shuts off the water flow, the problem is that the float isn't rising high enough in the tank. Carefully bend the float arm to raise the float. If this still doesn't fix the problem, unscrew the float and shake it to see if it's waterlogged; if so, replace the float. If water continues to come out of the ball-cock valve and adjusting the float doesn't affect it, the washers in the valve probably need replacing. Shut off the water supply and flush the toilet to drain the tank. Then remove the screws or pins holding the float arm to the valve. Pull out the small plunger centered in the top of the valve, remove and

replace the washers, and reassemble the valve. Instead of repairing the valve, you may want to replace the entire valve assembly with a new floating-cup ball-cock kit.

Adjusting a conventional float ball cock and tank ball

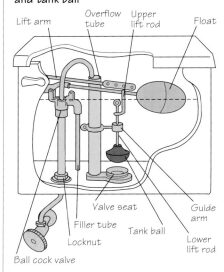

Adjusting a plastic floating-cup ball cock and chain-controlled flapper

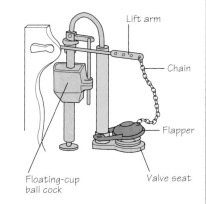

If the float and ball-cock valve seem to be operating correctly, water is probably running because the tank ball or flapper is not dropping fully into the valve seat (drain hole) in the bottom of the tank. Drain the tank before working on it. First close the shutoff valve under the tank; if there is no valve, turn off the main water supply valve. Then flush the toilet to empty the tank. If the toilet has a tank-ball assembly, make sure that the guide arm is aligned directly over the valve seat. If the guide arm needs adjustment, loosen the thumbscrew, move the arm to the right or left, then retighten the thumbscrew. Examine the tank ball; if it appears worn, unscrew it from the lift rod and replace it. If the lift rod is bent, causing the ball to drop crookedly into the valve seat, straighten it. If the ball doesn't drop far enough to seat tightly, move the upper lift rod to a different hole in the lift arm. If the ball or flapper is controlled by a chain, move the chain to a different hole, or hook it by a different link so that there is just a small amount of slack when the ball or flapper is seated.

If the tank ball seats properly but water continues to leak out, empty the tank and clean the bottom of the ball with detergent or a vinegar-and-water solution. Use water and a small wire brush or steel wool to clean the valve seat. Reassemble, turn on the water, and test.

▶ *Toilet doesn't flush completely.*

Check the water level in the tank. It should be about ½ inch below the top of the overflow tube. If it is lower than that, the tank may not be filling with enough water. To adjust the level, raise the float higher by bending the float arm, or replace the float if it is waterlogged (see left). If the toilet has a plastic

Tip *If the ball-cock valve or valve seat seems to require repair too often, replace both of them with a plastic floating-cup ball cock and a hinged flapper. Both are inexpensive and quite easy to install, following the simple instructions on the package.*

floating-cup ball cock, adjust the water level by squeezing the clip and raising the float.

If the water level is adequate, try to make the tank ball or flapper lift higher. If the overflow tube has an adjustable guide arm and it blocks the tank ball from rising any higher, loosen the thumbscrew and raise the arm about ½ inch. Also shorten the lift rods by bending the top hook over with pliers. If the ball or flapper is controlled by a chain, reduce the slack in the chain.

If the toilet never seems to flush completely, the problem may be a partial clog in the waste line (see page 17), inadequate venting (see page 16), or a low-flush model that requires a higher water pressure. Call a plumber.

▶ Handle is loose.

Tighten the nut inside the tank. If it is too corroded and you can't remove it, turn off the water at the shutoff valve and drain the tank by flushing it. On the inside of the tank, cut through the handle shaft with a hacksaw. Detach the inside piece from the lift arm, or if they are permanently connected, buy a new handle with a lift arm attached. To install the new handle, insert the shaft through the hole from the outside of the tank; attach the locknut or holding device from the inside. Because the handle is above water level, it doesn't require a tight-fitting gasket or seal around the hole. Tighten it enough to lift easily without wobbling.

▶ Toilet makes unusual noises when filling.

Take off the tank top, flush the toilet, and watch the ball-cock valve. The washers in the plunger may be worn, allowing water to squirt around it under pressure. If you see water squirting around the plunger, and you can confirm that it causes the noise, replace the washers on the plunger (see opposite page), or replace the ball cock with a floating-cup ball cock. If the noise is a splashing or gurgling sound, make sure the flexible filler tube is aimed into the overflow pipe and not the tank reservoir. There should be a clip on the end of the filler tube for attaching it to the top of the overflow tube. Adjust it so the water flows completely into the tube and does not splash out.

▶ Bowl is clogged.

If the toilet is the only fixture that is backing up, the clog is probably in the bowl trap. Use a plunger with a funnel cup to try to clear the blockage. If the problem remains after several minutes of regular plunging, snake a closet auger down the bowl. The bottom of the shaft of this kind of auger is protected to keep it from scratching the porcelain bowl surface. Retract the cable into the shaft by pulling up on the handle, then insert the shaft into the bowl and push the handle down to work the cable into the drain until it contacts the clog. Rock the handle back and forth gently while pushing and pulling slightly on it, keeping the shaft steady with your other hand. Be patient; it may take some time to break up the clog.

If the plunger and auger don't clear things up and you are certain that the clog is in the bowl, remove the toilet (see page 51). Be sure to drain the tank (if necessary, with a cup and bucket). If possible, carry the bowl outside and place it upside down. Use an auger or a piece of a wire clothes hanger to fish out the clog. Flush the trap with a garden hose. Put in a new wax ring when you reinstall the bowl.

Using a closet auger

Closet auger

▶ Water leaks around the floor.

First make sure that the water is coming from under the base of the bowl and not dripping from condensation on the tank or a leak from the tank or supply line (see page 50). Lift up the caps covering the bolts on each side of the toilet base to see if the nuts are loose.

Tip *If the handle on the toilet tank droops, or if it doesn't rotate far enough to provide a complete flush, look for a setscrew inside the tank where the handle connects to the trip lever, or lift arm. Loosen the screw, adjust the handle to its proper position, and tighten the screw.*

If so, tighten them carefully; over-tightening will crack the entire bowl. If the nuts aren't loose or tightening them does not stop the leak, you will have to lift the bowl from the floor to see what the problem is. Most likely the wax seal between the closet flange and the toilet has slipped or is damaged and needs to be replaced. However, the subfloor around the drain flange may have rotted or collapsed enough to cause the flange to shift, requiring more extensive repair. To remove the bowl and install a new wax ring, see opposite page. If you discover that the old wax ring shifted because the closet flange has come loose from the floor or the soil pipe, call a plumber.

▶ Tank sweats.

Condensation forms when warm moist air strikes a cold surface. A toilet tank surface remains cool from the cold water stored inside the tank. If the air is humid and warm, condensation will form. First try to control humidity in the bathroom by providing adequate ventilation. You can also keep the tank surface from cooling off by installing an insulation liner inside the tank; liner kits are available at hardware stores and home centers. Proper installation usually requires that the tank be completely dry. Trim the liner pieces to size and adhere them to the tank sides with the adhesive provided with the kit. A more expensive alternative is to install a tempering valve below the tank. It is connected to the hot-water and cold-water supply lines, allowing you to adjust the temperature so warmer water enters the tank, thus keeping the tank surface warm. This is a job for a plumber.

▶ You can't tell if the tank is leaking or sweating.

If there is water on the floor and the underside of the tank is damp, the problem is most likely condensation. If the tank is dry, you can rule out sweating or condensation as the problem. Clean up the water around the bowl and thoroughly dry the area. Then flush the toilet. If water appears from around the base, the wax seal is leaking. If the source of the leak remains a mystery, carefully examine and tighten all connections from the shutoff valve up to the tank (inside and out). Do the same with the nuts securing the bowl to the tank, but only if they are loose; overtightening will crack the bowl. See if the water level in the tank is too high, causing water to leak through the handle hole; and check to see if the refill tube isn't shooting water some place other than straight down the overflow tube. Examine the ballcock valve for a leak. Finally, look for cracks in the tank or bowl.

▶ Seat is loose.

Look under the top rim of the bowl for the tightening nuts connected to the seat bolts and tighten them. Check the rubber or plastic spacers that keep the nuts from tightening directly against the porcelain bowl. If they are missing, replace each with a rubber cone washer and fiber washer of appropriate size. Don't overtighten the nuts, as this will crack the porcelain. If the nuts are corroded and don't turn easily, squirt some penetrating oil on the bolt threads above the nuts and wait a few minutes for it to soak in. If the nuts are snug and the seat is still loose, check the screws that secure the hinges to the seat and cover; tighten any loose screws.

▶ Seat needs replacing.

To remove the old seat, loosen the nuts under the top rim of the bowl. If they are corroded and won't turn, apply penetrating oil to the threads above them and wait for it to soak in. If the nuts still won't turn, cut through the bolts with a mini hacksaw, being careful not to scratch the porcelain surface of the bowl (protect it with duct tape if necessary). With the nuts removed, lift off the old seat. Toilet seat sizes are highly standardized, but if you have a very old or unusual toilet, you might want to take the old seat along when you buy a new one. Seats are available in many styles, including solid wood, enameled wood, molded plastic, and fur. Install the new seat with the washers and nuts provided. Most seats have plastic bolts and nuts to prevent rusting. Tighten the nuts securely, but don't overtighten.

Replacing a toilet seat

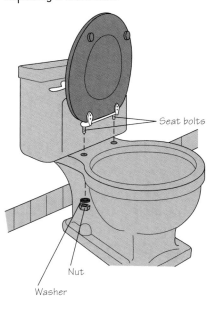

Seat bolts

Nut

Washer

Tip *If the caps that cover the closet bolts at the base of the toilet are loose, there are two ways to secure them. One is to dab some caulk or plumber's putty inside the caps so they will adhere to the closet bolts and nuts. The second is to buy plastic caps that include a separate snap washer. Unscrew the nuts from the closet bolts, slide a washer over each bolt with the grooved edge facing down, screw the nuts back on, and snap the plastic caps onto the washers.*

► *Toilet needs replacing.*

Shut off the water supply and drain the water from the tank and bowl (flush the toilet, then use a siphon or a cup and sponge to scoop out the remaining water). Remove the locknut securing the water supply line to the bottom of the tank, and remove the nuts holding the tank to the bowl; lift the tank off the bowl. Now loosen the nuts at the base of the bowl (they may be hidden under decorative caps). Lift the bowl off the closet flange (you may need to rock it back and forth), and carefully carry the bowl outside (spread newspapers along your route beforehand to protect carpets and floors). Stuff a rag into the flange to prevent sewer gas from entering the bathroom.

Clean off the wax residue from the closet flange with a putty knife. Slide out the old closet bolts and buy new ones. Clean the flange. If it is an old cast-iron flange and is cracked or broken around the bolt hole, check with a plumbing supplier for a short, curved repair strap for bolting to the flange; otherwise you should replace the flange. You will probably have to cut off the soil pipe below the floor, add a new section of pipe, and attach the flange to it.

Slide the new closet bolts into the slots on the flange. Use a dab of plumber's putty to hold them in place until you can set the bowl. Set the new bowl upside down on a towel or piece of old carpeting, and press a new wax ring onto the horn of the bowl. Some wax rings have a plastic sleeve that extends into the flange when the bowl is mounted on it, ensuring a better seal. Use this type especially when the flange lies below the level of the finish floor; if

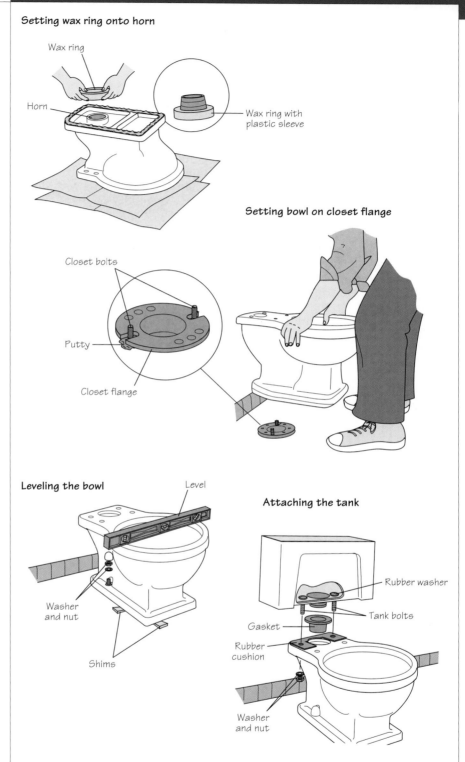

Setting wax ring onto horn

Wax ring

Horn

Wax ring with plastic sleeve

Setting bowl on closet flange

Closet bolts

Putty

Closet flange

Leveling the bowl

Level

Washer and nut

Shims

Attaching the tank

Rubber washer

Tank bolts

Gasket

Rubber cushion

Washer and nut

Tip   *Some communities, in an effort to promote water conservation, have programs for replacing toilets with low-flush models (1.6 gallons or less), free of cost. If you plan to install a new toilet, or wish to reduce water consumption, contact the water department to see if it offers this service.*

the finish floor is more than ¾ inch above the flange, stack two wax rings to make sure the gap will be sealed. Next turn the bowl over and gently set it onto the flange, using the closet bolts as a guide. Push the bowl down into the wax ring. Place the washers and nuts that came with the new bowl onto the bolts and tighten carefully. If a plastic disk is included for snapping the bolt caps onto, place it over the closet bolt first. Tighten each side a little bit at a time. Once they are snug, kneel or sit on the bowl with all of your weight. Check it with a level, using shims to level it if necessary. Then tighten the nuts again. Once the nuts are snug, don't tighten them any more. With a small hacksaw, cut the excess from the bolts and put on the decorative caps.

Next set the tank on the bowl. Make sure to align any washers, gaskets, or cushions exactly as specified in the installation directions. Normally, you will need to tighten the nuts from underneath while securing the bolt in the tank with a large screwdriver. Finally, reattach the water supply line to the tank, turn on the water, and flush a few times to check for leaks.

After a few days' use, if there are still no leaks, especially around the base, run a bead of caulk between the base and floor to prevent water from leaking under the bowl and damaging the floor. Some plumbers run a snake of plumber's putty around the bottom of the bowl before setting it if they are confident that the wax ring will seal perfectly. (The putty prevents water from leaking out from under the bowl, a warning that the wax seal is defective.)

▶ Flushing uses too much water.

Toilets are responsible for a large amount of water consumption, an issue of concern in many communities. Older toilets can use as much as 5 to 7 gallons of water for each flush. There are devices available that can limit the amount of water an older toilet uses, but often these toilets aren't designed to provide a complete flush with less water. Low-flush toilets are available that require 1.6 gallons of water or less per flush. Your community may require that you install one of these anytime you replace a toilet or add a new bathroom (check with the local building department). If you don't plan to install a new toilet and are otherwise happy with the one you've got, you can try installing a toilet dam, available at home centers and plumbing-supply outlets. Generally two dams are installed in the tank, reducing the amount of water that the tank holds. Do not place bricks in the tank to reduce water consumption, as they will slowly deteriorate and release grit that can foul up the functioning of the toilet.

▶ Porcelain is scratched, cracked, or stained.

Try covering minor scratches with appliance paint or auto-body touch-up paint. You may be able to stop a leak through cracked porcelain by sealing the crack with epoxy, but the solution will be only temporary as the crack will have weakened the fixture. The best solution is to replace the toilet. If stains in the bowl resist common household cleaners, pour some chorine bleach into the bowl, let it sit overnight, then scrub the stains again. For rusty stains, use a rust remover recommended for plumbing fixtures. If all efforts fail, consider replacing the toilet.

▶ Water trickles into bowl between flushes.

The tank ball or flapper that seals the drain hole in the tank bottom is probably not seating properly. If enough water leaks out and into the bowl, the tank will refill on its own with a rush of water, sounding like a phantom flush.

To correct the problem, check the alignment of the tank ball or flapper to be sure it settles securely over the drain hole after each flush. Correct the alignment of a tank ball by loosening the thumbscrew holding the support arm in place and rotating the arm until the ball is aligned. If a flapper is out of alignment, make sure it isn't torn or broken and that the hingelike mounting flange is securely attached to the overflow pipe. If alignment is not the problem, inspect the tank ball or flapper for nicks or wear; replace it if it seems worn.

If the problem persists, check the valve seat that the ball or flapper fits into. It may have mineral deposits or scratches that prevent a tight seal. To clean it, empty the tank and scour the valve seat with steel wool (if it's brass) or a nylon pot scrubber (if it's plastic).

▶ Water seeps from under tank.

The bolts that hold the tank to the bowl may be loose, or their rubber washers may have deteriorated. Try tightening the bolts by turning the nuts located behind the toilet and beneath the tank. Be very careful—overtightening will crack the bowl. If the nut is stuck to the bolt and they both turn, steady the bolt with a screwdriver from inside the tank (you may need a helper). If the nuts don't need tightening, turn off the water supply, flush the toilet to drain the tank, and replace the tank bolts, nuts, and rubber washers with new ones.

Tip *If the tank doesn't empty completely after flushing, the flush valve is closing too soon. This problem occurs most often with toilets that have a flapper-type flush valve. To fix it, take some of the slack out of the chain that connects the flapper to the handle lever.*

▶ Septic system backs up.

The septic tank may need pumping. Tanks should be pumped out every two or three years. If yours hasn't been pumped out for a while, call a professional tank pumper. Before the tank is closed back up, flush the toilets and run water down the drain to see if the clog has been removed. If it hasn't, use an auger to find and remove the clog. Run the auger from the tank inlet pipe, or from the sewer-line cleanout near the house foundation (if there is one).

Septic systems can also back up if too much water is run into the tank too fast—it runs directly into the leach field, clogs the soil, and fills the pipes. A larger tank or drain field may solve this problem if it is recurrent.

Finally, the leach field may not be functioning properly (see right).

Pumping a septic tank

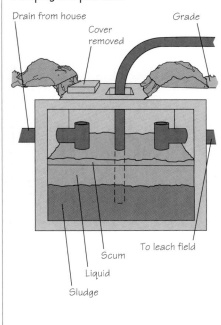

Drain from house
Cover removed
Grade
Scum
Liquid
Sludge
To leach field

▶ Odors emanate from ground.

Odors coming from the tank, or the house side of the tank, may indicate a crack or hole in the tank or a leaking drainage pipe. An expert should be called to try to determine the source of the leak and suggest corrective action.

▶ Leach field is marshy.

The leach field isn't draining properly. This will be particularly evident on dry days if you see patches of especially green grass above the leach pipes. If the problem is infrequent, and especially if it follows particularly heavy rainfall or spring thaw, it may not be worth fixing. But if it is persistent, the gravel in the leach field may have to be replaced and the pipes cleaned out.

▶ Pump cycles on and off erratically.

The pressure switch is probably defective and should be replaced. Drain the tank or, if there's a valve isolating it from the switch, close it. Turn off the power. Remove the switch cover and label the wires (or draw a sketch of the electrical connections). Then disconnect the wires from the terminals, unscrew the locknuts that attach the armored electrical cables to the switch box, and remove the cables. Unscrew the switch from its riser nipple, then wrap pipe joint tape on the nipple threads, and thread on the new switch. Reconnect the wires and turn on the power. The pump should shut off after it builds up pressure in the system. Open a faucet to test the switch; it should turn the pump on after a short time, when the open faucet has drained pressure from the system. Watch the pressure gauge while the pump runs; the switch should turn the pump

on when pressure falls below 40 pounds and shut it off when pressure builds up to 60 to 65 pounds. If the pressure gets too high because the switch leaves the pump on too long, or the pressure falls too low because the switch doesn't turn the pump on soon enough, adjust the pressure switch by turning the adjusting nut at the end of the spring.

Replacing a pressure switch

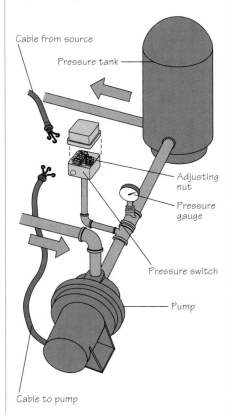

Cable from source
Pressure tank
Adjusting nut
Pressure gauge
Pressure switch
Pump
Cable to pump

Tip *The normal interval for having a septic tank pumped is between two and three years.*

Tip *Typical requirements for a septic-tank drain field: (1) minimum of 10 inches of soil above the drainage pipes, (2) no pipes within 10 feet of the house foundation or within 5 feet of any other structure, (3) no pipes within 10 feet of a property line, and (4) no pipes within 10 feet of a water supply pipe or within 100 feet of a well.*

▶ Pump cycles on and off frequently.

If the pump turns on every time you run water out of a faucet, the pressure tank isn't holding air pressure. First check the pressure with a tire gauge at the small threaded valve that looks like a tire valve. If it is less than recommended by the manufacturer, add the necessary amount of air with a tire pump. Add only a little at a time, checking regularly with the gauge.

If the tank is an older style of pressure tank without an air valve, it has probably lost air pressure from becoming waterlogged. To recharge the air, shut off power to the pump, then open the drain valve on the tank (attach a hose if necessary). Open a faucet in the house to drain the water out of the tank so it fills with air. Then turn off the faucet, shut the drain valve on the tank, and turn the pump back on. The water will compress the air into a cushion at the top of the tank, which pressurizes the system. Over time the air in such a tank does become waterlogged. If this happens frequently, replace the tank with a newer model that keeps the air separated from the water by an expandable bladder or diaphragm, which can be recharged without draining the tank.

If recharging the tank doesn't solve the problem, or solves it for only a short time, the tank is losing pressure because of leaks. First check for water leaks in the plumbing system: leaking faucets or pipes or a running toilet. Then check the pressure tank for an air leak. Spray soapy water around the tank surface. If you see bubbles indicating a leak, the internal diaphragm or the whole tank may need to be replaced. If you can't find a leak and the tank still does not hold pressure, the check valve for the pump, which keeps water from draining back into the well, may need replacing. This requires that the pump be pulled from the well if it is a submersible pump. Call for repairs.

▶ Pump won't run.

Check for a tripped circuit breaker or blown fuse. Well pumps require a large draw of amperage to start up and may overload the circuit. If the breaker trips frequently, have an electrician rewire the circuit. Also, with the power off, check that all wires are connected securely.

If a fuse or breaker isn't the problem, check the pressure switch, usually located near the pressure tank. The spring on the switch may have weakened over time; compensate by tightening the adjusting nut at the end of the spring. Also see if the switch contacts are dirty or discolored; if so, shut off the power and sand or file them (a nail file or very fine sandpaper works best). Restore power and draw some water. If the pump still doesn't come on, you probably need a new pressure switch (see page 53).

There may be an obstruction in the piping to the pressure switch or in the pump mechanism itself. Shut off the power and inspect the pipes and fittings. If they are clear, check the pump. Some kinds of pumps you can turn manually; if you encounter resistance while turning the shaft, there is some kind of obstruction in the impeller. Have the pump inspected and repaired by a professional.

If you have a well pump with a control box located near the pressure tank, the box may have a capacitor or capacitor coil that is the source of pump failure. If the pump is totally dead, both should be checked for an open relay or a short. Have a professional do this, as a capacitor can discharge a dangerously high level of voltage even when the power is off. If either component is defective, it will have to be replaced.

Cleaning pressure-switch contact points

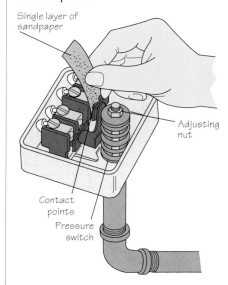

Single layer of sandpaper

Adjusting nut

Contact points

Pressure switch

▶ Pump won't stop running.

It's possible that the pump has lost its "prime" and is running continuously to try to catch up. Turn off power to the pump and restore the prime by pouring water into the priming hole. However, it's more likely the problem is in the pressure switch. It may be set too high; to adjust the setting, turn the adjusting nut at the end of the spring counterclockwise. If that doesn't work, turn off power to the pump and inspect the contact points; if they appear to be stuck together, gently pry them apart with a screwdriver and smooth them with sandpaper. If the switch still doesn't work, replace it (see page 53).

Tip *Wells run dry when the water table drops below the intake, often during severe drought or following particularly heavy usage. If the problem happens at other times, you should either have the well drilled deeper or have a new well drilled in a better location. Consult an experienced well driller.*

▶ Impeller on pump isn't working.

If you have a deep-well centrifugal pump, commonly called a submersible pump, the pumping suction is created by a rotating impeller, which is often made of either nylon or brass. If a centrifugal pump runs dry, heat buildup can quickly melt the blades. The pump will have to be pulled from the well and repaired or replaced.

▶ Well water may be contaminated.

There are dozens of biological and chemical contaminants that may be found in drinking water. Federal standards set allowable limits. Some contaminants can be detected by sight or smell, but most cannot. Some can cause acute health effects (diarrhea, nausea), whereas others can cause long-term, chronic problems. Contact the county extension service or a water-quality expert for advice on testing and treating. All water from wells should be checked periodically for coliform bacteria. Don't install any water treatment equipment until you have discovered what, if anything, you want to treat.

If you have had any work done on your well recently, you should chlorinate the whole system. Use regular, unscented laundry bleach. Mix at least 1 cup in 5 gallons of water, then pour the solution into the well casing. Turn on faucets in the house until you smell the bleach. Let the chlorinated water sit in the pipes for a couple of

hours, then run the water out of each faucet until long after the bleach smell has disappeared. If your drains run into a septic tank, empty the chlorinated water into buckets, let them sit for a few days, then dispose of the water elsewhere (it shouldn't be harmful to any but the most sensitive lawn or garden plants).

▶ Water needs softening.

Water containing high amounts of calcium, magnesium, or iron, called "hard" water, should be treated with a softener. Water softeners filter water through a granulated resin that causes an ion exchange, trapping the hard ions of the minerals and exchanging them for soft sodium ions. Salt is then filtered through the resin to rejuvenate it. Salt must be added to the container on a regular basis.

A water-softening system contains a resin tank and a brine tank, sometimes combined inside one self-enclosed unit. An automatic water softener will also have a time clock control that is programmed to siphon the brine into the resin tank to replenish its effectiveness. Generally, the only work required of the homeowner is to add salt to the brine tank from time to time.

There are two methods of installing water softeners, and the one you choose may depend on the degree of hardness in your water. For moderately hard water, which prevents soap from lathering easily but does not stain fixtures, you can choose to soften only the hot water, providing softened water where it is most needed (laundry and bathing). This is the simpler option and it has the added benefit of not adding sodium to your drinking water, which can be a health problem for some.

If your water is hard enough to stain fixtures and build up scale in pipes, fixtures, and appliances, you'll have to soften the water in the whole house.

For a hot-water-only installation, install the softener on the cold-water inlet line that runs to the water heater. To soften water on the whole system, install the softener near the water meter, before the hot- and cold-water lines branch off, though you might wish to avoid softening lines to sillcocks, as softened water can damage lawns and gardens. Installation should be done by a professional, as water pipes may have to be resized or a bypass system added to keep the water pressure up—adding a softener usually reduces it.

You can also rent a water softener, which will save you from having to install one, but will cost more in the long run.

Typical water-softening unit

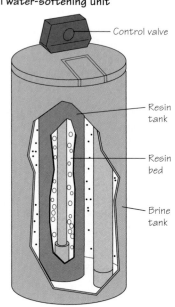

— Control valve

— Resin tank

— Resin bed

— Brine tank

Tip *To see if your water is hard enough to require further testing or a softener, fill a jar halfway with cold tap water. Then sprinkle in a few flakes of pure detergent or soap (unscented, with no additives). Screw a lid onto the jar and shake it. If little or no lather forms, the water is hard. Hard water will also leave a residue on your finger if you dip it into the solution.*

SOLVING PLUMBING PROBLEMS

▶ *Sprinkler pipe is leaking.*

Most lawn sprinklers today are installed using plastic pipe, either flexible (polybutylene or poly-ethylene) or rigid (PVC or ABS). They can be damaged by digging in the yard or garden. First dig a trench to expose 1 to 2 feet of pipe around the leak, removing dirt from the sides and bottom of the pipe as well as the top. Shut off the water supply. If the pipe has a small hole or crack, you can make a permanent repair with a dresser, or repair, coupling (see page 12). First cut through the pipe where it is damaged. Then carefully pull the cut ends apart far enough to slide the coupling over one end (the coupling nuts should be loose). Slide the coupling over the other end, tighten the nuts, and turn on the water to test the repair.

If the damage extends along the pipe too far for a repair coupling to cover it (1 inch for ½-inch pipe, 2 to 3 inches for ¾-inch pipe), cut out the damaged section and replace it with tubing of the same size and material. If it is solid pipe with solvent-weld joints, see page 14 for joining techniques. If it is flexible polybutylene or polyethylene pipe, there are several types of fittings available to join the replacement section of tubing to the rest of the pipe. Choose the same type of fitting that was used on the rest of the sprinkler system. Join push-fit fittings by simply pushing the tubing into the fitting. To join clamp fittings, tighten the setscrew with a screwdriver. Join crimped fittings by squeezing them together with pliers.

▶ *Sprinkler head is clogged.*

Some heads can be cleaned by clearing out the holes with a thin piece of wire. Heads that include a large cartridge body have an internal screen that you can remove and clean by disassembling the cartridge. You may need to dig around the cartridge a bit to grip it so you can unscrew the head, and to keep debris from falling into the exposed cartridge chamber. If cleaning does not solve the problem, replace the head (see below).

▶ *Sprinkler head doesn't spray far enough.*

First check for clogs (see above). Then adjust the force of the spray: Some sprinklers have an adjusting screw in the middle of the head; others have an allen-head setscrew. If the head sprays far enough but doesn't cover the required area of lawn, it may not be the right head for that spot. Some heads cover a full 360-degree sweep, others cover 180 degrees (useful along the sides of buildings or walks), and yet others cover only 90 degrees (one quarter of a circle) and are used in corners. Some types of sprinkler heads can be adjusted for changing the coverage arc. They are usually plastic and have a canister extending into the ground below the head. Consult the manufacturer's instruction sheet for your type of heads to see if you can adjust them; otherwise replace the head with one that has the coverage you desire. To install it, turn off the automatic timer for the system. Remove a few inches of grass and dirt from around the sprinkler head and unscrew it from the riser pipe (use two wrenches or pliers). If the

head has a deep body, dig carefully around it to expose the connection to the riser pipe before unscrewing it. If the new sprinkler head is not identical to the old, attach whatever couplings or nipples are necessary to adapt it to the right height and screw it onto the riser pipe. (If you won't be installing the new sprinkler head immediately, screw a pipe nipple or pipe cap onto the exposed water pipe to keep dirt from falling into it.) Orient the new head, or adjust it according to manufacturer's instructions, so the spray will cover the desired area.

Removing old head

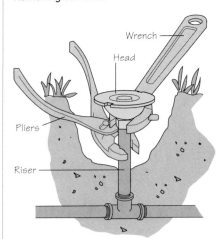

Installing new head

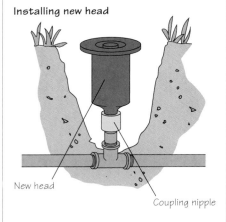

> **Tip**   *A simple way to test the water distribution of a sprinkler head is to set up a gridlike pattern of small, equal-sized containers on the section of lawn surrounding the sprinkler head. Run the sprinkler for a set time and measure the contents of each container with a ruler. A lawn generally needs from 1 to 2 inches of water per week.*

Electricity deserves respect, but it is not necessarily mysterious. The electrical system can be one of the simplest and most logical areas to work on, so long as you understand a few basic principles and safety procedures. This chapter presents guidelines for solving more than 130 problems. Before you attempt to solve a particular problem, browse through a few others to be sure you understand the principles involved.

SOLVING ELECTRICAL PROBLEMS

▶ *Electricity needs to be turned off.*

If you're turning off power to do any work on the electrical system, test your voltage tester first to make sure it works by inserting the probes into a receptacle. To shut off power to the entire house, locate the main circuit breaker, which is usually in a metal box near the electric meter, and switch it to *Off*. (It may be inside the main service panel in the house.) If there is no main breaker, shut off all the branch-circuit breakers. Older homes may have a fuse drawer marked *Main* that you pull out, or cartridge fuses that you can disconnect by pulling down a lever on the outside of the box (do not try to pull out the cartridges unless you are wearing rubber gloves or have an insulated fuse-pulling tool, and

the circuit is not drawing power). In some service entrances (the meter, main disconnect, and the circuit-breaker panel) there may be one or two other large breakers besides the main, labeled *Range* or *Air Conditioner;* they control those appliances independently of the rest of the house, and should be switched off if you want all power off.

To shut off electricity to only one part of the house—to a light switch you are replacing, for instance—shut off the circuit breaker or unscrew the fuse (make sure that it is not drawing power) for that particular circuit; it will deaden other fixtures and outlets as well. Then test the light switch or other device you are working on with a voltage tester to make sure it is dead.

Shutting off main disconnect

Breaker type   Cartridge fuse type   Fuse drawer type

Main breaker panel   Main fuse panel

▶ *Power goes off in whole house.*

Check to see if the main breaker is tripped. Examine the immediate area first for loose or dangling power lines; don't stand on damp ground, wear gloves, and take a flashlight. If the breaker is not tripped, phone the power company. If it is tripped, don't reset it. First turn off all the branch-circuit breakers; then reset the main breaker and, one by one, reset the circuit breakers. (To reset a breaker, turn it to *Off* first, then to *On*.) If the main breaker suddenly trips when you reset one of the circuit breakers, that circuit may be the source of the problem. Leave that circuit breaker off as you continue resetting breakers. If power is restored successfully, tape the problem breaker in the *Off* position and call an electrician. If the main breaker trips again as you continue resetting circuit breakers, the problem is probably an overloaded main breaker. No individual circuit is at fault, but the combined load is too much for the main breaker. Call an electrician. In the meantime reduce the load by turning off or disconnecting as many appliances as you can, especially an electric range or heaters; if you have to use one, turn off another first.

Be aware that occasionally a criminal may trip the main breaker to lure you out of the house. The box that contains the main breaker or fuse should be locked, and you should keep the key indoors.

▶ *Power goes off in part of house.*

Look for a tripped breaker in the circuit-breaker panel. The handle of a tripped breaker isn't always easy to notice; it may be in the center position, not the more conspicuous *Off* position. If the system has fuses instead of circuit breakers, shine a

Tip *Never replace a fuse with one that has a higher amperage rating. For protection, buy an S-type fuse of the proper rating and an adapter that matches it. The adapter screws into the fuse socket and will accept only S-type fuses of the same rating.*

Tip *For working with electricity safely:*
(1) Test your voltage tester before shutting off power.
(2) Always shut off power to any circuit you plan to work on and post a warning sign for others at the breaker panel.
(3) Test exposed wires or fixtures with the voltage tester before working on them.

flashlight into the glass center of each fuse until you see one that is smudged or has a broken internal bar. Do not reset the tripped breaker or replace the blown fuse yet; instead switch off or unplug all of the appliances and lights affected by the dead circuit, then reset the breaker or replace the fuse. If the breaker or fuse immediately trips again, call an electrician. If it does not, turn the lights and appliances back on, one by one, until the breaker or fuse trips. If it trips suddenly, the problem is almost certainly a short circuit in the last appliance turned on. To be sure, unplug it and reset the circuit breaker again; it should stay on. Turn on the rest of the appliances. If the breaker goes off again (there might be a delay), the problem is an overloaded circuit. Plug some of the appliances, especially those with heating elements, into other circuits. If the electricity stays on, the isolated appliance is the problem. Have it repaired.

▶ Power is off but breakers look fine.

If a few receptacles are dead (not necessarily in the same room), they may have been deadened by a tripped GFCI receptacle that they are wired into. These sensitive receptacles are subject to "nuisance tripping," and sometimes control outlets in other rooms. Check all GFCI receptacles, starting with the one closest to the dead outlets. Push the reset button on each one until electricity is restored.

If the problem isn't a tripped GFCI, there may be a subpanel of which you're not aware that controls the areas without power. Look in closets, under sinks, and in other hidden places. The main breaker

panel may have a breaker marked *Subpanel* or *Sub,* which confirms its existence if not its location. Even labels like *Addition, Basement,* or *Kitchen* are strong hints of a subpanel somewhere. If you can find it, look for a tripped breaker and proceed as described on opposite page. If not, call an electrician.

▶ Circuit breaker trips repeatedly.

The problem is probably an overloaded circuit. Follow the same procedure as for fuses (see below), except that the breaker gives no visible clues. Therefore, start with all appliances and lamps unplugged.

▶ Fuse blows repeatedly.

The problem is a short circuit or an overload. Examine the blown fuse to find out; if the window is blackened or discolored, the cause is a short circuit—either in the house wiring or in an appliance or fixture. Unplug all appliances and lamps on the circuit and try a new fuse. If it blows immediately, call an electrician. If it doesn't, plug in each device until the fuse blows again. The last appliance was the culprit. Replace or repair it.

If the fuse windows are clear but the internal link is broken, the cause is circuit overloading. It may be temporary overloading from a heavy motor starting up. Install a time-delay fuse of the same amperage; it allows temporary surges that aren't at dangerous levels. Or the overload may be caused by too many appliances plugged into the

same circuit. Redistribute the load by plugging some appliances into other circuits, or call an electrician. Do *not* attempt to solve the problem by installing a larger fuse.

Reading a blown fuse

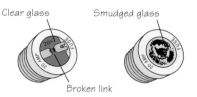

Clear glass   Smudged glass

Broken link

Identifying types of fuses

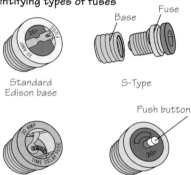

Base   Fuse

Standard
Edison base   S-Type

Push button

Time-delay   Breaker fuse

▶ Circuit-breaker handle won't budge or flaps loosely.

A breaker can wear out. Replace it with a new one of identical amperage from the same manufacturer, or a compatible model. To remove the old one, first turn off the main circuit breaker. Take off the panel cover to expose the wiring inside. Remove the old breaker by pulling first one end straight out, then the other, until one of them comes loose. Loosen the setscrew that holds the wire in place. Insert the wire into the new breaker, tighten the setscrew, and snap the breaker into the panel. Replace the cover

(4) Never stand on a wet or damp surface when working with electricity. Place dry rubber mats or boards over damp areas.
(5) Never touch plumbing, radiators, or metal duct work while working with electricity.
(6) Use a wood or fiberglass ladder (not metal) near overhead wires.
(7) Use tools with rubber- or plastic-coated handles.
(8) Wear safety glasses and, when working on service equipment (the main service entrance or circuit-breaker panel), gloves.
(9) Use only one hand when working on service equipment.
(10) Check your work with a voltage tester or receptacle analyzer.

and restore power. *Caution:* Wear gloves, use tools with insulated handles, don't stand on damp floor or ground, and keep fingers away from wires inside the box.

Removing old breaker

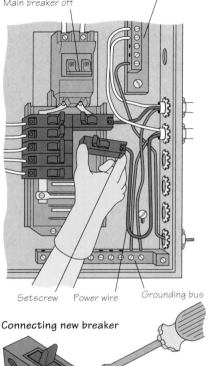

Main breaker off

Neutral bus

Setscrew   Power wire   Grounding bus

Connecting new breaker

Setscrew

Power wire

▶ Circuit doesn't have enough receptacles.

The number of receptacles on general-purpose circuits varies because capacity is determined by the total amperage draw and not the number of devices that can be plugged in. You can add new receptacles (see page 208) anywhere along a circuit (so long as it's not dedicated to a single appliance) by

running wire from any of the existing receptacles to the new one (provided the new wires don't crowd the electrical box; see "Number of Conductors Permitted in an Electrical Box" on page 151) or by splicing a junction box into the circuit wiring to provide a place to connect new wires. (You may have to install two junction boxes to make up for cable lost to splicing; see page 64.) Consult an electrician; obtain a proper permit.

Tying into receptacle at end of run

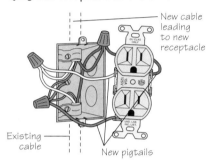

New cable leading to new receptacle

Existing cable

New pigtails

Tying into receptacle in middle of run

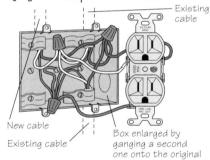

Existing cable

New cable

Existing cable

Box enlarged by ganging a second one onto the original

Tying into cable run

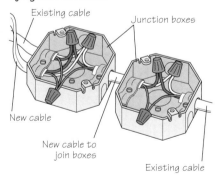

Existing cable

Junction boxes

New cable

New cable to join boxes

Existing cable

▶ Circuits are overloaded; not enough circuits.

If there are knockout blanks in the circuit-breaker panel or the breakers are the type that can be replaced with thinner ("wafer") versions, you can have new circuits run from the main breaker panel. If not, you will have to have a subpanel installed and run new circuits from it. In either case be sure that the increased load will not overload the main disconnect device (main breaker), that the new wire is sized large enough for the intended load, and that the circuit-breaker rating does not exceed the capacity of the wire size. The National Electrical Code (NEC) has specific requirements for various kinds of circuits. Consult an electrician or the local building department.

▶ Circuits aren't labeled clearly at breaker panel.

To prevent future annoyance during troubleshooting or to evaluate the house wiring system, map out the circuits by drawing a floor plan with all receptacles, switches, lights, and permanent (built-in) appliances. You'll need a helper and one or two plug-in lamps. If you work alone, use a radio that you can plug into different outlets throughout the house, turned up loud enough for you to hear from the circuit-breaker panel. If the circuits are not numbered, number them. Turn off the circuit breakers one by one and see which lights and receptacles don't work each time. On the floor plan, write the number of the circuit breaker next to each receptacle, appliance, or fixture it serves. Label the breakers themselves to identify which rooms or devices they control. Post a copy of the map inside or near the breaker panel.

Tip   *A tripped circuit breaker helps you diagnose the problem. If you switch it on and it suddenly trips with an angry buzzing sound, the problem is a short circuit where a hot (black) wire is in direct contact with a neutral wire or a ground wire; the short may be in a faulty piece of equipment, an electrical box, an electric fixture, or along a wiring run. If there's a delay before the breaker trips, it is an overloaded circuit.*

Note: You can also perform this test without turning off any breakers, by using a circuit-breaker locator tool. You may find it worth buying just so you won't have to reset digital clocks, VCRs, and other timers disturbed by turning off the circuits.

▶ Lights dim throughout house from time to time.

Occasional dimming may be caused by electrical storms or voltage drops in the power lines. More persistent dimming is probably due to heavy appliances, such as a refrigerator or washing machine, cycling on and off. These appliances should have their own circuits. Otherwise, try plugging them into a circuit that doesn't have lights on it.

▶ Appliances don't seem to run at full power.

The circuit that they are on is overloaded, but not to the point of tripping the circuit breaker or blowing a fuse. Reduce the load on the circuit by plugging some appliances into other circuits and using shorter extension cords wherever possible. If the problem continues, the entire electrical system should be inspected by a qualified electrician.

▶ TV picture shrinks.

The circuit is overloaded, probably by an appliance with a heavy-duty motor or a large heating element. Reduce the load on the circuit by plugging some appliances into other circuits, or plug the television into another circuit.

▶ System isn't grounded or is improperly grounded.

An electrical system must have a backup path that allows errant charges of electricity—from a disconnected wire, for instance—to flow at maximum available current so the circuit breaker or fuse can respond and shut off the circuit. Otherwise, the charged wire or appliance is a hazard to anyone touching it; it's also a potential fire hazard if the loose connection causes sparking. All receptacles, switches, lights, and built-in appliances should be connected to a ground wire (bare copper or green) or rigid metal conduit as part of their wiring. The entire system, in turn, should be grounded at the service-entrance panel by a continuous wire connected to at least two separate "grounding electrodes." These might be a metal water pipe (with bonding wires around the water meter and water heater), an 8-foot copper-clad ground rod, a 20-foot length of ½-inch-diameter reinforcing steel buried in the foundation (Ufer ground), or other approved means.

If your electrical system has partial or improper grounding, you should have it inspected and upgraded by a qualified electrician. In the meantime there is a stopgap measure you can undertake immediately: Replace ungrounded, two-prong outlets with GFCI receptacles, which work without a ground wire. They protect against shock by shutting off current so quickly that for all practical purposes the receptacle is dead *before* a hazard exists. If you can't afford one for each outlet, protect all outlets on the same circuit by installing a GFCI receptacle in the one closest to the breaker panel and attaching the wires that feed the other receptacles to the "load" terminals of the GFCI. Do not connect a ground wire between the GFCI and any downstream receptacles. See also page 70.

Providing grounding electrodes for a service panel

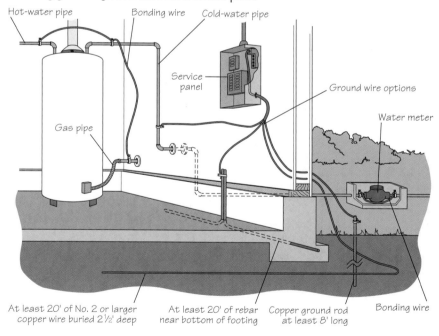

Hot-water pipe   Bonding wire   Cold-water pipe

Service panel

Ground wire options

Water meter

Gas pipe

At least 20' of No. 2 or larger copper wire buried 2½' deep

At least 20' of rebar near bottom of footing

Copper ground rod at least 8' long

Bonding wire

Tip *Plug fuses are color-coded: brown is less than 15 amps, blue is 15 amps, red is 20 amps, and green is 30 amps. Do not use a fuse rated above the capacity of the circuit wires. Unless the wires are labeled otherwise, assume that they are No. 14, which has a maximum capacity of 15 amps (blue fuse). Be very suspicious of a green (30-amp) fuse. Only some appliance circuits have wires large enough for such a load.*

▶ Power surges from time to time.

Except for the potential catastrophe of a rare lightning strike, power surges were never considered a serious problem until recently. Now homes have computers, electronic entertainment systems, appliances controlled by microprocessors, and other delicate (and expensive) equipment that is vulnerable to power surges. Although utility companies monitor and adjust voltage constantly, surges are unavoidable and no community is immune. At the very least you should protect your most expensive equipment (especially a computer) with a surge protector, readily available at electronics dealers or computer stores. Get one with a response time less than 10 nanoseconds (10 billionths of a second), a "clamping voltage" (threshold at which it reacts) between 120 and 300 volts or as close to normal house voltage (120 volts) as you can afford, and an energy-absorbing capability of at least 100 joules (more where lightning is common). For cheaper but less reliable protection, hardware stores and home centers carry plug-in power strips with surge suppressors, which usually have multiple receptacles. It is also possible to have an electrician install surge-protection devices that protect your entire electrical system.

▶ System is grounded to water pipes, but some are plastic.

A system grounded to water pipes alone may not be grounded sufficiently. There is no assurance of a continuous path of uninterrupted metal piping to provide adequate contact with the soil; the path may be broken by sections of plastic piping or plastic bushings (sleeves or gaskets that separate metal pipes electrically) within some metal fittings (for instance, connections to water meters and water heaters have such fittings). Although bonding wires can and should be attached to metal pipes to bypass such obstructions, to be completely safe you should install a secondary grounding electrode. For most soil conditions you can use an 8-foot-long copper or copper-clad rod, ½ inch in diameter. Drive it into the ground next to the electrical service entrance until it is flush with the finished grade. Scoop some soil away from the rod and clamp No. 6 or larger copper wire to the top, then to the water pipe, and finally to the neutral bus bar in the circuit-breaker panel (which is bonded to the grounding bus bar if they are separate). Wear gloves and avoid touching both the ground wire and service equipment at the same time unless they are securely bonded together and the wire is grounded. Consult the local building-inspection department about permits and code requirements.

▶ Old service entrance is rated at less than 100 amps.

The minimum size for new service-entrance equipment is 100 amps—more if certain loads, such as air-conditioning or electric heating, are included. If your home has a smaller service entrance (30 amps is typical for many older homes), you are probably inconvenienced by frequent overloads. Unless you choose to revert to a 1920s life-style, you should have the service entrance changed by a qualified electrician. Aside from being under-sized, a 30-amp system may have improper grounding, no 240-volt capability, and fatigued wires with worn or cracked insulation. Some older homes have a 60-amp service, which is almost always a three-wire service that was installed to accommodate an electric range. Such a system, if grounded properly, usually doesn't need upgrading unless you are adding electric heating loads. It often has sufficient capacity even for a major kitchen remodel; just replace the electric range with a gas one and use the range feeder wires for a new subpanel. Do not try to upgrade a system only by installing a larger main breaker or fuse. The entrance wires between the weatherhead and main breaker must also be replaced, and probably the mast as well.

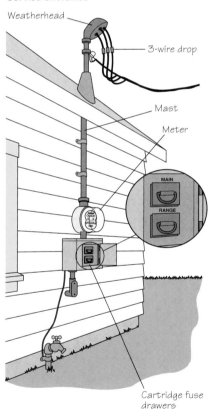

Identifying an older, 60-amp service entrance

Weatherhead

3-wire drop

Mast

Meter

MAIN

RANGE

Cartridge fuse drawers

Tip *Where a grounding electrode for an electrical system is buried in the ground, the soil must have some moisture. In a few areas the ground may be so dry that a water pipe or 8-foot copper rod is not sufficient grounding. In this case, a Ufer ground should be used. It consists of at least 20 feet of No. 4 copper wire or ½-inch-diameter reinforcing rod buried in the concrete foundation footing of the home.*

▶ House is wired with aluminum wire.

Aluminum wiring, which was installed in many homes between 1965 and 1973, has been the cause of many residential fires, according to the Consumer Product Safety Commission. Symptoms such as warm cover plates, metallic odors, and even sparks or smoke can occur spontaneously. To tell if the wiring in your home is aluminum, look in the attic, basement, or garage for exposed wiring. If the cable has plastic sheathing that says *AL* or *Aluminum*, call the builder or an electrician certified to work on aluminum wiring. The system should be inspected and possibly replaced with copper wiring. Do not try to work with aluminum wiring yourself. Connections can corrode or overheat unless they are made carefully and with materials specified for use with aluminum wire.

This caution does not apply to aluminum wire used for the large service-entrance wires inside a mast or underground conduit. It is used widely and is not hazardous if connected properly. Aluminum wiring that poses the greater hazard is smaller-gauge circuit wiring inside the home, with multiple connections to receptacles, switches, and lights.

▶ House has old knob-and-tube wiring.

In this system, which was used in homes when they were first electrified, the wires are kept separate from each other and are fastened to the house framing with porcelain knobs and tubes. Most codes do not require replacing it, but any new wiring must use modern materials. Knob-and-tube wiring has the advantage of not overheating, but the disadvantage of no ground wire. If you tap into this type of wiring to extend a circuit, first verify that the two

wires are indeed a hot wire and a neutral wire by testing them with a no-contact voltage tester. (The wires aren't color-coded and two parallel wires aren't necessarily a hot and a neutral—they could be separate legs of a switch loop.) Then turn off the power and install two junction boxes close to the wires. Cut the wires, test them with a neon voltage tester to be sure they are dead, and thread them through knockout holes in the junction boxes. If the box is metal, slide some sheathing or "loom" over the wires to protect them. Run a short length of No. 14, two-wire NMC cable between the boxes. Then run the cable that feeds the new receptacles or lighting into one of the boxes and join the wires. If you tap into this type of wiring to feed new receptacles, use a GFCI receptacle in the first box, and wire all additional receptacles into it. No ground wire should be used with this arrangement.

Installing boxes

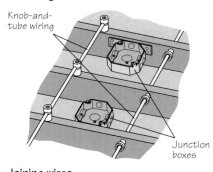

Knob-and-tube wiring

Junction boxes

Joining wires

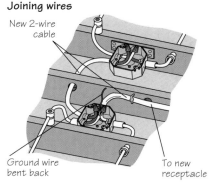

New 2-wire cable

Ground wire bent back

To new receptacle

▶ Ends of old knob-and-tube wiring are missing insulation.

The insulation on old wires eventually becomes brittle and frayed, especially near connections at the ends of wires. It can easily disintegrate when touched or rubbed, leaving wires dangerously bare. Turn off the power to affected wires, check them with a voltage tester, then wrap exposed ends with electrical tape. Where one wire crosses over another or enters a metal box, make sure it is enclosed in a length of loom (thick woven tubing used for insulation).

▶ Wire has splices or connections outside of electrical boxes.

This situation violates the NEC; all splices and connections must be made inside electrical boxes or other approved housings. Install a junction box in which to make the connections. First turn off the power to the wires; then disconnect them carefully and verify that the power is off by testing the exposed ends of both sets of wires with a voltage tester before proceeding. Mount a junction box where both sets of wires can be brought into it. Knock out a hole for each cable or wire, tighten the internal clamps over the wires, and connect the wires inside the box with wire connectors. If the wires aren't long enough to connect inside the box, move it toward one set of wires, install a second box for the second set, and join the boxes with new cable. (See page 64.) Screw a cover onto the junction box and leave it accessible (for example, do not bury it in a wall).

Tip *Treat electricity with respect. (1) Buy several neon voltage testers so you always have one handy; it's very cheap insurance. (2) Test the tester on a live receptacle before using it to test wires, just to make sure it works. (3) When testing, be sure that your fingers don't touch the metal probes of the tester or any other metal objects. (4) Consider all wires, terminals, and fixtures live until your voltage tester verifies that they are dead.*

▶ Cable is not long enough to reach electrical box.

Install a junction box at a convenient place along the cable run. Turn off the power and cut the cable so the "line" end of it (end originating at the power source) is long enough to be clamped into the box with 6 to 8 inches to spare. Discard the cutoff section. Thread the cable through a knockout hole in the box, strip off the sheathing from the portion inside the box, and tighten the box clamp onto it. With wire connectors, join a new cable to it inside the junction box, long enough to reach the receptacle, light, or switch box you are feeding. Attach a cover to the box and leave it exposed for access.

Using a junction box to extend cable

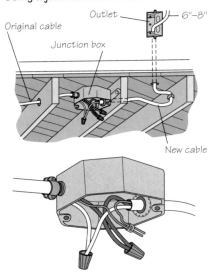

▶ Junction-box cover shows and is obtrusive.

Junction boxes (and covers) must be accessible. You cannot cover them with wallboard or other permanent coverings. Hang a picture over it.

▶ Wire connector doesn't grip wires tightly.

Check the chart on the connector package to make sure it is the proper size for the wires you are joining; you may need to use a smaller size. Also check manufacturer's instructions for how much insulation should be stripped from the end of the wire (strip length), and whether the wires are to lie side by side or be twisted together before screwing on the connector.

Joining wires with connector

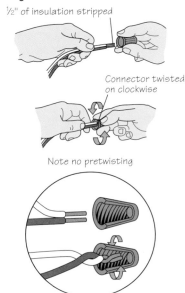

½" of insulation stripped

Connector twisted on clockwise

Note no pretwisting

▶ Wires are not colored properly.

Although common wiring practice is to use black or red wires for hot conductors, white wires for neutral, and green or bare wires for ground, you should never assume that you can tell the polarity of wire by its color. Occasionally a white wire is used as a hot conductor—when wiring a switch loop with nonmetallic-sheathed cable, for instance. Such wires are often wrapped with black

tape or colored with a black pen at the ends to indicate that they are hot, but this practice is not universally observed or even required by the NEC. Sometimes all wires are black, as with knob-and-tube wiring or service-entrance conductors.

With a voltage tester you can check the polarity of a wire by touching one probe to it and the other probe to a ground wire or known ground, with the power on. (Be sure your fingers are not touching any metal, including the probes.) A hot wire will light up the tester; a neutral wire won't. To identify wires in the middle of their run, such as knob-and-tube wires, use a no-contact voltage tester.

▶ Wire is not attached to anything; can't trace it to source.

If you run across the end of a mysterious wire or cable that you can't account for, you should find the other end so you know whether to remove the wire or connect it properly. Treat it as a live wire until you are absolutely sure it is dead. Try to trace the wire visually; note its location on the wall and look directly above that location in the attic (or below it in the basement) to see if the wire emerges. If it does, continue tracing it; if it doesn't, poke a discreet hole in the wall next to the wire and use a flashlight to follow it as far as possible. Poke additional holes as necessary (to be spackled later) until you find the source. Then turn off the power to the house, disconnect the wire, and test it for continuity to verify that it is the wire you started with. If it is a cable with two or more wires, test continuity by joining two of them together at one end with a connector (with the power off). Then, at the other end of the cable, touch the two probes of a continuity tester (not a voltage tester) to

Tip *Wire connectors that twist onto the ends of wires, which are used to make connections inside electrical boxes, are often referred to as wing nuts or by the brand names Wire-Nut® or Scotchlok®. They have replaced soldering as a means of making such connections.*

the two wires that match the colors of those that you joined together. If the tester lights up, it's the same cable. Double-check by removing the connector and testing the same two wires again; the tester should-not light up. To test a single wire, connect a long wire to one end and run it to the other end via the shortest route possible (the power should be off). Touch one probe of a continuity tester to this jumper wire and the other probe to the mystery wire. If the continuity test verifies that you have found both ends of the mystery wire or cable and it does not have a use, remove it. Otherwise, call an electrician.

Testing continuity

Wire connector
Continuity tester
Jumper wire

*Power off

▶ Wire is wrong size for new circuit wiring.

Never use wire that is too small for the fuse or circuit breaker of a given circuit. Most circuits are 15 or 20 amps, which require No. 14 and No. 12 wire, respectively. Because No. 12 wire is larger than No. 14, it could be used to wire a 15-amp circuit. On the other hand, No. 14 wire could not be substituted for No. 12 for a 20-amp circuit. If the wires for an existing circuit are too small for the breaker or fuse, replace the breaker or fuse with one that has the proper rating for the wire size.

▶ Wires must be run inside a wall.

Electrical wires or cable should be run through holes drilled in the centers of studs, which means removing portions of the existing wall covering. The least obtrusive area is along the floor. Remove the baseboard along the path between electrical boxes; then remove enough wall covering along the floor to expose all studs between the boxes. Drill a ¾-inch-diameter hole through the center of each stud near its base and pull cable through the holes, feeding it into the electrical boxes (or, for a new box, a hole cut into the wall covering). Connect the devices, test them, get any required inspections, patch the wall covering, and replace the baseboard.

Although the shortest distance between two points is a straight line, it may not be the easiest or best. The least disruptive run may be through the attic or the basement (or crawl space). For runs through the attic, drill a ¾-inch-diameter hole down from the attic through the top plate of the wall framing into the stud bay of each

of the electrical boxes to be connected. Feed fish tape (stiff wire for fishing cable through walls) down through this hole to one of the boxes, attach new cable to it, and pull the cable up into the attic. Drill holes through the centers of the ceiling joists. Run the cable through these holes to the hole in the plate above the other stud bay, then down to the electrical box. If you encounter an obstruction in the wall, drill a second hole next to the first. Shine a flashlight into the wall cavity while looking through the first hole. You may be able to guide the wire past it; if not, choose another stud cavity or remove wall covering at the obstacle and drill a hole through it. For running cable through the basement or crawl space, use the same process as for running cable through an attic. Avoid running wire through exterior walls. If you encounter the complications of insulation, windows, fire blocking, and limited access under eaves and above foundation walls, see page 66.

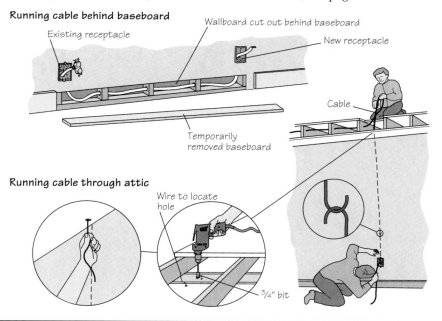

Running cable behind baseboard

Existing receptacle
Wallboard cut out behind baseboard
New receptacle
Cable
Temporarily removed baseboard

Running cable through attic

Wire to locate hole
¾" bit

Tip   *When using NM cable, be sure it is designated NM, Type B. This cable, which is rated for 194° F (90° C), is required by code and replaces older types of NM cable.*

Tip   *Nonmetallic-sheathed cable (NM or NMC) run inside a wall must be protected from nails that might be driven into the wall in the future. When drilling through studs and other framing to create cable pathways, locate the holes as close to the center of the framing members as possible. If the hole is within 1¼ inch of the edge of the stud, or you are able only to notch the framing member, nail a metal plate (stud guard) to the stud to protect the cable before patching the wall.*

▶ Wires must be run through ceiling or floor.

If the wiring runs parallel to a joist, fasten it to the side of the joist. If it runs across joists, drill holes in the approximate center of each and run cable through the holes. Cable strung below basement joists or across the top of attic joists must be protected by wood boards beside it or above it. Some communities allow an exception: In any area more than 6 feet from the opening to a "nonaccessible" attic (accessible only through a ceiling scuttle), cable can be strung across the tops of joists without guard strips. Check with local authorities.

Running wire parallel to joist

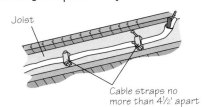

Joist

Cable straps no more than 4½' apart

Running wire perpendicular to joists

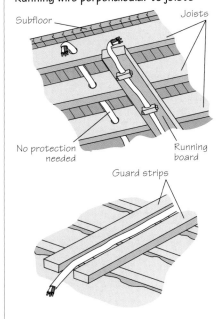

Subfloor

Joists

No protection needed

Running board

Guard strips

▶ Wires can't be run through wall, ceiling, or floor.

Run the wiring inside plastic or metal raceways that can be mounted on wall and ceiling surfaces. Systems designed for this purpose include channels, elbows, connecting devices, outlet boxes, and other components. Follow local code requirements and manufacturer's instructions—for instance, a system may require using individual wires and not sheathed cable; or surface-mounted wiring may not be allowed in certain rooms.

Using surface raceway

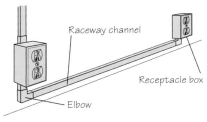

Raceway channel

Receptacle box

Elbow

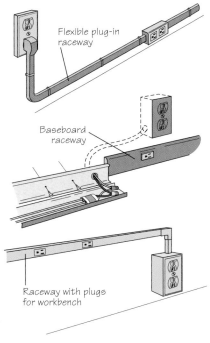

Flexible plug-in raceway

Baseboard raceway

Raceway with plugs for workbench

▶ Wires must be run outdoors or through garage or basement.

Wiring in these locations is often exposed to possible damage, thus requiring metal conduit. Be sure to use liquidtight connectors (which are tightened onto the conduit by compression nuts) for outdoor work. Check local codes for other requirements.

To run wiring underground, use rigid metal conduit with liquidtight fittings or nonmetallic cable specified for direct burial (for example, SE or UF cable). You can also use PVC (plastic) conduit wherever it will be buried at least 18 inches (it cannot be used for vertical segments where wiring emerges from the ground). Never bury ordinary NM or NMC cable, ordinary metal conduit (EMT), or flexible conduit.

▶ Receptacle doesn't have hole for grounding prong of plug.

Don't remove the grounding prong from a plug to make it fit an ungrounded, two-slot receptacle. Instead, buy a grounding adapter or a plug-in GFCI. An adapter has a short pigtail, or ground wire, intended to be attached to the cover-plate screw of the receptacle. However, this provides grounding only if the electrical box is metal and is itself grounded (look for a ground wire in the box or continuous metal conduit). If so, screw the pigtail to the cover-plate screw and leave the adapter in the receptacle for future use. If the box is not grounded, using the adapter will not provide grounding for the appliance. For immediate protection use a plug-in GFCI for the receptacle. Unless you plan to have all of the house wiring upgraded

Tip   *If you are working with armored cable (AC, sometimes called BX), connect it to metal electrical boxes with cable connectors specified for armored cable, or use a box with internal clamps designed for armored cable. Before connecting the cable, remove 8 to 10 inches of armor at each end by cutting with a hacksaw through one of the raised corrugations in the armor, being careful not to cut too deeply, and then bending the cable to release the cut end. Before connecting each end to an electrical box, insert a plastic antishort bushing into the end of the armor, and wrap the end of the internal ground wire around the metal armor so it will be in contact with the box clamp.*

with a system ground, you can provide more permanent protection by running a No. 12 wire from the electrical box to a grounded metal water pipe and plugging in an adapter, or replacing the ungrounded receptacle with a GFCI receptacle.

▶ Prongs of plug won't stay in receptacle slots.

Unplug the cord and, with pliers, carefully bend the prongs of the plug closer together or farther apart so they grip the receptacle slots better. If this doesn't work because the clamps inside the slots are too loose, replace the receptacle.

▶ Prong of plug is too wide for receptacle slots.

At one time the prongs of all lamp and appliance cords were interchangeable—the appliance would work whichever way the plug was plugged into the receptacle. Now appliances and electronic equipment often have internal switches or other devices that require correct polarization of the electrical supply to work properly, and to accommodate this, the prong on one side of the plug is wider and will fit only the longer, or neutral, slot of a receptacle. The receptacle, in turn, must be wired so the neutral side is connected to the neutral wire (usually white) of the branch circuit. An older receptacle, however, doesn't have a longer slot to ensure correct polarity, so a polarized plug won't fit. Replace the receptacle and wire the new one for correct polarity. Connect the neutral (white) wire to the silver-colored terminal beside

the wider slot, connect the hot (black) wire to the brass-colored terminal, and attach the ground (bare or green) wire to the green grounding screw (see page 68).

Wiring a receptacle for correct polarity

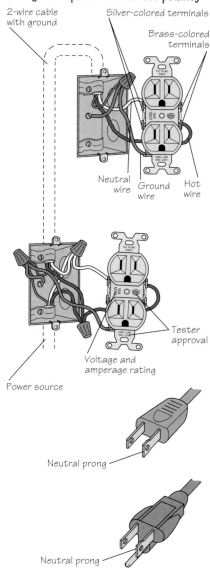

2-wire cable with ground

Silver-colored terminals

Brass-colored terminals

Neutral wire   Ground wire   Hot wire

Tester approval

Voltage and amperage rating

Power source

Neutral prong

Neutral prong

▶ Plug doesn't match receptacle.

Most household receptacles are rated 15 amps (even for 20-amp circuits), and accept almost any plug-in appliance or device intended for household use. Some large appliances and power tools have plugs that don't fit into an ordinary receptacle. This is to protect the circuit from overload and the equipment from insufficient power. Except for devices with 20-amp plugs, which can be plugged into any 20-amp receptacle wired into a 20-amp circuit, each appliance should be plugged into a matching receptacle on a dedicated circuit wired for that one appliance.

Matching plugs and receptacles

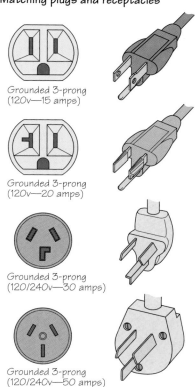

Grounded 3-prong (120v—15 amps)

Grounded 3-prong (120v—20 amps)

Grounded 3-prong (120/240v—30 amps)

Grounded 3-prong (120/240v—50 amps)

Tip *Receptacles with two outlets for plugs, which are the most common type available, are called <u>duplex receptacles</u>. Two duplex receptacles installed together in a double, or ganged, box provide outlets for four plugs. A <u>switch/receptacle combination device</u> has a single receptacle that is always hot, and a switch that controls a light or other device located elsewhere. Some receptacles are built into a light fixture or electrical appliance. A <u>clock receptacle</u>, for walls where a plug-in clock or other fixture will hang flush over the receptacle, has a recessed alcove for the plug.*

SOLVING ELECTRICAL PROBLEMS

▶ *Receptacle is dead; appliance or lamp won't work.*

After confirming that the receptacle itself is dead (not the entire circuit or the appliance), shut off power to the circuit, remove the screws holding the receptacle in place, and pull it free from the box. Then restore power to the circuit and carefully test the exposed wire ends with a voltage tester; if the tester lights up, the problem is the receptacle. Turn off the power and replace it with a new one.

If the tester indicates no voltage in the wires, the problem is a loose connection or defective receptacle somewhere else. Turn off the power and put the receptacle back. Then restore power and look for a nearby receptacle or light on the same circuit that does not work. If you find one, turn off the power and inspect that device for loose connections. Then repeat the diagnostic procedure for testing the receptacle and wires. If you can't find another dead receptacle or fixture, the problem is a loose connection or broken wire somewhere. Call an electrician.

Testing wires with voltage tester

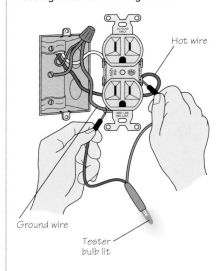

Hot wire

Ground wire

Tester bulb lit

▶ *Receptacle works only at certain times.*

In all likelihood, it is wired to a light switch. Plug a radio into the receptacle, turn it on, and test all the switches you can find to see which one operates the receptacle. Then label the switch so everyone will know what it's for, or rewire the receptacle (see opposite page).

▶ *Receptacle needs replacing.*

Turn off power to the circuit, remove the cover plate and screws holding the receptacle in place, and pull it out of the wall. If it has only two wires connected to it (besides a ground wire), disconnect them and wire the new receptacle to them in the same sequence: hot (black) wire connected to the brass-colored terminal, neutral (white) wire connected to the silver-colored terminal. To connect the wires, straighten the ends (make sure about ½ inch of insulation is removed) and push them into the round holes in the back of the receptacle. To release a wire from a push-in terminal, force a small screwdriver blade, finishing nail, or piece of No. 12 copper wire into the slot just above the terminal and pull the wire out.

If the old receptacle has two sets of white and black wires connected to it (a pair of incoming wires and a pair of outgoing wires), it means that the receptacle itself is part of the circuit. When attaching the new receptacle, connect only one wire to each screw, or wire the new receptacle to black, white, and grounding pigtails (short lengths of wire about 8 inches long). Then, using connectors, join each pigtail to the two wires of the same color that are in the electrical box.

After securing the new receptacle in the box, restore power and test it with an outlet analyzer—a small plug-in device that tests voltage, grounding, and polarity. If it indicates reversed polarity, the house wires were not properly color-coded. Turn off the power, disconnect the wires from the receptacle, and reverse them. Test again.

Connecting wires to receptacle in middle of run

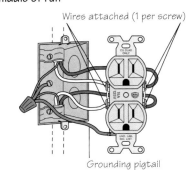

Wires attached (1 per screw)

Grounding pigtail

Connecting middle-of-run receptacle with pigtails

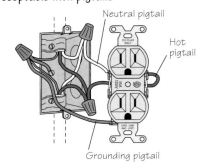

Neutral pigtail

Hot pigtail

Grounding pigtail

Using an outlet analyzer

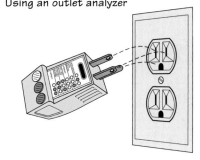

Tip *If you are replacing a receptacle in a location where a GFCI-protected outlet is required, such as in a bathroom or in a kitchen within 6 feet of the sink, be sure that the replacement receptacle is a GFCI type, even if the original receptacle was not. The electrical box does not have to be grounded in order for the GFCI to function.*

Tip *Whenever you run new wiring into an electrical box, leave at least 6 inches of each conductor extending out of the box to make it easy to connect receptacles and other devices.*

▶ *Polarity of wires to be attached to receptacle isn't clear.*

You can determine the polarity of a wire with a voltage tester. First make sure that the ends of the wires are exposed but not touching anything; then turn on the power. To test the polarity of each wire, hold one probe of the voltage tester on the ground wire; touch the other probe to one wire, then the second. The tester will light when it touches the hot wire; it won't light (or will only glow faintly) when it touches the neutral. Make sure your fingers don't touch anything metal, including the probes.

Testing for hot wire

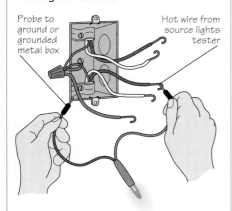

Probe to ground or grounded metal box

Hot wire from source lights tester

▶ *Receptacle makes sparks.*

It is normal for the prongs of a plug to arc slightly when you plug in or unplug an appliance that is switched on. However, if sparks occur around a receptacle at any other time, the problem may be caused by a defective receptacle or a loose wire. Turn off power to the receptacle and inspect it. If it's a loose connection with copper wire, tighten it. If it's aluminum wire, call an electrician. If the connections are not loose, replace the receptacle.

▶ *Switch-controlled receptacle needs replacing.*

Turn off the power. Verify that it is off by testing both the upper and lower halves of the receptacle with a voltage tester (insert one probe in each slot). Then remove the cover plate and screws holding the receptacle and pull it out. Wire connections will vary, depending on whether both halves of the receptacle are controlled by the switch (or just one), and whether the wires from the source come through the receptacle box or the switch box. Note how many hot (black) wires are attached to the brass-colored screws, and whether the tab between the screws has been broken off. Label or mark all wires so you won't get them confused, and note which end of the receptacle points up; then remove them. (*Note:* The hot wire for the switched half of the receptacle may be white because it is part of a switch loop and two-wire cable was used for the wiring.)

Before connecting wires to the new receptacle, break the tab on the hot (brass-colored) side of the receptacle if it was broken on the old receptacle. This isolates the two halves so that one can be controlled by the switch while the other remains hot. Connect the appropriate black (or white-made-black) wire to each brass-colored terminal.

Because the tab on the neutral (silver-colored) side remains unbroken, only one neutral wire is necessary. If two neutral (white) wires were attached to the old receptacle, connect a white pigtail (8-inch length of wire) to one of the silver-colored terminals and join it to the other two white wires with a wire connector. Connect the ground wire, secure the receptacle to the electrical box, and restore power. Test both halves of the receptacle with an outlet analyzer (with the switch in both positions).

Breaking receptacle tab

Tab between hot terminals

Connecting wires: power through switch

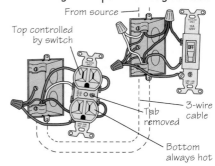

From source

Top controlled by switch

3-wire cable

Tab removed

Bottom always hot

Connecting wires: power through receptacle

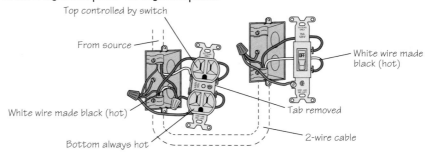

Top controlled by switch

From source

White wire made black (hot)

Bottom always hot

White wire made black (hot)

Tab removed

2-wire cable

Tip *The National Electrical Code requires that every habitable room, hallway, and stairway in a home have at least one light controlled by a wall switch at each entrance to that room. Most rooms fulfill this requirement with a permanently mounted ceiling or wall fixture, but a receptacle controlled by a switch, which is common in living rooms, dining rooms, and master bedrooms, is allowable in lieu of a light fixture (except in bathrooms and kitchens).*

SOLVING ELECTRICAL PROBLEMS

▶ 240-volt receptacle needs replacing.

A 240-volt receptacle is controlled by a double circuit breaker. Make sure both toggles of the breaker are off—they should be connected—before proceeding. Pull the appliance plug from the receptacle and plug it into the replacement receptacle to be sure that it is the right kind—prong configurations vary according to amperage. Then remove the cover from the old receptacle, loosen the screws that hold it in place, and pull it out of the electrical box. Note which wires are connected to which terminals (mark them if necessary), then disconnect the wires by loosening the setscrews. Connect them to the terminals of the new receptacle, tighten the screws, and attach the receptacle to the electrical box. Plug in the appliance and restore power.

▶ Receptacle needs GFCI protection.

The NEC requires that receptacles in certain locations be protected by GFCIs, which protect people from shock hazards; grounding alone is not sufficient protection. These locations include bathrooms, garages, basements, the area above countertops within 6 feet of a kitchen sink, and anywhere outdoors. Although there are several ways to provide ground fault circuit protection with various kinds of devices, individual GFCI receptacles are now inexpensive enough that the most convenient way to protect existing receptacles is to replace each one with a separate GFCI. Install them according to manufacturer's instructions, which typically involve connecting the black and white GFCI pigtails marked *Line* to the black and white circuit wires, respectively. If the GFCI has two more pigtails marked *Load* (often

a gray and a red wire), cap the bare ends with small wire connectors—they will be live and shouldn't be exposed. If the old receptacle had two pairs of wires connected to it, you have to identify which pair (black and white) are the "line," or source, wires and which two are "load"—going to other receptacles (see page 69). Join the "line" wires to the GFCI pigtails marked *Line*, and the "load" wires to *Load*. If the system is grounded, attach a ground wire to the GFCI. Otherwise, leave it unconnected. Read the manufacturer's instructions about testing the GFCI.

Installing a GFCI

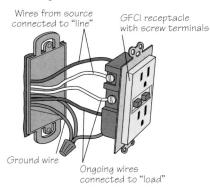

Wires from source connected to "line"

GFCI receptacle with screw terminals

Ground wire

Ongoing wires connected to "load"

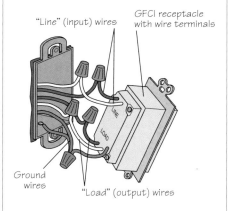

"Line" (input) wires

GFCI receptacle with wire terminals

Ground wires

"Load" (output) wires

▶ GFCI receptacle constantly trips or won't reset.

It may be wired incorrectly. Turn off power, disconnect the GFCI, and make sure the wire ends do not touch anything. Restore power and test the wires for polarity (see page 69). If the wires were reversed, turn off power and reconnect the GFCI correctly. If the wires weren't reversed, the problem may be a worn GFCI; install a new one. If tripping persists, the problem is probably a constant ground fault in the circuit. Call an electrician.

▶ Switch doesn't work.

Make sure that the problem is not a burned-out light bulb or tripped circuit breaker (or blown fuse). If not, replace the switch. First shut off the circuit breaker that controls the switch and light fixture. Remove the cover plate and the screws that attach the switch to the electrical box. Gently pull the switch away from the box, being careful not to touch the screw terminals. With a voltage tester, verify that the power is off by touching one probe to the ground wire and the other probe to each screw terminal of the switch, in turn. If there is no grounding screw or wire, touch the probes to the two screw terminals with the switch in both positions (be sure the light fixture has a functioning bulb in place).

If the switch is one of two switches controlling the same light, it has three screw terminals. Touch one probe to the terminal marked *Common* (bronze-colored) and the other probe to one of the two brass-colored terminals, with the switch in both positions *and* the other switch in both positions each time (four combinations in all).

Tip *If you use power tools outdoors, be sure to plug them into a GFCI-protected receptacle. If one isn't convenient, buy a portable plug-in GFCI. You can plug it into any receptacle, then run an extension cord from it to the outdoor location where you are working.*

Tip *The most common mistake when installing a GFCI is failing to attach the source wires from the circuit-breaker panel to the two terminals marked "Line." If these wires are hooked up to the two "Load" terminals, the receptacle will appear to work normally but in fact the GFCI will not trip when it is supposed to.*

The tester should indicate no power. If not, trip the correct circuit breaker. With power off, remove the switch (mark the wire attached to the "common" terminal if switch is three-way), and replace it with the same type. If the new switch does not work, the problem is in the wiring. Turn off the breaker and call an electrician.

Testing switch to verify that power is off

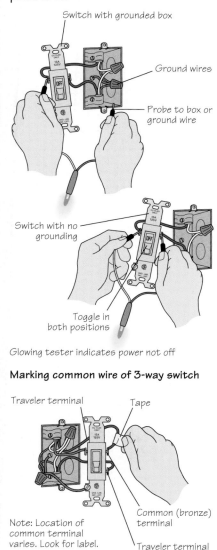

Switch with grounded box

Ground wires

Probe to box or ground wire

Switch with no grounding

Toggle in both positions

Glowing tester indicates power not off

Marking common wire of 3-way switch

Traveler terminal

Tape

Common (bronze) terminal

Traveler terminal

Note: Location of common terminal varies. Look for label.

▶ *Old switch needs replacing.*

Turn off power to the switch, remove the cover plate and screws that hold it in place, and carefully pull the switch away from the box. With a voltage tester verify that the power is off (see opposite page). Note how the wires are attached to the switch (mark them so you can remember), and disconnect them by loosening the side screws or, if they're wired to the back, releasing them by forcing a small screwdriver into the slot just above or below each wire. Before connecting the wires to the new switch, snip the curved ends off the wires and strip the insulation to expose ½ inch of bare wire. If you use the push terminals in the back of the switch, use the stripping gauge printed on the back of the switch to make sure enough insulation is removed. Keep the wires straight. If you connect wires to the side screws, bend them with needle nose pliers or by inserting the ends into the small holes in the blade of a wire stripper. Wrap them clockwise around the screw, making sure they engage it fully when it is tight. When all connections are made, fold the wires so you can push the switch into the box without kinking them. Secure the switch with the screws provided and replace the cover plate.

Back-wiring a switch

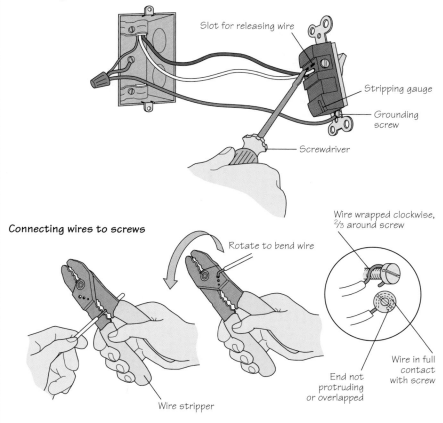

Slot for releasing wire

Stripping gauge

Grounding screw

Screwdriver

Connecting wires to screws

Rotate to bend wire

Wire stripper

Wire wrapped clockwise, ⅔ around screw

End not protruding or overlapped

Wire in full contact with screw

Tip *Switches should never be attached to neutral wires, thus interrupting a constant and safe path for electricity to flow back to the source. Only hot (black or red) wires should be connected to switches. In some cases white wires are used as hot wires and should not be confused with neutral wires; they often, but not always, have black tape or paint at the ends to designate them as hot wires.*

▶ Old and new switches have different number of terminals.

Both switches must be the same type: two-way, three-way, or (more rarely) four-way. In simplest terms, these designations refer to the number of terminals (not counting the grounding screw) on the back or sides of the switch. More accurately, a two-way (or single-pole) switch is for installations where only one switch controls a light or fixture (or multiple fixtures). It is the only switch with positions marked *On* and *Off*. It has two terminals, and the wires can be interchanged.

A three-way switch is for installations where two switches control a light or group of lights, and is always paired with another three-way switch. The toggle has no *On* or *Off* position because the light could be on or off in either position, depending on how the partner switch is set. A three-way switch has three wires connected to it (besides the ground wire); it is very important that the correct wire is attached to the bronze-colored terminal, marked *Common*. The brass-colored terminals are interchangeable for the remaining two wires.

A four-way switch is used together with two 3-way switches, so a light is controlled by three different switches. Additional four-way switches can be used to increase the number of control points, so long as they are all installed between two 3-way switches. A four-way switch has four wires (besides ground); it's important how they are attached.

You can use a replacement switch that has a different color, design, or specialty function (like a dimmer or pilot light switch), but it must have the same switching capability as the old switch. Use the switch diagrams that follow for hooking up the wires correctly.

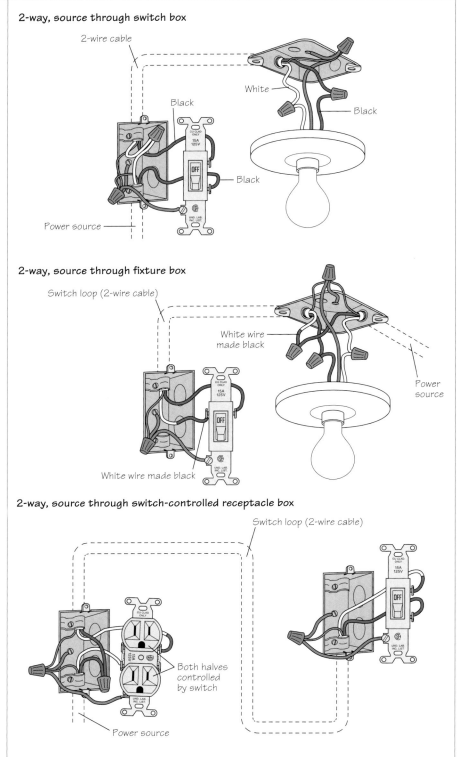

2-way, source through switch box

2-way, source through fixture box

2-way, source through switch-controlled receptacle box

3-way, source through central-fixture box

3-way, source through end-fixture box

3-way, source through switch box (central fixture)

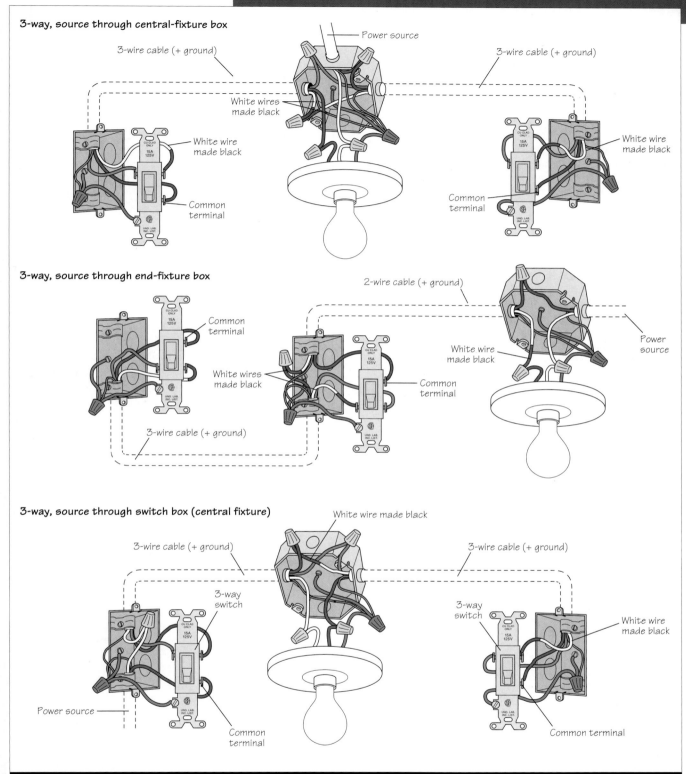

Power source

3-wire cable (+ ground)

3-wire cable (+ ground)

White wires made black

White wire made black

White wire made black

Common terminal

Common terminal

Common terminal

2-wire cable (+ ground)

White wire made black

Power source

White wires made black

3-wire cable (+ ground)

White wire made black

3-wire cable (+ ground)

3-way switch

3-way switch

3-wire cable (+ ground)

White wire made black

Power source

Common terminal

Common terminal

Tip   *The wire connected to the "common" terminal of a three-way switch must be either the hot wire from the source or the hot wire connecting to the light fixture. It's never one of the travelers, the two wires connected to the partner switch.*

3-way, source through switch box (end fixture)

3-way, source through switch box; receptacle beyond

4-way, source through fixture box

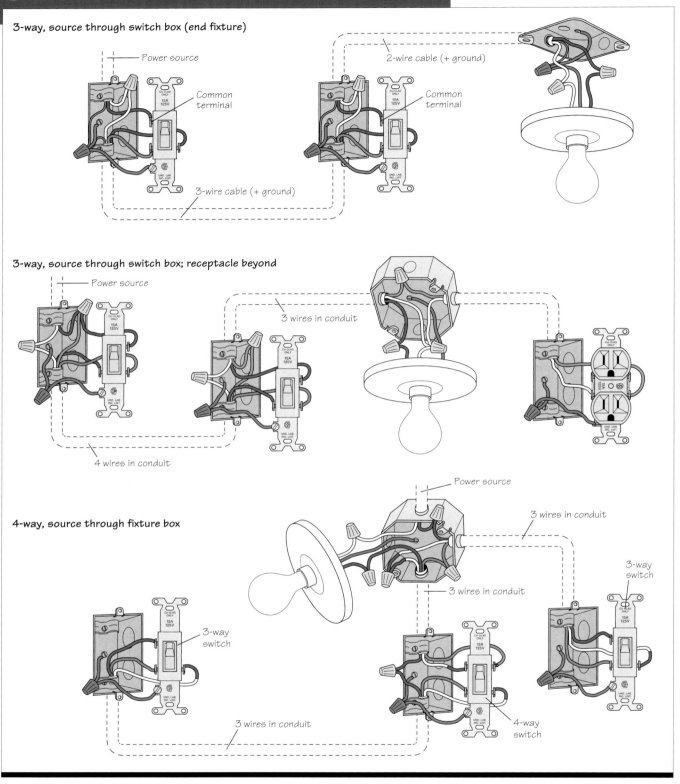

Power source

2-wire cable (+ ground)

Common terminal

Common terminal

3-wire cable (+ ground)

Power source

3 wires in conduit

4 wires in conduit

Power source

3 wires in conduit

3 wires in conduit

3-way switch

3-way switch

4-way switch

3 wires in conduit

Tip If you are installing a switch that does not have a terminal screw for attaching the ground wire to the switch, wrap the ground wire around one of the mounting screws used for securing the switch to the electrical box.

▶ *Wires weren't marked for attaching to terminals.*

If you lost track of which wires should be attached to which terminals of a switch, you can identify the wires with a voltage tester. The ground wire should be obvious; it should be bare or green and the only wire attached directly to a metal electrical box. For two-way switches, it doesn't matter which of the other two wires is attached to the top or bottom of the switch. Nevertheless, you can identify the "line" wire (from the source), if necessary, by turning on the power and touching one probe of the voltage tester to the ground wire and the other probe to the others, in turn. The "line" wire will light the tester. The other wire is "load" and goes to the light fixture.

For a three-way switch, hold one probe of the tester on the ground wire and test the other three wires, one at a time, with the partner switch in both positions (it's easier if someone helps). If one wire lights the tester no matter what position the other switch is in, it is the "line" wire and should be attached to the "common" (bronze-colored) terminal of the switch. The other two, which light the tester once each time, are "travelers" and are connected to the brass-colored terminals of the switch (either way). Be sure to turn off the power before making connections. If none of the wires lights the tester with the partner switch in both positions, identify the one that doesn't light the tester *at all*; this wire goes to the light bulb and carries power only when it's connected to the switch. It connects to the "common" (bronze-colored) terminal of the switch, and the other two wires to the brass-colored terminals. Turn off the power and connect them.

For a four-way switch, attach the two wires from one cable to the top two terminals, the two wires from the other cable to the bottom two terminals—in either order.

▶ *New switch doesn't operate correctly.*

If new wiring was involved, have a licensed electrician inspect the installation. If you replaced a working switch with a new one that doesn't work properly, there is the possibility that the new switch is defective. However, it is more likely, especially with three-way switches, that wires got reversed. This is almost certainly the case if the new switch works when the partner switch is in one position but not the other; the wrong wire is attached to the "common" terminal. To fix, turn off the power, remove the switch (test with a voltage tester first), and follow the procedure for identifying wires described at left.

▶ *Light or fixture needs an additional switch.*

Stairways, halls, and rooms with more than one entrance should have multiple switches so you can turn on the light no matter which way you enter. Adding a switch means running new three-wire cable between the existing switch, the light fixture, and the new switch location—most likely inside walls and through ceilings or floors. An alternative is to install a pair of radio-controlled switches. One of them replaces the existing two-way switch and requires no new wiring. The other switch is installed in the new location and requires no wiring; it communicates with the

master switch by radio frequencies. Look for this type of switch at a local electrical-supply house and install it according to manufacturer's instructions.

▶ *Switch is behind door and is hard to reach.*

Switches should be located on the latch side of doors where they can be easily reached. Sometimes doors are reversed after the house has been wired. The only solution is to install a new switch on the wall at the latch side of the door. Consult an electrician about running new wiring.

▶ *Switch has no "click."*

Old-style switches with a spring-activated toggle had a distinct snapping sound. New switches are quieter, although most have a distinctive click. If a switch has suddenly gone silent but still works, it should not be a problem. If the toggle flaps loosely, replace the switch.

▶ *Switch is hard to find at night.*

Replace it with an illuminated switch. The toggle contains a small light that glows when the switch is in the *Off* position. It requires that the electrical box or cable running to it be grounded, but the light operates at a slow, pulsating frequency that does not require a neutral wire, as lamps do.

▶ *Switch is too high to reach.*

Most switches are installed 48 inches above the floor, which may be too high for a child or a person in a wheelchair to reach easily. You can install another switch below it, using the original switch box for a junction box. If it's a two-way switch, replace it with a three-way one so you can operate the light

Tip   *If you are replacing a switch with three or more terminals (a three-way or four-way switch), be sure to mark the wires with tape or other identification before you disconnect them from the terminals so you can attach the wires to the same terminals of the new switch. The important wire to distinguish is the one connected to the "common" terminal of a three-way switch.*

from either switch; the new switch must be a three-way switch also.

To install the new switch, first shut off power to the old one. Drill a small hole at the new location and probe with a wire for obstructions. If there are none, trace the outline of a new box and cut the opening with a keyhole saw or wallboard saw. Cut carefully; there may be wires inside the wall. Remove the cover plate and screws holding the switch in place and pull it out of the box. If it is a three-way switch (three terminals), mark the wire that was connected to the terminal marked *Common*.

Next remove one of the knockouts from the bottom of the switch box. Cut about 3 feet of No. 14 sheathed cable and attach a wire connector about 8 inches from one end. Use three-wire cable (with ground) if the old switch was a three-way switch or you are installing two switches; use two-wire cable (with ground) if the old switch was two-way and you want only one switch. Remove the tightening ring from the connector, strip the sheathing from 8 inches of cable, and thread the wires through the new wall opening and up into the bottom knockout hole of the old switch box. From inside the box place the tightening ring over the new cable and screw the ring onto the connector threads. Thread the other end of the cable through a knockout hole in the top of the new cut-in box (using a wire connector for a metal box). Set the box into the wall opening and secure it by tightening the clamps or other devices attached to the box.

For a two-way switch, join the new wires to the old wires inside the original box with wire connectors, and the other ends of the new wires to a two-way switch in the new box. Mark the white wires black with electrical tape or paint.

To install a three-way switch in the new box, use wire connectors to join the three wires inside the original box to the three wires of the new cable, noting which new wire is connected to the "common" wire. Attach the other end of that wire to the terminal on the new switch marked *Common*. Connect the other two wires to the brass-colored terminals.

If you are replacing the old two-way switch with a pair of three-way switches, connect one of the original wires to the "common" terminal of one switch, and join the other wire to the red wire of the new cable. Connect the other end of the red cable wire to the "common" terminal of the other switch. Attach the black and white wires to the brass-colored terminals of both switches.

Cutting hole for new box

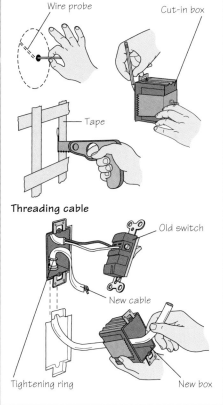

Wire probe

Cut-in box

Tape

Threading cable

Old switch

New cable

Tightening ring

New box

▶ Closet has pull-chain light and needs switch.

You can install a conventional switch on the inside or outside wall of the closet, close to the latch edge of the door; or you can install a door-activated switch that automatically turns on every time the door is opened. You can use the same pull-chain fixture (left in the *On* position) or replace it with a surface-mounted fixture approved for closet locations (see page 78). To wire the new switch, run two-wire No. 14 cable between the light fixture and the new switch location. Disconnect the hot (black) wire from the light fixture, attach it to one of the new wires, and attach the other new wire to the same light fixture terminal. Then connect the other end of the wires to a two-way switch; follow manufacturer's instructions for installing a door-activated switch.

▶ Mysterious switch doesn't seem to control anything.

Before testing the switch and analyzing wires, try some elementary detective work. If the switch is at the entrance to a room without a ceiling fixture, it most likely controls one of the receptacles in the room. Test every receptacle (both halves) by plugging a working lamp or radio into it and flipping the mystery switch to both positions. If none of the receptacles responds to the switch, one of them may have at one time been connected and then been rewired. Look for a receptacle that looks newer than the rest. If there is one, turn off the power, remove the cover plate and screws holding the receptacle, pull it out of the box, and look for unconnected wires in the box. To rewire the receptacle, see page 69.

Some switches, especially near doors to the garage, basement, attic,

Tip *When you remove a switch, you may find other wires in the electrical box that are not connected to the switch. There is no need to disconnect them or identify them for the purpose of replacing the switch. If all of the wires in the box are connected to the switch, it is at the end of a switch loop. The wires are all hot wires (not necessarily connected directly to the source, however), making the box an inappropriate one to tap into for extending the circuit.*

or outdoors, may control appliances that have timers or other automatic switching devices that must also be on for the appliance to work. Look for outdoor lighting with timers or motion-sensing devices, an attic fan that goes on only when the attic overheats, a furnace blower that can be switched on during hot weather, and receptacles for power tools.

If none of these investigations solves the mystery, carefully check the switch to see if it's hot. First turn off the power and pull the switch out of the box to expose the terminals, then restore power and touch one probe of a voltage tester to the ground wire and the other probe to all of the screw terminals of the switch, in turn. If the tester lights up, turn off the power, reattach the switch to the box, restore power, and call an electrician. If the tester doesn't light up, follow the procedure for tracing wires (see page 64).

▶ Bulb burns out too quickly.

Check the location for vibrations, such as a nearby door that slams frequently or a heavy appliance like a washing machine. Replace the bulb with an impact-resistant type designed for use in work lights for shops, available at lumberyards, auto-supply stores, or electrical-supply outlets. Another cause of frequent burnout may be overheating. The bulb wattage may exceed the limit recommended for the light fixture. Replace it with a bulb of less wattage. You could also

install a dimmer switch; running it at 90 percent capacity can double the life span of an ordinary incandescent bulb. On the other hand, dimming may reduce the life span of a halogen lamp.

▶ Bulb makes buzzing sound.

First be sure that it's the bulb and not a dimmer. If it's a dimmer, it may be overloaded and should be replaced with one that has a higher wattage rating. If a bulb is buzzing, especially in a recessed fixture that tends to amplify sound, replace it with a rough-service (impact-resistant) incandescent bulb; the tungsten filament won't vibrate as much. Otherwise, replace it with a compact fluorescent bulb; if there is a dimmer, be sure it's rated for fluorescent bulbs.

▶ Bulb is broken; base won't screw out.

Deaden the circuit, or unplug the lamp if applicable. Then, wearing gloves, remove as much glass from the bulb base as possible. With the glass removed, unscrew the base with needle-nose pliers. You may have to deform the base with the pliers to get a good grip—just don't deform the socket.

▶ Bulb is hard to reach.

You can buy an extension pole with a device on the end for gripping light bulbs. The ones for floodlights and spotlights work by suction; those for incandescent bulbs work by friction. Be sure to deaden the circuit first. Wear eye protection, and stay clear of overhead wires when changing bulbs outside. If you don't have access to such a pole changer, improvise one for incandescent bulbs by attaching a cardboard mailing tube to the end of a pole. Cut four slits

in the unattached end of the tube, as if sectioning an orange, and wrap a heavy rubber band around the end. Reach up and slip the tube onto the light bulb and unscrew it, then use the changer to install the new bulb.

▶ Ceiling light fixture heats up.

This is a problem that's difficult to detect but may be a serious fire hazard, especially with recessed fixtures. First make sure that the light bulbs do not exceed the wattage recommended for the fixture, which is usually written where you can read it after taking off the globe or removing the bulbs. If you aren't sure, use 60-watt (or less) bulbs. Next, if it's a recessed fixture, you should check the insulation in the attic. Most codes require that insulation be kept at least 3 inches away from the fixture on all sides, and that no insulation be placed above it. However, some fixtures are designed for zero-clearance insulation, and some codes allow you to insulate above the fixture under certain conditions. Check with the local building department and adjust the insulation accordingly.

Keeping insulation away from recessed fixture

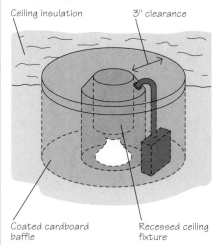

Ceiling insulation

3" clearance

Coated cardboard baffle

Recessed ceiling fixture

Tip *Because of higher efficiency standards now required for light bulbs, stores may be carrying bulbs that you aren't familiar with, such as compact fluorescent bulbs and various halogen lamps. Many of them have Edison bases, or standard screw bases, that make it possible to screw them into an incandescent bulb socket. When choosing bulbs, don't just compare wattages; look at lumens (amount of light output) as well so you can compare lumens per watt (the higher the better).*

SOLVING ELECTRICAL PROBLEMS

▶ Light in closet is too close to combustibles.

The NEC requires that incandescent surface fixtures in clothes closets be at least 12 inches away from the storage area, and fluorescent or recessed incandescent fixtures at least 6 inches away. In addition, a surface-mounted incandescent fixture must have the bulb completely enclosed by a glass globe. Pendant fixtures and bulbs not completely covered by a protective globe are prohibited in closets. The usual places to install closet fixtures are on the wall above the door or on the ceiling as close to the door as possible.

Meeting requirements for closet fixtures

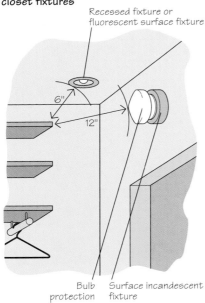

Recessed fixture or fluorescent surface fixture

6"

12"

Bulb protection

Surface incandescent fixture

▶ Light won't go on.

First check to see if the light switch is faulty (see page 70). If it works, the problem may be a loose wire in the light fixture. Turn off the circuit breaker and remove the globe and light bulbs from the fixture. Then loosen the screws or coupling nut that attach the fixture housing to the box; for a ceiling fixture have some coat hanger wire handy to hook onto the fixture and suspend it from the ceiling bracket after you loosen it. Inspect all of the wire connections between the light fixture and house wiring inside the box; tug at each wire to be sure it's not loose from its connection. If there are no loose connections, disconnect the wires from the fixture, restore power to them, and test with a voltage tester to see if the problem is in the wiring. Touch the probes to the hot (black) wire and the neutral (white) wire, or the hot wire and the ground wire. If the tester doesn't light up with the switch in either position, the wiring is at fault. Call an electrician. If it does light up, the problem is in the light fixture. Turn off the power and replace the fixture.

Testing wires for power

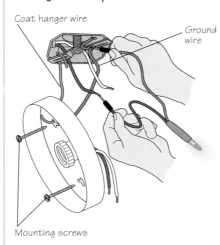

Coat hanger wire

Ground wire

Mounting screws

▶ Light fixture needs replacing.

Turn off power to the light fixture at the circuit breaker. Remove any globe or other decorative cover and the light bulbs. Loosen the mounting screws or coupling nut that attach the fixture to the ceiling box and lower the fixture. Attach a coat hanger to it and suspend it from the ceiling bracket while you reach above it and disconnect the wires. Now you can discard the fixture and install a new one, following these steps in reverse order. Be sure that the ground wire in the electrical box is connected to the box strap (if you use one) or the ground wire of the fixture, if it has one. Before joining the wires, install the mounting screws in the ceiling box or strap. Join the neutral (white) wires together and the hot (black) wires together with wire connectors; then slip the keyhole-shaped slots in the fixture housing over the mounting screws, rotate the housing, and tighten the screws. Install the bulbs, test the fixture, and attach the globe.

Connecting the ground wire

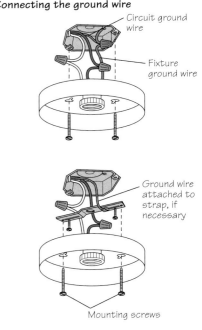

Circuit ground wire

Fixture ground wire

Ground wire attached to strap, if necessary

Mounting screws

Tip *For general lighting choose full-spectrum fluorescent bulbs—either tubes or compact bulbs that can be screwed into ordinary fixtures. They are extremely efficient and create very little heat. For reading, illuminating artwork, lighting bathrooms, and lighting food-serving areas, choose halogen lamps. They provide a whiter light with more contrast than fluorescent lights, and therefore reflect colors more accurately. Both types of lamps contribute much less heat to a home than incandescent bulbs, although halogen lamps are intensely hot at close range.*

▶ Several lights on same circuit don't work.

This will take time. First make sure that there is not another circuit breaker in a subpanel or a GFCI receptacle that has tripped. Look for hidden subpanels in closets, behind furniture or pictures, under sinks, and behind doors. Push the reset button on all GFCIs in the house.

If this doesn't work, the wiring for part of the circuit may be going through a fixture that is defective or has loose connections. Turn off the circuit, then check for loose wiring connections at the fixtures. Also make sure that none of the fixtures has more than one circuit wire screwed to the same terminal. Wherever this condition exists, remove the wires from the terminal, screw a pigtail (8-inch length of No. 14 wire of the same color) to the same terminal, and use an electrical connector to join the pigtail to the wires that you removed.

If the lights still don't work, there could be a broken wire in the circuit wiring between them and the source. Tracing it requires deadening the entire circuit and testing the run of wires between the affected fixtures and the source with a continuity tester (not a voltage tester). That run may be hard to identify, so you'll probably have to test several runs. To test continuity of any given run, disconnect the fixtures or switches at both ends of the run and, at one end, join the wires of the disconnected cable (except ground) together with a connector. Then go to the electrical box at the other end of the cable and touch the probes of the continuity tester to the other end of the same cable wires. If you find a combination that doesn't light the tester, and you are sure that the run doesn't have a switch or other device along it, one of the wires is

broken and should be replaced. Remove the connector, identify the wires, and replace them. If all of the wires test successfully for continuity, call an electrician.

▶ Older pendant fixture may not have ground wire.

All light fixtures must be grounded, especially hanging fixtures that are easy to reach. A chain alone is not sufficient to provide a continuous ground. Look for a bare wire or, if the light hangs on a cord, a green ground wire coming out of the bottom end of the cord. To add a ground wire to a fixture suspended from a chain, turn off the power, then twine bare stranded wire through the chain; connect the bottom end to the metal housing of the fixture and the top end to the circuit ground wire above the canopy. For fixtures suspended by cord, turn off the power and replace the cord with No. 16 cable that has a ground wire; attach the bottom end of the green or bare ground wire to the metal fixture housing and the top end to the circuit ground wire above the canopy.

Connecting ground wire to pendant fixture

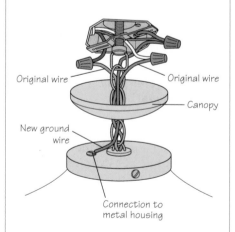

Original wire

Original wire

Canopy

New ground wire

Connection to metal housing

▶ Globe for light fixture attached to ceiling fan comes loose.

Vibrations from the fan can cause the setscrews that hold the fixture globe to work loose, causing it to rattle or even fall. With the power off, loosen the setscrews and remove the globe. Slip a wide rubber band around the outside of the neck of the globe, wide enough for the ends of the set screws to make full contact with it when the globe is in place. Tighten the screws snugly against the rubber band. It creates enough friction to keep the screws from backing out.

▶ One light of chandelier doesn't work.

Turn off the light, switch bulbs between the dead socket and one that works, and turn the light back on. If the socket still doesn't work, it probably has a broken or disconnected feeder wire. Mark the dead socket with tape. To fix it, you need access to where all the socket wires are joined, which is usually reached by removing the decorative cap under the center of the fixture; otherwise you must disconnect the canopy from the ceiling (have one or two helpers hold the chandelier). First turn off the power. Remove the cap to expose the wires and inspect the connections, tugging on each wire to be sure it is secure; if one is loose, remake the connection. Then restore power, test the light, and replace the cap. If none of the wires is loose or if the light still doesn't work, turn off the power. Touch one prong of a continuity (not voltage) tester to each end of the wire. If the tester doesn't light, replace the wire; attach the new wire to one end and

---

Tip   *When using a ladder to change bulbs in a ceiling fixture, there's usually no place to set the bulbs and glass globe that must be removed first. To solve this problem, tie two straw baskets or plastic pails to the top of the ladder before you go up. Use one to hold the new bulb, the other for the globe.*

feed the new wire into the tubing by pulling the old wire out. If the tester lights for both wires, remove the socket itself and replace it with the same kind.

Replacing socket wires

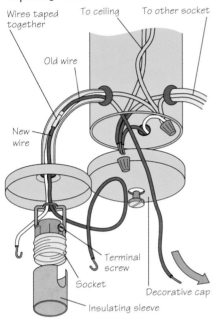

▶ Light is hard to turn on when arms are full.

Place a lamp with a touch-sensitive switch near the entrance to the room. Activate it by just brushing the base with your elbow. You can also replace a two-way switch with a motion-sensing switch that turns on the light as someone approaches. A number of additional features are available, such as manual override for normal operation, a dormant mode for deadening the switch during daylight hours, and options for setting the length of time the light stays on before turning off automatically. These switches are for indoor use and are similar to those used for outdoor security lighting.

▶ Fluorescent light flickers.

If it's a brand-new tube, leave it on for a few hours to stabilize. Cold temperatures (below 50° F) can also cause a bulb to flicker; allow several minutes for the bulb to warm up, or wait for the room to warm up before turning on the light. If flickering persists, the pins may be misaligned or have oxidation on them. Turn off the light, remove the tube, and clean the pins with a dry scouring pad or sandpaper. Install the tube again, rotating it in the pin holders a few times to clear the surfaces. Make sure all four pins snap into place securely. If the lamp still flickers, try a new bulb. If that fails, replace the fixture.

Aligning pins

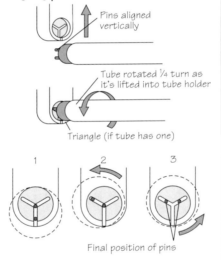

▶ Fluorescent light blinks on and off.

If the bulb is old, replace it. If the bulb is new, check to see if the pins are aligned properly. If they are, the problem could be a defective starter; replace it (see opposite page). If a new starter doesn't solve the problem, turn off the power and inspect the wires for loose connections. Finally, replace the ballast or entire fixture.

▶ Fluorescent fixture hums.

Most ballasts inevitably create a low humming sound. If it's too loud, check the mounting screws that secure the ballast to the fixture and tighten any loose ones. If the ballast has an acrid smell besides the humming, it's defective and should be replaced. If not, be sure that the ballast is the right size for the number and wattage of the tubes in the fixture; check the rating plate. Also check the wiring diagram printed on the ballast and make sure that the wires are connected properly. You may also have to check the polarity of the circuit wires in the electrical box. With the power off, expose the ends of the wires. Then turn the power back on and touch one probe of a voltage tester to the ground wire, the other to the hot (black) wire. The tester should light when the switch is on but not when it's off. It should also light with one probe touching the neutral (white) wire and the other probe touching the hot wire when the switch is on. It should not light when one probe touches the ground wire and the other probe touches the neutral wire. If the wiring is correct and the humming persists, check the sound rating of the fixture. If it's not an A or B, which are the quietest on a scale of A to F, replace the fixture with one rated A.

▶ Fluorescent tube is dark at ends and glows in center.

Some grayness is normal an inch or two from the ends. If the ends are black and the tube is old, replace it. If only one end is dark, switch the tube around. If the tube is new, replace the starter. If this doesn't work or the fixture has no starter, check the wiring for loose connections. Finally, replace the ballast or entire fixture.

Tip *Compact fluorescent bulbs have an Edison base that screws into an ordinary (incandescent) light bulb socket. The ballast and other electronics are built into the bulb. Although costly, they use less than half as much energy as an incandescent bulb of the same brightness.*

▶ *Fluorescent light won't go on.*

First check the circuit breaker or fuse box, then try a different bulb, one from another fixture that you know is working. Make sure it is the same type of bulb—some have two pins at each end, others have one. Position the bulb so that the triangular marking on both ends is visible, not concealed by the sockets. Also check the specifications printed on the ballast, where the wires are attached, to make sure that the bulb is the correct wattage. If the light still doesn't work and the fixture is the preheat type with a starter, which is a metal cylinder about the size of a film canister, remove the starter (turn it counterclockwise) and replace it with a new one. It should have the same wattage rating as the tubes. If this doesn't work or the fixture doesn't have a separate starter, the problem is probably the ballast, which is a box inside the fixture that contains a transformer. You can replace the ballast, but it may cost no more to replace the entire fixture.

Removing a starter

Power source
Canopy
Ballast
Ground
Replaceable starter of preheat fixture
Cover plate
Tube

Replacing a ballast

Power source
Ballast
Ground
Instant start fixture
Tube-holder wire cut and joined to new ballast lead

▶ *Fluorescent tube is dark in center and glows at ends.*

Try a new tube. If that doesn't work, replace the starter if the fixture has one. Finally, replace the ballast or entire fixture.

▶ *Fluorescent tube burns out too quickly.*

You may be turning the light on and off too frequently. Leave the light on for longer periods of time. If the bulb still wears out fast, replace the starter if there is one. Otherwise, check the wiring connections for loose wires. Finally, replace the fixture.

▶ *Fluorescent fixture needs a dimmer switch.*

Only certain fluorescent fixtures can be controlled by a dimmer switch. They must be rapid-start fixtures with a ballast designed for dimmers and a grounded reflector mounted within 1 inch of the tube. The dimmer, in turn, must be specified for fluorescent fixtures and labeled clearly as such. The dimmer can control more than one such fixture, but not a combination of fluorescent and incandescent fixtures. Also the wiring between the switch and fixture must have three conductors (besides a ground wire). Consult an electrician for other wiring requirements.

▶ *Fluorescent light makes things look ghastly.*

If the colors are too green or blue, change the tube to a warm white or deluxe warm white. If the colors are too orange or red, change the tube to a cool white or deluxe cool white. You may also find with full-spectrum tubes that things appear different because you are seeing things in true color rather than in the familiar warm colors created by incandescent lighting.

Tip *Wattage is not a measurement of light, but of power consumed. A 40-watt fluorescent bulb produces six times as much light as an ordinary 40-watt incandescent bulb (and lasts up to five times longer).*

Tip *A fluorescent light consumes more energy when it is switched on and off several times during a short period than when it is left on the whole time.*

SOLVING ELECTRICAL PROBLEMS

▶ Lamp switch won't click.

Replace the socket-and-switch assembly. Unplug the lamp, remove the top half of the socket shell, disconnect the wires from the switch, unscrew the bottom half of the shell from the lamp base, and install the new socket-and-switch assembly. See below.

▶ Lamp doesn't work.

Be sure that the bulb isn't burned out, then check the circuit breaker. Plug the lamp into a receptacle in another room. If it still doesn't work, unplug the lamp and inspect the plug and cord for breaks; replace the plug or cord as necessary (see right and opposite page). If they appear sound, unscrew the light bulb and disassemble the lamp socket by squeezing where it says *Press*. Now check the cord for hidden breaks by testing each wire with a continuity tester. Touch one probe to a terminal screw and the other probe to each prong of the plug. One prong should make it light. The tester should also light when you touch the other terminal screw and the prong that didn't light the first time. If either wire fails to show continuity, replace the cord and plug.

   If the wire tests for continuity, test the switch by touching one probe of the continuity tester to the silver-colored terminal and one probe to the brass-colored socket body. Test it with the switch in both positions. If the tester doesn't light either time, replace the socket-and-switch assembly. Be sure to attach the ribbed (neutral) side of the cord to the silver-colored screw of the

new switch. After connecting the wires, reassemble the socket by slipping the insulating sleeve over the switch and pressing the top shell into place until you hear it click.

Testing wire continuity

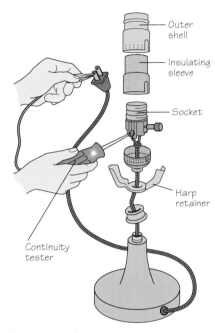

- Outer shell
- Insulating sleeve
- Socket
- Harp retainer
- Continuity tester

Testing switch continuity

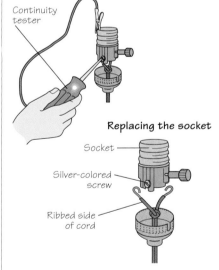

- Continuity tester

Replacing the socket

- Socket
- Silver-colored screw
- Ribbed side of cord

▶ Plug makes sparks when plugged in.

It is normal for the plug to arc slightly if a lamp or appliance is on while being plugged or unplugged from a live receptacle. If sparks occur under any other conditions, inspect the plug for loose connections and tighten them. If it appears sound, try it in a different receptacle. If the problem recurs, replace the plug. If it doesn't, check the original receptacle (see page 69).

▶ Cord needs new plug.

Replace any plug that has cracks, twisted prongs, a missing grounding prong, or frayed wires. Be sure to use a grounded (three-pronged) plug for a cord with three wires. All grounded plugs and some two-pronged plugs are attached to the wires with terminal screws; other two-pronged plugs connect to wires with clamps. For either type, pull the plug from the electrical receptacle and cut the cord about 1 inch above the plug. If the new plug is self-connecting, split the wires apart for the first ½ inch to 1 inch, depending on the style of connection. You do not have to remove any insulation. To attach, open the plug clamp, slide the cord into the plug body, and close the clamp. If one side of the cord is ribbed or otherwise identifiable as the neutral side, attach it to the side of the plug with the wider prong.

   To attach the cord to a plug with screw terminals, separate the wires about 1¼ inches at the end and strip about ½ inch of insulation off both wires. Remove the insulating barrier from between the plug prongs and slide the plug body off the prong assembly to expose the screws. Thread the cord through the body and attach the wires to

Tip *The old-fashioned round plug, with a cardboard insulator between the prongs, poses a hazard from potentially exposed wires and is no longer allowed. When replacing it, choose a plug with a plastic insulator.*

Tip *The cord of a lamp or small appliance is likely to wear out sooner than the plug. If the plug needs replacing, consider replacing both with a new polarized plug and cord.*

the screws—green wire to the green (grounding) screw, white or ribbed wire to the silver-colored (neutral) screw, and black or smooth wire to the brass-colored (hot) screw. To attach each wire, tightly twist the strands together clockwise, wrap the wire around each screw clockwise, and keep all of the strands together as you tighten the screw onto them. Slide the plug body back over the screw terminals and snap the insulating barrier between the prongs.

Attaching self-connecting plugs

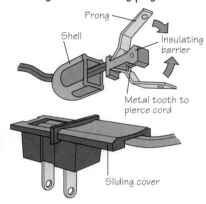

Tying an underwriter's knot

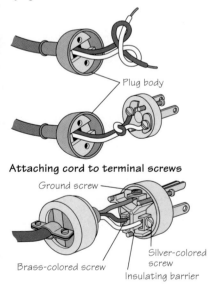

Attaching cord to terminal screws

Ground screw

Brass-colored screw

Silver-colored screw

Insulating barrier

▶ Cord needs switch.

Lamps, especially by bedsides, can be made more convenient by installing a thumb switch on the cord. The cord must be zip cord, which has a ribbed side and a smooth side. If it isn't, replace the entire cord first (see right). To attach the switch, unplug the cord. At the point where you'll install the switch, separate the cord wires for about 1 inch by slitting the groove between them. Cut the smooth (hot) wire of the cord, which should be attached to the narrower prong of the plug; do not cut the ribbed side of the cord. You do not have to strip insulation from the cut ends. Next separate the two shells of the switch by loosening the connecting screw. Place the cord into the bottom half of the shell so the cut side lies where the two sharp contacts will engage each segment of the wire. The ribbed (neutral) side of the wire should lie in a continuous groove of the shell and not be broken or punctured by the contacts when the two halves of the switch are joined. Then snap the two switch halves together and tighten the connecting screw. Test the switch.

Placing cord in switch shell

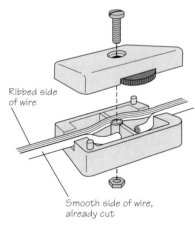

Ribbed side of wire

Smooth side of wire, already cut

▶ Lamp cord is frayed, burnt, or too short.

Replace the old cord with zip cord, which has a ribbed side and a smooth side. Most lamp cords are 6 feet long. Buy a new plug to match the cord. Unplug the lamp, remove the shade and bulb, then remove the top half of the socket assembly by squeezing where it says *Press.* Disconnect both wires from the screw terminals. Tape the wire ends to one end of the new cord and pull the old cord through the lamp. Remove the old cord and split the end of the new wire for 2½ inches. Tie an underwriter's knot (see left), strip ½ inch of insulation from the ends, and connect it to the socket terminals—ribbed side of cord attached to silver-colored screw. At the bottom of the lamp, pull the cord until the socket is snug. Reassemble the socket by slipping the insulating sleeve over the switch and pressing the top shell into place until you hear it click. Attach a plug to the new cord (see opposite page).

Pulling new wire through lamp

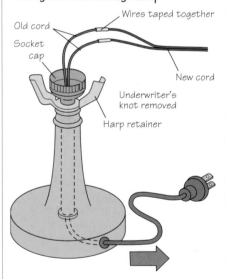

Old cord

Socket cap

Wires taped together

New cord

Underwriter's knot removed

Harp retainer

Tip *Lamp and small-appliance cord is referred to as flexible cord because the wires are multistranded, rather than single conductors. Most cords are 16 or 18 gauge and are called zip cord, fixture cord, or STP cord.*

▶ House lacks outdoor lighting.

Outdoor lights deter intruders, prevent people from tripping in the dark, make patios and backyards usable into the evening, and enhance the beauty of a home. With the widespread availability of low-voltage lighting systems, installing lights is inexpensive and relatively easy, especially if your home already has an outdoor receptacle. Pick the types of fixtures that best suit your needs. If you want to play nighttime badminton games in the backyard, mount a pair of floodlights under the eaves. If you're interested in subtle illumination to welcome guests, install low-voltage lights along the path to the front door. Use small spotlights to accent plants or sculpture. You can also sink lights into the lawn or recess them into a wall or into a riser on an outside step.

For safety, place lights at entrances and on each side of the house. Also light steps and pathways. Don't leave any shadows where intruders could hide, and make sure address numbers are well lit.

▶ Low-voltage lights need installing.

A typical low-voltage kit includes four to 14 or more fixtures, low-voltage cable, and a weatherproof transformer. The transformer plugs into a standard receptacle and reduces the 120-volt house current to a safe 12 volts. If you buy components separately, add the wattages of the fixtures and select a transformer that offers more than enough power.

Mount the transformer near a receptacle, either indoors or out. Attach the low-voltage cable to the terminal screw of the transformer, and plug in the power cord. Most fixtures, whether they are globes, floodlights, or tier lights, consist of a lamp head and ground stake.

Assemble the fixtures and wire them to the cable following kit directions. To avoid damaging the wire connections, don't drive the stake into the ground. Instead dig a hole, insert the stake, and pack the hole with dirt. Run the cable to the next fixture, covering it with mulch or burying it in a shallow trench. In places where the cable could be damaged by foot traffic or a lawn mower, bury it 1 foot deep. For best results, place lights no more than 200 feet from the transformer.

To turn lights on and off, install additional manual switches, a timer, a motion sensor, or a photoelectric eye.

Mounting transformer

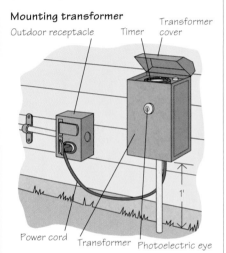

Outdoor receptacle · Timer · Transformer cover · Power cord · Transformer · Photoelectric eye · 1'

Installing low-voltage lights

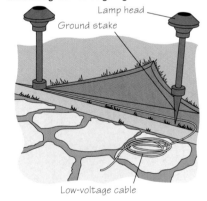

Lamp head · Ground stake · Low-voltage cable

▶ Lighting is too bright and not broad enough.

Your yard doesn't need to look like a nighttime ballfield to deter intruders. Several well-placed, low-wattage bulbs are more effective and less irritating to neighbors than a single floodlight. If you do use a floodlight, place it under the eaves and point it downward, or on the ground pointing upward toward the house. If you aim it out toward the street, the glare will prevent others from seeing an intruder in your yard. Avoid placing it directly above or below a window.

Mounting floodlights under eaves

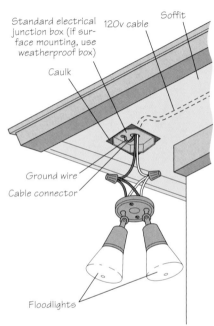

Standard electrical junction box (if surface mounting, use weatherproof box) · 120v cable · Soffit · Caulk · Ground wire · Cable connector · Floodlights

▶ Yard or garden needs a receptacle.

To install a remote receptacle, tap into a circuit at an existing outdoor fixture such as a porch light, or install a junction box on an indoor circuit (preferably in the basement

Tip *Many low-voltage fixtures use halogen bulbs, which should not be touched with bare hands. The oil from your skin will leave a residue on the bulb, causing it to heat unevenly and burn out too soon. Handle the bulbs with gloves or tissue paper.*

or attic) and feed cable to the outside through a hole in the wall.

None of the wiring can be exposed; it must be enclosed in walls or conduit or buried. If you run wires through conduit (along the house or a deck joist, for instance), use liquidtight connectors to join lengths of conduit, and secure it with straps every 10 feet and within 3 feet of any box. Check with the local building department about requirements for burying cable. In most regions you can bury rigid metal conduit (at least 6 inches deep) and plastic conduit (at least 18 inches deep) and fish Type TW or Type THW wire through it. Plastic conduit cannot be used for vertical segments where wiring emerges from the ground; use threaded rigid metal conduit instead. Type UF (underground feeder) cable can be buried directly in the soil so long as it's at least 12 inches deep. Cover the UF cable with sand or redwood boards. Where conduit turns to rise to a receptacle, lower a concrete block into the trench and bring conduit up through the hole in the block, stabilizing the conduit by filling the hole with gravel or concrete (see right); fill the trench with dirt. Enclose exposed UF cable in conduit where it exits the house and where it connects to the receptacle.

For the receptacle, mount a weatherproof box on a post or on the side of a shed. A box is not allowed to be supported by conduit only, unless there are two separate conduits connected securely to the box. Attach conduit to the box by screwing the end into the threaded holes in the box. Seal unused holes with coin-shaped screw-in plugs. Attach a receptacle to the wires (a GFCI receptacle if the circuit is not already GFCI

protected), secure it to the box, and attach a weatherproof cover with a hinged door that snaps shut.

Tapping into a light fixture

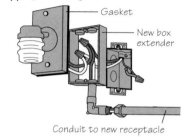

Gasket
New box extender
Conduit to new receptacle

Running conduit underground

Light fixture
Conduit
Liquidtight connectors
Conduit strap
12"
Type UF cable

Anchoring conduit

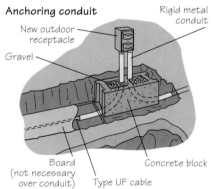

New outdoor receptacle
Rigid metal conduit
Gravel
Board (not necessary over conduit)
Concrete block
Type UF cable

▶ *House doesn't have outdoor receptacle.*

If you have to add a new receptacle outdoors, the easiest way is to install it on the side of the house. You can use an ordinary electrical box or a weatherproof surface-mounted box. The receptacle must have a weatherproof gasket and cover and a hinged door that snaps shut when the outlet is not in use. Outdoor receptacles must be GFCI protected.

To install, find a receptacle inside the house on an exterior wall, then shut off the power. Unscrew the cover, disconnect the receptacle, and remove one of the knockouts from the back of the box. Then, using a window or some other point of reference, measure and mark the location of the receptacle on the outside of the exterior wall. Make a second mark about 6 inches from the first (most walls are not thick enough to mount boxes back-to-back). Center the new receptacle over the second mark and trace its outline on the wall, making sure the outline isn't over a stud. If the house has board siding, position the box entirely on one board rather than on the joint between boards.

Cut the hole with a saber saw or reciprocating saw. On masonry walls use an electric drill and masonry bit to drill several holes within the outline, then knock out the remaining masonry with a hammer and cold chisel. Pull the cable from the indoor box through the new opening and into the outdoor receptacle box. Screw or mortar the box into the outside wall and caulk the gap between the box and wall. Wire the GFCI outdoor receptacle as you would an indoor

Tip *Before digging for underground wiring, especially near the curb, check with the utility company to see if there are any precautions you should take for buried gas pipes, power lines, or the like.*

receptacle (see page 70); connect the power supply cable to the receptacle leads marked *Line,* and connect the ground wires. Cap leads marked *Load* with wire connectors; tuck them into the box. Screw the receptacle into the box and attach the gasket and cover. Put the indoor receptacle back together and restore power.

Installing outdoor receptacle on an outside wall

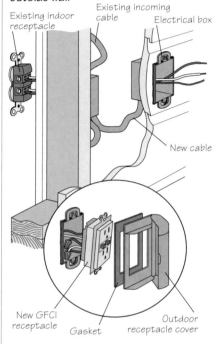

Existing indoor receptacle
Existing incoming cable
Electrical box
New cable
New GFCI receptacle
Gasket
Outdoor receptacle cover

▶ Outdoor receptacle or circuit is not GFCI protected.

The NEC requires that all newly installed outdoor receptacles be protected with a ground fault circuit interrupter (GFCI). The device prevents shocks by monitoring electricity flowing through the receptacle. If even a minuscule amount of voltage leaks, the device will "interrupt" or shut off the current within one-fortieth of a second. There are three ways to provide GFCI protection.

The easiest is to install a GFCI receptacle at each location where you need power. The second way is to use a GFCI receptacle at one location and protect all other receptacles that are on the same circuit and downstream from it by wiring them into its terminal screws or leads marked *Load.* A third way to achieve GFCI protection is to install a GFCI breaker at the circuit-breaker panel. Unlike normal breakers, the GFCI breaker includes a white neutral wire that must be connected to the neutral bus (the terminal strip in the breaker panel to which all the white wires are connected).

Protecting receptacles downstream from a GFCI device

GFCI circuit breaker
Incoming wires from source (line)
Outdoor electrical box
GFCI receptacle
Outgoing wires to regular receptacle

▶ Outdoor wiring is too complicated.

Install solar-powered lights that run on rechargeable batteries. They don't boost the electricity bill and are simple to mount because they are not wired to an external power source. However, solar-powered lamps may not be a good choice if you need hours of brilliant light. They often use less-bright, low-wattage bulbs, and most will operate for only six hours after being charged for a full day in sunlight. They work best in sunny climates.

▶ Lights lack automatic switches.

There are several ways to control outdoor lights without flipping a switch. One way is to install a clock timer, which will turn lights on and off at preset times. Mount the clock in a junction box on an inside wall near where the outdoor cable exits the house. If the timer doesn't have one, mount a switch nearby so you can manually override the clock. Following manufacturer's instructions, wire the switch to the clock and connect the clock to the cable leading from the power source to the outdoor lights.

Another option is photoelectric eyes, which automatically turn lights on at dusk and off at dawn. These sensors, which detect daylight, come in a variety of styles and can be wired directly into any outside circuit. You can also convert most single fixtures with a small photoelectric unit that screws directly into the fixture socket. The bulb then screws into a socket in the photoelectric unit.

If you want illumination only when someone comes near your home, install a light with a built-in motion detector. Using passive infrared sensors, these lights turn on when a vehicle or person enters a preset radius, and remain on until the person or vehicle leaves. Small animals will not trigger the sensor, but large ones will. Generally, motion-detecting lights don't operate in daylight. They come in floodlamp styles and in a variety of decorative fixtures; most include a photoelectric eye. A conversion kit, available at most home centers, will turn any outdoor light into a motion-sensitive light. Some outdoor motion detectors can be set up to trigger additional lights indoors.

Tip *There are three types of conduit for wiring: rigid metal, EMT (electrical metallic tubing, also called thin-wall), and PVC plastic. Rigid metal conduit is available in galvanized steel or aluminum. It uses threaded or threadless compression couplings and connectors, and can be used above ground and below ground. EMT is easier to cut and work with, but is restricted in outdoor use; it cannot be buried and, in some areas, cannot be used outdoors at all. Connectors are threadless and come in two types: setscrew (for indoors only) and compression, or "liquidtight" (for outdoors). PVC plastic conduit can be buried but not exposed; it is cut and joined like plastic plumbing pipe.*

▶ Motion-detecting light comes on too often and stays on too long.

If the motion-detecting light comes on with annoying frequency, shorten the range of the sensor using the control knobs on the fixture. Ranges among sensors vary from 1 to 75 feet. You can also adjust the time setting, which controls how many minutes the lamp remains on after it's been triggered.

If the lamp points at a busy sidewalk or street, unscrew the fixture and mount it in a different location or at another angle. If only an edge of the sensor field extends into a busy sidewalk, block that area by covering part of the sensor lens with duct tape or electrical tape. Have a helper walk in front of the sensor to isolate the part of the lens you should cover.

If the lamp on the fixture is mounted below the sensor, the heat from the bulb may be triggering the sensor. Replace the fixture with one in which the sensor is below the lamp. Power surges and vibrations can also trigger the sensor. Surges can't be controlled; vibrations might be if they're caused by a fan or some other appliance that you could move.

Adjusting time setting on motion-detecting light

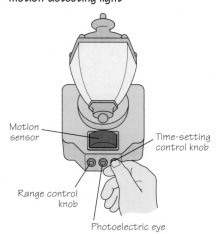

Motion sensor

Time-setting control knob

Range control knob

Photoelectric eye

▶ Lights don't turn on at the right time.

Timers must be reset periodically due to seasonal changes and daylight saving time. Because the timers are connected to the house current, they also need to be reset after power outages, unless the timer comes with a backup battery. If you don't want to reset the timer, consider installing a photoelectric eye, which automatically turns the lights on at dusk and off at dawn.

▶ Lights don't come on.

Check to see if the bulb has burned out; remove the bulb and screw in a new one that you know is working. If the problem is not the bulb, shut off power to the circuit and inspect the socket. Make sure it is clean and that nothing is preventing the bulb from making contact with the socket base. Remove the fixture from the wall to expose the wires. Make sure the black and the white wires from the house circuit are connected to the corresponding wires from the fixture. If the lamp includes a motion detector, make sure the red wire from the motion detector is connected to the wires from the lamp holders.

▶ Outdoor bulb won't unscrew.

Outdoor bulbs are prone to corrosion because the fixture is exposed to moisture and dirt. First shut off electricity to the fixture and try easing the bulb out of the socket again. If that won't work, break the bulb near the base, wearing thick gloves and holding a paper bag over the bulb. Then with needle-nose pliers unscrew the metal base of the bulb from the socket. (See page 77.) To reduce sticking problems in the future, smear petroleum jelly on the threads of the bulb before installing it, or use fixtures with coated-aluminum screw shells or ceramic sockets.

▶ Bulbs burn out too often.

See page 77.

▶ Doorbell won't ring.

First check to see if a fuse has blown or a circuit breaker has tripped. The problem may simply be no power. If the power is on, the trouble is in the push button, the bell, the transformer, or the wires. Inspect the push button first (you do not need to turn the power off to check the push button or the bell). Unscrew the unit from the wall and check the back to see if the two wires are touching. Connect any wires that may have come loose from a terminal screw. If the bell still doesn't ring, unscrew the wires and touch their ends together, holding them by the insulation; if the bell rings, the button is defective. Straighten and clean the contacts with fine sandpaper or an emery board; then rehook the wires and try again. If the button still does not work, replace it.

If touching the wires together produces only a faint ring or no sound at all, the problem is elsewhere. Unscrew the cover from the bell. Using a cotton swab and rubbing alcohol, clean off any dirt, paint, or grease that may have accumulated on the bell, the hammer, or the contacts. Also check for loose parts and inspect the wires where they connect to the screw terminals to see if any have broken or become loose.

If these steps don't solve the problem, check the transformer. (To find the transformer, see page 89.) This boxlike device reduces the 120-volt house current to a low-voltage

Tip *To make an outdoor bulb easier to remove, smear petroleum jelly on the threads of the new bulb before installing it.*

Tip *Replace standard incandescent bulbs with longer-lasting bulbs. High-pressure sodium or mercury vapor lamps last for years; fluorescent bulbs are also more energy efficient. All of these bulbs give off a quality of light different from incandescent bulbs, so check them in a natural setting before making a switch. Compact fluorescent bulbs screw into standard incandescent fixtures, but for other types of bulbs you will have to change the light fixtures too.*

current (usually under 20) for the doorbell system. You do not need to turn the power off to check the transformer or the wires. However, if checking reveals that you need to work on the transformer, you must

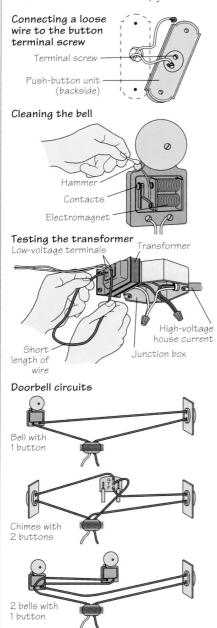

Connecting a loose wire to the button terminal screw

Terminal screw

Push-button unit (backside)

Cleaning the bell

Hammer

Contacts

Electromagnet

Testing the transformer

Low-voltage terminals

Transformer

Short length of wire

High-voltage house current

Junction box

Doorbell circuits

Bell with 1 button

Chimes with 2 buttons

2 bells with 1 button

turn the power off. Check the thin, low-voltage bell wires where they attach to the transformer screw terminals and tighten any loose connections. (The transformer wires that connect to the 120-volt current are usually enclosed in a junction box, safely out of the way; however, use caution, especially in older homes where connections could be outside of junction boxes.) If you have a voltmeter, touch a probe to each terminal screw; if the voltmeter doesn't measure any voltage, the transformer is broken and you'll need to replace it. You also can test for power by holding a length of wire to both terminals. If the transformer works, you will see a faint spark as you lift the wire on and off the screws (you may need to conduct this test in the dark). Just be sure that you are testing only the low-voltage wires.

If the button, bell, and transformer seem to be OK, check any wire you can easily get at. Wrap frayed areas with electrical tape and repair breaks by stripping the ends and twisting wires together or connecting them with wire nuts. If the bell is still silent, you'll have to replace all the wire.

▶ *Chimes won't ring.*

Most newer homes have chimes instead of a doorbell or buzzer. In a two-tone chime, when someone presses the front-door button, a striker hits the high-note chime. When the button is released, the striker springs back and hits the low-note chime, producing the familiar "ding-dong." The backdoor button sounds only the high-note chime. If the system isn't working, check the button, transformer, and exposed wires. (See page 87.)

If all of these are unimpaired, remove the cover from the chimes. Clean moving parts and connect any loose wires. If you have a voltmeter, place one probe to the terminal marked *Front* on the chimes. This terminal connects to the front-door button. Place the other probe on the terminal marked *Trans*, which connects to the transformer. If you get a reading, it means the chimes are broken and need to be replaced. If you don't have a voltmeter, hook the chimes directly to the transformer with two short lengths of wire. Attach the *Front* chime terminal to one terminal on the transformer; connect the *Trans* chime terminal to the other. The chimes should ring if they are OK.

Checking chimes with a voltmeter

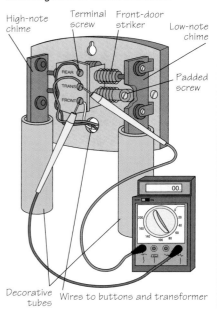

High-note chime

Terminal screw

Front-door striker

Low-note chime

REAR

TRANS

FRONT

Padded screw

Decorative tubes

Wires to buttons and transformer

▶ *Ding but no dong.*

If your two-tone chimes deliver only a single tone, remove the cover from the fixture and check to see if a striker is sticking or missing (see illustration above). If it's sticking,

Tip   *Connect doorbells to buttons with 18- or 20-gauge "bell wire," which has two insulated conductors wrapped around each other or encased together.*

lubricate it with powdered graphite. Never use oil; it attracts dirt, which muffles the sound. If the striker is missing, replace the chimes.

If the striker doesn't seem to be the problem, the trouble is either in the chimes or in the wires running to the buttons or the transformer. Try hooking the chimes directly to the transformer. If you get both tones, the chime unit is working fine, and you know the problem is in the wires. See page 87.

▶ Chimes ring but the sound is faint.

Remove the cover from the fixture and make sure the strikers that ring the chimes are not dirty or bent (see illustration, page 88). If that's not the problem, the transformer may be too weak to handle the doorbell system. Most bells require less than 10 volts, whereas many chimes need up to 24 volts. Someone may have replaced an old bell with a new set of chimes without installing a more powerful transformer.

Check how many volts the transformer delivers and how many volts the chimes need. The information should be written somewhere on the units themselves. If necessary, replace the transformer with a more powerful one. If the transformer is not the problem, you may need to shop around for louder chimes.

▶ Transformer is hard to find.

Most transformers are wired into one of the 120-volt house circuits at a junction box in the attic, basement, or a closet, often near a furnace or water heater. Check the wires coming from the bell. If they

head downward, the transformer is likely in the basement, mounted on one of the floor joists, possibly connected to overhead lights or receptacles. If the wires from the bell head upward, check for the transformer in the attic. If you still can't locate it, trace the wires from the button and see if you have better luck.

▶ Doorbell rings only sometimes.

Make sure all the wires are firmly connected at the button, bell, and transformer. There is likely a loose connection at one of these places.

▶ Doorbell rings continuously.

Carefully unscrew the push button from the wall and check the back to see if bare sections of the two wires are touching. If they are, separate the wires. Wrap frayed areas with electrical tape.

If the wires are not touching, unscrew them from the terminals and hold them apart. If the ringing stops, the push button is likely stuck in a depressed position. Pry up the button and make sure the spring works. If it's old and bent out of shape, replace the entire button.

Occasionally, the ringing does not stop when you hold the wires apart. This means that somewhere along the run the wires between the button and the bell are touching those between the button and the transformer. Trace the wires and wrap bare spots with electrical tape.

▶ One button rings doorbell but the other doesn't.

Test the button first and replace it if it's broken (see page 87). If the button works, check for loose connections at the bell and transformer. Finally, inspect and, if necessary, repair the wires that run

from the silent button to the bell and transformer.

Don't bother checking the wires running from the working button to the transformer or those from the transformer to the bell.

▶ House has no doorbell.

To install a bell or chimes, you will need to wire a transformer to the house circuit. You'll also have to run 18- or 20-gauge wires inside walls or under floors to connect the transformer to the button and bell. Attach the transformer to an existing junction box in an accessible location (the basement or attic are likely sites). Make sure the power to the circuit is off before you start working. Tap out a knockout hole from the junction box, and pass the transformer wires into the box. Then secure the transformer to the box by inserting the threaded lug into the knockout hole and screwing the locknut onto it from inside the junction box. With wire connectors, attach one transformer wire to the black 120-volt wire and connect the other transformer to the white 120-volt wire.

Install the bell in a central location so the sound can be heard throughout the house. Chimes generally hang about 6 feet off the floor. To mount the push button, drill a hole in the exterior wall about 4½ feet up from the ground and about 4½ inches from the outer edge of the door. Run low-voltage wire from the transformer to the bell, from the bell to the button, and from the button to the transformer. Use different-colored wires for each stretch, and you'll have an easier time isolating problems later on.

Tip *If you're still living in a ding-dong world you should visit your local lighting store or electrical supplier to see the variety of chimes available. You may be amazed at the astonishing selection of sounds—and sights—available for announcing your visitors. Popular songs, classical melodies, tunes you program yourself, and flashing lights are some of the options readily available.*

Bell wires are permitted by code to be exposed, so you can run the wires along the molding or under the edge of a carpet, but most people prefer them hidden inside walls (see page 65). Anchor the wires to joists or beams with insulated staples about every 4 inches, being careful not to pierce the wires. Closely follow manufacturer's instructions for connecting the low-voltage bell wires. Hook up the button and the bell first. If you're installing chimes, make sure the wires are clear of the strikers. Finally, screw the bell wires to the transformer, flip the power back on, and test the new bell.

Securing transformer to junction box

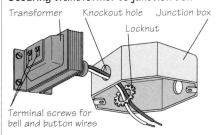

Transformer   Knockout hole   Junction box
Locknut
Terminal screws for bell and button wires

Connecting transformer to house current

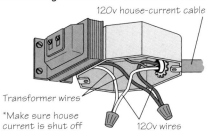

120v house-current cable
Transformer wires
*Make sure house current is shut off   120v wires

Anchoring the low-voltage wire

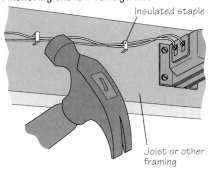

Insulated staple
Joist or other framing

▶ Doorbell is too complicated to install.

If you want to avoid the effort of wiring a doorbell, consider buying a battery-operated "wireless" unit. This is also a good solution for renters who do not have their landlord's permission to drill holes in the wall. You can find battery-operated doorbells at most hardware or electronics stores. Simply mount the push button, called the "transmitter," on or next to the door, and plug the chimes, or "receiver," into an existing outlet. Some models use portable chimes that run off 9-volt batteries. These chimes can be hung anywhere in the house so long as they're within 100 feet of the button. When you press the button, a radio signal is sent to the receiver, and the chimes will ring. The signal doesn't travel well through metal, so don't put the button on a steel door.

If the chime unit goes off when no one is pushing the button, it may be picking up a signal from a neighbor's doorbell or garage-door opener. Follow manufacturer's instructions on how to set the doorbell code; this may prevent the interference.

▶ Bell can't be heard from certain rooms.

Install a new bell in the part of the house where you have trouble hearing the existing one. Pick a spot, measure the distance from there to the existing bell, and buy enough 18- or 20-gauge wire to cover this distance. Mount the new bell on the wall and connect it to the existing bell with the wire. Carefully follow manufacturer's instructions for connecting the wires to each terminal of the new bell. You do not need to attach the new bell to the transformer.

▶ Back door has no button.

Adding another button to a doorbell circuit usually involves attaching a new button next to a door and running wires to both the bell and the transformer. Follow manufacturer's instructions for hooking up the button. If the wire from the new button ends up running alongside the wire from the existing button on its way to the transformer, you can splice the two lengths together. Cut the existing wire where it's joined by the wire from the new button, and twist the loose ends together with a wire connector.

▶ Smoke detector is chirping.

Most battery-operated smoke detectors will chirp when their battery runs down. Replace the battery and test the alarm. Not all smoke detectors deliver a low-battery signal; you will know the battery is dead only by testing.

▶ Smoke detector goes off frequently.

Don't disconnect the detector from the power circuit or remove the battery; you will likely forget to hook it up again. Instead open a window or turn on a fan to clear the air. Then at a more convenient time, determine what's triggering the alarm. It could be fumes from a toaster or moisture from a shower or clothes dryer. Try moving the detector farther away from the source of the problem. If the unit is in the kitchen or garage, move it just outside the door to these areas. If the detector runs on a battery, unscrew the mounting bracket and simply install the unit in its new location. Moving a direct-wired smoke detector is more complicated because you need to connect it to the house current. Call an electrician, or see page 91.

Tip   If you add new chimes to a system that uses a doorbell or buzzer, you can use the old buttons but you will likely need to replace the old transformer with a larger one. Chimes need up to 24 volts, whereas bells and buzzers use less than 10 volts.

Tip   Keep smoke detectors away from cooking fumes, fireplaces, bathroom showers, water heaters, and clothes dryers. Don't mount them in drafty areas or in corners where the air never moves. Also keep them far from fluorescent lights, and do not mount them on exterior walls.

► Smoke detector needs testing.

Smoke detectors either run off 9-volt batteries or are wired directly to the 120-volt house current. Some direct-wired units also use backup batteries. Change the battery once a year and test the alarm every two months. Most smoke detectors have a test button you can push, but this tests only the batteries. To test the entire unit, wave a lighted candle or cigarette under it and let smoke drift into the vent. If the alarm goes off, it's working. You can also buy a tester aerosol that simulates smoke (it doesn't deplete the ozone); spray it at the detector vents for a few seconds. Clean the unit periodically with the soft brush of a vacuum cleaner. If a smoke detector doesn't react to a test, replace it.

► Smoke alarm isn't loud enough.

People who are hard of hearing or who sleep soundly can buy a smoke detector with a louder horn. Some models on the market are twice as loud as the average 85-decibel alarm. You can also install additional alarms.

► Basement smoke alarm can't be heard upstairs.

Install a multiple alarm system in which each detector is linked to the others with low-voltage wire. If one goes off, they all will. To test, trigger each unit separately and check to see that all the others were set off. The indicator light will go off on the detector that is triggered first; the indicator lights on the others will remain on. To install this type of system, follow manufacturer's instructions.

► House doesn't have a smoke detector.

Every home should have a smoke detector in each bedroom and in hallways outside bedrooms. Homes with two stories or more should have a detector on each floor and at the top of each stairwell, including the one leading to the basement.

Alarm units use one of two detection systems. Photoelectric systems respond especially well to smoldering fires; smoke detectors of this type are best used in kitchen and bedroom areas. Ionization detectors are sensitive to rapidly developing fires. Use this type in furnace rooms and storage areas.

Installing a battery-operated detector is easy. Screw the unit into a wall or ceiling, slip in a battery, and snap on the cover. Wall installations should be within 12 inches of the ceiling.

To install a direct-wired detector, cut a hole in the wall or ceiling and mount a junction box. Making sure the circuit is shut off, extend a 120-volt house cable to the box. Attach the mounting bracket to the ceiling box. With wire screws, connect the black house wire to the black lead coming from the smoke detector, and the white house wire to the white lead. Finally, screw the detector into the mounting bracket.

If you are direct-wiring several smoke detectors, link them together in the same wiring circuit so that all of the alarms will sound if one of them is activated. Many codes now require that multiple detectors be interconnected in this way. Use "feedthrough," or "tandem," alarms. They have three wires: one black, one white, and one yellow or orange. Up to 10 such units can be wired into the same circuit. Use three-wire cable for the circuit wiring, connecting the black and white wires to the black and white leads of the smoke

detectors, and the red wire to the yellow or orange leads of the detectors. Make sure that the circuit wiring is not controlled by a switch or protected by a GFCI outlet or circuit breaker. For maximum security at least one of the units should be equipped with a 9-volt battery to provide a backup in case the house wiring has a power failure.

Installing a single direct-wired smoke detector

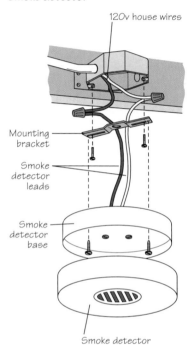

120v house wires

Mounting bracket

Smoke detector leads

Smoke detector base

Smoke detector

Tip *To provide extra protection for small children or people with limited mobility, consider a smoke detector that comes with a flashing red light. The unit is placed on the ceiling of the bedroom. The light attaches to a bedroom window with suction cups. When the alarm goes off, the light automatically starts flashing to indicate to rescuers the presence of someone in need of help. Another type of smoke detector includes a built-in light that comes on to illuminate an escape route when the alarm sounds.*

SOLVING ELECTRICAL PROBLEMS

▶ Phone is dead.

Make sure none of the cords between the telephone handset, the telephone base, and the wall jack is loose. If the system uses square plastic modular plugs, check to see that they are securely snapped into place. If a cord has been chewed by a pet or otherwise damaged, replace it.

If the cords are in good shape, test the phone itself by plugging it into a jack that you know is working, either in another room or at a neighbor's house. If you still get no dial tone, have the phone repaired.

If you do get a dial tone, the problem lies in the wiring. Check where the telephone line first enters the house; you will find either a lightning protector or a test jack. If there is a jack, plug in the phone. No sound means the problem is in

the outside wires, and the local telephone company will repair it.

If, on the other hand, the phone works in the test jack, you have a problem in the house wires. Unscrew the cover from the wall jack; you should see color-coded conductor wires. Make sure each wire is connected to the properly marked terminal screw. Also make sure no bare wires are touching; if any are, separate them and trim the excess wire. If a wire is broken (usually because it was nicked when the insulation was stripped), splice it or run a new length of wire.

Still no dial tone? Trace the phone wire (station wire) from the jack to where it enters the house, checking for breaks. If you find one, splice it or replace all the wire.

▶ Phone cord tangles easily.

Replace the phone cord between the telephone handset and base with a retractable cord. As you pull the handset away from the base, a small disc-shaped holder reels out up to 16 feet of cord. When you hang up, the cord automatically rewinds, much like a retractable tape measure. These can be purchased at hardware stores and at some office-supply stores.

▶ Phone reception is interrupted by static or humming.

Crackling sounds are usually caused by damp connections inside the jack. Dry the connections with a hair dryer. Remove the source of the moisture; if that's not possible, consider moving the phone jack.

If the phone hums, the red and green wires may be attached to the wrong screw terminals. Open the jack and reverse them. A loud humming sound that makes the phone unusable usually means that a bare phone wire is touching a metal water pipe or electrical conduit. Inspect the wires, especially where they run between floors. Staple them away from metal surfaces and wrap any bare spots with electrical tape. If that doesn't solve the problem, replace all the wires.

The poor reception could be caused by the phone itself. Make sure there are no kinks in the handset cord. Then check the contacts in the handset. Unscrew the mouthpiece, pull out the microphone disc, and gently bend the two contacts upward with your fingers or a small screwdriver. Clean them with a pencil eraser if necessary.

Phones that have additional features, such as automatic redial or call screening, are more sensitive to interference from radio frequency signals. Sometimes you can reduce static by using a couple of snap-on

Identifying damaged phone cord

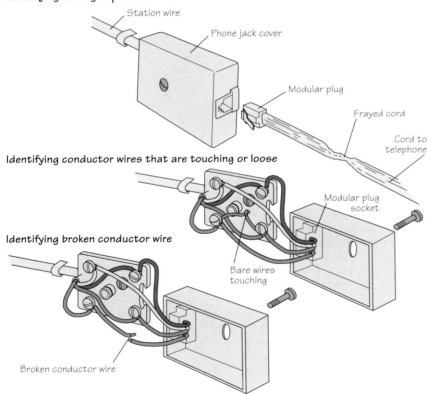

Station wire

Phone jack cover

Modular plug

Frayed cord

Cord to telephone

Identifying conductor wires that are touching or loose

Modular plug socket

Bare wires touching

Identifying broken conductor wire

Broken conductor wire

Tip *Phone wires conduct low-level electric current that is unlikely to cause harm. However, observe the following precautions: (1) Don't work on phones during thunderstorms or if you have a pacemaker. (2) Avoid touching bare wires or screws, and use tools with insulated handles. (3) Disconnect the house system from the company system before you work on a wall jack; if that's not possible, unplug all the phones in the house or take a phone off the hook while you're working.*

filter chokes, available at electronics or telephone-supply stores. Disconnect the handset cord, then wrap the handset end of the cord around one of the filter chokes as close to the handset connection as possible. Do the same with the second filter choke where the cord attaches to the base.

Cleaning mouthpiece contacts

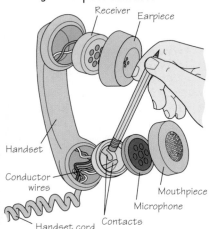

Receiver
Earpiece
Handset
Conductor wires
Mouthpiece
Microphone
Handset cord
Contacts

Placing filter chokes on handset cord

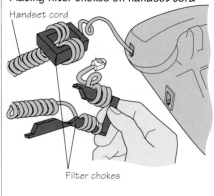

Handset cord
Filter chokes

▶ Phone dials out but doesn't ring on incoming calls.

If the phone doesn't ring or has a muffled sound, something may be jammed. Open the phone and look between the bells for the recoil metal and clapper. Free the jammed part with a knife or small screwdriver.

If the phone rings when it is plugged into another jack, you may have too many phones. The phone company provides enough power to run five standard phones on each line. If you overload the system, one or more phones may not ring. The amount of power a phone needs is expressed as a ringer equivalence number (REN) written on the bottom of the phone. Most phones are rated at 1, but some are higher (a computer modem may be as high as 3). Add up the RENs of all the phones and equipment on your line. If the total is higher than 5, you may have to unplug a phone to get them all to work.

Freeing clapper with a screwdriver

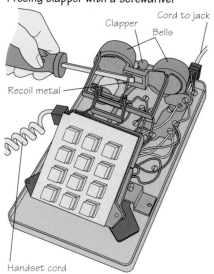

Clapper
Cord to jack
Bells
Recoil metal
Handset cord

▶ There is a dial tone but you cannot dial out.

If you hear a tone while you dial and the phone is a push-button one dating from the early 1980s, the green and red conductor wires may be reversed. Remove the jack cover and reverse the wires. If that does not work, take it to a repair shop.

▶ Portable cordless phone is dead.

Batteries may not be charging properly. First check that the base is plugged in, then clean the metal charging points on the base and handset with a pencil eraser or alcohol and a cotton swab. Place the handset in the base and let it charge. If the handset is still dead after 24 hours, replace the batteries. If the base unit of the cordless phone is dead, check the telephone wires and the power supply cord. Repair any frayed areas and if necessary replace the wires. (See page 92.)

▶ Portable cordless phone has noisy reception.

Try a regular phone on the same jack. If the noise persists, check the phone wires for problems. (See page 92.) If you get clear reception, the problem is with the cordless phone.

Crackling on the line may be caused by fluorescent lights or by electrical appliances near the base; move the base. Radio signals from a neighbor's cordless phone can also cause static. Most cordless phones have a security code that you can program into the handset and base that will prevent interference from nearby units. Change this code,

Tip *Once a month leave the handset of a portable cordless phone off the base until the batteries completely run out of power, then recharge. This will prolong the life of the batteries.*

Tip *Unplug the base of a portable cordless phone when you leave for vacation and during electrical storms. Power surges caused by lightning can disable a cordless telephone.*

following manufacturer's instructions. Make sure you enter the same numbers into the base and handset, or you will get no reception at all.

If you hear beep tones, you are too far away from the base. Move closer and try again. If the base is sitting on a metal surface or is near metal such as foil-faced insulation, the range will be shortened.

▶ Other callers can be heard.

If you hear other people's conversations in the background on your phone, one of your outside phone wires is probably touching a neighbor's line. Call the local phone company; this is not a problem you can fix yourself. If you hear other callers when using a portable cordless phone, try changing the security code (see page 93).

▶ Phone won't reach far enough.

Replace the cord between the telephone base and the wall jack with a longer one. Or buy an extension phone cord with a modular plug on one end and a modular socket on the other end. You can find these at consumer electronics or phone-supply stores. Unplug the cord from the wall jack, snap in the extension cord, then simply connect the two cords.

▶ Ringing phone near nursery wakes up baby.

Install a ring controller on the phone. This small, box-shaped device, which operates with a simple on-off switch, will silence the bell while still allowing you to answer a call on that phone if you hear another of your phones ringing. It can be used with rotary or push-button phones.

▶ New modular phone doesn't plug into old jack.

All new phone equipment uses square plastic connectors known as modular plugs. Older phones may be hard-wired into a wall jack—you can't unplug them. If so, buy a modular jack converter at a hardware store. Unscrew the cover from the old jack, leaving the base still attached to the wall. Snip off the wires that lead to the old telephone, making sure you don't cut incoming wires. Then snap the color-coded caps of the new cover onto the appropriate screw terminals. Screw the cover to the base, and plug in the new phone. Some converters may attach to the old base in a slightly different way—follow manufacturer's instructions.

Similar converters are available for hard-wired jacks that are mounted flush into the wall.

For older jacks that have four round holes, buy a modular adapter that plugs directly into the jack.

Converting to modular jack

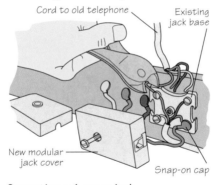

Cord to old telephone
Existing jack base
New modular jack cover
Snap-on cap

Converting a 4-prong jack

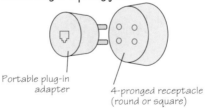

Portable plug-in adapter
4-pronged receptacle (round or square)

▶ Modular plug is broken.

To attach a new plug to a length of phone wire, you'll need a modular crimping tool. First lay the wire flat with the small lever on the damaged modular plug facing up. Mark the top side of the wire so you can attach the new plug in the same position. Next cut off the damaged plug with wire clippers, making sure the cut is at a 90-degree angle. Put the cut end of the cable into the wire stripper on the crimping tool; remove enough outer insulation to expose the colored wires. Then put a new modular plug into the crimping tool. Insert the trimmed phone wire into the plug and squeeze. Use this same method to shorten a phone cord.

Cutting off damaged plug

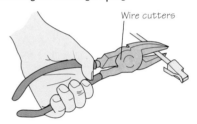

Wire cutters

Inserting new plug and wire into crimping tool

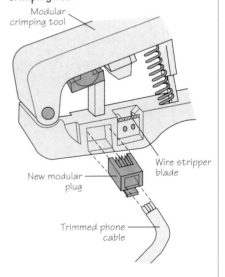

Modular crimping tool
New modular plug
Wire stripper blade
Trimmed phone cable

Tip *How many phones can you hook up? You may notice that newer telephones have an REN (ringer equivalence number) rating, which refers to the voltage required to ring the phone. A single phone line usually has enough power to ring the equivalent of 5 RENs. An older-style electromechanical ringer is equivalent to 1 REN; newer electronic ringers usually have lower RENs (for example, .5), but some are rated as high as 2 RENs. Therefore, one line could handle as few as three phones or as many as 10, depending on the total number of RENs of all the phones.*

From heating systems to major appliances, most homes contain complex mechanical systems with dozens of moving parts, electrical circuits, and electronic components. Manufacturer's manuals are the most complete source of repair information, but this chapter will help you diagnose and solve more than 200 of the most common problems associated with these systems.

▶ *Furnace needs inspection and maintenance.*

A furnace should be inspected and serviced by a professional annually, especially if it is more than 15 years old. An older furnace can develop potentially deadly carbon monoxide leaks. However, if your furnace is newer and you maintain it yourself, you can reduce professional inspections to once every three or four years.

Before attempting to work on your furnace, read the owner's manual. If you don't have a manual, contact the manufacturer to see if you can obtain one. Otherwise, have a professional inspect the furnace when you can be present. Ask the technician to tell you what the parts of the furnace are and how they work, and to show you how to light the pilot, reach and service the fan, and change the filters.

For annual maintenance, clean the furnace every autumn before turning it on. When the furnace is turned off and cool, open the furnace door (you may have to remove screws). Vacuum the fan compartment gently but thoroughly. Clean out the firebox or burner compartment, and use a vacuum brush attachment to gently remove soot from the walls of the chamber. If the furnace blower is not prelubricated, put a few drops of oil into each port (using a flex-nozzle oil can if needed). Inspect the fan and remove any obstructions or debris caught in it. Check the fan belt tension (it should "give" ½ to ¾ inch when pushed with a finger); the owner's manual should show you how to adjust the belt. Lubricate the fan and the motor bearings according to the instructions in the manual. Inspect the warm-air plenum (the sheet-metal box on top of the furnace) and repair any holes with duct tape. Put in a fresh filter. If the furnace includes a humidifier, clean the humidifier according to manufacturer's directions, and scrape away any mineral buildup from the unit.

For monthly maintenance, clean or replace the filters. Turn off the furnace and locate the panel that covers the filter near the blower (it will usually be in front of the return-air duct, a large pipe leading to the blower compartment). Slide out the filter and see if it's dirty. Dirty fiberglass filters must be replaced, but plastic-foam or metal ones are washable; use warm water and a mild laundry detergent. Let the filter dry thoroughly (use a hair dryer to speed up the process) before reinstalling it. Slide the cleaned or new filter into place, positioning it according to the airflow direction marked on it.

▶ *Fan motor hums but fan doesn't spin.*

Turn off power to the furnace, open the panel to the fan, and manually rotate the fan to make sure it's not frozen or obstructed. If it's frozen or very hard to move, lubricate it according to the owner's manual; usually a few drops of lubricant in the oil cup will be sufficient. Continue operating it by hand, and see if it begins to move more easily.

Now check the tension on the fan belt. When you press the belt with a finger, it should "give" about

Locating system components

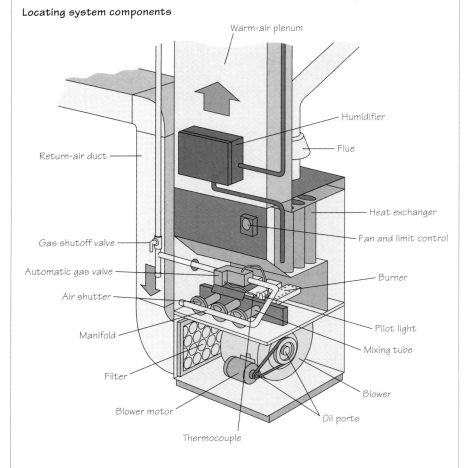

Warm-air plenum
Humidifier
Flue
Return-air duct
Heat exchanger
Fan and limit control
Gas shutoff valve
Burner
Automatic gas valve
Air shutter
Pilot light
Manifold
Mixing tube
Filter
Blower
Blower motor
Oil ports
Thermocouple

Tip *Most large appliance companies have toll-free "800-numbers" to provide customer service, including technical help in diagnosing and solving problems. All 800-numbers nationwide are listed with the "800" telephone information line: 1-800-555-1212.*

½ to ¾ inch. If the belt tension is incorrect, tighten or loosen the belt accordingly, following instructions in the owner's manual. If the belt is torn, remove it and replace it with a new one of the same size. Also check to see if the bearings are frozen; if so, oil them with the lubricant the manufacturer recommends, and use pliers to loosen them. Finally, check the mounting bolts for the bearings; tighten any that are loose.

If when you turn the furnace on again the fan still fails to work, the problem may be the blower control switch. Use a volt-ohmmeter to test whether the switch is receiving electric power. If it isn't, replace the switch or call for repairs. If the furnace is a new, solid-state model with electronic ignition, you won't be able to check or repair any function of the control module; it will have to be replaced.

Loosening motor tension

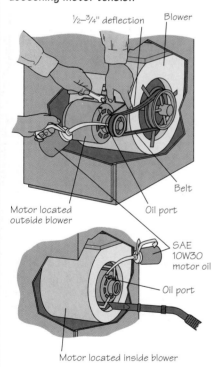

½–¾" deflection

Blower

Motor located outside blower

Oil port

Belt

SAE 10W30 motor oil

Oil port

Motor located inside blower

▶ **Gas furnace won't start.**

First make sure the furnace is turned on and receiving electricity. If your thermostat has a *Fan Only* switch, flip it to see if the fan comes on; if so, the furnace has power and the problem lies elsewhere. Otherwise, make sure all furnace power switches are on; many furnaces have one switch on or near the furnace, plus an emergency switch near the basement stairs. Check for a blown or loosened fuse or tripped circuit breaker. If the fuse blows or the circuit trips whenever you try to start the furnace, call a professional. If power checks out, press the red reset button on the furnace and see if the furnace starts. If this doesn't work, try holding down the reset button for about a minute.

If the furnace still doesn't start, check that there's gas. First make sure the manual gas valve is turned on; usually, in the *On* position the handle is aligned with the pipe. If it is, try another gas appliance (such as the stove) to see if there's gas to your building; if there isn't, call the gas company. Then check that the pilot is lit. Most furnaces have an inspection panel on the side or end; you can remove it to see the pilot. If the pilot is off, relight it, carefully following the instructions printed on the metal plate attached to the furnace (or as noted in the manual). If the pilot won't stay lit, see page 98.

Next look to the thermostat. (If the furnace is not controlled by a thermostat, check the manual to discover what type of controller it has. A modern, electronic set-back controller may merely have a dead battery or may be improperly programmed. If replacing the battery or reprogramming the thermostat doesn't revive it, have it repaired professionally.) To check a thermostat, see page 109.

If the thermostat works properly, the next step is to check the safety valve, which prevents gas from flowing to the furnace if the pilot goes out. To light a cold furnace, you can override the safety by pressing a spring-loaded red button, which allows gas to flow to the pilot only. Hold down the button for a minute or so; when it is released, the pilot should stay lit and the gas should flow as needed. (If the pilot goes out immediately, see page 98.) If the pilot stays lit but the burner still doesn't come on, either the millivolt generator or the transformer (depending on the type of furnace) is the next area to test. Use a volt-ohmmeter according to manufacturer's directions to see if there's electricity in the generator or transformer.

If the cause of the failure isn't any of the above, look at the limit switch, a temperature-activated electric safety switch. High temperatures above the safe limit cause the contacts to open, which shuts down the burner. If the contacts get stuck in the open position, there'll be no electrical flow and the furnace won't start. With the power off use a continuity tester or volt-ohmmeter to determine if the contacts are stuck open. If this is the problem, replace the switch. If the furnace still won't start, call a repair technician.

▶ **Pilot is lit but burner won't go on.**

A dirty or malfunctioning thermocouple is usually the problem. With the furnace turned off, clean the thermocouple (see page 98). If this fails to work, remove the thermocouple, buy an identical one, and install it. Make sure the sensor lines up in the path of the pilot flame.

Tip *How large should a furnace be? It used to be that homebuilders installed the largest size of furnace available because energy was cheap. Rising energy costs make it worthwhile to size a furnace more accurately, taking into account the size of the home, the local climate measured in degree days (how cold it gets and how often), the amount of insulation and window glass, and the amount of air infiltration into the home. If you have a new furnace installed, a heating contractor should make this calculation; in many areas local energy codes require it.*

SOLVING MECHANICAL PROBLEMS

▶ *Pilot won't light, relight, or stay lit.*

Before working on the pilot, make sure it has been out for at least five minutes and that the thermostat is turned to its lowest temperature setting. If the furnace is in a gusty area, the wind may be blowing out the pilot. Partially enclose the furnace to protect it from gusts. If this isn't the problem, try to locate the pilot adjusting screw (not all models have one); it is a cock-type device (rotates but does not tighten) that can get dirty or clogged. To clean it, rotate it completely a few times with a screwdriver. Now try to relight the pilot (you may have to try with the adjusting screw in different positions). If the pilot lights but won't stay lit, turn the adjusting screw so the flame burns strongly enough to stay lit. If the flame doesn't respond or the pilot didn't light in the first place, the pilot orifice may be clogged. Carefully clean out the orifice with a toothpick or toothbrush; blow or brush away any loose debris.

If the pilot still won't light, the furnace may not be receiving any gas. Make sure the manual shutoff valve is open. If it is, turn on another gas appliance (such as the stove) to see whether your household has a gas supply. If it does, test whether gas is reaching the furnace itself: First make very sure there are no open flames (such as a lighted cigarette) nearby. With furnace turned off, and using great care, loosen the connection of the gas pipe to the furnace only slightly. If you don't hear a hiss and can't smell gas after a few seconds, gas isn't reaching the furnace. Tighten the connection and contact the local gas company. If you can smell gas, *immediately* tighten the gas connection again; gas supply is not the problem.

Next check the thermocouple, which consists of a slim rod-shaped sensor in the pilot flame and a flexible connector that transfers heat from the pilot flame to a safety valve inside the control valve unit. If the pilot flame goes out, the thermocouple signals the safety valve not to release gas to the furnace. To test the thermocouple, press the spring-loaded red button, which allows gas to flow to the pilot only, and light the pilot. Hold down the button long enough to let the pilot heat the thermocouple (about 60 seconds). When you release the button, the pilot should stay lit and the gas should flow as needed. If the pilot won't stay lit except when you hold down the button, the thermocouple is the problem. Try cleaning the sensor tip with a wire brush and scraping it as necessary with a blunt knife. (Use no liquid.) If it is bent so that it is out of the pilot flame, bend it slightly back into place. If neither of these measures works, replace the thermocouple. Loosen the nut that connects one end to the combination control valve; at the other end loosen the nut that holds the sensor to the bracket, and slide the sensor out of the bracket hole. Connect the new thermocouple in the same way. If this doesn't work, replace the safety valve or call a repair person.

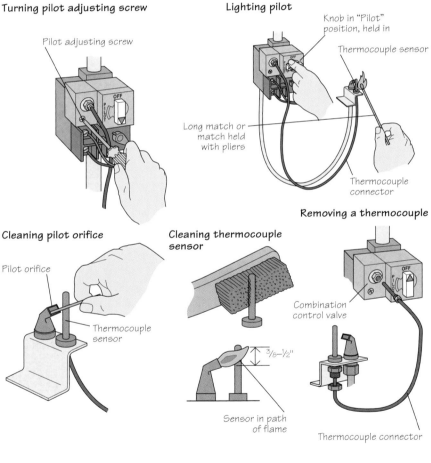

Turning pilot adjusting screw

Pilot adjusting screw

OFF

Lighting pilot

Knob in "Pilot" position, held in

Thermocouple sensor

Long match or match held with pliers

Thermocouple connector

Cleaning pilot orifice

Pilot orifice

Thermocouple sensor

Cleaning thermocouple sensor

3/8–1/2"

Sensor in path of flame

Removing a thermocouple

OFF

Combination control valve

Thermocouple connector

Tip   *A gas-burning appliance located in a closet or other enclosed space must have a source of combustion air. In the past a grille in the door was sufficient for providing the air; however, it meant that warmed air from the house was being drawn out through the furnace. Now it is common to provide outside combustion air directly to the furnace through a separate duct. The most sophisticated systems have an air-to-air heat exchanger as part of the house ventilation system. It prewarms air coming into the home by drawing it through an exchanger warmed by outgoing flue gases from the furnace (the two streams of air pass through separate tubes and don't mix).*

► Burner won't shut off.

Either the thermostat is defective or the safety valve is stuck open. Disconnect one wire of the thermostat and see if the burner goes off. If it does, replace the thermostat. If it doesn't, the safety valve is defective and should be replaced. Turn the manual shutoff valve to *Off* and call a furnace repair person.

► Furnace area has gas odor.

If the odor is strong, evacuate the house immediately, leaving doors open behind you; shut off the main gas valve and call the gas company or 9-1-1. For mild, nuisance odors, locate the source of the gas leak with soapy water: Mix liquid dishwashing soap and water in a spray bottle and spray all connections around the furnace until they drip; look for large bubbles, which indicate leaking gas. Tighten the leaking connection with two wrenches; check again with soapy water. Leaks from any other source, such as a cracked pipe or valve, should be repaired by a professional.

► Furnace air isn't warm enough.

First make sure that warmed air isn't escaping before it gets circulated through the ducts. With the furnace turned on, inspect the plenum for leaks at one or more of its corners. If you feel heat escaping, turn off the furnace, let it cool, and seal the leaks with metallic duct tape. Next check the blower. Turn off the furnace and examine the blower to see if it turns freely. Check that the belt is intact and has proper tension and alignment. Inspect the filter and, if it hasn't been replaced recently, install a new one.

If the air is initially cold and then warms up, or is chilly only at the end of the blower cycle, the fan control needs adjusting. It is located in a control box mounted on the furnace. Remove the cover; there should be two pointers, marked *Fan Off* and *Fan On,* clipped to the outside edge of a round wheel. (If there's a third pointer, labeled *Limit,* it should *not* be moved.) If the problem is cold air being circulated before it warms up, move the *Fan On* pointer a few degrees higher. If the problem is cold air being circulated after the warm cycle, move the *Fan Off* pointer a few degrees higher. (These adjustments may also decrease fuel efficiency, so you may have to settle for a trade-off.)

If none of these measures solves the problem, inspect the burners; look at the height, shape, and color of the flame from each burner. The flames should be similar to those on a gas stove: Most of the flame should be blue with yellow-orange only at the tip. Flames should be tapered—rounded at the bottom and narrowing to a point at the tip. If the color of the flame on one or more burners is wrong (too orange, for example), the burner is getting the wrong gas/air mixture. Protecting your hands with thick oven mitts, turn the adjustable shutter until the flame is the correct color, or call a technician. If the flame on one or more burners is short and flat looking, the orifice of the burner is probably clogged. Turn off the furnace, let the burners cool, and clean them. Using no liquids or cleaners, scour the burners with a stiff wire brush; use a dull knife to scrape off stubborn crusts, and finish by reaming out each orifice with pipe cleaners. Brush or vacuum away debris.

If the blower and burners are operating efficiently and air coming out of the registers still isn't warm enough, heat is being lost through leaking or poorly insulated ducts. Joints should be sealed tightly with metallic duct tape, and all ducts and joints should be insulated with at least 1 inch of blanket insulation or equivalent. See page 98.

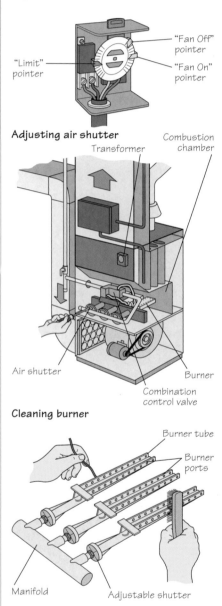

Adjusting fan limit control

"Limit" pointer
"Fan Off" pointer
"Fan On" pointer

Adjusting air shutter

Transformer
Combustion chamber
Air shutter
Burner
Combination control valve

Cleaning burner

Burner tube
Burner ports
Manifold
Adjustable shutter

Tip   *When sealing ducts with tape, use metallic duct tape rather than the more common fabric duct tape. The metallic tape is fireproof and forms a tighter seal.*

▶ Burners have sooty deposits.

Carbon deposits accumulate when the flame is not burning cleanly because of an incorrect mixture of air and fuel. With the furnace off and cooled, clean the burners as described on page 99.

▶ Ducts have asbestos covering over them.

Ducts in many older homes are covered with asbestos insulation, which looks like whitish gray plaster. If it is disturbed it releases tiny fibers into the air that may cause health problems over time. It's better to encapsulate or insulate asbestos than to try to remove it. Call a heating and cooling company or an asbestos abatement firm to have it done.

▶ Ducts aren't properly insulated.

You can increase heating comfort and energy savings significantly by making sure all of the ducts are sealed and insulated. Unless the ducts have asbestos insulation (a gray, plasterlike coating; see above), this is a job most homeowners can do if they are willing to put up with some mess and can work in tight, dark spaces (it's nice to have a helper for company). Buy a roll of metallic duct tape and several rolls of R-11 fiberglass duct insulation (buy extra, making arrangements to return what you don't use). Wear long pants, a long-sleeved shirt, a dust mask, and gloves. Make sure the furnace is turned off and cooled. Work outward from the furnace along each branch duct, whether in the attic or basement. Expose each joint, make sure it is secured with at least 3 sheet-metal screws, and seal it with metallic duct tape. Then wrap duct insulation around the duct, joints,

dampers, and other components so all exposed metal is covered. When you finish wrapping a section, secure the end of the insulation by wrapping wire around the duct or pinning the end of the insulation to itself with 16d nails, much like pinning two pieces of cloth together with straight pins; don't rely on tape. If the duct is in an area where it is exposed to contact, such as a basement or large attic, wrap plastic sheeting or bubble wrap around the insulation and tape it with duct tape.

Sealing and insulating ducts

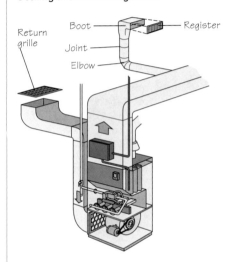

Return grille · Boot · Joint · Elbow · Register

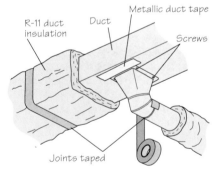

R-11 duct insulation · Duct · Metallic duct tape · Screws · Joints taped

▶ Filter hasn't been replaced for six months.

The filter should be replaced (or at least cleaned) at the start of the heating season and (depending on how much dust normally gets into the furnace area) about once every month or two for as long as the furnace is regularly turned on. For cleaning techniques, see page 96.

▶ Air is circulating too much dust, even with new filter.

Was the furnace cleaned and vacuumed before it was turned on? If so, look for leaks around the filter and in the duct work. You can also minimize circulating dust by creating cheesecloth filters for the registers throughout the house. Spread the cheesecloth and fold it over once or twice to form pads the size of the register grilles. Secure the pads to the backs of the grilles with rubber bands. Check the pads every month or so (when you change the furnace filters). Whenever they are dirty, wash them by hand and return them to the grilles when dry. Also consider upgrading to a more efficient filter, such as a HEPA or an electrostatic filter. You can also improve the air circulating in your home with a portable air cleaner.

▶ Whole house smells musty and unpleasant during winter.

Dirt and dust in the furnace may be causing the smell. Before turning the furnace on for the first time each autumn, vacuum it inside and out, or have a professional do this. Check the furnace air filters for dust and grime, and clean or replace them if necessary. Have the

Tip *The average life expectancy of a gas-fired or oil-fired furnace is 18 years, according to the National Association of Home Builders.*

furnace professionally cleaned if it hasn't been done recently (three or more years).

Merely heating a house may intensify normal, ambient odors (such as smelly pets, dirty rugs, and dusty drapes, blinds, and upholstery) that are not apparent when windows are open and rooms are cool. A thorough house cleaning solves this problem. Also consider obtaining an air purifier or portable air filter. (See discussion of ventilation, pages 116 and 117.)

▶ Air comes out too slowly or too fast.

There are three ways to adjust the flow of air from a warm-air duct system. One is at the registers, each of which should have a control for opening and closing the register baffles. If opening them doesn't increase airflow enough, or closing them yields loud whistling sounds, look for damper controls along the duct leading to the register and adjust them (see opposite). The third way to control airflow is to adjust the fan speed, which will affect flow throughout the entire system.

Most fans are driven by a belt connecting the fan to a pulley on the motor shaft. Some pulleys have a rotating adjustment to vary the belt speed. Loosen the setscrew and rotate the outer wheel of the pulley clockwise to increase speed, counterclockwise to reduce speed; then tighten the setscrew. If the pulley is not adjustable, replace it with one that is slightly smaller (for faster fan speed) or slightly larger (for slower fan speed). To remove a pulley, shut off power to the fan motor, loosen the motor mount adjusting bolt to release belt tension, and slip the belt off the pulley. Loosen the

setscrew on the pulley wheel and slide the wheel off the motor shaft. Reverse the process to install a new pulley. The pulley shaft should have a slotted keyway with a small key (shim) in it that aligns with a slot in the pulley. Be sure to save the key when you remove the old pulley and insert it into the keyway when you install the new one. It keeps the pulley from slipping on the shaft.

Adjusting fan speed with adjustable pulley

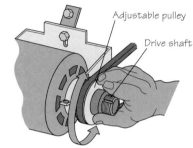

Adjustable pulley

Drive shaft

Adjusting removable pulley

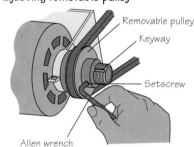

Removable pulley

Keyway

Setscrew

Allen wrench

▶ Some rooms are too hot and others are too cool.

Opening and closing wall air registers isn't sufficient to even out the heat in a house. (Closing a register only wastes heat.) Instead adjust the duct dampers to balance heated airflow evenly through all rooms. (A damper is a disk inside the duct that rotates on a pivot, controlled manually by a straight lever or butterfly lever on the side of the duct.) Look for damper controls along ducts in

the attic or basement. Most dampers have lever handles on the side; older types may simply have locking nuts. If the ducts are covered by insulation, look for telltale lumps. Depending on the type, you can loosen the nuts by hand or with a slotted screwdriver; adjust the dampers by hand and tighten the nuts firmly again.

To achieve the best results, adjust the angle of the dampers to between 45 and 90 degrees. Provide a slight flow (45-degree angle) through the ducts to rooms you rarely use, to rooms that are closest to the furnace, and to any rooms that are consistently too warm for other reasons. Fully open dampers (90 degrees, with handle parallel to the duct) on ducts that go to cool areas, especially those that are far from the furnace. If there are no dampers, consider installing them where two sections of duct are joined. The best locations are at the branches of a Y or T fitting, so you can adjust two dampers at the same spot.

Adjusting register and dampers

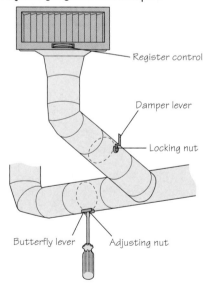

Register control

Damper lever

Locking nut

Butterfly lever

Adjusting nut

Tip   *If your forced-air heating/cooling system includes return-air registers at both ceiling and floor levels and you want to increase furnace efficiency, obtain or make magnetic sheets (made from the same material as flexible refrigerator magnets) to cover the metal grilles. (Look for lightweight magnetic sheeting at building-supply or crafts-supply stores). Because hot air rises, cover the ceiling-level return duct in winter so that only the cooler air near the floor is returned to the furnace. In summer, cover the floor-level return register so that only the warm air near the ceiling is returned.*

▶ Heat goes on and off at night.

If you don't want to turn off the heat at night or set the thermostat to a low temperature, you can adjust the thermostat so it doesn't respond so quickly to dipping temperatures. Inside the thermostat is a control called the anticipation-adjustment lever; it determines the actual temperature at which the furnace goes on and off. This temperature will be slightly different from the thermostat setting. For instance, if you set the thermostat for 65° F, you can set your anticipation adjustment to have the furnace come on when room temperature drops to 60° F, or 62° F, or 64° F. If the adjustment is set for a very narrow range (say, two or three degrees), the furnace will turn on and off frequently. If it is set for a wider range (five to seven degrees), the furnace will turn on and off less frequently.

To change the adjustment, turn off the power to the thermostat (if there is no thermostat switch near the furnace, trip the circuit breaker). Open the thermostat. The anticipation adjustment (also called a heat anticipator) is an arrow or dial, labeled either *More* or *Less*. Set the anticipation adjustment to a slightly wider range *(More)*. See also page 109.

If you have a type of thermostat that allows different settings for night and day, try setting the night temperature considerably lower (for instance, 55° to 60° F). The furnace will go on and off less frequently, and you'll save fuel costs as well. Set the timer to switch to the daytime temperature about an hour before you usually get up, so the house will be warm when you arise.

▶ Burner or combustion chamber is cracked.

Have it replaced immediately. A crack in the combustion chamber can be dangerous.

▶ Fan squeaks, or blower makes unusual noises.

Remove the cover to the blower compartment and inspect the fan to see if any obstacles are caught in it. On older fans, lubricate moving parts (following instructions in the manual). If the fan has a belt, check the belt tension and adjust it if necessary. (See page 96.) Check the bearings for side play and, if excessive, adjust or replace them. On modern models with direct drive (rather than a belt and bearings), the fan will probably have to be replaced.

▶ Small objects fall down registers into ducts.

The register grilles can be easily removed by unscrewing or in some cases merely lifting them. If you want the objects back, use a vacuum cleaner (with a long tube attachment but no nozzle) to retrieve objects from the ducts; when you're done, rummage inside the vacuum bag. To prevent future losses, obtain pieces of screening from the hardware store and use wire cutters to cut them slightly larger than the registers. Place the register on top of the screening and fold the edges of the screening so that it tightly hugs the register frame. Secure, if necessary, with string or thin wire, and replace the registers on the ducts.

▶ Steam heaters don't heat.

Make sure the thermostat (if you have one) is turned on and the setting is above room temperature. Check radiator valves; turn them to make sure they are open and not shut or stuck barely open. See if the boiler is turned on. Check the boiler gauge. If the level of the water is low, the boiler won't operate. Turn off the boiler and let it cool completely before refilling it. (Adding cold water to a hot boiler is likely to crack it.) When you've refilled and restarted the boiler, the heat may come on; however, call for a professional inspection to find out why the boiler went dry.

If none of these measures is successful, call a technician. Most steam radiator repairs require professional expertise because of the danger of scalds from the steam and the potential for boiler explosions. (If you are a renter, contact your building superintendent or landlord; landlords are required by law to provide heat.)

▶ Some steam radiators have heat and others don't.

If only some of the radiators are cold, the valves of those radiators may not be working. Check that the inlet valve (also called the shut-off valve) near the floor is open all the way. If your floor is slanted, the slant of the radiator may be causing the malfunction. Shim up the radiator legs (with pieces of wood or the equivalent) until the radiator is level. If the pipe doesn't move slightly as well, do not force it; you may loosen connections.

A radiator also may not work if the steam vent (also called an air vent) is clogged with mineral deposits. Turn off the inlet valve to

Tip *All heating systems have certain advantages and disadvantages. The advantages of a warm-air system (sometimes called forced-air, or heated-air) are: (1) circulating air can be filtered, humidified, or dehumidified; (2) the same duct work can be used for central air conditioning; (3) heat exchangers can be integrated with the duct system to bring fresh air into the home; (4) the furnace can be upgraded to a higher efficiency; and (5) air can be heated quickly. Disadvantages are: (1) the ducts are awkward and hard to conceal; (2) the system can be noisy and drafty; (3) the ducts transmit sound between rooms; and (4) the system warms the air but not the objects and surfaces of a room.*

the radiator (to make sure no steam comes in and scalds you). Unscrew the steam vent by hand (or with large pliers), inspect it, and attempt to wash it clean. If it is still clogged, buy a new vent (available at plumbing or heating outlets). Many models of vents offer adjustable air openings, so you can easily regulate the steam pressure in the radiator to adjust it to the room temperature. Coat the threads of the new vent with joint compound specified for steam radiators, screw the vent into place, and turn the intake valve back on.

Checking a cold radiator

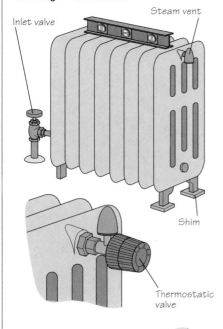

Inlet valve
Steam vent
Shim
Thermostatic valve

Setting an adjustable vent

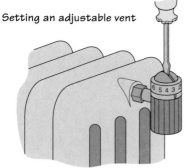

▶ Radiator valve leaks.

Using pliers, tighten the bonnet on the stem of the valve. If this fails to stop the leak, replace the valve. First shut off the system and let it cool. Loosen the steam vent at the top of the radiator and open the main drain for the system long enough for any water in the radiator to drain down past the valve. Loosen the valve connections, using two wrenches at each joint, and remove the valve. Coat the threads of the new valve or pipe connections with joint compound specified for steam radiators, then install it. Tighten all connections with two wrenches, making sure the bonnet on the valve is tight. Turn on the boiler, wait for steam to come out of the steam vent, then close it and inspect the new valve for leaks.

Removing a valve

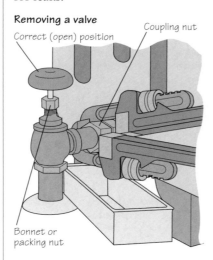

Correct (open) position
Coupling nut
Bonnet or packing nut

▶ Pipes knock.

The pipes may be knocking because the radiator is on a slant or the inlet valve is ajar. Try shimming the radiator (see left), and readjusting the valve so that it's fully open or fully shut. If neither step works, the problem is probably with the

steam-trap bellows, which is part of the steam-trap cap on valves of radiators connected to two pipes. A failed bellows allows steam and cold water to escape from the radiator together, producing the knocking sound. Turn off the inlet valve and let the radiator cool. Using a pipe wrench, take off the steam-trap cap. Inside the cap there's a flexible bellows. Use pliers or a small wrench to unthread the bellows from the cap, then take the bellows to a heating-supply store to help the dealer select a compatible new one. Coat the threads of the cap and of the new bellows with joint compound specified for steam radiators, thread the new bellows into the cap, and tightly fasten the cap to the radiator again.

Removing steam-trap cap

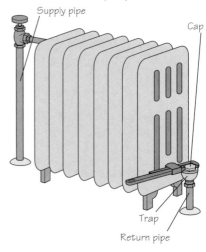

Supply pipe
Cap
Trap
Return pipe

Removing bellows

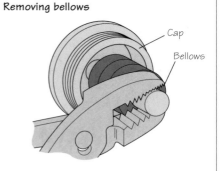

Cap
Bellows

Tip *The advantages of a steam radiator heating system are: (1) heat is distributed to the room by natural convection and direct radiation; and (2) the system is long lasting. Disadvantages are: (1) heat is difficult, if not impossible, to control; (2) the system is expensive to install; and (3) parts and service may be difficult to find or very expensive.*

SOLVING MECHANICAL PROBLEMS

▶ Steam-heated rooms are unevenly heated.

You can adjust the heat for an individual room by adjusting the inlet valve in its radiators to increase or decrease the steam. Remove any obstructions (such as drapes) that prevent warm air from reaching the center of the room. Consider replacing old steam vents with adjustable vents (see page 102) that will allow you greater control over the output of each radiator. To increase the general efficiency of a radiator, consider painting all metal parts with nonreflective, dark-colored paint to reduce heat loss. In a room that is chronically cold, place a sheet of heavy-duty aluminum foil between the radiator and the wall to reflect heat back into the room.

▶ Boiler pilot light stays on during summer.

Turning it off will decrease your energy bill. However, when the pilot is off in cool, moist weather, condensation can damage the unit's heat exchanger if it isn't corrosion resistant. Check with the dealer or manufacturer to find out if the unit is corrosion resistant.

▶ Radiator smells horrible and causes sneezing or coughing when first turned on.

The smell (and sneeze-production factor) is burning dust. Before turning on a radiator for the first time of the season, place some newspapers or rags under and around it to protect the floor. Thoroughly dust the top, the pipes, and (if possible) the back and then use a spray bottle filled with warm water to thoroughly rinse every part you can reach.

▶ Hot-water heating system heats unevenly.

In hydronic systems (which use hot water instead of steam), adjustable valves function the way dampers function in hot-air system ducts. Try tuning the valve adjustment for each room, opening or closing various valves slightly to see what changes; it will take several days to do this. If there are no valves, consider having a technician install some. If the system currently has a single thermostat controlling all heating to the house, consider having separate room thermostats or zone temperature controls installed. This installation will probably be costly, but may ultimately repay its costs in fuel savings as well as comfort.

▶ Hot-water heat doesn't come on.

Check to see if the boiler is turned on, that the gauge shows that hot water is flowing through the system, and that the valve on the radiator or convector (if there is a valve) is open. If none of these is the problem, call for professional service.

▶ Inlet valve leaks.

If the inlet valve for a convector leaks, tighten the bonnet to the valve with pliers or a small wrench. If this doesn't work, the valve needs replacing. Call a professional.

▶ Hot-water convectors in some rooms are cold.

Air is probably trapped in the chambers of those convectors (or radiators), preventing water from flowing into them. To "bleed" the air, look for the bleeder valves at the end of each radiator or baseboard convector. Place a thick layer of newspapers under the bleeder valve and have a cup or small

saucepan ready. Wearing oven mitts, use a hex-head key, allen wrench, or screwdriver to loosen the brass screw of the bleeder valve until it starts hissing; the hissing is the escaping air. Immediately place the cup under the valve. Once the hissing stops and a steady stream of hot water starts to pour into the cup, tighten the valve screw.

Opening a bleeder valve

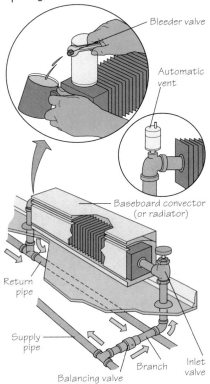

Bleeder valve

Automatic vent

Baseboard convector (or radiator)

Return pipe

Supply pipe

Balancing valve

Branch

Inlet valve

▶ Hot-water pump makes noises.

The bearings are probably dry and worn. Because modern pumps have sealed bearings, the entire pump must be replaced or rebuilt. Even a pump with accessible bearings should be rebuilt by a qualified technician; the seals are delicate membranes that must be installed and lubricated correctly to withstand constant water pressure.

Tip *To maximize the heating potential of convectors or radiators: (1) remove obstructions to airflow through the convector, such as draperies or furniture; (2) attach aluminum foil to the wall behind the radiator; and (3) paint a radiator (not convector, which has thin fins) flat black.*

▶ Convector fins are bent.

Bent convector fins interfere with airflow. You can straighten them using broad-nosed pliers or a tool called a fin comb that you may find in plumbing-supply stores.

Straightening convector fins

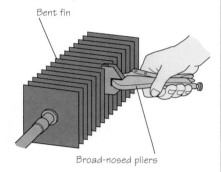

Bent fin

Broad-nosed pliers

▶ Pipes leak.

If you can see water under exposed piping, see if it is from a leaky valve, which you might be able to repair by tightening the bonnet. If the leak is from a loose joint or cracked pipe, and you don't have extensive experience in working with pipe and fittings, have it re-paired by a plumber. Simply tight-ening a connection may loosen other connections, and replacing a cracked pipe will involve cutting and threading pipe or soldering copper tubing.

▶ Relief valve on expansion tank leaks.

An expansion tank has an air chamber to absorb changes in water pressure as the water heats and cools. In some the air and water are in the same compartment; in others a diaphragm separates them. If the expansion tank is a diaphragm type (or you're not sure), have a profes-sional service it. For other types of tanks, replace the valve. First turn off the system, let it cool, and shut the valve between the boiler and tank. Drain the tank by attaching a garden hose to the combination relief valve and opening both parts of it. When the tank is empty, unscrew the old valve and take it with you when you buy a new one, to make sure the new one will be compatible. Screw on the new valve, close it, refill the system according to manufacturer's or installer's instructions, and restart the system.

Replacing expansion tank relief valve

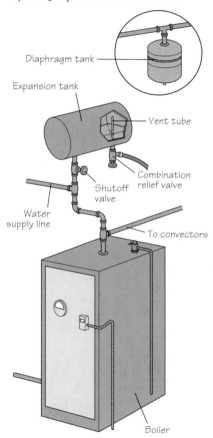

Diaphragm tank

Expansion tank

Vent tube

Combination relief valve

Shutoff valve

Water supply line

To convectors

Boiler

▶ Pipes in concrete slab are broken or corroded.

This ranks as one of the most diffi-cult problems in this book, first because it is almost impossible to pinpoint exactly where the problem is and, second, because the solution is a choice between destroying the floor and having a completely new heating system installed. Get help.

▶ Concrete slab may have pipes where you want to drill or nail.

Assume there's a pipe right where you want to drill or nail and aban-don the idea. However, if you have no choice and are willing to take some risks, there are two methods for guessing where pipes may be. One is to remove all floor cover-ing—carpet, pad, wood flooring, resilient sheet, whatever—to expose the bare concrete. Then turn the radiant heating system to the high-est setting. Moisten the floor and watch while the floor heats up. Areas that dry out first are most likely where the heating pipes are. Mark the pattern on the floor with chalk. Another way to locate hid-den pipes is with a magnet—so long as you know the pipes are iron or steel (many are copper or plas-tic). When you do find pipe loca-tions, you still won't know how far below the surface they are; they can be as little as ½ inch to more than 2 inches below the surface.

Tip *The advantages of a hot-water, or hydronic, heating system are: (1) quiet operation, (2) even heat, (3) efficient energy conversion, (4) ease of adjusting heat levels through zoning, and (5) ease of concealing pipes. Disadvantages are: (1) the system can't be used to filter or humidify the air, (2) it can't be integrated with central air conditioning, and (3) it requires a long start-up time.*

▶ *Oil burner stopped working and won't go back on.*

First make sure that the burner is getting electricity: it's plugged in, turned on, and the fuse isn't blown nor the circuit breaker tripped. Make sure, too, that there's enough oil in the storage tank. If these conditions check out, it's likely that the limit switch (near the heat exchanger) turned the burner off to prevent a fire because the fan wasn't working. Unplug the oil burner, open the panel, and inspect the fan. Remove any obstructions, lubricate the fan (according to manufacturer's instructions), check that the fan belt is intact, and check belt tension (see page 101). If the fan hasn't been cleaned recently, vac-

uum it gently; then plug in the burner again and see if it works.

If not, the furnace igniters may be defective, causing the safety switch attached to the stack control to turn off the pump to prevent the pump from spraying unlighted oil into the combustion chamber and possibly causing a fire. On the face of the stack (the large pipe leading into the chimney or flue), there's a reset button. Push the button firmly to get the stack control to recycle. It will remove any unburned oil from the firebox so that the unit can start again. The burner should go through its starting cycle once more, and should light this time. (If the

problem occurs again, the igniter will have to be replaced.)

If the burner still doesn't start, use a volt-ohmmeter to see whether the contacts on the limit switch are stuck open. (If that's the case, the meter will show there is no electricity in the switch.) Replace the switch if it is defective. If none of these measures gets the burner working, call for professional repairs.

▶ *Oil tank is filled but oil isn't reaching the burner.*

Trace the fuel path from tank to burner and make sure valves are open. If so, check the fuel filter. Turn off the electric circuit to the furnace, shut the fuel valve, and place a pan under the filter canister. Remove the canister by loosening the nut at the top; remove the filter cartridge, empty the canister, and wipe it clean. Check for blocked fuel lines at the canister top. Replace the filter and gasket and reassemble the filter unit. If there is no oil filter, look for a pump strainer on the end of the motor shaft; remove the cover and clean out the strainer with kerosene and a toothbrush. Next check the nozzle and nozzle filter (if it has one) inside the air tube. To remove the firing assembly (nozzle and igniters), mark its position in the air tube and disconnect the fuel line. Pull out the assembly and check for clogs in the fuel line and nozzle tip; carefully clear the tip with a piece of fine wire. If it won't clear, remove the nozzle tip and buy a replacement. If the problem still isn't solved, you may have to drain the oil tank to remove moisture.

Locating oil-burner components

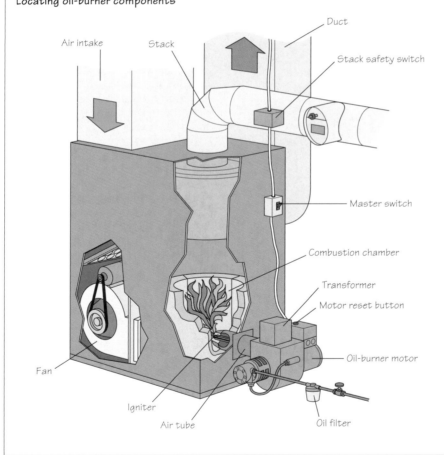

Air intake
Stack
Duct
Stack safety switch
Master switch
Combustion chamber
Transformer
Motor reset button
Oil-burner motor
Fan
Igniter
Air tube
Oil filter

Tip *If you have an old oil-burning furnace, consider having it converted to natural gas. Consult with local heating contractors and utility departments for a cost analysis of using oil versus natural gas.*

▶ Oil burner stops working just when it's coldest.

If the oil storage tank is located outdoors, at subzero temperatures the oil will thicken into a slow-moving sludge that won't flow through the transfer lines into the burner. If moisture gets into the lines, it may turn to ice and block the line entirely. Consider relocating the tank indoors (for instance, in the basement). For safety's sake, though, make sure the tank's new location is at least 7 feet away from the burner.

▶ Oil burner sounds like a backfiring car.

If the ignition is delayed, when the oil is ignited a small explosion occurs that sounds like a car backfiring. Soot or oil in the furnace room are other telltale signs of delayed ignition. To prevent it, check and clean all filters. Use a volt-ohmmeter to check that the voltages from the transformer (low voltage) and in the line (house voltage) are correct; if incorrect, call for repairs. If these steps don't work, you may have to drain the bottom of the fuel storage tank to reduce moisture, or you may have to replace or reset the electrodes, following instructions in the owner's manual. (Or you may prefer to have a technician complete these tasks.)

▶ Oil burner shoots out soot or oil spray.

The ignition is delayed. See above.

▶ Flame does not burn cleanly.

Heavy soot indicates a poor flame. First, with the burner and its power circuit both turned off, check the stack for heavy soot deposits and remove them with an old vacuum cleaner (or replace the stack pipe). Then make sure that the air intake is fully open; adjust by loosening the nut. Next remove the burner nozzle, screen, and igniters, clean them, then inspect them carefully; a visibly damaged burner nozzle or ignition assembly will require replacement. When you return the igniter assembly to the burner (whether it's new or the old one), set the gaps according to manufacturer's recommendations (or have an electrician do so). If these steps don't work, you'll need professional service.

Locating burner components

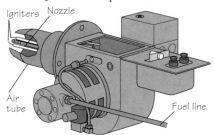

Igniters   Nozzle
Air tube
Fuel line

Removing nozzle and igniters

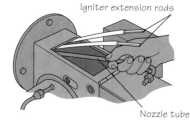

Igniter extension rods
Nozzle tube

Setting gaps

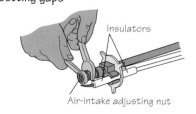

Insulators
Air-intake adjusting nut

▶ Electric baseboard heater won't go on.

Make sure the heater is turned on, that the thermostat is set higher than room temperature, and that the heater is receiving electricity. Electric heaters are more likely to trip circuit breakers and blow fuses than nearly any other appliance. (If fuses or breakers are difficult to reach, plug a lamp or small appliance into the wall receptacle for the heater to see if it works.) To decrease the frequency of electrical shutoffs, avoid using the heater at the same time as any other "electricity eater" (iron, toaster, electric stove or cookware, large numbers of electric lights), especially those connected to the same breaker or fuse. If this is impractical, consider having an electrician wire each element of the heater to a separate breaker in the household breaker box so that the electrical draw of the heater will be spread evenly throughout the house. If all of these factors check out, call for professional repairs. "Doing it yourself" on electric heaters and their thermostats isn't recommended, because these appliances typically operate on a 240-volt circuit, a voltage at which a shock can be fatal.

▶ Heat pump takes too long to heat or doesn't get house warm enough.

If you know that the heat-pump system is large and powerful enough to heat the whole house (because it's been sufficient in the past and the weather is normal), look for dirty filters. Turn off the pump and clean or replace the filters if necessary (usually this should be done about four times a

Tip *Increase the efficiency of electric baseboards by giving them a thorough cleaning at least once every heating season. Although they don't have fans, they depend on a free flow of air over the heating fins to warm the room. Disconnect or turn off power to the unit and remove the cover panel (usually attached with screws). Clean off the fins carefully with a dry paint brush (wear gloves); then, using a brush attachment, vacuum away the dust and debris.*

year). Clean condenser coils if they are dirty. If the fins are clogged with dirt, brush them with a stiff-bristled brush; do not use a wire brush or knife, however, because this can puncture the coil and allow the refrigerant to leak out (which is illegal, in addition to damaging the heat pump). Keep foliage well away from the outdoor coil. Check the fans for debris and clear any obstructions. Check fan belt tension, and lubricate the motor housing if bearings aren't sealed. Finally, check the level of refrigerant. The pump may need recharging; have this done professionally. If all these steps fail to work, call for professional repairs.

Heat pumps work best in mild-winter areas because their heat source (ground heat), although steady, cannot attain high temperatures. In an exceptionally cold winter, you may need to add portable space heaters. For the longer term consider having the system permanently linked to an auxiliary heat source. If you have a gas water heater, you may be able to extend hot-water pipes into a baseboard heating unit for convenient and efficient heating. Electrical heating can be hooked into the system quickly, but is usually expensive to operate. Probably the most economical auxiliary in the long term is a solar hot-water system.

You can also improve the performance of a heat-pump system by sealing air leaks throughout the house (windowsills and sashes, cracks, and the like) and improving insulation to the whole house.

▶ *Heat pump goes on and off constantly or runs constantly.*

Usually, this happens when the pump has no outdoor thermostats, or the outdoor thermostats aren't set correctly and are overreacting to changes in weather. You can install as many outdoor thermostats as your heat pump has strip heaters, but usually three or four are sufficient. Their cost will swiftly be repaid in energy cost savings. Consult a heat-pump dealer or technician about setting the trigger temperatures and anticipation adjustment on the outdoor thermostats; each one will require a slightly different setting to obtain the best results, and the settings will vary according to the climate in your area.

▶ *Thermostat does not activate furnace.*

See that the thermostat setting is higher than room temperature. If it includes a system switch, make sure it's set to *Heat*. If the thermostat area is dusty, remove the thermostat cover and blow strongly on the controls inside to remove any dust that may be preventing the contact points from closing. Further action depends on the type of thermostat you have.

One common type of thermostat uses a heat-sensitive bimetallic strip to open and close an electrical contact; if it does not close the contact, the furnace won't turn on. You can easily check it by taking off the cover and short-circuiting the two wire terminals inside the thermostat (they are low voltage—there's no danger of shock). Make sure the furnace switch is on so the burner will ignite. Then touch a screwdriver blade across the screw terminals for a minute or two. If the burner goes on, the problem is a broken thermostat. (You may need a helper to

watch the burner. Otherwise hold the screwdriver in place for several minutes until the blower comes on; you should be able to hear it.) If the burner or blower doesn't go on, the problem is a broken thermostat wire or defective furnace. You can check for a broken wire at the furnace: Short the screw terminals that are connected to the thermostat wire. If the burner goes on, the wire is broken and should be replaced; if it doesn't, see page 97.

An older type of thermostat uses a glass bulb partly filled with mercury, similar to a fever thermometer. This type won't function properly if it's mounted unevenly. Remove the cover and first check that the red and white wires are properly fastened to their terminals. (If not, turn off the power to the furnace, preferably at the breaker; remove the thermostat, refasten the wires, and reinstall it.) If the wires are correctly fastened, change the temperature setting to the coldest position, and watch to see if the mercury slowly flows to one end of the bulb. Now change the temperature setting to the warmest position. The mercury should move to the other end of the bulb. If it does not, try leveling the thermostat by remounting it. Check the screws on the wall plate; if they've pulled loose, that's probably why the thermostat isn't operating. Re-anchor them solidly; you may have to screw new holes a few inches from the old ones to do this. If the screws are intact, loosen them, and use a small carpenter's level to remount the thermostat evenly. Check again to see if the mercury flows back and forth when you change the setting. If not, replace the thermostat. If the mercury does flow correctly, reinstall the cover, set the thermostat for a warm temperature, and see if

Tip *A thermostat is an electric switch that is activated by changes in temperature. The moving part that makes and breaks contact to open and close the electric circuit is usually a strip of two different metals, bonded together, that react differently to temperature changes. For instance, as the temperature rises, the metal on one side of the strip expands while the other metal remains stable, causing the strip to bend. As it bends, the movable end separates from an electrical contact point, breaking electrical contact. As the temperature drops, the side of the strip that had expanded contracts, allowing the strip to return to its normal position and restore electrical contact.*

the furnace will turn on. If not, check for a broken thermostat wire by shorting the screw terminals at the furnace, as described.

Testing a thermostat by bypassing it

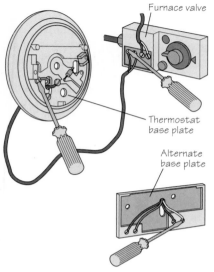

Furnace valve

Thermostat base plate

Alternate base plate

Leveling a mercury thermostat

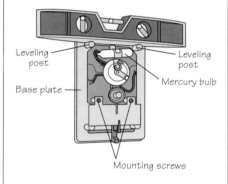

Leveling post

Leveling post

Base plate

Mercury bulb

Mounting screws

▶ Room temperature doesn't match thermostat setting.

You can expect a minor discrepancy between the thermostat reading and the setting you choose for it, but if the reading is significantly different from room temperature (5° F or more) the thermometer may be defective, or the unit may be located in an area that's warmer

or cooler than the rest of the house (for instance, a south wall is often warmer, and a drafty area will be cooler). First check to see if it is an older mercury thermostat that needs to be leveled (see illustration). Then consider relocating the thermostat. It should be placed on an interior wall at least 5 feet above the floor, away from any drafts or direct heat (including sunlight), and away from corners or dead spots behind doors. It should not be placed on a wall that has a duct or pipe inside. To relocate it, you will have to reroute the wires through the attic or basement into the wall of the new location (see page 65). It may be easier to run new wire from the thermostat to the furnace; thermostat wire is light gauge and relatively inexpensive.

If these minor adjustments don't solve the problem, the thermostat may have to be recalibrated. Read the instructions in the owner's manual, call a technician, or replace the thermostat.

▶ Thermostat lags in turning heat on or off.

Theoretically, a thermostat could activate the heating or cooling system every time the temperature varied only 1° F from your chosen set temperature. However, this would be annoying (and inefficient) because the system would be constantly cycling on and off. Therefore, thermostats have a range of a few degrees of change before they signal the heating or cooling system to go on or off. With most thermostats you can adjust this range yourself, to increase or decrease the time it takes for the thermostat to react to a temperature reading—except for electric resistance heaters (such as electric baseboards). In this case the thermostat is probably a high-voltage type, which could

cause fatal shocks; have it serviced professionally.

To adjust a thermostat, turn off the power to the furnace. (You may find a switch near the furnace; if not, trip the circuit breaker.) Remove the thermostat cover and look for the anticipation-adjustment dial or arrow (some thermostats may not have one). Set the adjustment to *Less* if you want to decrease the reaction time; *More* if you want to increase it.

If the house takes too long to warm up after the thermostat activates the furnace, it's probably the fault of the heating system, not the thermostat. The furnace may be too small to heat the house adequately, or the furnace may not be functioning properly. (See page 97.)

Adjusting anticipation control

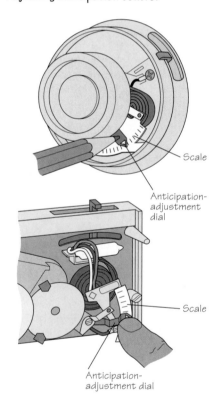

Scale

Anticipation-adjustment dial

Scale

Anticipation-adjustment dial

Tip *Where should the thermostat be located? Most experts recommend that it be mounted on a wall where it won't be in the path of a draft, and in a room where the desired temperature will be average for the whole house (or the rooms being heated by the system it controls). It should also be on a wall that is convenient to reach, near the main traffic path. Avoid placing a thermostat near a fireplace or on a wall that receives direct sunlight.*

► **Furnace cycles on and off too rapidly.**

Adjust the anticipation adjustment slightly in the direction of *More*. (See page 109.)

► **Thermostat needs testing.**

If you suspect that your thermostat is broken (see page 109) but want to pinpoint the exact problem, you can test it with a volt-ohmmeter according to the owner's manual for the thermostat.

Start by turning off the power to the thermostat and the appliance it governs. Hold the tester probes on the thermostat terminals. If the tester shows no continuity (circuit is not completed through the thermostat), the thermostat contacts are stuck open and it will have to be replaced. If the tester shows continuity, it indicates that the thermostat contacts are closed. To find out if they open properly, you will have to test the thermostat under live conditions by heating it to a temperature at which its contacts should open.

The easiest and safest way to do this is to heat it in a clean skillet. An electric skillet is easiest to use because you can determine its exact temperature. However, an experienced cook may be able to perform the test using a cast-iron skillet heated to approximately the right temperature. (This is particularly easy when testing a furnace thermostat, which should open its contacts at a very moderate temperature.) To test, turn off the power, disconnect the wires from the thermostat, and remove it from the wall bracket. Place it facedown (terminals up) in the skillet (unless it has a mercury capsule that should remain level, in which case prop it upright in the pan). Turn on heat to the skillet and let it reach the

required temperature (the temperature noted in the owner's manual or, for a furnace, a temperature that's warm to the touch). Put on oven mitts and hold the probes of the tester across the thermostat terminals. The tester should show no power, indicating that the contacts have opened and the thermostat is good. If not, the thermostat should be replaced.

Testing thermostat for open contacts

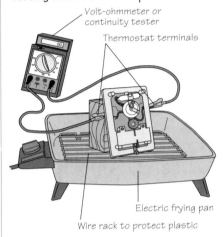

Volt-ohmmeter or continuity tester

Thermostat terminals

Electric frying pan

Wire rack to protect plastic

► **New thermostat doesn't work as well as the old one.**

You may need to experiment with the anticipation-adjustment control so the thermostat has the same lag period as the old one before turning the furnace on or off (see page 109). Also make sure that you have followed all installation instructions, including placing it in a proper location. If it still performs erratically, the new model may be defective. Thermostats are highly sensitive instruments and can fall out of adjustment. Immediately exchange it at the store where you bought it, trying a different model or brand.

► **New programmable thermostat needs installing.**

To remove the old thermostat, turn off the power to the furnace (and thermostat). Remove the thermostat cover to expose the wire connections and the mounting screws for the bracket. Remove the mounting screws to expose the wires. Before disconnecting the wires from the thermostat, mark each wire so you will know which terminal screw it should be attached to. To keep the wires from falling back inside the wall and to prevent accidental shorting, tape each one *separately* to the wall as you disconnect it. Install the new thermostat, following the instructions that came with the unit. Use hollow-wall fasteners to mount the bracket on the wall so the screws will not come loose. Carefully connect wires to the proper terminals; if you aren't sure, check on the furnace itself to see which wires are connected to which terminals. Use a continuity tester to trace wires if they aren't color-coded. After installing the thermostat, program it according to manufacturer's instructions.

Removing old thermostat

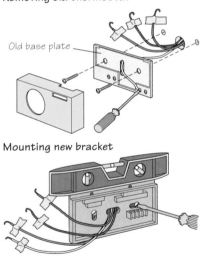

Old base plate

Mounting new bracket

Tip *A programmable thermostat saves on heating costs and increases comfort. You can program it to keep the house at a cool temperature at night and while you're at work, and to raise the temperature to a comfortable level before you get up or get home.*

▶ Humidifier unit leaks or overflows.

First use a carpenter's level to check that the humidifier is level both horizontally and vertically. If not, adjust the mounting. Then check the float valve; see whether its adjustment is set for the right water level and inspect its condition. If the valve is stuck open (usually because mineral deposits have made it too heavy to float), try cleaning it: Scrape off mineral deposits from the float and from the needle and seat on the inlet valve. If the float valve itself is leaking, or if the small rubber button that seals the outlet looks worn, replace the float valve. If this doesn't stop the overflows, the unit may be incorrectly installed or the media pads may need to be replaced or repositioned. Call for professional service.

Checking humidifier components

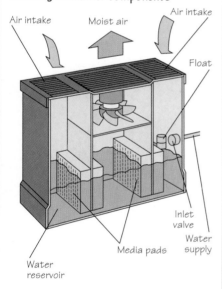

Air intake / Moist air / Air intake / Float / Inlet valve / Water supply / Media pads / Water reservoir

▶ Humidifier has corrosion or calcium buildup.

You can clean out buildup of calcium and lime by spraying a mild acid, such as vinegar, inside the humidifier. Start with a solution of 1 part vinegar to 3 parts water; strengthen as necessary. At least once a year, turn off the water, remove the humidifier element, and scrape off mineral buildup. Corrosion, however, will require professional repairs.

▶ Humidifier unit makes strange noises.

An occasional gurgle is probably normal. Check that water is running and inspect the float valve to make sure it's not stuck open or closed. Make sure that the duct edges to the unit are not bent; if so, straighten them. Otherwise, call for repairs.

▶ Portable humidifier won't run.

First check that the unit is plugged in and the receptacle is live. (Try another small appliance or lamp in the receptacle.) Make sure the cord is intact. If the air is already more humid than the setting of the humidistat (the humidity-sensing device), the unit won't work until the air is drier. (If the humidifier is new, it may take a few hours to adjust and start running.)

The machine may be jammed because of mineral buildup on the belt, rollers, drum, or (in newer ultrasonic models) the nebulizers. Start by unplugging the humidifier and emptying the reservoir. Lift out the belt and rollers (if applicable) or the drum. Change the evaporator belt at least once a year, and more often in desert conditions. Remove the pad from the drum. Scrub these parts with a solution of ¼ cup detergent in 1 quart hot

water, and return them to the humidifier. Add fresh water to the reservoir. In an ultrasonic model, once a week gently wipe the nebulizer with white vinegar, using a soft cloth, and rinse off. Check the air filter; if dirty, remove it and clean it with cool water. In hard-water areas, consider using bottled distilled water in place of tap water in any type of humidifier. If cleaning the unit doesn't start it, check for a broken or misaligned drive belt (see below). If this too fails to start it, take it in for service.

Checking components of a warm-mist humidifier

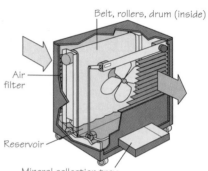

Belt, rollers, drum (inside) / Air filter / Reservoir / Mineral collection tray

Checking components of an ultrasonic humidifier

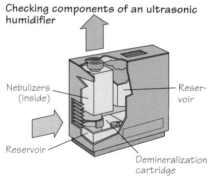

Nebulizers (inside) / Reservoir / Reservoir / Demineralization cartridge

▶ Portable humidifier's fan squeaks.

Manually rotate the fan blades to make sure the fan isn't frozen or obstructed. If it is frozen or very hard to move, lubricate it according to the owner's manual; usually, a

Tip *Adding humidity to the air makes people comfortable at lower temperatures. If the air is dry, most people are comfortable with an air temperature between 75° and 80° F. If the air has more than 50 percent relative humidity, the same people will be comfortable at a temperature as low as 70° F.*

SOLVING MECHANICAL PROBLEMS

few drops of lubricant in the oil cup will be sufficient. Continue operating it by hand, and see if it begins to move more easily. Lubricate the fan motor once a year (according to the owner's manual), more often if using the unit the year around. Check the tension and condition of the fan belt; it should give about ½ inch. Check the bearings; if they're frozen, oil them with the lubricant recommended by the manufacturer and use pliers to loosen them.

▶ Portable humidifier emits odors.

To kill odor-producing bacteria breeding in the reservoir, clean the reservoir at least once a week, using a solution of 1 tablespoon chlorine bleach per pint of water. Rinse with plain water. If odor persists, clean the evaporator belt with the same chlorine solution, and use water treatment tablets in the reservoir. (For special occasions or to purge the chlorine smell, you can add a few drops of rose water, orange-flower water, or a light cologne or aftershave to the reservoir water.)

▶ Portable humidifier won't stop running.

If the unit is new and the home is extremely dry, it may be necessary for the humidifier to run for a long time before the proper humidity is reached. Check for open windows or an open fireplace damper that may be pulling out the humidified air. Otherwise, it's likely that either the on-off switch or the humidistat (the humidity sensor) is broken. Disconnect the power cord, locate the humidistat, and test it with a volt-ohmmeter; then test the switch. Be sure you are testing in low-humidity conditions. If the meter registers an electric current (continuity) in either case, the electrical contacts of that part are

stuck in a closed position, keeping the machine running. Replace the broken part. If this doesn't work, have the machine repaired professionally. If you feel the machine isn't worth repairing, just unplug the humidifier whenever you want to turn it off and plug it back in when the air feels dry.

Testing humidistat

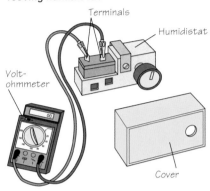

▶ Dehumidifier unit doesn't start or won't stay on.

Check that the unit is plugged into a live receptacle; if using it consistently blows the fuse or trips the breaker, try a different receptacle to avoid overloading a circuit. If the problem recurs, have the unit repaired professionally.

If room temperature is below 65° F, the unit may be blocked with ice; few models function well below 70° F. Try the unit again when the room is warm. If you've been repeatedly turning it on and off, turn it on and wait about two minutes to see if it starts again.

Check to see if the collector bin is full of water. If so, empty it and try it again. If the unit still doesn't start, unplug it and disconnect one lead to the humidistat. Simultaneously rotate the knob and test the humidistat with a volt-ohmmeter. If there's no current, the humidistat has to be replaced.

▶ Dehumidifier motor or fan squeaks.

Check the owner's manual to find out where the lubrication points are and what type of lubricant to use. (Most dehumidifiers have an oil cup for inserting lubricant.) Lubricate according to the manual. If the sound is more like a rattle than a squeak, tighten the screws on the fan hub. If this doesn't stop it, check the fan motor for worn bearings. Unscrew the mounting nuts and then unscrew the fan from the shaft. If you can move the shaft in any direction, a bearing is worn out, and the motor will need to be replaced. Consult the manual for specific instructions.

Tightening fan-hub screws

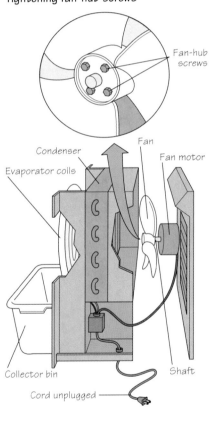

Tip *A dehumidifier should be cleaned periodically. With the power turned off, unscrew the panel(s) and vacuum the inside, including the fan and coils. Scrub mineral deposits from the coils with a stiff wire brush.*

▶ Dehumidifier has water under it.

Usually this means the collector bin is overflowing. Empty the collector. If the unit has a drain trough under the coils, remove any obstruction in the drain hole. If water continues to collect, check the owner's manual to see if the unit has an overflow-prevention switch. If so, disconnect it and test it with a volt-ohmmeter; if the meter shows no current (continuity), the contacts are stuck open and the switch will need to be replaced. If the problem recurs, corrosion may have eaten a hole in some part of the mechanism. Call for professional repairs.

▶ Dehumidifier evaporator coils collect frost.

Many models frost up when operated at a room temperature under 65° F. If it's warm, the problem may be dirty coils or too little airflow. Clean the coils by unplugging the unit, removing the outer cabinet, and letting moisture evaporate; then wipe the coils gently with a soft-bristled brush (such as a refrigerator-coil brush) and/or vacuum the coils. If the dehumidifier is right next to a wall, move it an inch or two away from the wall to allow better airflow.

If ice-ups continue, turn up the speed of the dehumidifier (if it has a speed switch). If the dehumidifier has a deicer control (a bimetallic thermostatic device attached to the suction line), it may be faulty. Obtain a replacement and clamp it over the suction line in the same place, according to manufacturer's instructions, or have a repair person do so.

▶ Window air conditioner needs routine maintenance.

Once a year when the weather is warming up, clean the unit or have it cleaned and inspected professionally. (In areas with high air pollution, a professional should clean the unit.) To clean it yourself, unplug the unit and, with a helper, remove it from the window. Set it outdoors on an improvised work table (such as on sawhorses); if that is impractical, set it on an up-ended heavy-duty plastic laundry basket (or equivalent) in the bathtub. Wrap all electrical components in heavy plastic bags secured with duct tape. Vacuum the evaporator fins clean, and then wash both the evaporator and condenser coils with a garden hose or handheld shower sprayer until clear water percolates through. Let drain.

Next pull out the filter; it is usually a thin sheet of foam rubber located behind the face grille. Check its condition and wash it with a mild detergent if it's dirty (and washable), or replace it if it's worn or isn't washable. Oil the fan motor according to the owner's manual. Remove the plastic bags and return the unit to the window. Don't try to add refrigerant yourself; call a professional. You risk not only ruining the system, but illegally releasing CFCs (chlorofluorocarbons) into the atmosphere.

The filter should be cleaned or changed at least once a month, more often in smoggy or dusty weather. In most areas the coils need a thorough cleaning just once a year, but if there's heavy air pollution, clean them about once a month.

Cleaning filter and coils

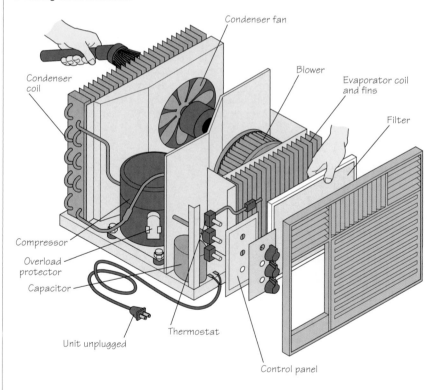

Condenser fan

Condenser coil

Blower

Evaporator coil and fins

Filter

Compressor

Overload protector

Capacitor

Thermostat

Unit unplugged

Control panel

Tip *Whenever you take the cover off an air conditioner, beware of touching the capacitor, as it stores an electric charge. You can discharge it and render it safe (so long as the unit is unplugged) by touching a screwdriver blade across the two terminals and holding it there for a few seconds; be sure the screwdriver handle is insulated. Don't touch the blade and don't let the blade touch anything else. Some capacitors discharge automatically, but assume it doesn't and perform this maneuver anyway.*

SOLVING MECHANICAL PROBLEMS

► Room air conditioner doesn't turn on.

If the fuse hasn't blown nor the circuit breaker tripped, check to see if the cord or plug is damaged; if so, replace it. If not, unplug the unit and check the switch with a continuity tester or volt-ohmmeter to see if the switch is stuck in the *Off* position (the tester will indicate no continuity). If the switch is faulty, replace it. If turning on the unit consistently blows the fuse or trips the breaker, try a receptacle in a different room; if the problem continues, call for professional repairs.

► Room air conditioner doesn't cool room.

First check to see if anything is blocking the front of the unit. Then close the door to the room and turn the thermostat to the coldest position and see if that works better. If not, check the filter; if it is dirty or ripped, clean it or replace it. Open the unit and see if the coils are dirty; if so, remove the unit from the window and clean the coils (see page 113), or have the unit professionally cleaned. If the unit is connected to the receptacle with a long extension cord, it may not be getting enough power to operate at full capacity; change the cord to a larger gauge (at least No. 14). Also check to see that the thermostat is working (see pages 108 and 109). The refrigerant level may be low; if so, call a professional to replenish it.

► Room air conditioner cycles on and off too rapidly.

Follow the procedures outlined above. In addition, the thermostat may be adjusted to go on and off in too narrow a temperature range (see page 110).

► Room air conditioner may be too small.

Before you buy a larger unit, for long-term savings consider reducing air infiltration and increasing shade. Caulking air leaks, adding window coverings, replacing single-glazed windows with double-glazed units, planting shade trees and installing trellises, and screening the porch are some of the steps you can take to cool your house while reducing energy use. Installing a ceiling fan or, even better, a whole-house fan can also diminish reliance on air-conditioning.

► Window air conditioner is subject to winter exposure.

Weather-induced corrosion of the case is usually a minor problem that can be repaired with touch-up paint, but if winters are severe or rain is highly acidic, you can protect the unit by covering the outside portion with a heavy-duty garbage bag or similar sturdy plastic sheeting secured with duct tape. If frequent hailstorms are damaging the case, make a double or triple layer of plastic foam or bubble wrap (available at office-supply stores), poke many small holes in it for ventilation, and tape it to the top of the unit.

If the main problem is the draft that comes through the vents, remove the inside front cover and place a piece of plastic between the unit and the front cover for the winter, or obtain a quilted air conditioner cover. Be sure to remove the plastic inside the unit before starting it up again.

► Central air conditioner doesn't turn on.

First make sure that the unit is plugged in, switched on, and receiving electricity (the fuse isn't blown or the circuit breaker isn't tripped). If the fuse blows or circuit breaker trips whenever you turn on the unit, call for repairs. After a power outage, do not use the air conditioner for at least six hours or you may damage the compressor.

Check the thermostat to make sure that the setting is below room temperature and set to *Cool* or *Auto*, and that the fan switch is set to *Auto* or *On*. Check the coil outside to see if the fan is running; if not, check the condition of the blades and belt (see page 115). Make sure that the filters aren't clogged with dirt. If none of this is the problem, check that the thermostat is working (see page 109). Otherwise, the problem is probably a jammed or frozen compressor unit. Call for professional service.

► Central air conditioner needs routine maintenance.

At the start of warm weather, give the air conditioner an annual checkup and cleaning, or have it done professionally. First trim away any shrubbery that's growing close enough to restrict airflow to the outside condenser unit. Before starting work on the air conditioner itself, turn off the main power switch and thermostat; during the work, don't touch the capacitor, its terminals, or the wires leading from it, because the capacitor stores a heavy electric charge (see Tip, page 113).

Tip *A coating of frost on air conditioner coils usually indicates overuse. There are several simple ways to reduce the air-conditioning load and decrease operating costs: (1) turn off the air conditioner when no one is home; (2) consider opening windows and using an electric fan when temperatures are semibearable; (3) have a whole-house fan installed to remove hot air from the house; and (4) seal or weather-strip all gaps around the air conditioner to keep the cooled air inside.*

Remove the cowl from the condenser. Cover the compressor and other electrical parts with large plastic bags secured with duct tape, and wash the fins and coils with a garden hose until clean water percolates through. If fins are bent, straighten them with broad-nosed pliers or a fin comb (available at plumbing or heating outlets); wear heavy gloves (such as oven mitts or garden gloves). Carefully inspect the coils with a flashlight; if they're still very dirty, call a technician to clean the unit (watch the operation closely, so you will be able to do it yourself next year). Lubricate the condenser motor and fan motor according to the owner's manual. Check the fan for dirt and check the fan belt tension (see page 96). Oil the fan and fan bearings, following the instructions in the owner's manual. If the cupped portion of the fan blade is heavily coated with dirt (more than 1/16 inch thick), call a professional to clean it. Replace the fan compartment cover tightly, and replace the cowl.

Indoors, clean the evaporator fins with a soft brush and, if necessary, straighten them with a fin comb. Change the air-intake filter. Rinse the drain pan with a solution of 1/4 cup chlorine bleach in 1 pint water to keep algae and bacteria from breeding. Every month check the air-intake filter and replace it (or wash it, if it's washable) when dirty, and rinse or spray the drain pan with a bleach-and-water solution.

If the level of refrigerant is low, only a professional can recharge it legally and safely. In regions with severe air pollution, have a professional perform the annual cleaning.

Cleaning air-conditioning components

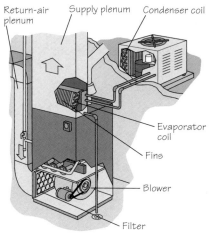

Return-air plenum · Supply plenum · Condenser coil · Evaporator coil · Fins · Blower · Filter

Cleaning condenser coil

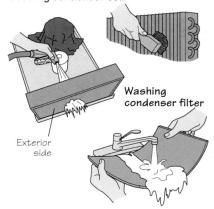

Exterior side

Washing condenser filter

▶ *Central air conditioner doesn't cool house enough.*

Make sure the thermostat and fan are set correctly, and check that the fan is running. Make sure nothing is restricting airflow. Check for unnecessary cool-air loss, such as open windows or doors. Close drapes, blinds, or shades in any room that doesn't require outside light. See opposite page for additional cooling strategies. Check the filters and condenser for dirt, and make sure nothing is obstructing the fan. If the compressor isn't turning easily, or if none of the above measures helps, call for professional repairs.

▶ *Outdoor compressor is exposed to weather.*

Clean and wax the cabinet with auto-body polish to protect the finish. Consider making or buying a ventilated protective shed or a tarp of breathable, water-repellent fabric (such as house wrap used in new construction) that you can use in winter and remove in summer. (Be sure there is ventilation to allow moisture to evaporate, or the compressor is liable to rust.) During air-conditioning season the compressor can't be enclosed because free airflow is vital to its functioning.

If severe summer hailstorms are denting the compressor, obtain a "breathable foam" mattress pad of the appropriate size; cut it to the exact size of the top of the compressor, and attach it by any means possible (such as crisscrossing duct tape or electrical wire). Monitor the pad to see how quickly it dries after a storm; if it remains wet after a day of sunshine, remove it, let it dry, and then poke many small holes in it with a barbecue fork or similar instrument before returning it to the compressor top. Continue monitoring, and be prepared to remove

Tip   For guidelines to size an air conditioner, you can obtain a "Cooling Load Estimate Form" from: Publications Department, Association of Home Appliance Manufacturers, 20 North Wacker Drive, Suite 15, Chicago, IL 60606; 312-984-5800. There is a nominal fee for the guidelines.

the pad to dry it out after storms. For more permanent hailproofing, consider building a box-shaped shed, a few inches taller and wider than the compressor, from sheets of windowscreening stitched together with thin wire; attach the mattress pad to the top to keep hailstones from breaking the screen.

▶ Air conditioner doesn't work properly following power outage.

Keep an air conditioner turned off for six hours after a power outage. Before then the compressor can't operate correctly and may be damaged if turned on. If you suspect that power outages occurred while you were asleep, don't use the air conditioner until the power supply has stabilized.

If your thermostat is electronic (setback) with no backup battery, a power outage may have erased the programming (along with that on your VCR and microwave clocks). Reprogram the thermostat.

▶ Air conditioner filter hasn't been cleaned for a month.

Clean it or change it. Filters should be cleaned every 30 days, unless your area has pure mountain air.

▶ Condenser unit makes strange sounds.

If the unit is new, be aware that it is normal for the condenser to make a few odd noises. However, if an older unit starts making strange noises, especially if it also stops cooling properly, call for repairs.

▶ Evaporative air conditioner doesn't cool enough.

Evaporative air conditioners are nicknamed "swamp coolers," but it would be more accurate to call them "desert coolers" because they work best in low humidity. The higher the humidity, the less efficiently they work, and in rain or heavy fog, they're useless.

If the humidity is low and the cooler still doesn't cool enough, check to see if the fan is working (see page 96). If the coils are dirty, clean them (see page 115). Make sure there's an adequate supply and flow of water. If the unit is clogged with deposits, clean it with white vinegar and rinse with water. If it shows signs of corrosion, you may have to have it patched or even replaced.

▶ Evaporative air conditioner emits foul odor.

To kill odor-producing bacteria in the water, mix ¼ cup chlorine bleach with 1 pint water in a spray bottle. Spray the solution onto the cooler, coils, and drain pan. Rinse by spraying them again with plain water. Repeat once a week.

▶ Evaporative air conditioner has squeaking or strange sound.

If the condenser is outside, look in the box to make sure no varmints (such as reptiles or small rodents) are living in it. (Proceed cautiously in rattlesnake country!) If it's infested, evict the squatters and their nests. Look on top; if birds are nesting there, you'll have to either evict them or put up with chirps until they fly south. Next check the alignment and tension of the pulleys; call for professional service if necessary. Lubricate the bearings, following the owner's manual instructions. Clear the fan of any obstructions, and lubricate the fan motor according to the manual. If the unit still makes noises, call for professional repairs.

▶ House has mold, mildew, or musty odors.

Musty, mildewy odors and visible mold are caused by water condensing inside the home. To address the immediate odor problem, scrub visible mildew and mold from walls and shades with mildew-killing or fungicidal cleanser (available at hardware stores) or a mixture of 4 tablespoons chlorine bleach in 1 quart water. Follow all label directions. If drapes smell mildewed, wash or dry-clean them. Be sure all clothing is clean and dry before storing it in closets. Weather and safety permitting, open some windows at night; if you obtain good cross-ventilation by opening windows on opposite sides of the house, the breeze will draw out much moisture. To minimize the problem in the future, install ventilating fans in the kitchen, laundry, and bathrooms (even those with windows); attach them to ducts to discharge moisture to the exterior. Make sure the clothes dryer is ducted to the outdoors. Whenever you paint interior rooms, have a mildewcide additive mixed into the paint by the paint dealer. Arrange furnishings and window coverings to allow maximum sunlight and cross-ventilation.

▶ ... especially in summer.

Moldy smells are especially common during humid summers in "tight" homes that have been caulked, weather-stripped, and/or insulated against heat loss. Improving air circulation should do much to solve the problem. If windows are "sweaty" and water puddles on the sill, open window coverings on bright days to let the sun dry the sills and frames. Thin the foliage of dense tree and shrub growth outside the windows if you don't need it for shade. In warm weather, if

Tip *Unlike auto air conditioners, household air conditioners should never be run when the temperature is below 60° F, as this may seriously damage the compressor.*

Tip *Freezing? Try turning the thermostat to a warmer setting and/or turn it off and substitute a fan at night.*

you have a forced-air furnace in the basement, open or remove the basement door and run the blower continuously for as long as necessary to dry out excess moisture. Also consider installing extra foundation and attic vents to dry out the crawl space and roof.

If your ceiling is at least 10 feet high, consider installing a paddle-style decorative ceiling fan; when run in reverse (counterclockwise), it will force warm air down from the ceiling to dry out the windows and walls. (Also consider, as a larger installation, a whole-house fan, which will drastically cut cooling bills and reduce some heating needs as well.)

To stop humidity in the crawl space from rising into the flooring, lay plastic sheeting (6 mil polyethylene) directly over the dirt. Overlap the sheets by about 6 inches, securing the seams with fabric duct tape. The soil surrounding the home should be graded away from the foundation. Water foundation plantings before 10 a.m. so soil can dry by nightfall, and consider drip irrigation or spot watering rather than wholesale sprinkling. The downspouts from the roof should, optimally, discharge into subsurface drainage pipes; a less costly alternative is a pipe extender (usually a flexible self-coiling tube) that can dump the water several feet away from the house.

▶ ... especially in winter.

In some climates, especially if the house is uninsulated and/or leaky, mildew and musty smells are worst in the winter when there are chilly fogs and winter rains. Dehumidifying crystals (calcium chloride, available at hardware stores and home centers) can absorb some excess moisture in bedrooms, living areas, closets, and storage rooms.

Half-fill open or ventilated containers (such as lidless plastic food containers or large powdered-sugar shakers) with the crystals; use at least 36 ounces of crystals for large rooms, 12 to 24 ounces in closets, and 8 to 12 ounces in mildew-prone drawers and trunks. Monitor the containers weekly to dump water and replace dissolved crystals. Also consider installing louvered doors on closets to minimize clothing mildew. Consider obtaining one or more portable dehumidifiers; inexpensive, low-wattage models that can not only function at cool room temperatures (around 65° F) but also provide a little warmth are most commonly found at boating-supply and RV-supply stores. Air-to-air heat exchangers can also help dehumidify in cold weather, but they are very costly and rather unreliable.

▶ House may have carbon monoxide buildup.

Virtually all combustion-based appliances (furnace, stove, fireplace, vehicles running in garage) vent carbon monoxide. An old furnace is liable to develop a dangerous leak in the heat exchanger, and a well-caulked, weather-stripped, and insulated house is more likely to have a buildup than one that is well ventilated (or simply leaky). Carbon monoxide is not detectable to the senses, but some possible indications are persistently stale or stuffy air, very high indoor humidity and "sweating" windows, accumulations of soot around the fireplace or furnace, and no draft or a hot draft in the chimney. Health symptoms are similar to those of a persistent severe flu.

To minimize gas buildup, have the chimney cleaned and cleared of any blockage every fall; check all indoor flue pipes for obvious cracks

and leaks. Make sure the water heater is properly vented and not leaking. Don't use kerosene heaters, unvented gas heaters, or the kitchen stove for space heating. Replace worn out or loose tailpipes and mufflers on vehicles that park in the garage, and never run a car inside the garage for longer than it takes to start it and move it to the driveway. Have the furnace professionally inspected in late summer every year (especially if it is old), and make sure the furnace has access to enough outside air (consult the owner's manual for recommended ventilating area). Replace furnace filters monthly, and check the color of burner flames on the furnace and gas stove.

You can also buy a carbon monoxide detector. Models are available for prices ranging from a few dollars to $100 and up. The least expensive ones don't have an alarm and must be monitored by observation; more expensive models sound alarms and may combine smoke, carbon monoxide, and gas detection, or may even shut off a malfunctioning furnace.

▶ Kitchen or bathroom lacks exhaust fan.

When buying a fan consider capacity and sound level. Fans are rated by their capacity to exchange air, shown in cubic feet per minute (CFM), and by their noise levels (sones). One formula used by some heating contractors to determine the minimum-sized fan is to multiply the square feet of the room (its length times its breadth) times 2 for the kitchen, and times 1.07 for the bathroom. If ceilings are high—or if you love long showers, have a big household, or cook a lot (or in large quantities)—choose a considerably larger-capacity fan than indicated by the CFM rating.

Tip *Health experts recommend that a home have enough ventilation for one complete air exchange every two hours. Older homes with leaks and drafts accomplish this fairly easily, but newer homes that are tightly insulated and weather-stripped should have a ventilating system to ensure a continuous supply of fresh air.*

A sone is equivalent to the sound level of a quiet refrigerator. Fans range from 1 sone (fairly quiet) up to 4 sones. The lower-sone-rated fans will cost more but will be more pleasant to use and may last longer. Lower-priced units usually have a propeller blade motor. Higher-priced fans usually have a centrifugal (squirrel-cage) motor, which is quieter and more efficient.

The size of the duct work venting the fan is just as important as the size of the fan. Never downsize ducts below the minimum recommended by the fan manufacturer. If in doubt, have a professional size the ducts. Also, in some areas a duct through an unheated attic or wall cavity will have to be insulated.

Ventilating a kitchen

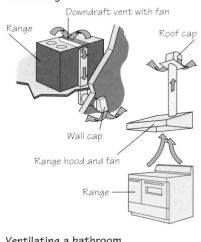

Downdraft vent with fan

Range

Roof cap

Wall cap

Range hood and fan

Range

Ventilating a bathroom

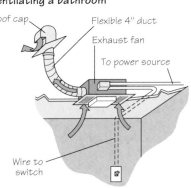

Roof cap

Flexible 4" duct

Exhaust fan

To power source

Wire to switch

▶ *Kitchen fan won't go on.*

If the problem isn't a tripped circuit breaker or blown fuse, see if the fan is getting power. First turn off the circuit breaker that controls the fan. Then find where the fan switch is connected to the house wiring (either at terminals on the switch itself or at connectors inside the fan junction box). If wires are joined by connectors in a junction box, carefully disconnect them and leave the house wires exposed so they are not touching anything. (Don't do anything to house wires if they're connected directly to the switch; you can test for power by touching probes directly to the screw terminals.) Restore power and, with a volt-ohmmeter or neon voltage tester, check the house wires for live voltage by touching one probe to the ground wire, the other to each house wire (or switch terminal), in turn. If no combination of wires indicates live voltage,

the problem is in the house wiring. Call an electrician.

If the wires do have power, the problem is in the switch or fan motor. Turn off the power and test the switch for continuity, either with the volt-ohmmeter or a continuity tester. Touch a probe to each switch terminal. (If there are more than two, make sure one probe touches the "line" terminal, where the house wire is connected.) If the switch shows no continuity in any setting, it is faulty and should be replaced. If it shows continuity, the problem is the fan motor. First make sure that the fan blades turn freely; if not, see if they are hung up on the housing or some other obstacle, or if they have frozen bearings. If not, remove the fan motor. Take it to a small-appliance parts dealer for a replacement. Install the new motor according to manufacturer's directions.

Testing for power

Note: Power on for this test.

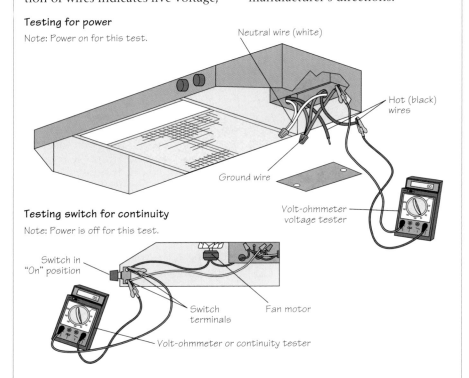

Neutral wire (white)

Hot (black) wires

Ground wire

Volt-ohmmeter voltage tester

Testing switch for continuity

Note: Power is off for this test.

Switch in "On" position

Switch terminals

Fan motor

Volt-ohmmeter or continuity tester

Tip *When choosing a kitchen fan, look for a model that's easy to clean. It should have a removable, washable filter.*

▶ Kitchen vent fan clears air too slowly or not at all.

Check (if you don't know for sure) that the fan is actually connected to a duct for venting; if not, it is just moving the grease and smoke around the room. Then check to see if the fan blade or cage may be loose from the motor shaft, causing it to spin less rapidly than the motor and to lag at the beginning and end of its run. Next check to see whether the exterior vent opening is obstructed. Also check for blockage in the duct by turning on the fan and holding a piece of lightweight paper over the vent opening; if the paper doesn't blow freely, the damper may be shut or there may be an obstruction in the duct.

To inspect the damper, which is usually installed between the fan unit and the first duct fitting, you may have to remove the fan itself to gain access. If so, turn off the circuit breaker for the fan and remove the cover. Remove the filter and wash it in hot soapy water and set it aside to dry out thoroughly. Disconnect the electrical connection: Some models have a plug you can pull; others have connections inside a junction box located next to the fan motor. Then unscrew the mounting bolts and remove the fan unit. The damper flap(s) should move freely with no resistance. If not, look for a bent flap that needs straightening, or stuck pivots that you should clean, straighten, or lubricate.

The fan may be operating below capacity if it's gummed up with grease. Clean every part that you can reach inside the duct, using a grease-dissolving household cleaner. If all this fails, you may need a more powerful unit and possibly a new duct.

▶ Kitchen hood light goes off.

If the bulb is burned out, replace it with an oven bulb to keep it from burning out so frequently. If it still goes out, or won't light, check the switch and all wiring connections. First turn off the circuit breaker that controls the hood. To make sure it's the right one, run the fan before turning off the breaker; it will stop running when you switch off the correct breaker. With power off, inspect the bulb socket, wire leads, wire connectors, and light switch terminals for loose or broken connections; you may have to loosen screws to remove cover plates. If no likely culprits emerge, check the switch for continuity with a volt-ohmmeter or continuity tester (with the power off). Touch one probe to the switch terminal with the house wire connected to it, the other probe to the terminal with a wire leading to the light(s). The tester should indicate continuity when the switch is in the *On* position. If not, replace the switch.

▶ Kitchen hood filter hasn't been cleaned for two months.

Check the filter (and fan blades, if possible) at least once a month (more often if you are a frequent fryer) and clean as needed with a grease-dissolving cleanser or hot sudsy dishwater. If the filter is missing, write down the make and model of the hood or measure the opening to the fan housing and buy a replacement filter at a hardware store, kitchen appliance dealer, or small-appliance parts dealer.

▶ Kitchen hood admits cold draft.

All ducts for kitchen and bathroom fans should be fitted with a damper that shuts automatically when the fan is not running. The easiest type to install when the hood and duct are already in place is at the exterior vent opening. Measure the interior dimensions of the duct where it terminates outside the house (either on the roof or exterior wall) and obtain a vent cap with a back-flow preventer of the same size; some are plastic, others metal. Install it on the exterior according to manufacturer's instructions. Make sure nothing interferes with the automatic operation of the damper, such as a bent duct or loose piece of siding.

▶ Kitchen fan is too noisy.

Make sure all screws and bolts are tight, and oil the fan motor according to manufacturer's directions. Make sure the fan is connected to a duct to the outside (if not, it will be extra noisy as well as useless). If the noise is a whistling sound, the duct may be too long and twisty and may have to be redone. Otherwise, consider upgrading to a fan with a lower sone rating. Also consider changing to the type of powerful fan (such as a restaurant-type fan) that is mounted at the exterior end of the duct, so that most of the noise occurs outdoors.

▶ Kitchen fan has only one speed.

If the kitchen has cross-ventilation or if the fan is sufficiently powerful at that speed, you may be able to get by with only one speed. Otherwise, contact the manufacturer to see if a multispeed switch is available to replace the one-speed switch for the model you have.

Tip *A kitchen fan is essential for removing household pollutants from the home. Normal cooking activities produce not only odors and steam, but in a year's time they can release into the air more than a gallon of vaporized grease.*

▶ Kitchen hood controls are hard to reach.

You can obtain an inexpensive remote-controlled device from a housewares or building-supply store, or from many housewares mail-order catalogs. These devices consist of a receiver unit that you install between the fan and power source, and a remote-controlled sending unit that you place wherever it is convenient to use. To connect, simply unplug the fan from its receptacle, plug the receiver unit into the receptacle instead, and plug the fan into the receiver unit. Turn the fan settings to those you use most often, and use the remote-controlled device to turn the system on and off.

▶ Kitchen hood gets in the way of cooking.

Unfortunately, you'll probably have to remove the hood and raise it, or replace it with one that is more functional. Otherwise, if the hood is built into the wall behind the stove and can't be moved, consider moving the stove out an inch or so. If it won't move because it is attached to rigid gas pipes, have the pipes replaced with a flexible connector and shutoff valve; it's safer as well as more convenient.

▶ Bathroom walls and ceiling have moisture.

Hot, moist air does considerable damage to bathrooms; it accelerates the deterioration of wallcoverings, wallboard, ceiling, insulation, and framing, and fosters the growth of mildew. The best solution to the problem is a ventilating fan, even if the bathroom has an openable window. An easier but less effective remedy for severe moisture is a de-humidifier. Small, low-priced, low-wattage dehumidifiers (including standing or hanging models) suitable for bathrooms may be found at boating-supply and RV-supply stores and in some housewares mail-order catalogs. Other partial remedies include bathing with the door or window open, wiping down the walls after each shower, switching to shower curtains made of a breathable fabric (such as a house-wrap used in home construction), using a small stand-alone fan, and using a small electric heater recommended for bathrooms.

If you already have an exhaust fan, it may not be drawing properly. If the fan has a flapper valve that opens when the fan is on, check to see whether the valve indeed opens. Check that the duct is free of obstructions. If the fan is operating properly, it may not be powerful enough to draw the air out of the room; consider upgrading. Alternately, let the existing fan run for 10 minutes or so after you have left the bathroom, with the door open so that dry air can enter the room. (You can install a timer switch to turn it off automatically.)

▶ Bathroom fan is vented to attic and not to outside.

A bathroom fan duct that terminates in the attic does considerable harm; it sends moisture into the attic, which can produce wet insulation and rot the ceiling and rafters. Attic venting also diminishes the ability of the fan to draw in fresh air and rid the bathroom of moisture. The fan should preferably be vented through the roof. Cut a 4-inch-diameter hole through the roof sheathing and roofing and install a roof cap (with a back-flow preventer) over it. Tuck the cap flange under the shingles above it (you may have to remove nails) and lap it over the shingles below it. Connect the fan duct to the bottom of the cap. If the duct is too short, buy a length of the same diameter (3- or 4-inch) flexible aluminum duct and join it to the old duct by slipping the ends of both ducts over a short length of rigid aluminum duct tubing of the same diameter. Secure each end with a hose clamp. If a roof termination is impossible, install a wall cap (with a back-flow preventer) on an exterior wall (except for one on a property line) and connect the duct to it.

Installing a roof cap

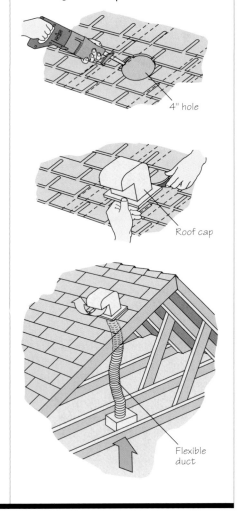

4" hole

Roof cap

Flexible duct

Tip *A downdraft kitchen ventilating system is about 75 percent effective in removing pollutants from the air that are caused by normal cooking. A traditional updraft system should remove 100 percent.*

▶ Bathroom fan duct admits cold air into room.

First look for gaps between the fan housing and the ceiling cutout. Caulk with a bead of silicone sealant along the edge of the opening. Buy a roof- or wall-mounted duct cap with a back-flow preventer and install it where the duct terminates outside. If you live where winters are very cold, consider switching to a type of ventilating fan with an insulated, motorized exhaust hood that opens only when the fan is on. Various models are available, some with the fan blower installed in the hood for quieter operation.

Installing an insulated ventilating hood

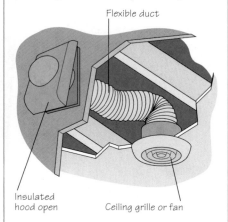

Flexible duct

Insulated hood open

Ceiling grille or fan

▶ Bathroom ceiling has mildew even though fan is always used.

Scrub the existing mildew with a mildewcide liquid or spray cleaner, or with a solution of 4 tablespoons chlorine bleach in 1 quart water. Follow all label precautions. If the infestation is severe, strip the paint before washing, and repaint with a mildew-retarding oil-based paint. To prevent future growth, see opposite page. The problem may

be especially acute if the bathtub or shower is in a corner; you may need a stronger fan to draw all the air out of the room, or you may have to leave the fan on longer, open the door during showers, or add a small dehumidifier to the room.

▶ Attic or roof fan doesn't come on.

These fans are controlled by automatic switches that activate the fan when the attic temperature reaches a certain point, or by timers for automatic operation. There should also be a manual switch—either in the attic or downstairs in the house somewhere—that controls power to the fan unit.

First check that the fuse or circuit breaker for the fan has not blown or tripped, then make sure the manual switch is on. Next be certain that the conditions activating the fan are met (right time or temperature). If the fan still does not come on, turn off the circuit breaker for the fan and look for obstructions or a broken belt.

Next test the wiring for power to the fan; expose the terminals or wires where the house wiring is connected to the fan unit, make sure that any wires you disconnect are not touching anything else, and restore power. With a voltage tester or volt-ohmmeter, carefully touch one probe to a ground wire and the other to the hot (black) wire of the house wiring (be sure the manual switch is on). If the tester shows no power for this wire or any other, the problem is in the wiring; call an electrician. If the tester shows power, the problem is in the switch or the

fan motor. The fan will have either a timer switch or a temperature switch. Test either switch by turning off power and using a continuity tester or a volt-ohmmeter (set for 4x1 ohms resistance). For a timer, adjust the clock so it shows time within the set limits and touch the tester probes to both power terminals. For testing the temperature switch, the temperature should be above the lower limit of the switch (usually around 90° F; choose a hot day or remove the switch and heat it up in a frying pan to make sure; see page 110). If either switch does not show continuity, replace it. If it does show continuity, the problem may be the fan safety switch or fan motor. Test the safety switch for continuity to see if the contacts are stuck open. It it's not faulty (needing replacement) the problem is probably the fan motor. Remove it and buy an exact replacement motor at a small-appliance parts dealer or fan specialty store.

▶ Attic fan hasn't been cleaned for six months.

Attics are often dusty; accumulated dust on the fan could impair its operation. Turn off the power to the fan and wash it with a sponge and warm water, cleaning every part that you can reach.

▶ Attic fan has no safety switch.

Should a fire break out, an attic fan that has no switch to cut off power at high temperatures (200° F) can feed the flames with air. Add-on safety switches are inexpensive. To install one, place a junction box along the power wires near the fan to house the switch connections. Splice the switch into the hot (black) wire between the fan thermostat and the power source.

Tip   *The cost of electricity for running an attic fan is about one-tenth the cost of running a central air conditioner. A fan doesn't replace the need for air-conditioning—at least for the hottest days—but it reduces the cooling load for an air conditioner significantly.*

▶ Whole-house fan hasn't been inspected for a year.

A whole-house fan is a powerful machine that should be inspected and serviced at least once a year. If you do it yourself, clean the fan blades and louvers, check the fan belt tension, tighten loose screws and bolts, and lubricate the bearings, motor housing, and fan as directed by the manufacturer. While you're at it, clean all the vent screens in the attic to increase potential airflow.

Servicing a whole-house fan

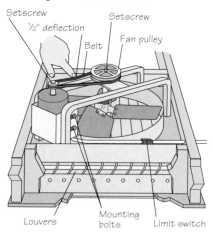

Setscrew
Setscrew
½" deflection
Belt
Fan pulley
Louvers
Mounting bolts
Limit switch

▶ Ceiling fan doesn't circulate air properly.

Check the condition of the paddle blades; repair any obvious damage. Some fans have blades with adjustable pitch; follow manufacturer's directions to slant them properly. If the fan is a model with a reverse switch, change the rotation of the blades with the change of seasons. The fan should direct air downward in summer to create a breeze and upward in winter to move the warm air from the ceiling.

▶ Ceiling paddle fan wobbles or is working loose from ceiling box.

Correct the immediate problem by turning off the circuit breaker for the fan and tightening all screws and bolts that connect the fan to the ceiling box. Check to see that the box itself is not loose and that it is heavy enough to meet the fan manufacturer's recommendations; if not, replace it with a stronger box. Then inspect the fan blades and observe operation at a slow speed to see if they wobble due to loose screws, missing hardware, or unevenly balanced paddles. Make necessary corrections (for example, replace a nicked paddle with a new one). If the fan still wobbles, the problem may be a bent shaft or worn shaft bearing in the motor. Have it professionally repaired.

▶ Ceiling box for paddle fan is working loose from ceiling.

Electrical boxes for paddle fans have stricter requirements for reinforcement than other ceiling electrical boxes. If the box is loose, remove it entirely and replace it with a reinforced box approved for ceiling fans. First turn off the circuit breaker for the fan and disconnect it from the box (you will need a helper to support the fan while you disconnect the wires). Then test all wires in the box with a voltage tester to be sure the power is off. If you have access to the box from the attic, proceed from there. Otherwise, to remove wires from the box and the box itself you will have to

cut away some of the ceiling. If so, cut it back to the centers of the joists on either side of the box so you will have framing for attaching a wallboard patch. Secure the bracket for the new box to each joist with two 1¼-inch wallboard screws (nailing may disturb the ceiling); slide the box into position, and secure it in place by tightening the screw clamp. Patch the ceiling opening (if applicable) and install the fan. Secure the holding strap to the box with two screws and the central lug provided with the box; then connect the wires and screw the fan canopy to the holding strap.

Installing a new ceiling box

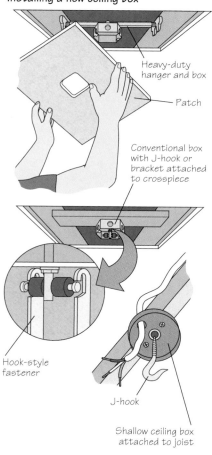

Heavy-duty hanger and box
Patch
Conventional box with J-hook or bracket attached to crosspiece
Hook-style fastener
J-hook
Shallow ceiling box attached to joist

Tip It's easy to think of ceiling paddle fans as cooling devices, but they serve a useful function during cold weather, too. Running the fan in reverse mode forces air upward toward the ceiling and down the surrounding walls. This distributes the heat more evenly around the room and prevents condensation from building up on the inside of windows.

▶ Range or cooktop controls are within child's reach.

Until the child is old enough to learn not to touch the controls, you can disable the range when you're not actually using it: For any type of range, pop the control knobs off and keep them in a handy yet childproof place; for a gas range with electronic ignition, unplug the range; for a 240-volt electric range, turn off the circuit breaker. Also consider installing a childproof shield (usually heatproof plastic, and available at some range dealers, children's furnishings stores, and housewares mail-order catalogs) at the front of the cooktop to keep the toddler from being able to touch pots or flames on the range.

▶ Range controls are hard to turn.

Grease may be gumming up the knobs and valves. Pop off the knobs by tugging them outward. (You may need to slip a dishcloth behind the knob to help you pull it off.) Soak knobs in warm water with a strong, grease-cutting detergent; then ream them out with wet, soapy pipe cleaners and rinse well. While knobs are off, spray the parts of the valves that are reachable with spray-on no-rinse cleanser and rub them clean with paper towels or a small, sturdy brush. Return the knobs to the rods. If this isn't sufficient, clean the valves themselves. Turn off the gas and unplug the range (the knobs may have electronic-ignition controls). Take the valves apart with two wrenches and clean them with steel wool and paint thinner. Lubricate them with a high-quality long-term lubricant, and then reassemble.

If controls are hard to turn because they're hard to grip, replace them. Find new knobs at an appliance parts dealer or large building-supply store. Bring an old knob with you to make sure the new knobs will fit.

▶ Gas burners with electronic ignition don't light.

If you have a modern range with electronic ignition (no pilot light; just a clicking sound before the burner lights), check that the stove is plugged securely into the electrical receptacle and that the circuit breaker isn't tripped or the fuse blown. Try turning on a burner and holding a lighted kitchen match to it. If it doesn't light, the stove is probably not receiving gas. Check the gas shutoff valve to make sure it's on. (The valve may be located under the cooktop, at the bottom of the cabinet, or behind the stove. When the handle is in line with the pipe, the valve is open; at right angles, it's closed.) You can verify the lack of gas by *carefully* loosening the gas connection to the stove only slightly, first making sure there are no open flames nearby (such as a cigarette or pilot light). If you hear no hiss and smell no gas, there's no gas supply. Retighten the connection and call the gas company. If you do smell gas, *immediately* tighten the connection. The problem is most likely in the range. Call for professional service.

If the burner will light with a match, check that the igniter is working: Remove the range top (after taking off the grates), turn off the lights, and turn on a burner. If you don't hear clicking and don't see sparks, the igniter is faulty and needs to be replaced. If the igniter sparks, the pilot light electrode may be dirty. To clean it, unplug the range and remove the metal bridge

or cover from above the pilot electrode (a small pointed metal rod between the tubes that lead to the burners). Clean the electrode with a soft cloth or small brush. If this doesn't work, call for professional service.

Cleaning electronic-ignition electrode

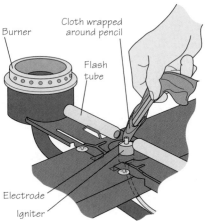

Burner
Cloth wrapped around pencil
Flash tube
Electrode
Igniter

▶ Gas burners with pilot don't light.

First check to see if the pilot light is on. It may be hidden under the range top; remove the grates and lift it up like a car hood. Some cooktops have one central pilot light for all burners, others have a pilot for each burner. If the pilot light is out and won't relight when you hold a match to it, look for the pilot adjusting screw along the tube that feeds gas to the pilot, near the gas manifold, and rotate it with a screwdriver while holding a match to the pilot. If the pilot still won't light, the cooktop may not be receiving gas (see above). If there is gas, the pilot orifice may be clogged. Clean the pilot and its

Tip *Electronic, or "pilotless," ignitions have replaced standing pilot lights in new ranges and cooktops. Because they don't require a continuously burning pilot flame, they save energy. Electronic ignitions also provide a safety factor: They reignite a burner if the flame is blown out accidentally. In addition, they reduce heat buildup in the appliance, which is a welcome relief on hot days.*

cover, using a small copper wire or a pipe cleaner for the pilot; clear the pilot orifice with a straight pin or sewing needle (the actual orifice may be at the end of a feeder tube, not where the flame occurs). If the pilot still won't light, call for professional repairs.

If the pilot is lit and burners won't light, check the flash tubes radiating from it to each burner, making sure each tube is aligned in the slots or tabs that hold it in place (be careful—they may be hot). If the burner still won't light, you may need to increase the flame on the pilot; turn the pilot adjusting screw until the flame is robust. If you are successful, readjust the pilot to the lowest flame required for lighting the burners. If the burners won't light, try turning on one burner and lighting it with a match. If it lights, check the flash tube between it and the pilot again for misalignment or obstructions. If that's not the problem, call a repair technician.

Adjusting pilot

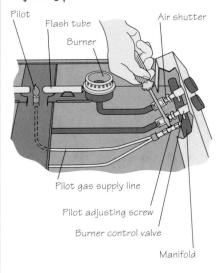

Pilot
Flash tube
Burner
Air shutter
Pilot gas supply line
Pilot adjusting screw
Burner control valve
Manifold

▶ One burner on gas range won't light.

Remove the range top. Check the flash tube (the tube leading from the pilot light to the burner). It may be knocked askew, so that gas can't reach the burner; jiggle it into place so slots, tabs, or other "feet" are aligned (be careful—it may be hot). Check it for obstructions, clear out any blockage with a pencil or pipe cleaner (depending on the diameter of the tube), and scrub the tube with a strong grease-cutting detergent. If it's too hard to remove from the stove, try reaming it out in place with a cleanser-soaked pipe cleaner or paper towel wrapped tightly around a pencil. If the burner still won't light, it may not be receiving gas due to clogged orifices or a faulty control valve. Clean out any clogs (see right). If that doesn't help, call a technician.

▶ Gas pilot light keeps going out.

The pilot flame is probably too low. Trace the gas supply tube running from the pilot light to the gas manifold (pipe with branches to burners); there should be an adjusting screw along the supply tube. Use a screwdriver to adjust the height of the pilot flame; the adjusting device is a cock (rotates without unscrewing) so you can turn it either way. Also check for drafts that may be blowing out the pilot: open windows, an open entryway without a curtain, frequently slammed doors, or a kitchen fan without a backdraft preventer.

▶ Gas burner has weak or uneven flame.

The burner is probably clogged with spilled food or grease. Remove the range top. If the burner has a removable cap, wash the cap in hot water and a grease-cutting detergent; rinse well, dry, and replace. If not, use pipe cleaners dipped in a no-rinse grease-cutting cleanser to ream out all the flame holes in the burner. If this does not clean out the grease sufficiently, lift out the burner assembly (removing any retaining screws from the support, if necessary) and wash it in hot sudsy water. Rinse well, immediately wipe dry, and use a hair dryer to dry the holes. If it still burns weakly, the control valve may be defective. Call a technician.

▶ Gas burners aren't hot enough.

Assuming the burners have been cleaned (see above), look at the flames themselves. They should be steady, tapered, and mainly blue with a little orange at the tip. If the flames are short and flat, too orange or yellow, or all-blue and roaring, the mixture of air to gas is incorrect. To adjust the gas/air mixture, look for an air shutter below each burner. Loosen the shutter retainer screw and open or close the shutter until the flame is steady, shapely, and blue with orange at the tip. Wear an oven mitt and be prepared to turn off gas to the burner should it go out suddenly while you are

Tip *The maximum output of individual burners for gas ranges and cooktops, measured in BTUs, varies from around 5,000 for small burners to 15,000 for burners on commercial-style ranges for residential use. Most older cooktops and range tops have two burners rated at 6,000 or 7,000 BTUs, and two burners rated around 9,000 BTUs. Now, it is more common for cooktops to have two burners rated at 8,000 or 9,000 BTUs and two at 11,000 or 12,000 BTUs.*

adjusting it. On some cooktops you can also adjust gas flow to each burner. If the gas flow is not already at maximum, increase flow by turning the adjusting nut located where the gas supply line for the burner branches off from the manifold.

If the burner flames grow weak only when the oven or broiler is on (or is set to a high temperature), the gas pipes in the house may not be sized correctly. Have a qualified plumber or heating specialist check them. If the pipes are not the problem, the range does not have a high enough BTU (heating capacity) rating to support both the stovetop and the oven at once. The only solutions are to replace the range with one that has a higher BTU rating, or to use an auxiliary appliance (such as a microwave oven or other electric cooker) in place of the oven, broiler, or a burner. Also consider obtaining a heat-powered oven convection fan to increase the efficiency of the oven so you can bake or roast more quickly or at a lower temperature.

Adjusting the burner air shutter

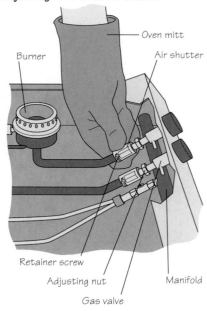

▶ *Electric burner heats up only halfway or not at all.*

First see if the burner element is defective. Turn off power to the range. Slightly raise the edge of the burner element; pull it straight out. Switch it with another element of the same size that works, restore power, and turn on the burner. If there isn't another burner to switch it with, test it with a continuity tester or volt-ohmmeter (set at 4×1 ohms resistance). First touch the probes to the terminals to make sure current flows through the coil. Then touch the probes to each terminal and the outer shell of its coil, in turn; current should *not* flow.

If the suspect element does not test or work properly, buy a new one to replace it. If it does, the

problem may be a faulty receptacle in the original burner cavity. Turn off power to the range, remove the drip pan from the defective burner, and locate the receptacle. Remove the bracket screw and pull the receptacle out (the wires will still be attached). If it's caked with crud, clean it off; use an emery board or sandpaper to clear the slots. If the receptacle is broken or the wires charred, replace it; disconnect the wires from the terminal screws in the back of the receptacle and take the old one to an appliance parts dealer for an exact replacement (bring the burner element too). If the wires are burned or the burner still doesn't work, call a technician.

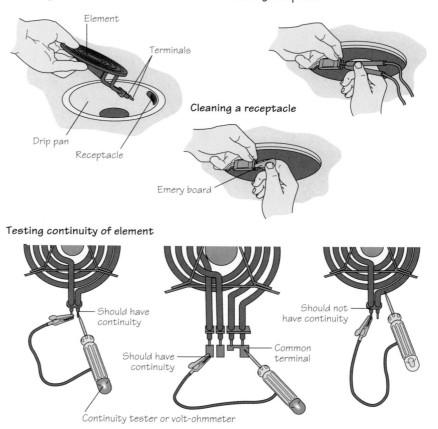

Removing a burner element

Testing receptacle

Cleaning a receptacle

Testing continuity of element

Tip *When using a volt-ohmmeter (sometimes called a multitester) always recalibrate the zero setting before testing continuity. Set the selector dial for 4×1 ohms resistance, and touch the probes together. The electricity should flow effortlessly through the probes, with no resistance, yielding a 0 reading on the ohms scale. If the needle doesn't rest at the 0 mark, turn the ohms adjusting knob until it does. Now the tester is ready to use.*

► Electric range is dead; nothing works.

Check that there's electric power: Is the range plugged in? Have the circuit breakers been tripped or the fuses blown? Electric ranges are 240-volt and receive service from a pair of fuses or circuit breakers (which have their handles linked together). With some electrical installations the circuit breaker or fuse block for the range may be located with the main electrical disconnecting device, not in the circuit-breaker panel. If the range has a pull-out fuse block with cartridge fuses in it, the only way to check if they have blown is to test them. Pull out the fuse block, remove the cartridge fuses, and touch the probes of a continuity tester (or volt-ohmmeter set for R×1 ohms resistance) to each end of the fuse. If the stove is receiving power but won't work, call for service. At 240 volts, a shock can be fatal.

► Electric burner has only one temperature—hot!

The switch that controls the electricity to the burner is probably stuck in the full-heat position and should be replaced by a technician.

► Electric self-venting range doesn't have hookup for duct.

No duct hookup or connection is required. The hood and blower on the ceiling (or wall) should take care of the oven as well as the cooktop exhaust. A down-draft range, on the other hand, which has a vent and blower mounted on the cooktop, must be connected to a duct. Such ranges are usually ducted through the floor or out the lower part of the wall behind the range.

► Gas oven burner won't light.

First make sure that the unit is receiving gas: Light a burner on the cooktop; if it won't go on, check the gas shutoff valve. (See page 123.) If no gas is reaching the range, call the gas company.

If the oven has electronic ignition, make sure it's plugged in and receiving power. (Try a burner on the cooktop, or a small appliance plugged into the same receptacle as the range.) Local fluctuations in electric power can briefly disable electronic ignitions; try again in a few minutes. If you don't hear any clicking when you turn on the oven, or if there's a lot of clicking followed by silence (and still no burner ignition), the igniter is broken and needs to be replaced. Some oven igniters are sparkless and don't make a clicking sound; you can tell if they are working because they glow red-hot.

If the oven has a gas pilot light, the pilot has probably gone out. The oven pilot is often at the bottom rear; you'll have to pull out the broiler "drawer" to reach it. Look for a red reset button; it should be near the front, but if it's back near the pilot light, you'll need a long pole, such as a broom handle, to reach it. Have some long fireplace or barbecue matches and a set of tongs or long-handled pliers handy. Kneeling by the open oven door, light the match (and keep it lit) and grasp it in the tongs or pliers. Keeping your head out of the oven to protect hair and eyelashes, press the red button with one hand (or with the broom handle) while with the other you apply the lighted match to the oven pilot until it lights. This may take several tries; persist. Once the pilot is on, the burner should light. If the pilot light goes out frequently, it may be set too low. Look for a pilot

adjusting screw for the oven pilot under the range top (not all ranges have one). With a screwdriver, set the screw for a higher flame.

If the pilot works but the burner still won't go on, call a technician.

Checking sparkless igniter

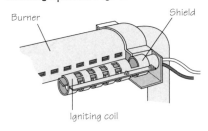

Adjusting oven pilot flame

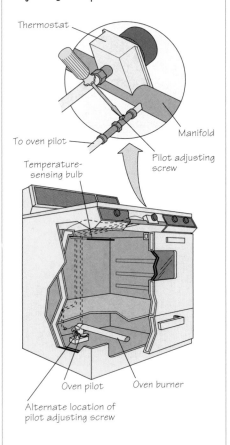

Tip *Caution: Whenever you work on a gas appliance, be sure to turn off the gas supply to the appliance before disassembling any tubes, valves, or lines. Reassemble the components with pipe joint compound at all connections, and before igniting the pilot test the unit for leaks by spraying the connections with soapy water.*

▶ **Gas broiler won't light.**

The thermocouple (a sensor device attached to the pilot light that prevents gas flow unless the pilot is on) may be dirty, out of place, or broken. If you can reach it, you may be able to clean it and reposition it. (see page 98). Otherwise, have a technician repair or replace it.

▶ **Gas broiler flame is too weak.**

If the broiler heats unevenly or poorly, grease spatters may have clogged many of the burner ports. Turn off gas to the appliance to extinguish the pilot and let it cool. If possible, remove the burner unit to clean it: Unscrew the brackets that hold it in place and gently place it on a work surface covered with newspapers. Ream out all the burner ports with pipe cleaners and clean the surface. If necessary, scrub it with a no-rinse household cleaner and dry it immediately; dry out the portholes with a hair dryer. If you can't remove the burner, clear the holes with pipe cleaners.

▶ **Gas oven light doesn't work.**

Make sure the stove is receiving electricity. Replace the bulb with an oven-rated type designed to withstand high temperatures (available in most supermarkets). Turn off power to the oven at the fuse or circuit-breaker panel, and let the bulb and its housing cool before beginning to work. If the bulb has a cover, remove it carefully; replace the bulb and restore the cover. Restore power and try turning on the bulb again. If this fails, the door switch is defective. Turn off power, open the oven door, and remove the switch by gently prying it out from the door frame (use a screwdriver on each side). Disconnect the wires and test the switch by touching each probe of a continuity

tester or volt-ohmmeter to the switch terminals. It should have continuity when you push in the switch button. If it does not, replace the switch. If the light still doesn't work, call a technician.

Removing an oven light switch

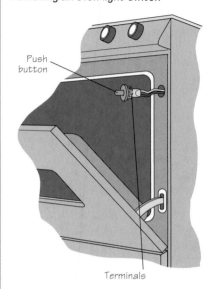

Push button

Terminals

▶ **Gas oven vents directly into the room.**

Old-fashioned woodburner and trashburner ovens had flue pipes, but modern gas and electric ovens don't need them. Many of them vent to the cooktop, which in turn is vented by the hood and blower unit. In urban areas many residences (especially older multifamily rental properties) have no stove hoods, vent fans, or duct work, and hence only vent into the kitchen; in this situation, a window fan set to exhaust (and cleaned frequently) can do much to clear the air.

▶ **Gas oven doesn't hold its set temperature.**

If the oven cools down (even when the door has not been opened), inspect the door gasket. If the gasket is worn, torn, or cracked, replace it. In some models you can just pull it off and attach a new one. In others you'll need a repair person to loosen the oven liner or remove the door.

If the oven overheats consistently, check if it has an exhaust vent at the back of the cooktop or under one of the cooktop burners. Clear any obstructions from the vent, and make sure that the hole in the stovetop reflector pan is aligned with the hole of the vent.

The thermostat may need to be recalibrated, the temperature sensor may need replacing, or the oven may have lost insulation (due to rodents tearing it out for their nests). In such events, call for professional repairs.

▶ **Gas oven thermostat does not maintain set temperature.**

The control knob that governs the oven thermostat may have drifted slightly into a setting that's too high or too low. You can adjust the control knob, although it may take several tries over several days to get it precisely right.

First obtain a high-quality oven thermometer (or better yet, a precise temperature tester, available at appliance parts stores), place it in the middle of the center oven rack, and record what temperature the oven reaches after 20 minutes at each of several temperature settings. (You'll probably have to let the oven cool and start over again to get a full and accurate range of readings.) The temperature regulator is a complicated spring-loaded device located behind the oven

Tip   *For energy efficiency choose a convection oven, which uses a fan to blow heat over the food. Such ovens use about one-third less energy than conventional ovens.*

SOLVING MECHANICAL PROBLEMS

control knob. Remove the knob but do *not* remove the control (it's difficult to reassemble once the spring has sprung). In some ovens there will be a pointer and notches on the back of the knob; by moving the pointer a notch, you'll change the oven temperature 10° F. (You may have to loosen screws on the back of the knob, or use a screwdriver to lift the pointer slightly, before you can move the pointer.) On other ovens there'll be nothing on the back of the knob, but you'll see an adjusting screw at the front of the control; use a screwdriver to move it just a hair. Now turn on the oven again and see what temperature it reaches after 20 minutes at a moderate setting (350° F). Try it again at higher and lower settings. Be prepared to make several trial-and-error attempts before the oven performs precisely as desired.

If altering the temperature regulator fails, the oven thermostat may have to be replaced or recalibrated professionally.

Adjusting oven temperature regulator

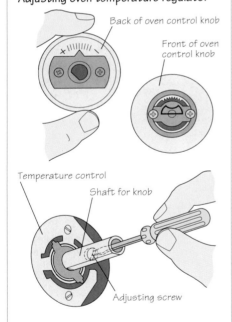

▶ Gas oven sweats.

Check for a worn-out gasket and replace it (see page 127).

▶ Baked food is often burned or soggy.

If food is often burned, the oven is probably running hot; if soggy, it's running cool. Obtain a high-quality oven thermometer, place it in the middle of the center rack, and compare the temperature to that of the setting to verify. Adjust the control knob (see page 127) and/or replace or recalibrate the thermostat (or call a technician to do so). Until the oven is repaired, if it is running cool, bake food at the back and well to the side on a high rack; if oven is too hot, use a low rack and place food in the center front area. Consider obtaining a heat-activated convection fan to keep the air circulating evenly in the oven and eliminate hot and cool spots.

▶ Baked food tastes awful.

Assuming neither the cook nor the recipe is at fault, it's probably residue from a caustic oven cleaner turning to vapor and settling on the food. With oven turned off, fill a spray bottle with hot water and spray all over the oven (including broiler); wipe with clean rags or paper towels. Heat the oven to 400° to 450° F and then open the door. If an unpleasant smell persists, let the oven cool, wash it with hot water again. Refill the spray bottle with bottled unsweetened lemon juice (or vinegar) and spray and wipe once more. Consider switching to a lye-free oven-cleaning product in which the active element is baking soda, vinegar, or citrus oil.

▶ Electric oven bakes food unevenly.

There may not be sufficient air circulation inside the oven. Consider installing a heat-activated portable convection fan or a permanent convection fan unit.

▶ Electric oven consistently overbakes or underbakes food.

The temperature regulator is no longer accurate. Turn off power at the circuit breaker and detach the oven control knob. You may be able to adjust the temperature regulator (see page 127). If not, the temperature regulator will have to be replaced; call a technician.

▶ Electric oven light doesn't work.

Assuming that the oven is getting power, the bulb may be loose or burned out. Obtain an oven-safe appliance bulb (available at supermarkets). Turn off power to the oven at the fuse or circuit-breaker panel, and let the bulb and its housing cool before beginning work. If the bulb has a cover, remove it carefully. Replace the bulb and return the cover. Restore power and try turning on the bulb again. If this fails, the problem may be the switch (see page 127).

▶ Automatic oven-cleaning feature doesn't work.

It's likely that either the temperature regulator is broken or the oven door latch is broken (see opposite page). Both should be professionally repaired, especially the latter: Don't try to overcome the door-lock mechanism to force the oven to clean itself, because the influx of air into the oven when the temperature is at flash point (550° F) can

Tip *The power for an electric oven is controlled by a separate circuit breaker. Because the oven is a 240-volt appliance, it has a double breaker consisting of two 120-volt breakers connected together.*

cause a flaming explosion of vaporized grease.

If you decide to ignore the self-cleaning feature for the present, when you clean the oven by hand make sure to rinse off all traces of oven cleaner, because chemical residues will damage the porcelain if you later decide to have the self-cleaning feature repaired. Choose a noncaustic, kitchen-safe type of cleaner (for example, one based on citrus oils, vinegar, or baking soda rather than lye) to minimize the danger of chemical residue.

▶ Electric oven door latch is broken.

Check the manufacturer's directions for the oven to see if you can correct the problem. If not, call for professional repairs; along with the lock itself, the fault could lie in the front door-lock switch or lock solenoid.

▶ Electric oven or broiler doesn't work.

First make sure power is on for the oven (see page 126). Next check the burner element for the oven or (if different) the broiler. To test the element, turn off power to the oven at the circuit-breaker or fuse panel, and then carefully remove the element according to manufacturer's directions. Test the element for continuity by removing the wires and, with a volt-ohmmeter (set for 4×1 ohms resistance) or a continuity tester, holding a probe to each terminal of the element. If there is no continuity, it is defective. If there *is* continuity between one terminal and the outer covering of the element, the element has a short circuit and should be replaced. Inspect the wires; if they're burned, call for

professional repairs. If the element and wires are in good condition, the thermostat control is defective and will have to be repaired or replaced.

Removing an oven heating element

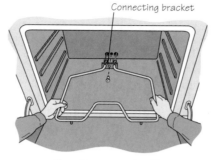

Connecting bracket

Note: Power must be off.

Testing an oven heating element

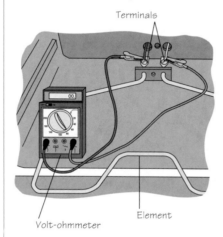

Terminals

Volt-ohmmeter

Element

▶ Microwave oven has lingering odor from burned food.

Pour a cup of water into an oven-proof bowl and add 1 tablespoon of lemon juice. Place in the microwave and bring to a boil at the highest setting. Lower the temperature to "simmer" (or equivalent) and lightly boil for three minutes. Remove the cup and wipe dry the inside and door of the microwave. If this doesn't remove the odor, repeat the process.

▶ Microwave oven heats intermittently.

The air vents may be blocked, causing the oven to overheat and turn off. Check the owner's manual for locations of the air vents, and (with the unit unplugged) inspect them and clean them if clogged. Let the oven cool one hour, then try again. If this doesn't work, the thermal cutout switch may be defective. Have it professionally repaired, assuming that the estimated repair cost is markedly less than that of a new machine.

▶ Microwave oven takes longer to cook than cookbook says.

Various models of microwaves have different wattages. The less expensive models usually have a lower wattage than higher-priced ones. This means that foods cook more slowly or require a higher setting. Aside from defrosting or keeping hot foods warm, routinely use the highest setting for cooking.

If the microwave is operating on the same circuit with any other appliance, cooking time will increase when the other appliance is also in use. If you are remodeling your kitchen, provide a dedicated circuit for the microwave oven (not because it draws so much power, but to avoid having other appliances interfere with its operation). Fluctuations in local voltage will also prolong cooking time.

Tip   *Just how does a microwave work? A transformer steps up 120-volt house current into high-voltage current, which enters a magnetron (electronic tube) that converts it to electromagnetic waves. These waves are guided into the oven compartment, where a fanlike stirrer at the top spins and bounces them around. Another fan keeps the magnetron cool. The waves agitate molecules in the food, causing friction that produces heat.*

SOLVING MECHANICAL PROBLEMS

▶ Microwave oven needs installing over a range.

A combination microwave oven and exhaust hood will let you exhaust kitchen odors while having all your cooking appliances in a single area. These combinations, which cost considerably more than standard microwaves, can either vent back into the kitchen or connect to the existing duct work. The steps you will need to take to install them are: removing the existing range exhaust hood; installing a ventilating duct, if required; running a new 20-amp electrical line that places the microwave on its own circuit (or having an electrician do this); and installing the new unit.

Disconnect the power and remove the old range hood before buying the new unit so you can measure the distance from the wall to the center of the exhaust hood and choose a model with similar dimensions.

▶ Microwave oven may be leaking radiation.

There are several inexpensive microwave radiation detectors on the market (including one with magnetic backing that you can leave attached to the side of the unit). To use a detector, turn on the oven and move the probe over the vents, the door, and the door cracks. If radiation is leaking, the probe will glow bright red. Have a leaking unit repaired professionally or replace it.

▶ Microwave oven emits sparks.

See whether grease has collected on the heads of the screws that hold a shelf. If so, wash the screws with warm soapy water, using a sponge or dishcloth. Metal (or metal-trimmed) containers or utensils, including dishware trimmed with gold, silver, platinum, or cobalt blue, shouldn't be used in the microwave; nor should plastic-coated metal bag ties. A temperature probe will cause sparks if it's plugged into the microwave but not inserted into food. And if the unit has a metal cooking rack, it will cause sparks if it's not firmly hooked into place or if it's left on the oven floor while the unit is operating.

If none of these possibilities is causing the problem, have the machine serviced professionally; however, get an estimate for repair costs first, as a new microwave may cost little more.

Identifying components of a microwave oven

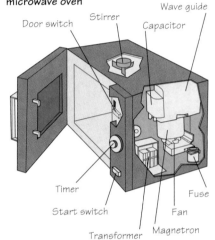

Door switch · Stirrer · Wave guide · Capacitor · Timer · Start switch · Transformer · Fan · Magnetron · Fuse

▶ Dishes don't get dry.

Make sure the *Power Dry* (or *Hot Dry*) button is fully depressed and is not popping out again. If machine is very heavily loaded or is loaded incorrectly, some items may not dry. (Check the owner's manual for proper loading.) Open door immediately after drying cycle is complete, to vent any remaining water vapor before it settles onto the dishes again. If all this fails, call for service.

▶ Dishwasher is spewing suds.

When suds erupt from all orifices, immediately turn off the dishwasher, leaving its door shut. You can now take as much time as you need to clean the foam from the floor and sink cabinet before proceeding further. Dishwashers can cope only with the nonsudsing dishwasher detergents designed for them. Eruptions occur whenever even a small amount of a foaming cleaner (such as regular dishwashing liquid, laundry detergent, or even many types of general-purpose household cleaners) gets into a dishwasher. This is one of the most common reasons for service calls; fortunately, the repair is easy.

Turn off the water supply to the dishwasher; then turn the unit on again (still without opening the door), and immediately set it to the *Drain* or *Exhaust* portion of the cycle. (If there's no specific *Drain* button, rotate the timer dial until you can hear draining noises or, in a portable model, can see the exhaust; normally, this occurs during the last minute or so before the drying cycle begins). Let the unit drain completely, turn it off, and remove the dishes. The bottom of the machine will be filled with suds. Remove the bottom basket and scoop out and discard as much foam as possible. To purge the remainder, start the dishwasher again (still without water), immediately setting it to *Drain*. Once draining is complete, fast-forward to *Off*, and then to *Drain* again. Repeat six or seven times or until all foam is purged from the bottom of the dishwasher.

To prevent a recurrence, use only dishwasher detergent. If dishes have been soaking in the sink (or have been filled with household cleaners), rinse thoroughly before loading them in the dishwasher.

Tip *Microwave ovens have fairly complex components that should be repaired professionally. However, if you are comfortable with analyzing circuits and working on electronic equipment, you may be able to diagnose and replace faulty switches, a broken door latch, or defective fan on your own. Consult the owner's manual if you wish to attempt repairs yourself.*

▶ Dishwasher needs routine maintenance.

Dishwashers clean dishes but not themselves. Grease-wads, glass shards, pottery chips, and suicidal measuring spoons will eventually affect a dishwasher's functioning. Every month, on a regular schedule, remove all baskets. If they are grimy, clean them in the sink or bathtub. Repair any nicks in the basket coatings or on walls with dishwasher-epoxy coating (from a hardware store). Remove any rust spots with rust-removing compound. With a screwdriver, wrench, or fingers, loosen the nut attaching the spray arms. Shake arms vigorously under very warm running water and/or use pipe cleaners to remove all foreign matter (broken glass, food bits) from the holes.

Clean the tub of debris and then clean the pump screen (it's in the depression in the bottom of the dishwasher, usually under the lower spray arm). With many models, you'll have to feel around carefully to find and pick out the broken glass and small utensils that may be lodged in the pump area. If it's necessary to use a cleaner on any dishwasher part, rinse very well. Wash the door of the dishwasher with hot water and use a slightly abrasive soapless scouring sheet dipped in hot water to clean under the door-crack and along the unit's lower front wall (the areas you can't actually see, where a sticky grease-and-soap sludge collects). Scrape out any dried soap from the soap dispenser cups, and if the cover doesn't move freely, rinse off any dried soap that's impeding it. If the machine has an air gap, remove its cover and clean any grime collecting there. Return everything to its place, and refill the rinsing agent dispenser (if applicable).

▶ Dishwasher won't start.

First check to make sure electric power is getting through. Make sure that the unit is turned on, that the circuit breaker hasn't tripped or the fuse blown, and that the door is latched properly. On some portable models the machine won't start unless the faucet is turned on. If the dishwasher is plugged into a receptacle under the sink shared by the garbage disposer, make sure the plugs aren't reversed; the disposer outlet may be controlled by a switch that is off. If none of these is the problem, verify that the dishwasher receptacle is receiving power by plugging in a lamp or small appliance. If there's no power, see page 68. If the dishwasher is wired directly to a junction box, with no plug, turn off power to the circuit, remove the junction box cover, carefully disconnect the wires, turn the circuit back on, and test the circuit wires for power. If there's no power, call an electrician.

If power is getting through and the unit still won't start, the door latch, the door switch, or the motor may be the problem. If the latch doesn't engage completely, it may not be tripping the door switch. Have the latch replaced. If the latch works, test the door switch. Turn off power at the circuit breaker and remove the control panel: Open the door, remove the screws that hold the inside door panel, take off the panel, and remove the exposed screws at the top of the door that hold the control panel to the front of the door. Steady the control panel with one hand and close the door, then lower the panel carefully to expose the door switch. Disconnect

Locating dishwasher components

Upper arm
Spray tower
Lower arm
Float
Door latch
Selector switch
Soap dispenser cups

Cleaning the spray arms and pump screen

Pump
Motor
Water inlet valve
Pump screen
Heating element
Power cord
Drain hose
Hot-water line

Tip *The average dishwasher lasts about 11 years, according to the Association of Home Appliance Manufacturers, but many models can last as long as 20 years with proper use and care.*

SOLVING MECHANICAL PROBLEMS

the two wires from the switch and latch the door shut. With a continuity tester or volt-ohmmeter (set for 4×1 ohms resistance), touch the two probes to the two terminals. If there is no continuity, replace the door switch. If there is, call for repairs to the motor.

Removing control panel

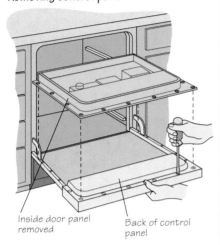

Inside door panel removed

Back of control panel

Testing door switch

Volt-ohmmeter

Door switch

Switch terminals

Door latch closed

Selector switch

Wires removed

Timer

Control panel

▶ Dishwasher won't stop filling.

Immediately turn off the water and leave the dishwasher door shut. Allow the machine to complete its cycle. After dishwashing is complete, check the float switch; the float should move up and down freely. If jiggling it doesn't make it function, shut off all power to the dishwasher, disconnect the wires from the switch, unscrew the float switch, and replace it with a new one.

If the float switch works, the problem may be in the timer or in the inlet valve. Remove as much water from the bottom as possible. Lift the pump filter and clean it; pumps often collect broken glass, lightweight utensils, long-lost earrings, and the like, which can interfere with functioning. Replace the filter, shut the door, and turn the water on again. Start the washer and turn it off after a few seconds. If the water doesn't stop, the inlet and/or drain valve is the problem and should be replaced; call for repairs. If the water does stop, continue running the dishwasher through its full cycle. If it overfills again, complete the cycle, turn off the water, and check the timer (see page 133), or call for repairs.

Removing float switch

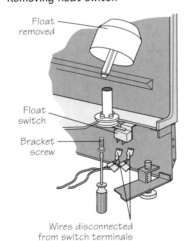

Float removed

Float switch

Bracket screw

Wires disconnected from switch terminals

▶ Dishwasher leaks.

If the machine isn't overfilling (see left), and if the leak is clear, not foamy, check to see that the machine is level by opening the door and setting a carpenter's level on the ledge (or hold the level against the edge of the door opening). To level the machine, open the bottom access panel and use a wrench to turn the adjusting screw on one or more legs (you may have to loosen locknuts first; retighten them when the machine is level).

If the leak persists, check the float valve; the float should move up and down freely. If there are trickles around the door, the door may not be tight. Loosen the screws in the lock strike, then readjust the strike so that it will be firmly aligned with the door latch. If there is a gasket around the door, check that it is in place and not cracked, broken, or caked with debris; if it is faulty, replace it. Also check the water supply tube and drain hose; tighten the clamps, if applicable. If the leak persists, call for service.

▶ Dishwasher won't fill or continue cycle.

Make sure that the water is turned on and that the water valve is open. (The water valve may be located under the sink, under the floor in the basement, or in a closet or garage behind the wall.) Also look to see whether the dishwasher float valve is stuck; the float should move up and down freely. If not, it will need replacement or servicing.

Water pressure should be between 20 and 120 psi; if it's too low, the machine can't fill sufficiently to run. To test, with no other water running in the house, place a ½-gallon container under the hot-water faucet nearest the dishwasher. Turn on the faucet; the container should fill in 14

Tip *A normal dishwasher cycle has two washes and three rinses. An energy-saving cycle, which is intended for lightly soiled dishes, has one wash and two rinses. A heavy-duty cycle usually consists of three washes and four rinses.*

seconds or less. If pressure is too low, contact the local water company to learn if this is an areawide problem or if your house pipes need to be replaced. You may be able to operate the dishwasher in a low-pressure area by avoiding use of the dishwasher when any other water in the house (including toilet) is in use. If the house pressure is adequate, the water line to the dishwasher may be blocked. To check, close the shutoff valve, remove the front access panel, disconnect the water line from the dishwasher, place a bucket or pan under it, and open the shutoff valve slowly to see if water sprays out in full force, then close it. If pressure is weak, disconnect the line from the valve and either clear the line or replace it.

Finally, a faulty timer may be closing the inlet valve too early, or the automatic shutoff valve may be faulty. Read the owner's manual to learn whether you can readily reach these parts or will need a service call. Checking the timer involves turning off power, removing the panel from the inside of the door, loosening the control panel screws, closing the door, and pulling the control panel out from the door front (with the wires attached). The timer consists of a motor that runs a clock that trips a series of switches, in sequence. Disconnect the motor wires from the wires leading to the power source and test the motor by touching the probes of a continuity tester to the two motor leads; if there is no continuity, the motor is faulty and the timer must be replaced. Next check the switch terminals for continuity. Unplug the block of wires from the switch to expose several pairs of terminals. With a continuity tester or a volt-ohmmeter (set for 4×1 ohms resistance), test each pair for continuity, turning the timer knob to the dishwashing cycle that those terminals control. (Consult the owner's manual or wiring diagram on the door to identify which terminals control what cycle.) If any pair fails the continuity test, replace the timer.

Checking float valve

Float cover

Float

Testing timer motor for continuity

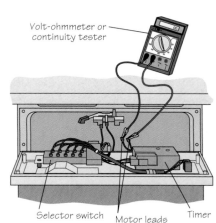

Volt-ohmmeter or continuity tester

Selector switch Motor leads Timer

Checking for clogged water line

Front panel removed

Automatic valve

Testing timer switch terminals for continuity

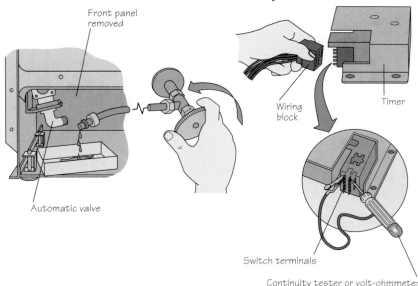

Wiring block

Timer

Switch terminals

Continuity tester or volt-ohmmeter

Tip *Many dishwashers have an internal mechanism for grinding up food scraps, just like a garbage disposer, and ejecting the remains with the drain water. It is located in the center of the tub floor, over the pump, and has a screen guard that prevents dishes (but not silverware) from getting snagged by the disposer blades.*

▶ Dishwasher won't drain and leaves standing water in bottom.

A small amount of water must always remain at the bottom of the dishwasher. If a lot of water is left, check and clean the pump filter or screen. Also check for a kink or clog in the drain hose; you may be able to work the clog free by pushing it through to the end. If not, turn off power to the machine, remove the front access panel, detach the hose from the drain valve by loosening the hose clamp (be ready for an outflow), detach the other end from the air gap (or sink drain, if there is no air gap), and poke a long wire through it to clear it; or call for service. If the hose isn't blocked, the air gap (usually located on the countertop or sink deck) may be clogged with debris. Remove the debris with tweezers, a brush, or a wire. Also check for blockage in the sink P-trap or drainpipe. If these steps don't solve the problem, call for service.

Disconnecting drain hose and cleaning air gap

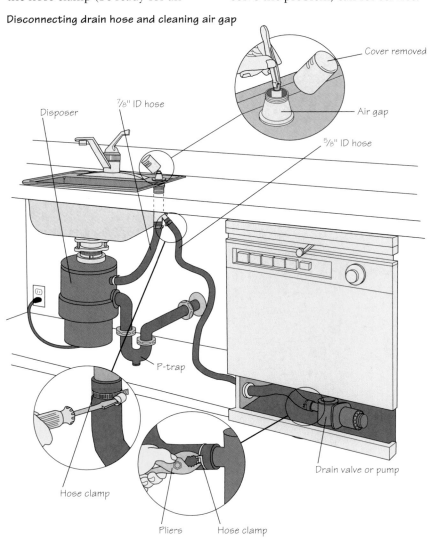

- Disposer
- 7/8" ID hose
- Cover removed
- Air gap
- 5/8" ID hose
- P-trap
- Hose clamp
- Pliers
- Hose clamp
- Drain valve or pump

▶ Dishwasher air gap leaks.

Make sure that the hoses are properly connected. The hose from the outlet side of the dishwasher pump goes to the inlet tube (smaller diameter) of the air valve. The hose from the outlet side of the air gap (larger diameter) goes to the sink drain or disposer. Check the hose to the sink drain to make sure there is no kink or debris in it, and clear it or replace it if necessary; also check the sink P-trap and drain to make sure they aren't blocked. If none of these is the problem, the air gap may be defective. To replace it, disconnect the hoses from the bottom of the gap; remove the cover and tightening nut from the top of the gap and slip it down through the sink or countertop opening.

▶ Dishes don't get clean.

Poor performance may be caused by food particles and other matter clogging the spray arms and pump. Perform the maintenance routine (see page 131), cleaning arms, pump screen, door area, and soap cup. Add rinsing agent if cup is empty (the rinsing agent reduces spotting on glassware). When you load the unit, make sure that dishes aren't tightly nested and that no tall dishes interfere with the action of the spray arms. (Rotate each arm before you start the machine to be sure it's not impeded.) Make sure no silverware is sticking out of the bottom of the silverware basket. Fill soap cups less than completely full, and don't wet the detergent before starting the machine.

Water that isn't hot enough can cause poor performance. See that your water-heater thermostat is set to the temperature recommended in the owner's manual. If dishes are washed just after someone has filled a bathtub or taken a long shower,

Tip *If the dishwasher drain hose is not connected to an air gap above the sink counter, make sure the hose is secured in such a way that it loops as high as possible under the counter close to its connection with the drainpipe. Secure the top of the loop to the bottom of the countertop with a hose bracket.*

the hot-water supply may be used up; run the dishwasher only when there's plenty of hot water.

If the problem persists, the heating element may be faulty. Use an immersible thermometer (such as a confection or deep-fry thermometer) to check how hot the tap water is after it has been running for about a minute. If it is considerably below the water-heater thermostat setting, the problem is with the water heater. If not, measure the temperature of the water inside the dishwasher when it is partly full. If it is below 150° F, call for service.

▶ *Dishwasher is too noisy or makes unusual noises.*

Unusual noises are caused by spray arms whacking dishes or utensils, dishes or utensils whacking each other, and fallen utensils getting whacked or ground up by the pump; utensils may also be poking out the bottom of the silverware basket. Check the owner's manual for proper loading of the machine. Load tall items at the edges of the baskets, where they can't interfere with the rotation of the spray arms. Load other items carefully to minimize their chances of escaping from their slots or racks and colliding with each other. Lightweight items (such as shallow aluminum mixing bowls, shot glasses, and plastic measuring cups) often float up and interfere with the spray arms or else plunge down into the pump area. You can obtain enameled wire-mesh minibaskets (at hardware and housewares stores) to lock up small items; a lightweight bowl can be anchored by placing a large wire-mesh colander or sieve firmly over it. Some

items (such as tiny plastic measuring spoons) may simply have to be washed in the sink.

As soon as you hear strange noises (thuds, crunches, grinding) unlatch the dishwasher door and wait a few seconds for the machine to stop completely. Open the door and check for loose utensils. Wearing rubber gloves to protect against hot water, correct the loading. If something has broken, turn off power and temporarily remove the bottom basket so you can fish out all the shards from the pump area and the baskets; broken glass or ceramic is liable to damage the pump. Turn on power and lock the door again to resume dishwashing.

If the dishwasher makes a sound like a distant tambourine, spray arms may be full of food bits or broken glass. Remove arms and clean them (see page 131). For grinding noises check and clear the pump area. If grinding sounds persist, there may not be enough water in the machine (at least 1 inch above the sump) when the dishwasher is running. If this is the problem, call for service.

▶ *Silverware gets tarnished.*

Real silver, silver plate, and any other precious metal (including fine china edged with gold, silver, platinum, or cobalt blue) shouldn't be washed in a dishwasher, precisely because the process does produce tarnish. However, if you must, wash them separately from other dishes on a short cycle and immediately dry each piece by hand with a soft dish towel.

If the silverware is actually stainless steel and you're getting black streaks, it's not tarnish. Aluminum cookware often creates black streaks on other utensils in

the dishwasher; it should be washed separately, or kept well away from other utensils. Throwaway aluminum baking pans are prone to melt in hot water and should not be dishwasher-cleaned at all.

▶ *Soap dispenser won't open.*

See whether a buildup of dried soap is caked in the cup; if so, clean it out. If someone packed in and tamped down too much soap, the soap may have formed a hard lump when it got wet, sealing the dispenser shut. If you can't jiggle the cup open again, wash dishes using the short cycle for a few weeks, or use the long cycle by adding soap manually at the end of the fill cycle. After a dozen or so loads, the soap lump will have dissolved and the problem should correct itself. Otherwise, replace the dispenser.

▶ *Dishwasher basket has lost plastic coating.*

You can dip the worn spots into the rubberized plastic dip used to coat tool handles, and/or cover worn spots with hot-melt glue or dishwasher epoxy. Alternatively, buy clear flexible tubing (¼-inch OD, ⅛-inch ID) at the hardware store. Cut ¼-inch pieces and slide them over the exposed tips of the racks.

▶ *Dishwasher emits odor resembling melting wax.*

Some plastic item (such as a container lid) may have fallen into the bottom of the unit and gotten wedged up against the heating element. Unplug the dishwasher. When it's cooled, inspect the area around the element, feeling around for the unseen object.

Tip *To diminish routine noisiness, consider sliding a layer or two of rubber-backed carpet (for instance, low-priced samples or scraps from a carpet store) or a rubber doormat or thick bath mat under the machine.*

▶ Light doesn't come on when door is opened.

Make sure the switch next to the light unit (if it has a master switch) is set to *On* and that the refrigerator is actually plugged in and running. Unplug the unit and replace the bulb with an appliance bulb of the same wattage specified for refrigerators. If this doesn't work, the door switch or the light circuit may be defective and need replacing. To check the door switch, unplug the refrigerator and carefully pry out the switch with a putty knife. Disconnect the wires and touch the probes of a continuity tester or volt-ohmmeter (set for 4×1 ohms resistance) to the terminals of the switch. It should show continuity when the plunger is out. If there are four terminals, test one pair at a time with the plunger in both positions. One pair should test for continuity with the switch on, the other pair with the switch off. If the switch doesn't test accordingly, replace it. If the light still doesn't work, call for repairs.

Testing the door switch

Leads disconnected

Continuity tester

Terminals

Switch in "On" position

▶ Motor doesn't run.

Assuming the unit isn't in its defrost cycle, check that it is plugged in and receiving power. (If the interior light doesn't come on when you open the door, see if another small appliance will work when plugged into the refrigerator receptacle. If not, check the circuit breaker or fuse.) Check that the temperature control is turned on; turn it off and on several times to see if the compressor starts. If it doesn't, call for service. If it starts but then turns off again, remove all other appliances from the circuit and see if it starts again. If so (or if the plug feels hot) the problem may be voltage drops on the circuit or house electrical system. Turn off power to the circuit and call an electrician.

▶ Refrigerator doesn't keep food cold enough.

If the refrigerator is located next to a range, a heating vent, or in direct sunlight, consider relocating it. Check that the thermostat control is set to a temperature between 34° and 40° F. If not, adjust it one notch or number and allow the temperature to stabilize for 24 hours before changing it again. Make sure there is nothing (such as a food package or partly opened or crooked bin or compartment) that's preventing the door from closing solidly. Make sure the base grille is not blocked, and check whether the condenser coil behind the grille is clogged with dust. (In a very old refrigerator, the coil may be in the back.) At least once a year, vacuum the coil gently with a crevice-cleaning tool or dust carefully with a refrigerator-coil brush. Also make sure the compartment fan is running.

Heat may also be coming from the refrigerator light if it is not turning off when the door is shut. Push each switch button (the one at the light and the one near the door). If one of the switches does not turn the light off, it is faulty. With power off, remove the switch and test it for continuity with a volt-ohmmeter or continuity tester (see left).

Cleaning condenser coils

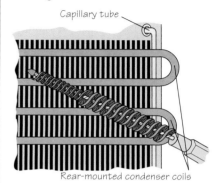

Capillary tube

Rear-mounted condenser coils

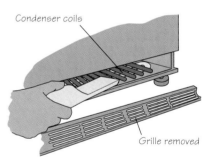

Condenser coils

Grille removed

▶ Refrigerator or freezer is running too cold.

Check that the thermostat is set for the correct temperature (38° to 40° F). If not, change it one number or notch and let it stabilize for 24 hours before adjusting it again. Otherwise, the thermostat may be faulty or the temperature-sensing bulb may be defective or improperly positioned. Call for service to have both replaced at the same time.

Tip *The coolant used in most refrigerators is freon or a similar chlorofluorocarbon (CFC). Because of environmental concerns about CFCs, refrigerator manufacturers now offer optional coolants.*

▶ Refrigerator runs constantly.

If the thermostat control is adjusted for a very cold temperature (34° F or under), try keeping the refrigerator at 40° F instead. Also check the condenser coils for dust and dirt and clean if necessary. If large amounts of hot food are placed in the unit, it may cause the motor to run, as could hot weather. Locating the unit with insufficient clearance behind or above it (minimum 2 inches), next to a range or hot-air vent, or in direct sunlight could also be a cause. Leaving the door open too long or opening it too often makes the refrigerator run; make sure nothing is keeping the door from shutting solidly. Finally, carefully inspect the door gasket; if cracked, broken, or loose, replace it. (Another sign of a problem gasket is water collecting in the lower bins.) To test, close the door on a piece of paper. When you pull the paper out, you should feel tension. If you don't, replace the gasket (see right).

▶ Water drips onto floor.

First see whether the drain from the freezer is clogged. To clear the drain, remove ice from the floor of the freezer; mix 1 teaspoon baking soda in 2 cups hot water, and pour it down the drain using a bulb baster.

If the refrigerator is located in a cool area (garage, utility room), condensation from the heat given off by the freezer motor can build up and drip onto the floor. To check, place a small room heater near the unit and keep it turned on for a day or two. If this stops the dripping, move the refrigerator to a warmer spot. Also note that when a self-defrosting refrigerator/freezer

is kept in an area that's near freezing, the freezer portion may turn off, and food inside will spoil. If the room with the refrigerator is merely chilly at night (in the 60° F range), turn the freezer temperature up one notch.

Also examine the tubes leading to and from the motor. If they are coated with frost (which in turn melts and leaks), try insulating the suction line (near the compressor) with foam tubing insulation or wraparound plumbing insulation (from a plumbing-supply store).

Check the drain pan under the refrigerator for cracks and replace if necessary.

▶ Ice builds up too quickly in bottom of freezer.

First make sure that nothing is keeping the freezer door from shutting completely. Warm air entering the freezer causes massive condensation, which freezes into ice (which in turn pushes the door even more ajar, causing more ice to form). Defrost the freezer and some of the food in it and rearrange the remaining food. Also clear the drain (see left).

In certain refrigerator/freezer models, if the insulation around the drain hole in the freezer gets wet, it never dries. The frozen moisture then clogs the defrost hole, so defrost water settles on the freezer deck and turns to ice. A factory-authorized technician may be able to install a low-wattage heater that will keep moisture from icing up the drain hole.

▶ Frost forms too quickly in standard refrigerator.

The door is not sealing properly or is being opened too often. First make sure that the refrigerator is level and tilted slightly backward, so the door shuts automatically. (See page 138.) Examine the gasket; if it is cracked, torn, or loose, replace it. (See below.)

▶ Refrigerator door gasket needs replacing.

Unplug the refrigerator and roll the gasket back to see how it's attached to the door. It may be attached by retainer strips, by screws along with retainer strips, or by screws only. If it's secured by retainers only, pull the gasket out of the grooves and take it to the appliance store to be sure you get a comparable replacement. If the new gasket is wrinkled, soak it in hot water for 15 minutes before installing it. Start at a top corner and work toward the other, pushing the narrowest edge of the gasket into the groove. Then work down the sides, one at a time, and finally press the bottom into place.

If the gasket has screws as well as a retainer, use a screwdriver (or nut driver if applicable) to loosen the screws. Slip out the gasket and take it with you when you buy a new one. Slide the edge of the new gasket under the retainer at the top corners of the door. Tighten the center screw just enough to hold the gasket. Work down one side, then the other, and then across the bottom, tightening the center screw of each side just enough to hold the gasket. Now gently tighten the screws at the corners, and then the remaining screws.

If the gasket is held by screws only, use a nut driver or screwdriver to remove all the screws. Pull the

Tip *Most refrigerators need clearance behind them for air to circulate through the condenser coils. Built-in refrigerators, which fit flush with the cabinetwork around them, have the compressor and condenser coils mounted on the top of the unit, with air circulated through a front grille.*

gasket off the door and take it with you when you buy a replacement. Install the new gasket, starting in a top corner and working toward the opposite corner, putting the screws back in as you go. Work down each side in turn and then across the bottom. Do not overtighten the screws.

Removing an old door gasket

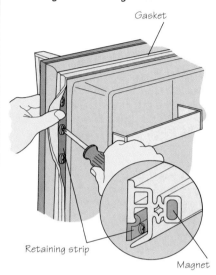

Installing a new gasket

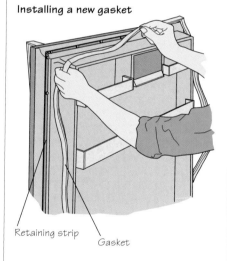

▶ Refrigerator makes strange noises.

If the noise is a rattling or vibration, it may indicate the refrigerator is not resting solidly on the floor, because either the floor or the legs are uneven. Place a carpenter's level on top and see if the horizontal line is straight. If not, adjust the roller screws or front leveling legs by turning them clockwise with a wrench to raise the appliance or counterclockwise to lower it. If the drain pan is rattling, move it so that it's clear of the compressor. If you have some strong-backed helpers, you can put a layer or two of rubber-backed carpeting (such as thick bath mats, large rubber doormats, or inexpensive carpet scraps from a carpet store) under the refrigerator to diminish noise.

If the unit is aging, note that older refrigerators develop strange noises. Usually, it's one of the fan motors imitating a jet taking off or a panicky jungle bird. Listen to the condenser fan motor and the evaporator fan motor, and if you have an ice maker, listen to that motor as well. Replace whichever one is making the noise. If the unit is very old, consider replacing the refrigerator.

▶ Refrigerator door wanders when open.

The refrigerator should be level but tilted slightly back so the door closes by itself. To adjust it, remove the front access panel near the floor. Place shims under the front legs or, if they have adjusting screws, turn the screws to extend the feet slightly (you may have to loosen a locknut first). To make adjustment easier, have a helper use a crowbar to lift the front of the refrigerator slightly near the leg you are adjusting; place some padding and a scrap of plywood under the

crowbar to protect the floor. Be very careful—don't put your fingers under the unit while it is raised.

▶ Refrigerator emits strong, caustic odor.

If the refrigerator is very old it may be leaking a sulphur dioxide refrigerant. Open windows, evacuate the room, and call for service. With more modern refrigerators the refrigerant is odorless and not likely to be causing the odor. Try the strategies for eliminating food odors (see below), or call for service.

▶ Refrigerator has unpleasant odors inside and in drip pan.

Prepare a solution of 1 gallon hot water, ½ cup baking soda, and 3 squirts dishwashing detergent. Turn off the unit and remove all food. Wash the whole interior (including bins, door trays, and shelves) with the cleaning solution. Pull out bins and wash the refrigerator floor.

If you have seen evidence of spilled liquid, also check the drip pan under the refrigerator; remove it and, if it is dirty, wash it with the solution. Return it to position and search for a drain trap on the bottom shelf. Pour more of the solution down the trap; then rinse the drip pan again. (If it is moldy, see next paragraph.) Inspect the former contents of the refrigerator and discard red-haired butter, black spinach, orange sour cream, green cheddar, and the like. Return bins and food to the unit and turn it back on.

If the drip pan has smelly mold, scrub with a solution of hot water and mildew-killing cleaner or chlorine bleach, using a scouring cloth or pad. If possible, let dry in hot

Tip *Washing the gasket frequently with soapy water prevents mold. If it's already moldy, you might try washing it several times with a liquid detergent, a mildew-killing cleaner (check label before buying, in case cleaner can't be used on rubber), or a mixture of 4 tablespoons chlorine bleach in 1 quart hot water.*

sun (or wipe dry). Check and clean the drip pan frequently (about every two weeks at first, then every three or four months if mold does not return). If refrigerator is leaking heavily into the drip pan, encouraging mold, check the door gasket for looseness or cracks; excess condensation due to a loose seal may be causing the leakage.

▶ Refrigerator cord won't reach wall receptacle.

If you can't move the refrigerator closer to the receptacle, use a heavy-duty extension cord (no smaller than No. 14 wire) and set the controls slightly colder. Alternatively, replace the cord or install a new receptacle.

▶ Refrigerator finish is chipped or color is undesirable.

Touch up small chips with appliance-repair paint (available at hardware stores in several standard colors). To change colors entirely, use auto-motive spray paint or have the unit painted by an auto-body shop.

▶ Inside of door has crack.

For tiny cracks, clean the crack with cleanser and dry thoroughly. Spread a thin bead of silicone sealer (available in tubes at hardware stores) along the crack. (Most caulks specify a minimum temperature before applying. Check the label; you may need to shut off the refrigerator, empty it, and let it warm up before applying the caulk.) With a wet putty knife, press sealer into the crack. Then scrape off excess sealer. For large cracks, have the liner replaced by a trained technician. If it's not done correctly, the liner may pull away from the door completely when the door shelves are filled with food.

▶ Refrigerator damages flooring when moved.

The best way to move a refrigerator is with an appliance dolly, which any rental agency should have. Otherwise, protect the floor with clean pieces of plywood or other paneling ($\frac{5}{16}$-inch flooring under-layment works well). Tip the refrigerator back and slide the first piece under it. Spray the bottoms of the feet or casters with furniture polish to make them slick, and slide or roll the refrigerator over the plywood. Have at least one helper.

▶ Ice maker doesn't work.

Check that the stop arm is in the *On* (down) position and that the water supply is connected and turned on. Check water pressure in the house (see page 132) and the unit. Ice cubes piled in the bin will cause the ice maker to shut off. Finally, the freezer may be too warm to make ice. Use a refrigerator/freezer thermometer to check the temperature, or see whether ice cream in the unit is melting. If so, set controls a notch colder.

Checking ice-maker stop arm

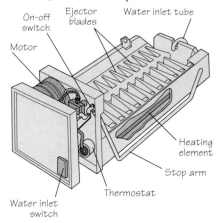

On-off switch — Ejector blades — Water inlet tube — Motor — Heating element — Stop arm — Thermostat — Water inlet switch

▶ Motor of standard standup freezer groans.

Before calling for service, see if the freezer is overfilled and/or ice en-crusted, or if a package is keeping the door from closing all the way. Defrost the unit and remove some of the food.

▶ Warm air flows out from under refrigerator.

The compressor under the refrigerator normally emits warm air. Clean the compressor coils if they are dirty and hence overheating, and return the bottom grille so that it is firmly in place. If the bottom grille has vanished, obtain a replacement to minimize dust accumulation.

▶ Automatic defrost doesn't function.

The automatic defrost system has a number of components, any one of which could be causing the problem. Obtain a repair manual for the brand and model of your refrigerator if you wish to diagnose and repair it yourself. Otherwise, call for service.

▶ Washing machine won't start.

Make sure that the machine is plugged in and that the circuit breaker hasn't tripped or the fuse blown. Check to see whether a small appliance will work plugged into the same receptacle. If absence of power is not the problem, see that the lid is closed and check the lid switch (see page 140). Try turning the dial to a different cycle or a different stage of the cycle. If this starts the machine, the timer is probably faulty and will need replacing. If it doesn't start the machine, the motor is defective and may need to be replaced. Call for repairs.

Tip To reduce odors in a refrigerator, place an open or vented container of baking soda or activated charcoal in a corner. Check it every few months and replace it when it starts to smell bad.

Tip To prevent door cracks, avoid overcrowding the door shelves or placing sharp-edged items on them.

▶ Tub fills but motor won't start or makes noises.

Make sure the lid is firmly latched. If the motor makes no noise, test the lid switch, with the lid down, by inserting a pencil or wood chopstick under the indentation on the lid and pushing the switch. If this starts the motor, the lid-latching mechanism needs to be replaced. If it doesn't, the switch itself may be defective. To remove it for testing, unplug the machine, open the lid, and lift up the top panel. Remove the two screws that hold the switch in place and disconnect the wires from the switch (mark or label them). Touch the probes of a continuity tester or a volt-ohmmeter (set for R × 1 ohms resistance) to the two terminals. It should show continuity when you depress the switch button; if not, replace the switch. If the lid safety switch is not the problem (or the motor is making noises), call for service.

Removing lid safety switch

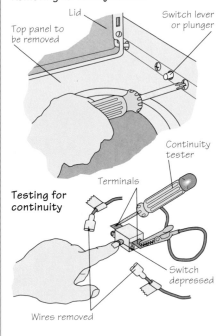

Lid
Switch lever or plunger
Top panel to be removed
Continuity tester
Terminals
Testing for continuity
Switch depressed
Wires removed

▶ Tub doesn't fill.

Make sure that the hose bibbs are turned on all the way, and that the water valve is turned on. Check to see that the control button for the desired water level is fully depressed. Check for clogs in the hose filters and clean them. (See right.) Also look for (and straighten) kinks in the inlet hoses. Next see if the timer is the problem by moving it up a notch or two and pressing the start button. If the machine starts filling, the timer is faulty; replace it.

If these steps don't solve the problem, check the solenoid of the inlet valve with a volt-ohmmeter or continuity tester. First unplug the machine, shut off the hose bibbs, and disconnect the hoses. If the inlet valve is accessible through the back panel of the machine, release the valve by removing the screws that hold it to the bracket, and pull it out from the bracket with wires attached. Otherwise, gain access by removing the top panel and the splash guard that surrounds the tub rim. With the valve in view, note which wires are connected to the four terminals; disconnect them. Test continuity between the terminals of each pair (if you use a volt-ohmmeter, set it for R × 100 ohms resistance). If there is no continuity, the solenoids don't draw current and are unable to open the valves; replace the valve.

If the inlet valve works and shows continuity (around 800 ohms on each test), check the water temperature switch. Look for it inside the control panel behind the temperature button. Note how the wires are connected to the four terminals and detach them. Check each pair of terminals with the switch on *Cold*. If neither pair shows continuity, replace the switch. If one pair shows continuity, verify that it is the correct pair

by studying the wiring diagram in the owner's manual or on the back of the control panel; the probes should be touching the terminals designated for cold water. If the water temperature switch is not the problem, call for service.

Checking continuity of inlet valve

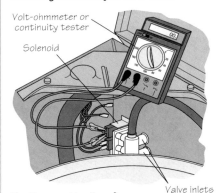

Volt-ohmmeter or continuity tester
Solenoid
Valve inlets

Testing continuity of water temperature switch

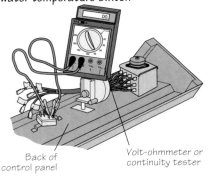

Back of control panel
Volt-ohmmeter or continuity tester

▶ Tub fills very slowly.

Check whether both the hot- and cold-water bibbs are fully open. If so, the hose filters (or the pipes) may be plugged up. At the back of the machine are hose connections marked *Hot* and *Cold*. Close the bibbs and unscrew the hoses from the washer. (If necessary, carefully use pliers to loosen them;

Tip *If you need to move a washing machine or other heavy appliance to gain access to the back, always get help. To keep from damaging the floor, tilt the machine back and place pads of carpet or heavy cardboard under each front leg. Do the same for the rear legs as soon as you have access; then slide the machine on the pads. If you need to check the bottom of the machine, tilt it against a wall or other barrier and prop it up firmly. Be sure to unplug the machine, disconnect water lines, and empty all water before moving or tilting it.*

don't squeeze the hose end out of shape.) There may be filter screens just inside; clean them with a cotton swab or a small dishwashing brush dipped in hot water (if they are very dirty, use some dishwashing detergent as well). Replace them if they are bent or crushed. If the fitting has dome-shaped removable filter screens, clean them or replace them. Also disconnect the hoses from the bibbs to see if they have filters that need cleaning or replacement. While they are off, hold a bucket under each faucet and turn it on. If water doesn't come out full force, the problem is probably poor water pressure. (See page 19.) If the water comes out with normal force but the tub still fills very slowly, the problem could be a defective inlet valve or water temperature switch (see page 140).

▶ Tub won't spin.

If the washer stops when it's full of water, lift the lid, redistribute the laundry, and close the lid; if it starts again, the load was merely unbalanced. If the machine starts again only after several minutes' wait, it may not be receiving enough voltage to work well. Check voltage with a volt-ohmmeter, following directions in the meter manual, or call for service. If the tub stops spinning entirely but the motor runs, the problem is probably a loose or broken drive belt or faulty transmission. You can probably replace a belt yourself (see right). In older machines with direct drive, the friction material that locks the brakes, clutch, and spin wheel together may have dried out, making the transmission slip. Get an estimate before repairing it; the cost of reconditioning the unit will probably be close to that of replacing it with a new one.

▶ *Motor hums but nothing happens.*

Consult the owner's manual to find out whether your model has a drive belt or a transmission. If the machine has a drive belt, it may be broken. To repair it yourself, if the owner's manual does not include a diagram of the drive belt, see if you can obtain a repair manual (through the appliance dealer or the customer service department of the manufacturer). Pull the unit away from the wall and disconnect it. If the belt is accessible from the rear, unscrew the rear access panel. If it is accessible only from the bottom, with a helper lay the machine on its side on carpet or other padding (water may drain out).

Check the belt tension by pressing the belt. The correct tension varies in different models and makes; check the manual for its recommendation. If the belt is loose, tighten it according to manufacturer's directions. For most models this involves using a socket wrench to loosen the mounting nuts, then pulling the motor back against the belt and retightening the nuts. Also check the pulleys by taking hold of each of them in turn and trying to shake them from side to side. If a pulley is loose, tighten its setscrew. If the belt or pulley is worn or torn, replace it. In many models this may require major disassembly; call for service and get an estimate before authorizing the repair—it may approach the price of a new unit.

If your unit has direct drive, the transmission may have failed. Transmission repairs are extremely expensive; get an estimate and compare it to the cost of replacing the unit.

Adjusting belt tension . . .

. . . from back

. . . from bottom

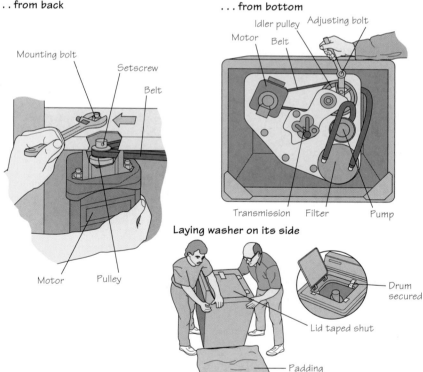

Laying washer on its side

▶ Clothes come out wet or tub won't drain.

For weak spin, first check to see if the machine is overloaded or if the load has become unbalanced. If clothes come out wet or machine fails to drain, unplug the washer and check the drain hose for clogs or kinks and remove them. Bail out most of the water, plug in the unit, turn it on again, and set the control to *Spin*. If the machine still doesn't spin or drain properly, look to the drive belt and pulleys (see page 141). If agitation is slow as well, the unit may have a faulty transmission or brake, requiring professional repair.

An uncommon but possible cause of failure to spin is binding, caused by dried detergent or grease coating the gasket around the tub or by clothing trapped between the basket and the tub; check for and correct these conditions. Other possibilities include motor carriage needing lubrication, a broken motor carriage roller, a damaged water pump, or a defective tub bearing. Get an estimate for repairs.

▶ Agitator doesn't work properly.

Check to see if the unit will agitate on other cycles or other stages of the cycle. If not, the drive belt or transmission may be faulty (see page 141), or the timer may be defective. To test the timer, unplug the machine and remove the back plate from the control panel (you may need to unscrew the control panel first). Locate the mechanism behind the timer knob and disconnect the wires leading to the motor from the wiring plug. With a continuity tester or volt-ohmmeter (set for R × 1 ohms resistance), test the continuity of the timer motor by touching the probes to the two wire leads that you disconnected. If the tester shows no continuity, the timer motor is defective; replace

the complete timer unit. If the motor shows continuity, check the switch terminals of the timer. Mark and disconnect the wires (or pull out the block with all wires attached) to expose several pairs of terminals. Test each pair for continuity, turning the timer knob to the cycle that those terminals control. (Consult the owner's manual or wiring diagram on the door to identify which terminals control what cycle.) If any pair fails the continuity test, replace the timer.

If, when you tested the agitator on another cycle, it started up, the problem may be a faulty water-level switch. To test it, unplug the machine and locate the switch inside the control panel behind the selector knob. Detach the plastic air tube (the air pressure in this

tube changes as the water level in the tub changes). Mark and disconnect the wires from the switch terminals. With a volt-ohmmeter (at R × 1) or a continuity tester, check all the terminals in pairs (three combinations in all). If no pair, or more than one pair, has continuity, replace the switch. If one pair has continuity, note it and proceed to testing the other pairs with different air pressures. To do this, blow lightly into the hole you disconnected the tubing from (or attach tubing of the same diameter and blow into it) until you hear a click. Test the terminals at this setting; a different pair should show continuity. Repeat the process; the third pair should now show continuity. If not, replace the switch. If the problem persists, call for service.

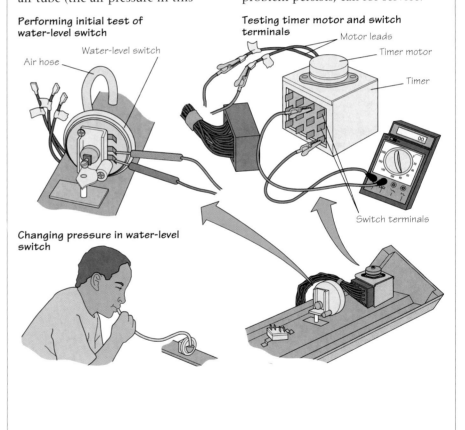

Performing initial test of water-level switch

Air hose

Water-level switch

Testing timer motor and switch terminals

Motor leads

Timer motor

Timer

Switch terminals

Changing pressure in water-level switch

Tip *Although washing-machine hoses are designed for heavy use, there's always a chance an old one will weaken and burst. To avoid this, you can shut off the hose bibbs when you're not using the machine, to take pressure off them and eliminate the chance of leaks or bursting while nobody is home.*

▶ *Water is too cold or too hot.*

Check the hose bibbs to be sure both are fully open; if the hoses are connected to a sink faucet, be sure the shutoff valves under the sink are fully open. Check the water hoses to see if they are reversed; disconnect both hoses from the bibbs, switch them, and test. If water is too cool, check the setting on your water heater; if it's under 120° F, raise it slightly. Note that if you run the washing machine right after someone has filled the bath, taken a long shower, or done dishes, there may not be enough hot water left to service the washer.

Clean the filters in the hoses and replace them if they are bent or crushed. If there is still a problem, test the hose bibbs or faucet by disconnecting the hose, holding a bucket underneath, and turning on the water. If little or none comes out, the pipe itself is probably clogged and needs to be replaced. The final possibility is that the temperature selection switch is faulty and needs to be replaced.

▶ *Water doesn't shut off automatically.*

First turn off the machine and un-plug it. If water continues to run into the machine, the inlet valve is faulty and should be replaced. Turn off the bibbs, empty the tub (bailing it out by hand, if necessary), and replace the valve. Consult the owner's manual to learn whether the valve is accessed by removing the cabinet top or the rear service panel. Leaving the machine unplugged, disconnect the inlet hoses and remove the screws holding the valve in place; lift out the valve assembly. Loosen the clamp connecting the nozzle hose with the

valve outlet and remove the hose. Mark and disconnect the wires from the valve solenoid terminals. Install a new valve by reversing the procedure.

If the water stops flowing when you pull the plug, the timer may be faulty. Plug the machine back in and advance the timer knob. If the water stops, replace the timer (or have it done by a repair person). If water doesn't stop, the water-level switch is probably faulty. Test it (see opposite page) or call for service.

Removing the inlet valve

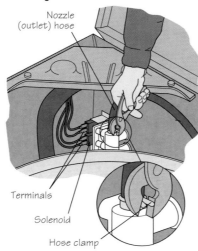

Nozzle (outlet) hose

Terminals

Solenoid

Hose clamp

▶ *Drainpipe overflows.*

The tub could be overfilling (see right), the branch drain that the washing machine is on may have a sudden discharge from some other plumbing fixture (such as the dishwasher or a draining bathtub), or the standpipe may be clogged or improperly sized or plumbed. To check for clogs, work a drain auger down the standpipe. Also look for a cleanout plug under the floor or behind the wall where the standpipe is located; open it carefully and have buckets handy. Use the auger to clear obstructions down-

stream from the cleanout. If you don't encounter anything but the standpipe still overflows, it is probably plumbed incorrectly. It should be 2 inches in diameter, terminate at least 34 inches above the floor, have a P-trap below it between 6 and 18 inches above the floor, and have a vent pipe connected to the drain line within 3 or 4 feet of the trap, depending on local code requirements. If it shares a branch drain with the kitchen, the drain should be 3-inch-diameter pipe. All horizontal drainpipes should be sloped ¼ inch per foot. If you find substandard plumbing conditions or aren't sure, call a plumber.

▶ *Washing machine leaks.*

First try to figure out when and where it leaks. If the leak occurs behind the washer, check the inlet hoses for cracks, and if necessary replace the hoses. Check the hose bibbs; if the leaking comes from there, tighten the packing nuts and hose connections with a wrench. Inside the machine check the nozzle hose (connected to the inlet valve) and replace it if it is cracked.

If the machine leaks when it's full, check the pump hoses for loose connections or cracks. For access, unplug the machine, turn off hose bibbs, remove supply hoses, and remove the rear service panel. If the hoses and connections are all intact, the pump may be leaky and need replacement, or else the water-level switch (which turns off water intake when the machine is full enough) may be faulty, allowing excess water to leak out through the overflow tube. To stop the leak, have the

Tip *The drain hose of a washing machine, also called a purge hose, usually discharges into a vertical pipe located behind the machine. This standpipe should be at least 36 inches above the floor to provide enough capacity to serve as a small catch basin for discharged drain water. It also holds the discharge end of the drain hose high enough so water gets trapped in the bottom of the hose between washings, ensuring that the rubber seals in the drain valve do not dry out and crack. To keep the drain hose from popping out of the discharge pipe or splashing water onto the floor, connect it to the pipe with a rubber friction cap made for this purpose: Simply slide it onto the top of the pipe, tighten the hose clamp provided with it, and force the end of the drain hose through a hole in the top of the cap.*

pump or switch replaced by a technician. (However, if the leak is slight, repairs may not be worth the cost. If the leak is from the overflow tube, just place a small container under it to catch the drips.)

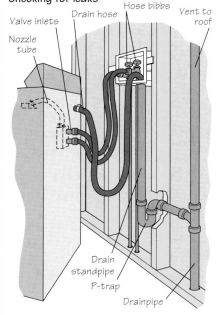

Checking for leaks

Valve inlets
Nozzle tube
Drain hose
Hose bibbs
Vent to roof
Drain standpipe
P-trap
Drainpipe

▶ Suds end up on roof.

The drain is partially clogged downstream from the vent pipe, allowing water to drain away but causing suds to back up through the plumbing vent until they spill out onto the roof. Clear the drain with a drain auger, working down through the standpipe, the roof vent, or any cleanouts located along the drain line and branch drain that serve the washing machine. Or call a plumber.

▶ Machine is excessively noisy.

A quick way to diminish washing-machine noise is to slide a layer or two of rubber-backed carpeting under the machine or the drip pan. (Check at a carpet store for low-priced samples and scraps.) Make

sure the machine is level (see below) in case vibration is contributing to the noise.

Also check to see if a bobby pin, small nail, or similar object has gotten stuck through one of the bottom holes in the basket; it could be hitting the antiswirl device on the pump hose and causing a clattering sound.

▶ Machine shakes and vibrates.

First level the machine: Screw the adjustable legs as far down as possible so the machine is close to the floor. Using a carpenter's level and open-ended or adjustable wrench, adjust the legs so the machine is level back-to-front and side-to-side. After leveling, tighten the locknuts on each leg. If leveling the machine doesn't correct vibration problems, check to see whether the installers left the retaining bolts (for shipping) on both sides of the service panel. If so, the bolts are compressing the springs, so they can't absorb vibration; remove them.

The bolts that hold the gear case to the support braces may be loose. Check the owner's manual or a repair manual for exact procedure. For most models the procedure is to unplug the machine, disconnect the hoses, move the machine away from the wall, and remove the rear service panel. Tighten all the nuts holding the gear case to the support braces (the gear case is under the tub, attached to a large mounting plate). Reattach the service panel and hoses and restore power.

If this doesn't work, replace the snubber and spring rod. The snubber is a piece of plastic that holds the spring rod, which (in

turn) reduces vibration. Unplug the washer, lift the top, and find the snubber and spring rod (usually in a rear corner). Pull up the spring rod to release it from the snubber, then unscrew the snubber. Remove the nut and bolt attaching the spring rod to the frame. Press the bolt down to release it; the rounded end of the spring rod will also come free. Slip the hook end of the rod out of the holes. Install the new snubber and spring rod (by reversing the whole process).

Leveling a washing machine

Locknut

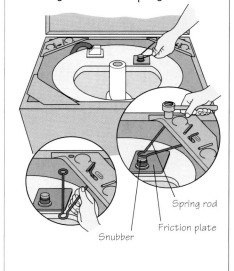

Removing snubber and spring rod

Spring rod
Friction plate
Snubber

Tip *For a washing machine located in the house, especially in bedroom areas or upstairs areas directly over living space, have a sheet-metal shop fabricate a 2-inch-deep drip pan to place under the washer, just slightly larger than the outside dimensions of the machine. For maximum overflow protection, install a drain fitting in the side of the pan and run $\frac{3}{4}$-inch pipe from it to a safe discharge point (such as a floor drain or outdoors).*

▶ Water pipes bang when washer shuts off.

A washing-machine inlet valve snaps shut quickly, causing water rushing through the pipes to stop suddenly and create a hammering sound. To suppress the noise, install water-hammer shock absorbers (available at home centers or plumbing-supply stores). Get the kind that can be installed on the hose bibbs (as opposed to those installed on the water pipes, usually inside the wall). Shut off the hose bibbs, unscrew the hoses carefully, and screw the shock absorbers onto the bibbs. (Make sure the washers from the hoses and the shock absorbers are still in place.) Reconnect the hoses.

Installing water-hammer shock absorbers

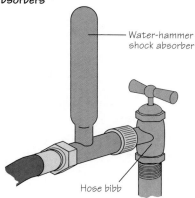

Water-hammer shock absorber

Hose bibb

▶ Washer screeches as spin cycle ends.

The brake seals are probably dry. To service the brake, unplug the machine, shut off the hose bibbs, and disconnect the hoses. Open the lid and secure the tub with fabric duct tape fastened from the top panel into the inside of the tub at several points. Close the lid and tape it shut. Place a rug, blanket, or beach towels over the floor and

(with a helper) tip the washer and lay it gently on its side. Using a squirt-gun oil can, lubricate the brake with the lubricant recommended in the owner's manual. (There should be an opening in the transmission pulley that lets you reach the brake.) Turn the pulley clockwise for two turns to distribute the lubricant. Now return the machine to operating position and operating condition.

▶ Machine spins when it's not in the spin cycle.

The main bearing may be damaged or the solenoid may be faulty. In either case you'll probably need professional repairs. Especially if the machine is aging, get an estimate before committing; repair costs may be close to those of buying a new machine.

Lubricating brake seals

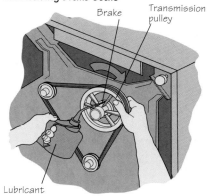

Brake

Transmission pulley

Lubricant

▶ Washer screeches as spin cycle starts.

This is usually caused by a drive belt glazed to a shiny hardness by a pulley spinning against it while it's stuck in place. To replace, see page 141. Some belts are much harder to replace than others, so you may need to call for repairs. Get an estimate first.

▶ Clothes dryer won't start.

Make sure the door is shut firmly, the switch is turned on, and the unit is plugged in. Check for a blown fuse or tripped circuit breaker. Electric dryers draw 240 volts and have a pair of fuses or circuit breakers; both must be functioning for the unit to run effectively. If you reset the breaker or replace the fuse but it blows again as soon as you start the dryer, call an electrician or appliance repair person.

The most common reason a dryer won't start is that lint is plugging up the exhaust hose and air vent. Go outside and see if there's lint all the way to the end of the duct; if so, just pull out as much of it as you can. If there is a damper, turn it parallel to the duct and clean off lint with a straightened-out wire coat hanger. (If the duct is long, use rubber bands to attach securely a two-tined cooking fork to a long stick or broom handle, and use the tines to "comb" out lint from well back in the duct. If duct is very long (20 feet or so) you may need professional service to clean it all the way; also look into renting an industrial vacuum cleaner. Return to the dryer, remove the exhaust hose, and shake out lint. Also clean the lint from the lint filter. If exhaust vents are severely clogged, disassemble the vent pipes, run a rag through each piece, and wrap joints with fabric duct tape when reassembling. Now try the dryer again.

If it still won't run, try poking the door safety switch with a chopstick or pencil while the door is closed. If the dryer starts up, the switch plunger is faulty; replace

---

Tip *Most washers and dryers have self-adjusting rear legs for leveling the machine front-to-back. Simply tilt the machine forward to raise the legs off the floor, then let it down slowly. If the machine is still not level, raise or lower the front legs with a wrench and repeat the process. When the machine is level, press down on opposite corners for a final check. It shouldn't rock.*

the switch. If the dryer doesn't turn on, test the switch to make sure it's not the problem. First turn off the power, then remove the top panel to gain access to the switch. Remove the wire leads and test for continuity by touching the probes of a continuity tester or volt-ohmmeter (set for 4×1 ohms resistance) to both terminals and pushing in the switch button. If there is no continuity, replace the switch. If the switch has continuity, reconnect the wires and test the start switch in the same way (with power off). If none of this works, call for repairs. The timer may have failed or the motor may have burned out.

Removing top panel

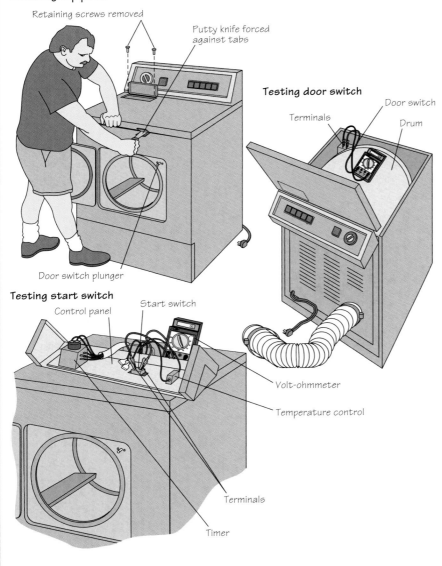

Retaining screws removed

Putty knife forced against tabs

Door switch plunger

Testing door switch

Door switch

Terminals

Drum

Testing start switch

Control panel

Start switch

Volt-ohmmeter

Temperature control

Terminals

Timer

▶ Clothes dryer attracts mice.

Attracted by warmth and lured by lint, the creatures are coming in through the duct and the exhaust vent. If you have a draft preventer (flapper) on the vent pipe indoors, check to see whether it is staying open when dryer is off; if so, replace it. Also consider installing an automatic vent flapper designed for the outdoor end of the duct (this will make the duct harder to clean, however).

▶ Electric dryer won't heat enough or at all.

Electric dryers normally run on two fuses or circuit breakers. If one of the two is blown or tripped, often the dryer will run but won't heat. If a breaker or fuse continues to trip, call an electrician or appliance repair technician. If the breakers or fuses are sound, the problem may be a faulty thermostat (see page 148) or broken heating element (call for repairs and get an estimate).

▶ Dryer takes too long to dry clothes.

If the machine is overloaded, the clothing doesn't toss well and does not dry. If the washing machine is ultralarge and the dryer is compact or normal, one washer-load will make two or three dryer-loads. If a few items (rugs or large towels) are large, heavy, and/or very wet, they should be dried separately on a longer or hotter cycle (following label directions for the fabric).

If loads are normal and still take a long time to dry, check that the flapper on the vent duct hood is wide open when the dryer is on; if it isn't, loosen or replace the flapper. Also check for lint clogging the filter, exhaust vents, and duct, and clear them out as needed.

Tip *If the bulb in your clothes dryer keeps burning out, make sure it matches the specifications for your model (check the owner's manual). The bulb should be an appliance bulb, not a regular light bulb. Other possibilities: If the cover over the bulb has vanished, if the door to the dryer is left open, or if the dryer isn't level, the bulb is liable to burn out quickly. If other bulbs in the house also burn out quickly, check with the electric company to see if there have been power surges in your area.*

▶ Clothes dryer motor needs replacing.

If the dryer does not run and the switches are not at fault, the problem is most likely a defective motor. Installing a new dryer motor is not a difficult repair. Unplug the dryer (or shut off the circuit breakers) and move it away from the wall. Remove the screws that hold the lint screen in place. With a screwdriver tip protected by a rag, pry up the top (see opposite). Then remove the front panel and (if applicable) the toe panel. Remove the drive belt by pushing the idler pulley toward the motor. Lift the drum out of the dryer. You can now reach the motor. You'll need two open-end wrenches. Place one of them on the hub of the blower wheel (fan)

at the rear of the motor. Place the other on the motor shaft holding the pulley. Holding the blower wheel hub steady, turn the belt pulley wrench clockwise to disconnect the blower wheel from the motor. Now check the floor of the dryer; in some models the motor is secured to the floor by two clamps. Unscrew these clamps. Then disconnect the wires attached to the motor; you can now remove the old motor. Install the new motor in reverse order. However, if the new motor doesn't have a belt pulley included, remove the pulley from the old motor (either unscrew it or pull it off with a wheel puller), and attach it to the new motor.

▶ Dryer won't turn off when door is opened.

The door safety switch is defective. It is usually behind the cabinet front, near the door hinge. To repair it, first unplug the dryer or shut off the circuit breakers. If the dryer is gas powered, shut off the gas valve for the dryer (by turning the handle 90 degrees) and proceed very carefully when moving the dryer, to avoid causing a dangerous gas leak.

Assuming the switch is located behind the cabinet front, remove the screws at the rear of the appliance and take off the cabinet front. Inspect the switch area. If a wire has fallen out of the switch, reattach it, turn on the electricity, and see if dryer works now. If wires are intact, disconnect them from the switch, remove the screws holding the switch in place, and install a new switch (from an authorized dealer or repair facility). Turn the power and gas back on and relight the pilot.

▶ Gas dryer won't heat although drum turns.

Avoid moving the dryer during diagnosis and repair, to avoid causing a gas leak. First check to see if the pilot light is out. Look for the pilot behind the lower access panel (if it does not open easily, look for a release spring). Read the directions printed on the inside of the panel. Usually, you can relight a pilot by holding down the reset button for about 30 seconds while holding a long fireplace match to the pilot. The pilot should remain lit. If it goes out, repeat the process. If it still won't stay on, replace the thermocouple (see page 98).

If the pilot is not out, check for lint blocking the exhaust vent and duct and clean it out.

The dryer may not be heating enough because the burner has

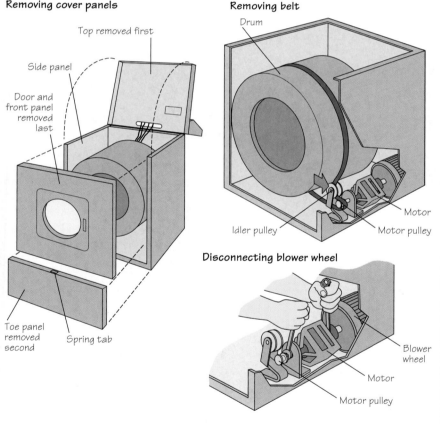

Removing cover panels

Top removed first

Side panel

Door and front panel removed last

Toe panel removed second

Spring tab

Removing belt

Drum

Idler pulley

Motor

Motor pulley

Disconnecting blower wheel

Blower wheel

Motor

Motor pulley

Tip   *Dryer lint, which is highly combustible, poses a fire hazard if it is not cleared out of the lint trap and exhaust duct periodically. Clean the trap before each use. Disconnect the vent duct from the back of the machine and check for lint buildup at least twice a year—more often if the duct vents upward.*

SOLVING MECHANICAL PROBLEMS

an improper gas/air mixture. If the flame has a yellow tip or a lot of orange, there's too much air in the mixture; if it's all pale blue and roaring, there's not enough air. To adjust, turn off the dryer and let the burner cool. Loosen the small screw on the air vent, then, wearing an oven mitt, turn on the dryer and adjust the air vent to create a steady, quiet, tapered blue flame.

Finally, one of the thermostats may be faulty. Clothes dryers use several thermostats. High-limit (safety) thermostats open the circuit to shut off the heat whenever the temperature reaches a preset point, to prevent overheating. If the contacts of such a thermostat are stuck open, the heat won't go on. Turn off electric power to the unit, and look for high-limit thermostats in the heating element or burner. To test one of them, disconnect the two wires attached to it, and join them to one another with a jumper wire (short length of wire with alligator clips attached to each end). Restore power and start the dryer; if the dryer starts to heat up, the thermostat is bad. Turn off the dryer immediately and install a new thermostat. If there is more than one high-limit thermostat, test the other in the same way. *Do not run the dryer with jumper wires except as a test.*

Cool-down thermostats work by closing their contacts while dryer heat is on, and opening them when drying is completed, so the heat turns off while the dryer is still on (providing a cool-down period). If this thermostat fails, the dryer will not warm up. Test this thermostat in the same way as for the high-limit thermostat.

Temperature-control thermostats close and open to maintain a correct drying temperature. They are usually connected between the timer and the heating unit. Turn off power to the unit, remove the thermostats, and test them with a volt-ohmmeter and an electric skillet (see page 110).

Adjusting gas-air mixture

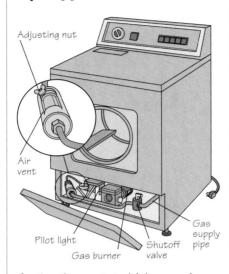

Adjusting nut

Air vent

Pilot light

Gas burner

Shutoff valve

Gas supply pipe

Testing thermostat with jumper wire

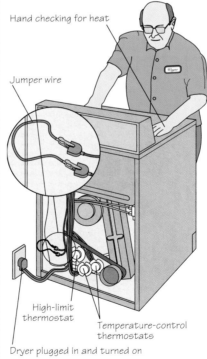

Hand checking for heat

Jumper wire

High-limit thermostat

Temperature-control thermostats

Dryer plugged in and turned on

▶ Drum doesn't turn.

The drive belt is probably broken. To quickly tell, rotate the drum by hand and listen for the loose belt thwacking against the side. The location of the belt and the method for replacing it depend on the make and model of the dryer; it's best to consult the owner's manual and, if possible, a repair guide for the model (see also page 147). Some models (those that have a single long belt that wraps around the drum and runs to the motor pulley) require that the whole cabinet be disassembled to replace the belt; these are better repaired by a professional. After learning from the manual how to reach the belt, also check to see if the problem might be a loose pulley instead of a defective belt. Tighten the setscrew of any loose pulley, and see if the dryer works now.

If the belt needs replacing and it's feasible for you to do it, note the model number of the dryer so you can buy an exact duplicate. Follow manufacturer's directions for replacing the belt. The process usually involves releasing a tension spring and threading the new belt onto the pulley.

▶ Drum is rusty and stains clothes.

Some manufacturers make custom touch-up paint (available from authorized appliance repair shops) that differs from regular appliance touch-up paint because it can withstand high heat. To repair the rust, first pull the plug or turn off the electric current. Remove all rust with fine-grade sandpaper. Vacuum the dust from the inside of the drum and wipe the sanded spots with a rag moistened with vinegar. Let dry. Then spray on the paint, covering all the rust spots, and let dry for 48 hours. Run the dryer

Tip *If the dryer makes excessive noise, check for coins, buttons, and other objects inside the drum. For thudding sounds, check for sneakers in the dryer (they are harmless, just noisy). If the noise is due to the machine vibrating or rocking back and forth, level it by adjusting the feet. Also consider placing rubber-backed carpet scraps or a rubber doormat under the legs to reduce noise.*

empty on high heat for 30 minutes; then soak a large, clean white rag in water, wring it out, place in dryer, and dry on high heat for 30 minutes. Inspect the rag for paint. If any paint appears, let the drum dry another 48 hours and test again. When no paint comes off on the rag, you can use the dryer.

▶ Dryer stops before clothes are dry.

If the dryer has an electronic system that senses when clothes are dry and shuts off the unit, try adjusting the load. Remove items that can be hung to finish drying, and shake out large items like sheets. Restart the machine. If it still will not continue until clothes are dry, the sensing system should be checked. Call for service.

For a dryer with conventional timing, assuming you have set the timer for a long-enough drying period, see page 146.

If the dryer has a defective timer, it will stop early only once, then stop completely. To check a timer, unplug the dryer and remove the back plate from the control panel (you may have to remove the front of the panel instead; look for screws on the bottom front corners). First check the timer motor for continuity; mark and remove the wires connected to the motor terminals and touch the probes of a volt-ohmmeter (set for R × 1 ohms resistance) or a continuity tester to the terminals. If there is no continuity, replace the timer unit. If there is continuity, mark and remove the wires attached to the switch terminals. Set the timer control to *Off* and test all pairs of terminals; if any tests for continuity, the timer is defective and should be replaced. Then switch the control

knob through all the cycles; a different pair of terminals should show continuity for each setting (except *Off*). If not, replace the timer.

Testing timer motor

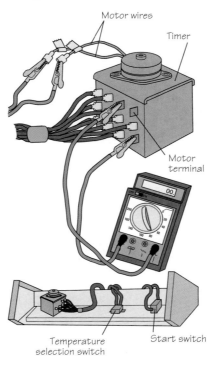

Motor wires
Timer
Motor terminal
Temperature selection switch
Start switch

Testing timer switch

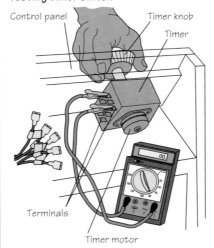

Control panel
Timer knob
Timer
Terminals
Timer motor

▶ Dryer is unvented and leaves air too humid.

If the dryer is close to an exterior wall, buy a dryer vent cap to install in the wall and a length of 4-inch-diameter flexible dryer duct to connect it to the exhaust duct behind the dryer. Before cutting the wall, make a small hole and explore with a piece of wire to make sure there are no obstructions. Mark a cut line on the interior wall by tracing around the duct, and cut out the opening with a wallboard saw. Remove insulation, if necessary, to expose the back of the exterior wall sheathing. Drive a nail through the wall sheathing at the center of the hole; use it as a reference for marking the hole on the outside of the wall and cutting through the siding. After cutting the hole, caulk around it, insert the vent cap, and secure it to the siding with HDG screws. On the inside, caulk around the duct where it extends through the interior wall, slide the decorative collar over it, and attach the flexible dryer duct to it with a hose clamp. Attach the other end of the duct to the dryer exhaust vent. Push the dryer into place.

If you can't vent it to the exterior, obtain a vent bucket (from an appliance store or repair shop) and attach it to the exhaust outlet at the back of the dryer.

Installing a dryer vent

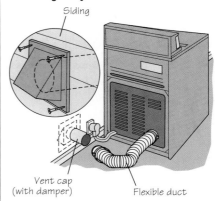

Siding
Vent cap (with damper)
Flexible duct

Tip *Vinyl ducts are not ideal for a clothes dryer because if they are long, they can accumulate enough lint to become a fire hazard. If you are using vinyl, keep the duct short. If you have a choice, use aluminum.*

▶ Copper Wire: Sizes, Ampacity & Use

For aluminum wire, use two sizes larger.

Wire Gauge Number	Ampacity Type T, TW wire (cable assemblies)	Ampacity Type THW wire (individual connectors)	Use
18	7		Cords, low-voltage, bells
16	10		
14	15		General circuit wiring for lights and receptacles
12	20		
10	30		Individual appliances: heaters, ranges, dryers, water heaters, ovens; branch-circuit feeders
8	40		
6	55		
4	70	85	
2	95	115	
1	110	130	
0 (1/0)	125	150	Main service conductors and branch-circuit feeders
00 (2/0)	145	175	
000 (3/0)	165	200	

Note: Receptacles and switches have ampere ratings that are to be matched to the type of wire being used. Most of them are stamped *15 amp,* which means they should be used with No. 14 wire. However, the NEC permits the use of No. 12 wire, which has an ampacity of 20 amperes, for use with 15-amp receptacles and switches.

▶ Color Coding of Wires & Terminal Screws

Function	Wire Color	Terminal Screw Color
Grounding	Bare copper Green Green and yellow	Green
Neutral (grounded)	White	Silver
Hot	Black Red Blue White made black*	Brass Bronze (common terminal of 3-way switch)

*Occasionally, when wiring is done with cable, the white wire must function as a hot wire (for example, a switch loop between a light fixture and 2-way switch, or the traveler wires between two 3-way switches). Common practice is to mark both ends of such a wire with black paint or electrical tape.

▶ Wire Talk: What Labels Mean

AC	Armored cable, which is flexible metallic sheathing
ACT	Armored cable that has wires with thermoplastic insulation
AWG	American Wire Gauge; a system of wire sizes
BX	Old trade name for flexible armored cable
NM	Nonmetallic cable for dry locations only
NMC	Nonmetallic cable for dry or damp (aboveground) locations
R	Rubber insulation
SE	Service-entrance wire; has plastic sheathing over neoprene insulation
T	Thermoplastic insulation
THW	Thermoplastic, heat- and water-resistant insulation
TW	Thermoplastic, water-resistant insulation
UF	Underground feeder cable with thermoplastic sheathing for direct burial
USE	Underground service-entrance wire with rubber and neoprene sheathing
w/G	With ground; designates cable with ground wire

Note: Wire refers to single- or multi-strand conductors. *Cable* refers to two or more conductors, insulated from each other, wrapped in sheathing.

► Number of Conductors* Permitted in an Electrical Box

Box Size (Metal)†		Maximum Number of Conductors		
Inside Dimensions	Cu. In.	No. 14	No. 12	No. 10
Round or Octagonal				
4 × 1¼	12.5	6	5	5
4 × 1½	15.5	7	6	6
4 × 2⅛	21.5	15	13	12
Square				
4⅝ × 1¼	25.5	12	11	10
4⅝ × 1½	29.5	14	13	11
4⅝ × 2⅛	42	21	18	16
Device Box				
3 × 2 × 1½	7.5	3	3	3
3 × 2 × 2	10	5	4	4
3 × 2 × 2¼	10.5	5	4	4
3 × 2 × 2½	12.5	6	5	5
3 × 2 × 2¾	14	7	6	5
3 × 2 × 3½	18	9	8	7
Junction Box				
4 × 2⅛ × 1½	10.3	5	4	4
4 × 2⅛ × 1⅞	13	6	5	5
4 × 2⅛ × 2⅛	14.5	7	6	5

*When Counting Conductors:

Each hot wire	=	1 conductor
Each neutral wire	=	1 conductor
Total of all ground wires	=	1 conductor
Each switch or receptacle	=	1 conductor
Each cable clamp or fixture stud	=	1 conductor

†For plastic boxes refer to capacity, in cubic inches, stamped inside box.

► Recommended Locations of Electrical Boxes

Type of Box	Location of Center of Box
Switch	48" above floor
Receptacle	12" above floor; 44" above floor if over a countertop
Baseboard heater	Usually 6" above floor; varies
Ceiling fixture	Center of ceiling (find by measuring diagonals)
Junction box	Wherever accessible; cannot be concealed

► Minimum Requirements for Electrical Fixtures

The following specifications will help you to place light fixtures, switches, receptacles (outlets), and appliances. Consult National Electrical Code (NEC) or your local building department for additional restrictions. Code requirements are minimum; when going to the trouble and expense of installing new wiring, it is good practice to increase the number of fixtures and receptacles in anticipation of future needs.

Lights. Every room, hallway, stairway, outdoor entrance, and attached garage must have at least one permanent light fixture controlled by a wall switch located at each entrance. The light can be mounted on the ceiling or any wall, and you may use as many individual fixtures as you wish. The following list includes some exceptions to this rule:

• A wall receptacle controlled by a wall switch at the entrance to a room may be substituted for a permanent light fixture in any room except the kitchen or a bathroom.

• Light fixtures for utility rooms, crawl spaces, and attics without stairs can be controlled by pull chains instead of wall switches.

• Lighting for hallways, stairways, and outdoor entrances can be activated by specialized switches. These include remote, central, or automatic switches.

• Additional recommendations. Lighting fixtures should also be installed to illuminate the front of a furnace, laundry equipment in a basement or garage, bathroom mirrors, and clothes closets. Fixtures in clothes closets must be located on the ceiling or on the wall above the door. Pendant fixtures are not allowed—most codes assume that fixtures of this type could cause an overstuffed closet to become a fire hazard.

Switches. The switch for the main light fixture of a room should be located at the entrance to the room—at each entrance, if there is more than one. The switch must be on the latch side of a hinged door so the door does not interfere with the access to the switch. Do not locate switches in bathrooms where it is possible to reach them while using the shower or bathtub. Attic stairs must be illuminated by a light that is controlled by a switch at the foot of the stairs. Lights for basement stairs must have a switch at the head of the stairs as well as one at any other entrance.

Receptacles. Receptacles, also called convenience outlets, must be located in every room no more than 12 feet apart. (The NEC actually requires that no point along the floor line of any wall be more than 6 feet from an outlet.) On a wall with more than one door opening (including closets), there should be at least one outlet between the doors unless that section of wall is less than 2 feet wide.

Place receptacles for a kitchen counter no more than 4 feet apart. Standard practice is to install at least one outlet for each foot of counter.

Laundry rooms must have at least one receptacle positioned within 6 feet of any appliance.

Bathrooms should have at least one receptacle adjacent to the washbasin. All bathroom outlets must be protected by GFCI devices.

There must be at least one receptacle outdoors, as well as one in the garage and one in the basement. They must all be GFCI protected.

Appliances. Any 240-volt appliance or permanent 120-volt appliance should have its own receptacle or junction box.

▶ Drain, Waste & Vent Pipe Sizes

Codes specify the exact size of all drain-pipes; the sizes are not minimums. The size of fixture outlet, trap (outlet and trap must be the same size), and vent depends on the amount of water flowing through the fixture. Codes measure the flow in *fixture units*. The chart summarizes typical code requirements. Remember that codes specify pipe sizes in fixture units, not by fixture type.

Typical Code Requirements

Fixture	Fixture Units	Trap Size (in inches)	Vent Size (in inches)
Toilet	4	3	2
Washing machine	3	2	1½
Shower	2	2	1½
Bathtub	2	1½	1¼
Kitchen sink	2	1½	1¼
Washbasin	1	1¼	1¼
Kitchen or laundry	varies	2	1½
Bathroom	varies	3	2
Whole house	varies	3 or 4	total = drain size

▶ Which Supply Stop (Shutoff Valve) to Use

Inlet Options	For Connecting to . . .
½" compression fitting	Copper tubing
½" IPS (coarse) female threads	Threaded galvanized pipe or threaded adapter on copper tubing
IPS male thread (or ⅜" "coarse-threaded nut")	½" threaded pipe fitting (IPS female threads)

Outlet Options	For Connecting to . . .
¼", ⅜", or ½" compression fitting	Smooth end of ¼", ⅜", or ½" OD supply tube Flexible tubing with fine-thread compression nut on one end
⅜" or ½" slip-joint fitting with rubber cone washer	Smooth end of ⅜" or ½" OD supply tube (smooth end of tube should be flared)

Optional Configurations	For . . .
Angle stop	Changing direction of piping
Straight stop	Keeping piping in straight line
Double outlet/triple outlet	Controlling 2 or 3 fixtures

▶ Recommended Minimum Fixture Clearances

(Verify against local codes)

Toilet

From centerline to side wall	15"
From tank to basin on side	4"
From back wall to obstruction in front of toilet	48"

Washbasin

From side to side wall	4"
From side to toilet tank	4"
From side to bathtub	6"
Clearance in front	24"

Shower

Clearance inside, between walls	32"
Clearance in front for door swing	28"

▶ Rough-In Dimensions for Bathroom Fixtures

	Toilet	Basin	Bathtub	Shower
Distance of below-floor drainpipe from back wall	Varies; 12"	—	6"–10"	Center of stall
Height of drain stub above floor	—	15"–17"	—	—
Height of supply shutoff above floor	5"–10"	19"–21"	—	—
Distance of shutoff from centerline of fixture	6"	8"	—	—
Height of faucet above finish floor	—	—	26"	46"
Height of tub spout above finish floor	—	—	20"	—
Height of showerhead above finish floor	—	—	65"–76"	65"–76"

DWV (Drain-Waste-Vent) Fittings: Which Fitting to Use?

	Drain & Waste Pipes	**Vent Pipes**
Joining Pipes at a Change of Direction		
Horizontal to vertical	Short- or long-sweep ¼ bend Two ⅛ bends Sanitary tee Double tee, or elbow with side inlet (where 2 horizontal pipes join at a vertical pipe)	¼ bend or 90° vent ell Sanitary tee (inverted), wye (inverted)
Vertical to horizontal	Long-sweep ¼ bend Two ⅛ offset bends Wye and ⅛ bend (combo wye) Closet bend (for toilet connections only)	¼ bend or 90° vent ell Two ⅛ bends (offset)
Horizontal to horizontal	Long-sweep ¼ bend ⅛, 1⁄16, or 1⁄6 bend Wye or combo wye	¼ bend or 90° vent ell ⅛, 1⁄16, or 1⁄6 bend
Joining Pipes, No Change of Direction		
Same type of pipe, identical size	Coupling or no-hub coupling	Coupling or no-hub coupling
Same type of pipe, different sizes	Reducing coupling	Reducing coupling
Different types of pipe	Adapter (glued plastic fitting to threaded fitting, plastic to copper, and such), or no-hub connector	Same as drain
Miscellaneous Joints		
Joining pipe to fitting of larger size	Reducing bushing	Reducing bushing
Joining fitting to fitting	Street fitting to street fitting; or hub fitting to hub fitting, with close nipple	Same as drain
Offset bends	Various combinations of bends	Same as drain
P-trap (rough in)	Adjustable P-trap: solid joints Adjustable P-trap: slip joints (where allowed)	
Cleanout: vertical pipe	Wye and cleanout fitting Sanitary tee and cleanout Test tee	
Cleanout: horizontal pipe	Cleanout fitting (end of run) Wye and cleanout fitting Cleanout tee	

ABS (acrylonitrile-butadiene-styrene) Black plastic pipe used for drain-waste-vent pipes in plumbing systems; pipe is joined to fittings with solvent.

Air gap A device through which a pump-drained appliance (dishwasher, washing machine) must discharge its waste water before that water enters the drain system; prevents waste water from siphoning back into the appliance.

Amp, ampere A unit of measurement of electric current, used in quantifying the rate at which electrons flow past a given point in a wire or other conductor.

Ampacity The capacity of a conductor for carrying electricity, measured in amperes.

Antiscald valve (faucet) A tub and/or shower valve that automatically balances the hot and cold water to maintain an even temperature.

Ballast A magnetic coil that provides the starting voltage or stabilizes the current in a circuit (as of a fluorescent lamp).

Basin wrench Tool for removing or installing nuts or bolts in hard-to-reach places, usually under sinks.

Bearings Movable rings placed over the ends of a motor shaft or other arbor (shaft) to eliminate friction as the shaft rotates in its mount.

Bibb A faucet with male threads that allow a hose to be attached; also called hose bibb or sillcock.

Bonnet The packing nut of a bibb or faucet that holds the valve stem in place.

BTU (British thermal unit) A measurement of heat; specifically, the amount needed to raise the temperature of 1 pound of water 1° F, starting at 39° F.

Bus bar A rigid conductor at the main power source to which three or more circuits are connected.

BX Electrical cable sheathed in a flexible metallic covering.

Capacitor An electronic component that stores and intensifies electrical current for an instantaneous discharge.

Cartridge The replaceable unit in some washerless faucets; controls the flow of water.

Centerset faucet Faucet design in which spout and controls are built into a single unit.

Channel lock pliers Large pliers with adjustable parallel jaws.

Chase An enclosed space, such as inside a finished wall, for running duct work or vent pipes between floors.

Circuit The complete path of an electric current, leading from a source (generator or battery) through components (for example, electric lights), and back to the source.

Circuit breaker A safety device used to interrupt the flow of power when the electricity exceeds a predetermined amount. Unlike a fuse, a circuit breaker can be reset.

Circuit breaker panel In an electrical system, the main service panel where electricity is distributed to branch circuits through a series of circuit breakers.

Circular saw A power saw with a circular blade.

Cleanout Easy-to-reach opening in the drain system; used in removing obstructions.

Closet auger A drain auger for cleaning obstructions out of a toilet drain.

Closet flange A plumbing fitting that connects a toilet to its waste pipe and the floor.

Code A set of regulations that specifies how buildings must be constructed or the electrical, plumbing, and mechanical components installed; local codes are usually based on model codes widely adopted throughout the region or across the country.

Compressor A machine that compresses air for use with air tools; or the part of a refrigerator or air conditioner that compresses fluid as part of a cycle to create temperature changes in that fluid.

Continuity An uninterrupted electrical path.

Continuity tester A tool for testing whether electric current can flow through a wire or electrical device; used to test the wire or device when power is turned off.

Convector A heating device, consisting of water pipes encased in multiple metal fins, that uses hot water to heat the surrounding air, which then rises and circulates through the room in natural air currents.

CPVC (chlorinated polyvinyl chloride) Plastic used to form rigid gray- or pastel-colored pipe from which hot-water supply lines are made.

Crawl space The area under a house, usually with a dirt floor and not enough headroom for a basement.

Diverter Valve for changing the flow of water from one outlet to another.

Downspout Vertical pipe, metal or plastic, for carrying water down from roof gutters.

Drain auger A coiled wire device, with a crank and hooked end, for unclogging drains; also called a plumber's snake.

Ducts Pipes that carry air from a furnace or air conditioner to the living areas of a structure, or that carry exhaust air from a fan or ventilator.

DWV (drain-waste-vent) All or part of the plumbing system that carries waste water to the sewer and gases to the roof.

Electrical box A metal or plastic box used to contain wire terminations where they connect to other wires, switches, or receptacles.

Electrical conduit Tubing used to enclose electrical conductors; the most common types are EMT (electrical metallic tubing, or "thin-wall"), rigid (thick-walled, like steel water pipe), and plastic.

Electrical connector A device with a threaded metal sleeve inside an insulating cap, that screws onto the ends of two or more electrical conductors to make a firm connection; commonly referred to as wire connector or solderless connector.

Escutcheon Ornamental plate for covering a wall opening where pipe penetrates, or the part of a faucet that covers the stem.

Fish To feed wires through tight spaces, such as wall cavities.

Fish tape Flat steel spring or nylon wire with hooked ends; used to pull wires through conduits or walls.

Flange A rim that allows one object to be attached to another object.

Float valve   A valve, regulated by a hollow float, that shuts on and off automatically when water reaches certain levels, used in toilets, sump pumps, dishwashers, and other fixtures with variable water levels; also called ballcock valve.

Flue   In a chimney or vent, the opening through which smoke and other gases pass.

Fluorescent bulb   A bulb in which a coating on the inside of a glass tube is made to glow by an electric current.

Flux   An acid-bearing substance spread on a metal surface so solder will bond to the metal.

Forced-air heating   _See_ Warm-air heating.

Gas cock   The type of valve used for gas lines; has a lever or lug handle that, when parallel with the pipe, indicates that the valve is open and, when perpendicular to the pipe, indicates that the valve is closed.

GFCI (ground fault circuit interrupter)   An electrical safety device that monitors a receptacle or circuit for minute leakages of current and that deadens the receptacle or circuit whenever there is a potential for electrical shock.

Ground   A conducting connection between an electrical system and the earth that usually does not carry current unless a short circuit occurs.

Ground wire   The safety wire (green or bare) in a circuit intended to provide a safe path for voltage surges or disconnected hot wires. Its purpose is to allow the voltage to discharge rapidly enough to open the circuit breaker or other overcurrent device.

Hard-wire   To wire a fixture or appliance directly into the electric circuit rather than attach it with a removable plug.

HEPA (high efficiency particulate air) filter   Used for vacuum cleaners or respirators to remove dust with microscopic fibers.

Hot wire(s)   The wires of a house circuit that are not connected to a ground and that carry power to receptacles and appliances; usually identified with black, blue, or red insulation.

HVAC (heating, ventilation, and air-conditioning)   Mechanical systems that are often grouped together and installed by the same tradespeople.

ID   Inside diameter of a pipe.

Incandescent bulb   A bulb that produces light when electricity heats a metal filament to incandescence; a standard household lamp emitting a yellow-white light.

IPS (iron pipe size)   Uniform sizing of threaded pipe fittings.

Jigsaw   A portable power saw with a narrow reciprocating blade, usually used for cutting curves; also called saber saw.

Jumper wire   A short length of wire used temporarily while testing for electrical continuity.

Leach field   The drain field for a septic system, where perforated pipes are buried in the ground to disperse the water.

Low-voltage lighting   Lighting that operates on 12-volt current rather than on the standard 120 volts (a few systems use 24 volts). Power is supplied by a transformer, which is connected to 120-volt current.

LP (liquid propane)   Bottled gas used for heating and cooking.

Main disconnect   The electrical device for disconnecting a home electrical system from the main conductors connected to the utility company's wires.

Manifold   A chamber that distributes a fluid or gas from a single pipe to several other pipes, tubes, or conduits.

Mast   Electrical conduit that encloses the main conductors of a home electrical system.

Masthead   _See_ Weatherhead.

Media pad   An evaporation pad in a humidifier that wicks moisture from the reservoir and releases it into the air.

Needle-nose pliers   Pliers with a long, very slim nose.

Neutral wire   In a circuit, any wire that is kept at zero voltage. The neutral wire completes the circuit from source, to fixture or appliance, to ground. The covering of neutral wires is always white.

Nipple   Short length of pipe, externally threaded at both ends.

NMC (nonmetallic-sheathed cable)   Electrical cable consisting of two or more insulated wires, sheathed in plastic or nonmetallic material; used indoors; often referred to by the trade name Romex®.

OD   Outside diameter of a pipe.

Ohm   A unit of measurement used in electrical wiring to indicate resistance to electrical current in a circuit or electrical device; equal to the resistance in a conductor in which 1 volt of potential difference produces a current of 1 ampere.

Orbital sander   An electric sander that vibrates in a tight oscillating pattern (as opposed to the wider circular pattern of a disk sander).

O-ring   A rubber ring used as a gasket and having a circular cross section.

Packing string   String impregnated with flexible watertight material; used for wrapping around valve stems to provide a leakproof seal.

Phillips head   Describes a screwdriver with an X-shaped tip or a screw with an X-shaped slot.

Pigtail   In an electrical installation, a short length of wire used to connect a device to an electrical box or the circuit wiring.

Pilot   In a gas appliance, a continuously burning flame that ignites the burner.

Plenum   A large chamber in warm-air heating systems where ducts converge at the furnace.

Plumber's putty   Putty used when installing plumbing fixtures for sealing drain fittings, gaps around faucets, and similar watertight joints.

Polarity   Alignment of electrical conductors or terminals to ensure the safe and continuous flow of electricity; maintained by the use of color-coded wires and terminals: white wire and silver-colored terminals for neutral conductors; black, red, or blue wire and brass-colored terminals for hot conductors; and green or bare wire for ground wires.

Pressure-balancing valve   An anti-scald tub-and-shower valve that senses the water pressure of the hot- and cold-water inlets and keeps them balanced should the pressure in either one suddenly change.

Programmable thermostat   A thermostat with a microprocessor that can be programmed to switch on the cooling or heating system at set times.

Psi (pounds per square inch)   A measurement of water or air pressure.

P-trap A curved plumbing fitting, resembling a broken letter "P" and usually consisting of two pieces, that connects a fixture tailpiece to the drain system; designed to trap enough water to prevent sewer gas from entering the house through the drain line.

PVC (polyvinyl chloride) A rigid, white or beige plastic used for plumbing pipe for supply and DWV systems.

Radiant heating Heating system that utilizes electrically heated panels or hot-water pipes in the floor or ceiling that radiate heat to warm the room surfaces.

Receptacle A device, commonly called an outlet, through which an electrical plug can make contact with an electric circuit; most devices are duplex, with two receptacles.

Screw terminal A means of connecting wiring to electrical devices using a threaded screw.

Scuttle A hatch for access into an attic.

Septic tank An underground tank that receives water and waste from a house sewer, in which the solids settle and are transformed into a rich sludge through the activity of anaerobic bacteria.

Service entrance The place where the electrical system of a building is connected to wires from a utility company; components include the mast, conductors, meter, main disconnect, and service-entrance panel (circuit-breaker or fuse panel).

Set-back thermostat A thermostat that can be adjusted to switch on a heating system at set times by means of moving stops on a clock wheel.

Single-pole switch An electrical switch in which the internal mechanism either breaks the flow of electricity or directs it to one pole, or terminal; commonly called a two-way switch.

Solenoid An electromagnet that moves a rod into and out of a position in which it engages some other mechanism.

Splice A connection made by joining two or more wires.

Stack A 4-inch vertical pipe that serves as the main plumbing vent and drain for a bathroom.

Standing pilot A pilot flame for a gas appliance.

Standpipe A vertical drainpipe for washing machines.

Starter A device used with many fluorescent fixtures to strike an arc between the electrodes when the fixture is turned on.

Sump A pit in the lowest area of a basement floor for collecting water from the surface of the floor.

Sump pump A pump for removing water from a sump.

Temperature-balancing valve An antiscald tub or shower valve that senses the temperature of the incoming hot and cold water and makes adjustments to keep them balanced.

Terminal A screw or other structure for connecting wires to an electrical device.

Thermocouple A device for gas burners that monitors the pilot light and deactivates the main gas valve if the pilot light goes out.

Three-way switch An electrical switch in which the internal mechanism directs the flow of electricity to one of two poles; used in pairs to control a single fixture.

TPRV (temperature-pressure relief valve) A safety valve for water heaters that prevents steam from building up in the tank should the heater malfunction.

Transformer A device that converts current of one voltage into current of another voltage; used with doorbells and low-voltage lighting systems.

Trap In plumbing, a U-shaped fitting that allows water and sewage to flow through it while blocking the flow of air and gas from the other direction.

Traveler wires Pairs of wires, used in the wiring connections for three- or four-way switching systems, that connect the switches together but don't connect to the light fixture or the electrical source.

Two-way switch *See* Single-pole switch.

UL label A label applied to manufactured devices that have been tested for safety by Underwriters' Laboratories, Inc., and approved for placement on the market. These laboratories establish safety standards and are supported by insurance companies, manufacturers, and other parties interested in electrical safety.

Underwriter's knot A knot used to tie two insulated conductors at the terminals inside an electrical plug or fixture; used to relieve strain on the terminal connection.

Valve grease Lubricant for the internal parts of a faucet or valve.

Vent In plumbing, a pipe that goes through the attic to the roof to allow sewer gases to escape and air to enter the plumbing system to prevent the siphoning of the fixture traps; any opening for air circulation, usually into an attic or crawl space.

Vent stack In plumbing, the largest vent pipe; branch vents may be connected to it; also called the main vent.

Volt A unit that measures electrical pressure; comparable to pounds of pressure in a water system.

Volt-ohmmeter An electrical testing device that measures the live voltage of connected circuits (alternating current or direct current) or the impedance (in ohms) of disconnected wires or devices.

Warm-air heating Heating system consisting of a furnace and a network of ducts and registers to distribute heated air; also called forced-air heating.

Watt A unit that measures electric power; the unit by which utility companies meter electrical consumption. Volts × amperes = watts of electric energy used.

Weatherhead A weathertight fitting at the top of a mast where the main conductors are connected to the overhead wires from a power pole; also called masthead.

Wire connector *See* Electrical connector.

U.S./Metric Measure Conversion Chart

	Symbol	When you know:	Multiply by:	To find:	Rounded Measures for Quick Reference		
Mass	oz	ounces	28.35	grams	1 oz		= 30 g
(weight)	lb	pounds	0.45	kilograms	4 oz		= 115 g
	g	grams	0.035	ounces	8 oz		= 225 g
	kg	kilograms	2.2	pounds	16 oz	= 1 lb	= 450 g
					32 oz	= 2 lb	= 900 g
					36 oz	= 2¼ lb	= 1000 g (1 kg)
Volume	pt	pints	0.47	liters	1 c	= 8 oz	= 250 ml
	qt	quarts	0.95	liters	2 c (1 pt)	= 16 oz	= 500 ml
	gal	gallons	3.785	liters	4 c (1 qt)	= 32 oz	= 1 liter
	ml	milliliters	0.034	fluid ounces	4 qt (1 gal)	= 128 oz	= 3¾ liter
Length	in.	inches	2.54	centimeters	⅜ in.		= 1.0 cm
	ft	feet	30.48	centimeters	1 in.		= 2.5 cm
	yd	yards	0.9144	meters	2 in.		= 5.0 cm
	mi	miles	1.609	kilometers	2½ in.		= 6.5 cm
	km	kilometers	0.621	miles	12 in. (1 ft)		= 30.0 cm
	m	meters	1.094	yards	1 yd		= 90.0 cm
	cm	centimeters	0.39	inches	100 ft		= 30.0 m
					1 mi		= 1.6 km
Temperature	°F	Fahrenheit	⅝ (after subtracting 32)	Celsius	32° F		= 0° C
					68° F		= 20° C
	°C	Celsius	⅑ (then add 32)	Fahrenheit	212° F		= 100° C
Area	in.²	square inches	6.452	square centimeters	1 in.²		= 6.5 cm²
	ft²	square feet	929.0	square centimeters	1 ft²		= 930 cm²
	yd²	square yards	8361.0	square centimeters	1 yd²		= 8360 cm²
	a.	acres	0.4047	hectares	1 a.		= 4050 m²

Formulas for Exact Measures